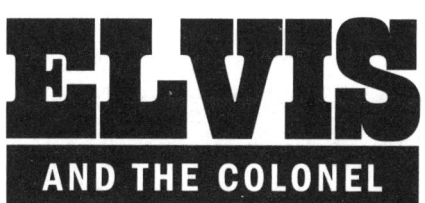

Courtesy of Joseph A. Tunzi / JAT Publishing

ELVIS
AND THE COLONEL

An Insider's Look
at the Most Legendary Partnership
in Show Business

GREG McDONALD

and

MARSHALL TERRILL

ST. MARTIN'S GRIFFIN
NEW YORK

Published in the United States by St. Martin's Griffin, an imprint of St. Martin's Publishing Group

ELVIS AND THE COLONEL. Copyright © 2023 by Greg McDonald. All rights reserved. Printed in the United States of America. For information, address St. Martin's Publishing Group, 120 Broadway, New York, NY 10271.

www.stmartins.com

Designed by Omar Chapa

The Library of Congress has cataloged the hardcover edition as follows:

Names: McDonald, Greg, author. | Terrill, Marshall, author.
Title: Elvis and the Colonel : an insider's look at the most legendary partnership in show business / Greg McDonald and Marshall Terrill.
Description: First edition. | New York: St. Martin's Press, 2023. | Includes bibliographical references and index.
Identifiers: LCCN 2023016804 | ISBN 9781250287496 (hardcover) | ISBN 9781250287502 (ebook)
Subjects: LCSH: Parker, Tom, 1909 June 26–1997. | Presley, Elvis, 1935–1977. | Singers—United States—Biography. | Impresarios—United States—Biography. | Concert agents—United States—Biography.
Classification: LCC ML429.P33 M33 2023 | DDC 782.42166092/2 [B]—dc23/eng/20230509
LC record available at https://lccn.loc.gov/2023016804

ISBN 978-1-250-89228-7 (trade paperback)

Our books may be purchased in bulk for promotional, educational, or business use. Please contact your local bookseller or the Macmillan Corporate and Premium Sales Department at 1-800-221-7945, extension 5442, or by email at MacmillanSpecialMarkets@macmillan.com.

First St. Martin's Griffin Edition: 2025

10 9 8 7 6 5 4 3 2 1

I dedicate this book to my beautiful and loyal wife, Sherry, and my three loving children—Gregory, Tommy, and Suzie. I am also dedicating this to Colonel Tom Parker and Elvis Presley, who were nothing but good and kind to me in the years I spent with them. I'd also like to remember Marie Parker and Loanne Miller Parker, who were like family to me.

It was all a blessing.

Greg McDonald

CONTENTS

Introduction 1
Prologue: All in a Day's Work 7

1. Dutch Boy 15
2. The High Seas 30
3. The Road to Success 45
4. Pulling Rank 64
5. Artist of the Century 82
6. Elvis Presley Inc. 101
7. G.I. Blues 117
8. Fame and Fortune 134
9. We Are Family 144
10. Lucky Streak 154
11. Elvis in the Age of Aquarius 172
12. Reel to Real 181
13. Viva Las Vegas 199
14. 20,000,000 Elvis Fans Can't Be Wrong 214
15. The Colonel's Crew 229
16. Aloha from Hawaii 247
17. T-R-O-U-B-L-E 257
18. Prescription for Disaster 266

19.	Auld Lang Syne	284
20.	Way Down	292
21.	Baseball, American Pie, and Chevrolet	302
22.	Under New Management	308
23.	Always Elvis	319
24.	Colonel Parker Reconsidered	335

Acknowledgments *353*
Selected Bibliography *355*
Index *357*

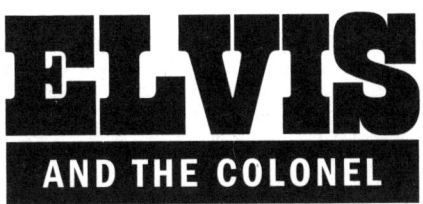

INTRODUCTION

Colonel Tom Parker has gone down in history as a malevolent leech, the Svengali-like, cigar-chomping, ironfisted manager of the King of Rock 'n' Roll. That's the myth . . . the man he, in fact, wanted the world to see. He chose to play the heavy when the situation called for that.

"The artist always wears the white hat," Parker said more times than I care to remember.

The artist, of course, was Elvis Aaron Presley. The mantle Colonel Parker wore—rightly or wrongly—for decades was easy for the press and public to digest, offering a clean and palatable story with no shades of gray. Elvis could remain a saintly figure if Colonel Parker remained the heavy. Despite his carnival barker demeanor and P. T. Barnum–like façade, the real Tom Parker was nowhere near his public persona.

He conveyed that image because he constantly had to do battle with businessmen, bean counters, and lawyers who had Ivy League backgrounds and lots of credentials hanging on their walls. The Colonel had only his street smarts and his reputation to fend off the wolves, and he used both to his advantage. His negotiations were great theater because he elevated them to an art form. I've always contended that the Colonel was a much better actor than Elvis Presley ever was. He created a persona to instill fear in his opponents across the table so he could get the best deal possible for his client.

So, what is truth, what is legend, what is misunderstood or misjudged, what is totally false?

What history and countless other books on Elvis Presley don't tell you is that Colonel Parker was the first mega-manager who made forays into today's multimedia world of music, film, television, publishing, and Las Vegas–style entertainment. Parker, along with his once-in-a-millennium star, Elvis Presley, blazed many paths in the span of two decades. Elvis (the artist) and Parker (the enigmatic manager that made it happen behind the scenes) were the greatest pairing in entertainment history.

Though the Colonel may have appeared to many to be shrewd, flamboyant, crass, and brash, in actuality, he was fair-minded, loyal, funny, a twenty-four seven workhorse, a man whose word was his bond, and even philanthropic in private. Many of Presley's artistic endeavors had a charitable aspect to them thanks to Colonel Parker's prompting. The two men provided major support—through financial contributions and raising awareness—for several charities throughout their two decades of success, including the USS *Arizona* Memorial in Hawaii, March of Dimes, the Salvation Army, St. Jude Children's Research Hospital, and the Kui Lee Cancer Fund. Colonel Parker was also a lifelong animal lover and even once worked for the Humane Society in Tampa, Florida.

Colonel Parker made sure to give fans, concert promoters, and business clients their full value while at the same time leaving them wanting more. Conversely, he got his client the best possible deals for the maximum amount of money. He was getting Elvis nearly $1 million a movie and 50 percent of the box office net when the biggest stars in Hollywood might have gotten 10 percent at most. Colonel Parker got those extraordinary deals because of his savvy and smarts. He was also strategic and Zen-like in his feats: getting his client the maximum deal while saving enough gravy for those who sat across the bargaining table from him.

Others wanted his services too: the Beatles. Frank Sinatra. George

Hamilton. Ann-Margret. Tony Orlando. Tanya Tucker. They all wanted Colonel Parker to manage them. I remember when one of the Beatles (I believe it was Paul McCartney) called the Colonel at his Palm Springs home shortly after the death of Beatles manager Brian Epstein in late August 1967. He took the call, excusing himself to another room. After he got off the phone, he said he couldn't take them on because of his loyalty to Elvis. It was a testament to his greatness as a manager that the Beatles wanted him. The fact that he turned them down was a testament to his belief in his client.

All business dealings were done with military-like precision and secrecy. Parker kept his mouth shut for several reasons. What he concealed was far more astounding and complex than has ever been revealed. Although an uneducated Dutch farm boy who grew up in a modest apartment above horse stables, he had an innate knack for creating a spectacle and weaving the public's heart and soul into it. The Nashville music scene, Hollywood, and Las Vegas were not going to be a match for him.

Before he got to the top, Colonel Parker rode the rails as a hobo, sailed around the world in the merchant marine, served four years in the United States Army, and spent a decade as a traveling carny perfecting his act. He understood human behavior and learned how to squeeze a nickel out of all of it, making him the perfect power behind the entertainment throne.

Colonel Parker arrived in the United States a penniless immigrant who had to overcome a language barrier and battled discrimination and bias; yet he came to befriend US presidents and CEOs, and he created a cultural icon for the ages who generated $4 billion in his lifetime, all the while managing to keep a low profile.

There have been hundreds of books written about Elvis and a few about Colonel Parker. None of those writers and biographers were ever in the room when the deals went down.

But I was.

I knew Colonel Parker for almost four decades from the time I was a teen. I drove him around Los Angeles when Elvis was making movies in Hollywood, hung out with him when Elvis started his Las Vegas residency, traveled with him when Elvis started touring again, and spent countless hours with him in his home office in Palm Springs, California. I saw firsthand how Colonel Parker worked, how he played (which was not very often; he was a workaholic), how he negotiated contracts, and how he made sure there was enough honey to go around. And I know how the deals were made. I can tell you this: nothing went down without Elvis's knowledge and consent, and Colonel Parker earned every penny of whatever went in his pocket. Rest assured, way more money went into his client's pockets.

Many biographers and people in Elvis's inner circle have inaccurately portrayed their business and personal relationship because of their lack of knowledge. They knew only a fraction of the story. They did their best to investigate or find out; however, they couldn't peer into the character of Tom Parker, which is essential to the story.

First and foremost, Colonel Parker never talked business to outsiders. While he might have hyped his client to the press, he never spoke of the details of their business. The same also went for Elvis. Their business dealings were strictly private and between them. These two men will be forever intertwined in history like other famous business partnerships: Henry Wells and William G. Fargo, William Procter and James Gamble, Bill Hewlett and Dave Packard. They made beautiful music together, metaphorically speaking.

But Elvis has gone down as the bright half of the pairing whereas Parker has always been tarred by a reputation as the dark half. My hope is to dispel that myth and all the negative feelings associated with a man who was nothing but kind to me and my family.

This is a story of a man who could give P. T. Barnum a run for his money—the grand vizier of aggrandizement, the pasha of pizzazz, the baron of ballyhoo. Ever wonder where concert rain checks, concert T-shirts, tour books, and mass music merchandise came from? The answer is Colonel Parker. He could sell tickets to see two flies wrestling

Introduction

on a windowpane, and the line would go around the block. His is the all-American immigrant's tale: a poor Dutch farm boy who came to the United States seeking and achieving the American Dream, and introducing modern history's greatest entertainer in the process.

And it's better than any movie you could imagine.

PROLOGUE

All in a Day's Work

Elvis's success was almost instantaneous once he signed with Colonel Parker and RCA Victor. Just two days after his twenty-first birthday on January 10, 1956, Elvis was in RCA Studios in Nashville, a facility they shared with the Methodist Church's Television, Radio & Film Commission Studios, recording a batch of songs. The dark and brooding "Heartbreak Hotel," one of three tunes recorded during this eight-hour session, was released as a single just seventeen days later. Produced by Steve Sholes, RCA's artist and repertoire man, the song was an instant smash.

"Heartbreak Hotel" sold more than 300,000 copies in the first three weeks. It rocketed to the number one spot on *Billboard* magazine's pop single chart faster than any recording in history and remained there for over two months. It would also hit number 1 on the country charts and number 5 on the rhythm-and-blues charts. It was the first of Elvis's 110 gold, platinum, and multi-platinum albums and recordings.

Even though many radio stations refused to play "Heartbreak Hotel" (it was said the song was too suggestive; others believed the truth was that it was rooted in Black music and would tear down the cultural divide in America), the Colonel's old carny buddies loved it and blasted it over the midway sound systems. It seemed to get people in a toe-tapping, money-spending mood.

The day after "Heartbreak Hotel" was released, Elvis appeared on

Stage Show, the first of six Tommy and Jimmy Dorsey shows produced by Jackie Gleason on CBS-TV. These shows were part of the RCA Victor buyout contract negotiated by the Colonel. Elvis received $1,250 for each of the first four shows and $1,500 for the final two.

From January 28 through March 24, 1956, Elvis had six straight weekly *Stage Show* appearances that resulted in some minor reviews and some major press grumblings. Even Gleason himself was less than impressed with Elvis.

"Presley can't last," Gleason roared to the media. "I give him one year at the most. He'll have a brief period of popularity and then it's back to the country dances, the fairs, the carnivals, and the cooch shops. It's hard for a legitimate star to make it today. What can a freak do for an encore?"

Six years later Gleason's opinion of Elvis had done a 180-degree turn. On June 5, 1962, he wrote to Colonel Parker, telling him that his client has "developed into one of the real fine performers and nice guys in show business. You can certainly be proud." Gleason ended the letter with, "I think he's 100% thoroughbred."

Gleason's initial criticism of Elvis seemed to have no lasting impact on the Colonel, who appeared to welcome the controversy. He never cared what the media wrote or said about Elvis as long as they got his name right.

"The more they talked and wrote about Elvis, the better," the Colonel once confided in me. He learned to live with bad press because he knew that whatever was written or said, it made Elvis all that much cooler to the fans who bought his records. He also knew that country and western was slowing down and rock 'n' roll was heating up. And so was the Colonel.

Before the ink was even dry on the RCA contract, the Colonel was negotiating a deal with the Hill and Range publishing company in New York to establish a spin-off company called Elvis Presley Music, Inc., which would share the publishing rights to all the music Elvis would ever record. Hill and Range, the largest independent music publishing company in its day, was owned by a pair of Viennese refugee brothers named Jean and Julian Aberbach. The company employed many of the top songwriters of the day such as Doc Pomus, Mort Shuman, Phil Spector, and Leiber and Stoller.

They struck a deal in 1955 that set up an unprecedented arrangement in which the publishing rights to all songs recorded by Elvis were split 50/50 between Hill and Range and Elvis Presley Music. They employed writers (including Leiber and Stoller) to provide songs for Elvis's films and albums. Elvis seemed happy with the arrangement according to Julian Aberbach.

"I gave Elvis a check for $2,500, an advance against royalties of his stock ownership, and he promptly went to the Cadillac dealer and got a pink one—his first one," Aberbach recalled.

Elvis's sixth and final appearance on *Stage Show* came on March 24, and Gleason let everyone know that he would not be welcomed back. Fortunately, Milton Berle wasn't quite as cynical as Gleason. In fact, as soon as he heard that Elvis would not be signed for another run on the Dorsey brothers' show, he immediately contacted the Colonel and struck a deal for two appearances on Berle's popular Tuesday night *Texaco Star Theater*. His first appearance with "Uncle Miltie" was telecast on April 3, 1956, from the deck of the USS *Hancock* at the San Diego Naval Air Station. Elvis played before the aircraft carrier crew, their wives, and dates. Other stars appearing with Elvis were Esther Williams, comedian Arnold Stang, and Harry James and His Orchestra.

Not one to miss an opportunity, the Colonel booked Elvis into the huge San Diego Arena for the next two nights. He drew 11,250 screaming fans for the pair of performances. The navy's shore patrol backed up the local police, and they still couldn't control the crowd. Elvis was trapped in the building for nearly a half hour after the second concert until the Colonel convinced the police to form a "flying wedge" to get him to his car. Reporters saw the police escort and reported that Elvis had been arrested after the show. His critics around the country must have been all smiles, thinking that law enforcement finally did something about his outrageous onstage antics.

Elvis was still under contract to the *Louisiana Hayride*, a popular Southern-based radio show, but it was becoming increasingly difficult to travel back to Shreveport, Louisiana, every weekend. His current contract ran through November 1956, which meant he was still obligated to do twenty-five shows. He was now making $200 a performance, so the Colonel arranged a $5,000 buyout and Elvis agreed to do one final show on December 15, 1956.

On one early tour through the South, a local politician thought it would be a great idea if Elvis would perform at one of his major speaking engagements. He felt it would assure a bigger audience. The Colonel had a swift reply to that request.

"If Elvis goes on first, the fee will be $2,000," the Colonel said. "If he goes on second, the fee will be $2,500." When asked the difference in price, the Colonel would drawl, "Well, it all depends on how large a crowd you want at your speech. If Elvis goes on first, possibly most of his fans will leave after he entertains. But, if you speak first, they will hear your speech and they will stay 'round to hear Elvis sing."

In addition to his expanding tour dates, another entertainment frontier awaited Elvis: the glittering desert town of Las Vegas. The Colonel booked him as the opening act for comedian Shecky Greene and Freddie Martin and His Orchestra for two weeks (April 23 through May 6, 1956) at the New Frontier on the famed Strip. It was the only open spot in his schedule and fit in perfectly.

After his Las Vegas debut in 1956, the Colonel realized they needed more technical help on the tours and consulted Tom Diskin, Parker's longtime and loyal employee, who recommended Al Dvorin. At first, Dvorin said he was much too busy with his booking agency to leave the office for any length of time. But the Colonel was insistent. Dvorin had booked an announcer for the tour; the Colonel wasn't happy with his selection and asked him to take over as public address announcer. Dvorin and Colonel Parker had met several times since Diskin left the Chicago agency to join the Colonel's team, and they had become close friends, but Dvorin did not meet Elvis until May 14, 1956, in La Crosse, Wisconsin, when he became Elvis's official announcer.

All in a Day's Work

Dvorin hated speaking in front of large crowds and told the Colonel as much.

"Al, who's the boss here?" the Colonel replied in a playful yet serious tone. Dvorin soon found himself standing in front of a large mirror, rehearsing his lines. He even wrote notes to himself so he wouldn't forget.

Dvorin nervously walked onstage, notes firmly in hand, to open the show. His voice was shaking slightly as he took the microphone and announced, "Ladies and gentlemen, welcome to the *Elvis Presley Show*." Suddenly, the house lights went down, and a spotlight hit him in the face. He was blinded by the light and couldn't see his notes. He had to ad-lib the entire show, which he managed to do without embarrassing himself. The next night, things were much calmer. It was while on tour in Minneapolis on November 5, 1971, that the Colonel told Dvorin to say something like "Elvis has left" to the audience as soon as he saw Presley was safely in the limo and on his way back to the hotel. Dvorin thought about it for a moment, and the famous phrase, "Elvis has left the building!" was born.

Unfortunately, teenage girls can't shoot craps and didn't hang around Las Vegas much, so Presley's first Sin City engagement primarily went unnoticed. Vegas crowds in those days were more interested in seeing Liberace, who was playing at the same time for $50,000 a week. Elvis was making $7,500.

It was the Colonel's future Palm Springs neighbor, Liberace, who helped save the day. Elvis dropped by to see the flamboyant showman perform one night and later went backstage to meet him. The late Jerry Abbott, a Las Vegas News Bureau photographer for forty-four years, was there and took what turned out to be one of the most famous photos to ever originate from Las Vegas—a laughing Liberace strumming the guitar with Elvis sitting next to him playing the piano and singing. It went worldwide on the wire services and garnered Elvis lots of great publicity.

Elvis's second Milton Berle appearance on June 5, 1956, originated in the ABC Studios in Los Angeles and was the first time he was backed onstage by the Jordanaires, a quartet who started as a gospel group and provided Elvis with backing vocals live in concert and television appearances and on recordings for nearly fifteen years. This time he was joined by two of Hollywood's most beautiful women: Debra Paget, his future co-star in *Love Me Tender,* and Irish McCalla, star of TV's *Sheena, Queen of the Jungle.* His torrid bump and grind rendition of "Hound Dog" drove the audience insane and, once again, the media responded with intense outrage.

"Popular music has reached its lowest depths in the 'grunt and groin' antics of one Elvis Presley," wrote Ben Gross in the New York *Daily News.* And *The Catholic Weekly* piped in, "His one specialty is an accented movement of the body that hitherto had been primarily identified with the repertoire of the blonde bombshells of the burlesque runway. If the agencies (TV and others) would stop handling such nauseating stuff, all the Presleys in our land would soon be swallowed up in the oblivion they deserve."

But Elvis was far from oblivion. His appearance on Berle's show was seen on approximately 25 percent of all television sets in the United States. That night, for the first time that season, Berle beat out the top-rated *Phil Silvers Show.* Other TV hosts took notice and responded.

Steve Allen was running second to Ed Sullivan in the ratings for the valued Sunday night TV viewing audience, but he beat out his archrival by a large margin when he booked Elvis for a July 1 appearance for $5,000.

The whole point of Allen's show was to crush Sullivan's ratings. Most of the skits and gags you see on late-night TV today got their start with Allen. He had music and dancing, like Sullivan, but with sight gags, a recurring cast of in-house comedians doing "man on the street" bits, and other jokes like dramatic comedy readings of real "letters to the editor" from New York City newspapers. Allen himself was a droll, deadpan comedian, seemingly unfazed by the zanies he surrounded himself with on air.

The contract with Allen's show had a strange exclusivity clause negotiated by Colonel Parker. It prohibited Elvis from appearing on any other TV show prior to his Allen performance other than his June 5th date with Berle. However, he was also permitted to appear as a "mystery guest on quiz panel programs." The Colonel was obviously negotiating for Elvis to appear on the very popular TV program *What's My Line?* but it never took place. My assumption is they never met the Colonel's asking price.

Elvis more than held his own in a comedy sketch with Steve Allen, Imogene Coca, and Andy Griffith, whom he hadn't seen since the touring days in 1955. He even wore black tie and tails while he sang "Hound Dog" to a basset hound named Sherlock. The fans weren't crazy about the skit, or Elvis's tuxedo for that matter, but the exposure was priceless.

A few years later, the Colonel was asked if Elvis would do a walk-on for *The Joey Bishop Show*.

"Sure thing, for $2,500," said the crafty Colonel with a twinkle in his eye. When asked why the price was so low, he replied, "Because it will cost you $47,500 for him to do a walk-off."

While Elvis was leaving audiences around the country all shook up, the Colonel, with his master plan now running at full throttle, was off to Hollywood to start a new phase of Elvis's eye-popping career. Like any entertainment manager worth his salt, the Colonel was always ten steps ahead of everyone else.

1

Dutch Boy

When most people today think of Colonel Tom Parker, the image they conjure most often is of a balding, rotund man with steely eyes and a grand, knowing grin, sporting a blazer, buttoned-down shirt, porkpie hat, and a victory cigar protruding from the side of his mouth. That, of course, is the carefully crafted myth perpetuated by the man who was the power behind the throne of rock 'n' roll's king: Elvis Presley.

The real person behind that myth began his life as Andreas Cornelius van Kuijk on June 26, 1909, in Breda, Holland—a beautiful small, bustling seaport village near the North Sea, in the southern region—born to hardworking people who struggled to make a living and feed their nine children. They lived above a stable where his father, Adam, tended to horses that pulled barges along the canals. His father spent a dozen years in the Dutch army and was a disciplinarian. He wielded a heavy hand in dealing with his children and seldom laughed and could barely crack a smile. Ever-present poverty, a large family, and the endless rotation of farm work probably had something to do with that.

Maria van Kuijk was a housewife whose job never seemed complete; she was an excellent cook who knew how to stretch the family's food budget. Andreas (nicknamed "Dries") was right in the middle of the line of children—Joseph, Adriana, Marie, and Nel were older and Engelina, Adam, Jr., Johanna, and Jan were younger. Two others died at birth. Adam Jr. was the only member of the family to visit his brother in America. As for the rest of his siblings, he saw them only once after he left the country.

Even in his youth Andreas was different. He had intelligence, imagination, courage, and an uncontrollable case of wanderlust. He felt the adults in his life never fully understood him. One exception was his grandmother, who lived in a small cottage nearby. Neighbors called her a "witch" because of her amazing healing powers and keen insight into people.

"Now, she understood me," he told his second wife, Loanne, his voice softening.

Andreas also had a deep devotion to his mother, but there was a part of him that resented her because she did not protect him from his harsh father. And like his grandmother, his mother had a sixth sense about him.

"She was amazing. She always knew what I was thinking, and I could never figure out how she could do that when others couldn't," he recalled. "Maybe it was because I never thought like a child. Even when I was a child I thought like an adult. I guess that's why no one understood me."

Conversely, he held an opposite view of his father and would grow rigid when speaking about him to Loanne.

"He was no good, no good," he said. "He was a bad person."

One trait young Andreas picked up from his father was his legendary stubbornness. Andreas hated his blond curls and didn't want anyone to touch them. In fact, he never wanted anyone he didn't know well to touch him, another trait that followed him into his adult life. Once, when he knew his two overly affectionate aunts were coming over for a visit, they went into their usual coddling tone, telling him how cute he was, making a big fuss over his golden locks. Andreas quickly looked for an escape. He spotted his mother's sewing scissors and promptly cut his blond hair down to a few scraggly nubbins.

"Now," he triumphantly told his aunts, "no one will be playing with my hair!"

Andreas's hometown of Breda is a harbor city in the Marylandsized country that borders Germany and Belgium and is located directly across the North Sea from Great Britain. It boasts its own fourteenth-century castle and a fifteenth-century Gothic church. As is common in Holland, Breda has more canals than roads,[1] and they were used for both transportation and for shipping goods throughout the country. Below sea level, the city is protected from flooding by manmade dikes, affording pedestrians the unique view of ships passing by twenty feet above them.

Life certainly was not easy for Dutch citizens of that time. Shortly after Andreas's fifth birthday, most of Europe was embroiled in the conflict of World War I. Belgium, situated to the south, was the first country to fall as invading troops advanced on France. Holland was a relatively weak nation in contrast to the European powers of that time and not considered a threat to Germany or the Austrian-Hungarian Empire. Although they had an army, the Dutch government enforced strict neutrality.

"Friendship with all, alliances with none" was the country's motto. With a large overseas colony, Holland stood to lose a lot if it entered the war. Life, while not as enjoyable as it once was, would go on. The army was mobilized for the duration to enforce neutrality. While this meant a lot of young Dutchmen stood guard in the rain for four years, for Holland the war was a distant rumbling.

The Dutch were serious, earnest, and hardworking people though they had two national pastimes that seemed to offset their weighty lives: music and the circus. The latter impacted Andreas at a very young age. Whenever the traveling circus came to Breda and set up their tents in the town square, the van Kuijks would rent a bed to one of the clowns, Thomas, a distant relative. Thomas made a big impression on young Andreas, who emulated every move and mannerism to the point of picking up his discarded cigar butts, snipping off the end, and lighting them. This, of course, he did in secret, knowing

---

1 Canals and rivers make up over 2,700 miles of the country's inland waters. Much of the land was reclaimed from the sea.

his mother would punish him if he was caught; he dared not think of what his father would do. In his mind, anyone who smoked cigars was *somebody*, and he very much wanted to be somebody the world would recognize and remember. It would be his future, but not for many years to come. (Try to find a photo of Colonel Parker in his prime *without* a cigar.)

Andreas attended the circus at every opportunity. He liked the clowns and the acrobats, but he was especially fond of the animals, elephants in particular. When Thomas was in town, he'd tag along and get to know the lay of the land. Other times he'd go by himself and volunteer, lending a hand with the chores. He'd carry water for the animals without being asked and was soon given a job helping with the small duties around the camp. Instinctively, he learned at a young age to start helping and working of his own initiative. But, even more important, Andreas discovered a real love for show business. He may have been doing nothing more than carrying water and cleaning up after the animals, but he was in show business and part of a working team. I believe Colonel Parker recognized this same trait in me when I was barely a teen, and that is where our bond was formed.

The circus sparked Andreas's imagination, and soon he began creating tents out of newspapers and charging neighborhood children the equivalent of a penny to experience his "backyard circus." After the children had all paid their admission and were allowed inside the "big top," Andreas treated them to songs, acrobatics, and a special show with trained beetles, a goat, and a crow named Blackie. These critters followed directions (to a certain degree). Blackie was smart but stubborn. He did not always follow instructions and every performance was different, depending on Blackie's mood.

"Guess he was too much like me," Colonel Parker confessed to Loanne.

Andreas, like most circus promoters, learned to think fast on his feet. His most difficult days came when it rained, which was often in Breda. Usually the tent would collapse, causing his youthful patrons to ask for their pennies back. Andreas, ten steps ahead of everyone else, may possibly have been the first kid in the Netherlands to use the "rain check" method. To him, money went in only one direction. That direction was not out.

Andreas's love for animals had developed at a very early age and remained for the rest of his life. He worked with his father in caring for the huge draft horses used to pull heavy loads along the canals. Adam van Kuijk suffered from asthma and, having to work so closely to oats and hay, he sneezed and coughed constantly. So, Andreas was given the task of feeding and watering the horses before dawn each morning. He usually got up at 4:30 A.M. to shovel oats and pump water into large drinking troughs. Adam shoveled the stalls while Andreas raked in fresh hay. He grew very fond of these huge animals and was amazed that the horses were careful never to step on him. But life at the stables wasn't always rosy. The smells emanating from below and the constant flies in the summers were punishing on the senses as well as the skin.

Because of the war, food was very hard to obtain throughout most of Europe. The Germans occupied neighboring Belgium, and everyone feared Holland would soon fall next even though it declared itself a neutral country. Even the nearby North Sea was not safe as German U-boats controlled everything from the Baltic Sea in the north to the vast North Atlantic. Dutch vessels were sunk by submarines occasionally. Holland was virtually isolated from the outside world and dependent upon its own meager resources, made even scarcer by exporting food to both England and Germany during the war.

The van Kuijks were extremely proud people and would not accept food or charity from relatives even though they had wealthy ones living nearby. The family, however, dined well on Sunday afternoons when they visited Andreas's uncle. He was an executive with a major shipping company, so these visits almost always included meat as well as the ultimate luxury: indoor plumbing. On every visit, Andreas stood in front of the porcelain toilet in amazement and repeatedly pulled on the chain to watch it flush. How great it would be, he thought, to go to the bathroom without having to trek downstairs, past the stables, and brave the blustery winter storms blowing in off the North Sea. It was during these Sunday visits that he discovered the various luxuries that were available to those who worked diligently for them, and he vowed to have them someday.

Bread was a staple of life during these hard times, and rationing was in effect throughout most of Europe. Andreas would hitch rides (or "borrow" a bicycle from someone in the neighborhood) and ride out to a farm situated in the flat grasslands just on the outskirts of Breda. Two brothers and their sister lived and worked on the dairy farm, selling milk to many local cheese factories in the area. He quickly learned which day the weekly baking was done and appeared whenever he could get away from his chores around the stables. For hours he would work, doing whatever tasks they had for him, helping to feed the chickens and dairy cows, and cleaning the barns. Of course, he was invited to share their noon meal and received a loaf of fresh-baked bread as his day's pay.

One day the sister gave him two loaves of bread to take with him. On the way home he pedaled as fast as he could, baggy britches flopping in the breeze, imagining how happy his family would be to see him with the extra loaf. He was sure his father would be very proud, shake his hand and tell him what a clever young man he was. His mother would give him a hug and tell him how much the family appreciated the extra food.

The reality was starkly different from what he had imagined. His parents were horrified, fearing the authorities would arrest them for having extra bread rations, which were *verboten*. Over and over, they exclaimed, "What if you had been caught? Have you no consideration for your family? How could you put us in such danger?" Instead of praise, he received punishment. He always remembered that time with resentment and bitterness.

After the bread incident, Andreas continued to feel less and less appreciated by his family. He felt they took and took and never appreciated what he tried to give. His eldest sister, Adriana, was the only exception. She often acted as a second mother to her younger siblings and would listen to his problems, trying to give him the best possible advice. Adriana shared her rare treats and consoled him when he was reprimanded.

Life during the war, however, wasn't so bad for Andreas, despite the lack of food and other necessities. He and his friends swam in the canals in the summer months even though the average high temperature was sixty-six degrees. And they skated on the frozen canals in winter.

Other than the fawning, Andreas enjoyed visits from his aunts because they brought special food that the family could not afford. His older sisters loved and nurtured him, often giving him part of their own treats even though he was different.

He was often teased about wishing for things that could be rather than accepting what was. "It's not Andreas's fault that his mind is too fast for the other children to follow," his sisters said in his defense. His mind was not a place that had borders.

One of Andreas's aunts was an opera star in Europe, and he attended some of her performances with his mother when the opera came to Breda. He was enthralled with the beautiful music, costumes, and overall aura of the performance. In later years, he'd sit for hours in his lounge chair at his home in Palm Springs listening to classical music.

When he was seven, Andreas often had to cross a small pine forest near their home to reach a deep blue lake on the other side. It was surrounded by large homes with balconies and porches where the owners would sit on warm summer evenings and enjoy their splendid natural surroundings, a safe distance from the war raging nearby.

Andreas took the opportunity to walk to the edge of the placid waters and sing some of the operatic arias he learned from his aunt. When he finished, folks on the balconies around him applauded. It was his first opportunity to experience just how satisfying it was to please people with his talents. Here, at least, he was appreciated by somebody. Unfortunately, his voice soon began to change, and he could no longer perform his favorite arias for the "lake people."

Raised Catholic in a predominantly Protestant country, Andreas often questioned why a priest should have the final decision regarding his actions or beliefs. He resented it when he took communion, as it was presented as the blood of Christ when everyone knew it was only wine.

"Do you really believe everything the priest tells us?" he'd ask his older sister.

"Andreas, God wants us to believe the Father, and we must believe if we want to go to Heaven," she'd respond.

He'd shake his head, wondering how such a smart person could accept wholesale these teachings that made no sense to him. He chalked it up to the fact she was a girl.

Part of the reason he found religion hard to swallow was the strict punishment doled out by the nuns who taught school. Of course, it didn't help that he was the class clown and cynic. While in the sixth grade, he questioned a lesson of one of the nuns. She responded by rapping him hard on the knuckles, which made him bleed. In turn, he bit her on the leg and ran out of the classroom and never returned.

Running away was a theme in Andreas's life—seventeen times in a two-year span. Initially, he did it because he felt he wasn't getting enough attention from his mother. When this occurred, she grew concerned and sent all his siblings out to look for him, which pleased him. At least, he thought, they cared.

When they found him in a nearby shack or barn and took him home, he was the center of his mother's attention. This ploy worked in the beginning but had diminishing returns on subsequent trips. It reached a point where the family just stopped looking for him at all. He determined his mother really didn't love him. The overworked woman didn't have enough time to indulge this one son in his games. She knew, of course, that eventually his appetite would send him home.

While he might have been starved for attention, his physical state was robust. Because of the hard work in his youth and his vigorous swimming and skating activities, he was much sturdier than his peers. Andreas was also taller than most of them, making him a standout. At the age of twelve, he began taking odd jobs around Breda, working stints in a grocery store, a jam factory, or running errands around Breda's cobbled streets. Andreas never held one job for too long and usually returned home to assist his ailing father in the stables when out of work.

He also knew many people handling the barges and found work on these cargo vessels carrying the tulip bulbs for which Holland was famous, sugar beets, and hundred-pound wheels of cheese from the dairies to the shops throughout Holland. Later in life, he believed his chronic back pain was a direct result of carrying those large blocks of cheese. However, he never lost his taste for it, and loved a large piece of cheddar.

Working long hours on the barges by day was not easy or pleasant, and if Andreas found a nearby carnival or circus, he'd slip away and volunteer to do whatever work was available.

Europe rebounded after the war ended, but that prosperity did not extend to the van Kuijk household. Adam's health had been in decline for some time. His litany of ailments, including diabetes, lung problems, rheumatism, and major swelling in his feet, made it difficult for him to perform his daily duties at the stables. In 1925, he was confined to St. Ignatius Hospital.

Andreas, now sixteen, went to see Adam, not to comfort him but to seek permission to move to Rotterdam. The city, about twenty miles away, held more opportunities and fewer responsibilities. There wasn't much his father could do, barely clinging to life as he was. He reluctantly gave his blessing, knowing the family needed whatever financial support Andreas could contribute.

On July 6, 1925, fifty-nine-year-old Adam van Kuijk died while Andreas was en route to Rotterdam where he would live with his uncle, Jan Ponsie, and his family in a middle-class suburb called Spanjaardstraat, not far from the docks.

In the beginning, the idea of city life was exciting to a teenage boy on the precipice of manhood. Being the second largest city in Holland and the largest seaport in Europe, Rotterdam boasted a population of two million people, many immigrants from Russia, Poland, Germany, and Ukraine, all seeking a better life.

Large cruise ships, ocean liners, and freighters floated in and out of the docks from around the world, and many of the seamen were Andreas's age; two of whom he befriended. Beyond the docks, the dynamic city was broken up into small boroughs and villages but interlinked through riverways, tunnels, bridges, and railroads. Each neighborhood offered churches, cathedrals, restaurants, cafes, shops, and bars. In spring, the colorful bulb fields with tulips and hyacinths filled the air with a wonderful scent.

But the postcard held more promise than the reality. Even though Andreas had a roof over his head, life in Rotterdam consisted of an endless cycle of menial work in blue-collar jobs. He found employment in retail, at the docks, and in a shipping office after his uncle called in a favor. But he found sitting in an office too confining.

The world came to Rotterdam every day, and he saw it—a world where a successful man smoked a cigar and ate meat every single day, a place that held everything he dreamed of. And he was determined to find it.

Who could blame Andreas for not being sentimental? There wasn't much about his past to be sentimental about. Grinding poverty. Menial jobs. Parents who didn't understand him. An entire culture whose ethos didn't seem to match his or his unstinting ambition. Nothing in Holland gelled for young Andreas. He was just one of those people who must see what's on the other side of the horizon. He was an adventurer, an explorer. So, he split without saying goodbye to his immediate family in Breda or the Ponsies in Rotterdam. Though he did remain in touch with his family through letters and postcards and sent his mother money right up to the end of her life (I was usually tasked with that chore, which was done bank to bank at the time; Colonel Parker didn't trust the US or Dutch mail system, especially with money), he left Holland in the rearview mirror and didn't look back.

It didn't require much effort to leave the country. With the help of his two friends, he boarded the Holland America Line ship. He slipped aboard their freighter in the middle of the night and hid in the bowels of the ship. His friends managed to sneak him small portions of food and water during the nearly two-week Atlantic crossing. Sometimes, in the middle of the night when one of them was on watch, they brought him on deck for a few minutes to catch a breath of fresh air. Then he'd have to return to the rats and stench of the hold.

The ship made a few stops en route to the States and eventually docked in Hoboken, New Jersey. Getting Andreas off the ship wasn't quite as easy as sneaking him on board; however, he managed to walk down the plank and to the dock without detection.

What happened after that has never fully been explained. That part of the Colonel's story died with him. However, a few months after he disappeared from the Ponsies, he received a letter from a well-to-do Dutch family who had immigrated to New Jersey. Andreas managed to secure a room in their house. He spent a short period with his new family, and then, just as suddenly as he had appeared, he disappeared.

Frightened that he would be caught and deported back to Holland, Andreas headed for the rail yards and caught the first freight train out of town. For the next several months, he traveled the country compliments of the American rail system.

Following World War I and right into the Great Depression, America was not a place where the streets were paved with gold as so many immigrants had heard. Many young men were forced to travel from town to town, stopping long enough to find an odd job and earn a little extra cash for food. Some were turned out by their own families because there simply wasn't enough to feed everyone. Some headed out for the adventure of it, planning to become cowboys out West or to ship out and see the world. At the height of the Depression more than two million men and a quarter million teenagers lived on the road. (It's estimated about eight thousand women took up hobo life, as well.)

Mostly, it was miserable. The danger of being arrested or beaten by railroad detectives, cold nights, days without food, begging at farmhouses was the way of the hobo life. They would leave a mark on the wall or fence of a generous farmer to signal to others there was a good chance of a meal. If teenage boys did find work, they were paid far less than adults. But there was one upside to this scenario: Andreas was able to disappear into the interior of the country and learn about it at the same time.

He spoke little English but quickly learned the new language by reading newspapers, continually asking questions, and conversing with other rail riders. Andreas also learned to stay away from the rough hobos and hang around with the more kindhearted ones. They'd share their meager stocks while sitting round the campfires at night, swapping stories about their travels. Still, Andreas was a loner at heart and never teamed up with other hobos while riding. He preferred to come and go as he liked. However, he came to understand two important rules for life on the road: make friends fast and share with them.

The road was harsh and filled with plenty of rough characters. Loners like him were usually the first targets. Once, the Colonel recalled to me a time when he encountered a gang of bullies who wanted everything he had. While he didn't have much, he wasn't eager to part with the belongings he did have. For that, he was severely beaten. It was one of the low points of his life. He was lost, hurt, and hungry. He figured it couldn't get much worse, but then it began to rain. He continued down the narrow dirt road until he saw a house with the lights on. In desperation, he stopped, knocked on the door, and asked if he could sleep under their front porch until it stopped raining.

The occupants of the home insisted he come in out of the rain, genuinely concerned about his condition. He informed them of his plight, and the women of the house cleaned his wounds and fed him. He was sincerely moved by their generosity. They were a poor Black family and had several young mouths to feed, yet they were willing to share whatever they had with him. They insisted he remain with them until the rain stopped and he was strong enough to travel.

Several days later, he thanked the family and left, refusing to take the food they had offered to him. A short distance from the house he ran into a group of white men who surrounded him.

"[N-word] lover!" they shouted. "You've been living with *them*!"

Once again, he was savagely beaten and left lying in the road. Years later, he recalled the encounter to me; it made him realize how hard it was for Black people to live in America, especially in the Deep South. "I never forgot that experience," he told me. "Kindness and goodness can be any color. Meanness and cruelty can also be any color. What counts is what is within."

When he finally recovered, Andreas continued his westward journey, riding the rails and taking any job available. All the early training and skills he learned in Holland came in handy. He could cook, operate and repair machinery, handle animals, or do manual labor. His tall build, sparkling blue eyes, ready smile, and willingness to work made him a likeable young man and won him many jobs that others did not get. Hobos knew to look for work that others didn't want to do. They also made a point of keeping themselves and their clothes as clean as possible, often spending a day or two in a hobo "jungle"—a camp on the outskirts of a town, usually next to a creek, where they could wash up, shave, and boil their clothes—before going into town to look for work. Housewives often hired them to wash windows or sweep sidewalks, paying them with produce from their kitchen gardens.

Andreas hopped off the train in a sweltering little southern Nevada desert town called Las Vegas. He remained there for a few days, hanging around the Northern and other small saloons on Fremont Street by the railroad tracks. Nevada would not legalize gambling until 1931, but it was thriving, nonetheless. He remembered the miners riding their horses into town with their dogs following closely behind. While they drank and gambled, employees brought out steak scraps and water for the dogs and feed for the horses, ensuring that their owners would not have to leave the gaming tables to take care of their animals. What the Colonel saw there was possibly the first form of "comps" for which Las Vegas would eventually become famous, and he never forgot it. After a few days in Vegas, he caught the next train west to Los Angeles.

When he arrived at the coast, he worked a few days at a tent revival meeting held by Canadian-born radio evangelist Aimee Semple

McPherson. He was duly impressed—not by her drawing power, or her ability to whip up crowds by speaking in tongues or by delivering faith-healing demonstrations by laying hands on people, helping the blind to see or the halt to walk again—but how she could make it rain money. He was awed by the sheer volume of dollars and food she collected from the followers of her International Church of the Foursquare Gospel. He was offered a full-time job working in her five-thousand-seat Angelus Temple, but after a few days, his wanderlust set in again. Since he couldn't go any farther west, he decided to head back to the East Coast and experience more of what the country had to offer.

Traveling by boxcar, he discovered a magazine another hobo had left behind. He spotted an ad for a hotel in Chicago that featured ice water in each faucet of every room. He dreamed of the day when he could have ice water available any time he wanted. He never forgot those blistering summer days in the railcar when he would have traded his entire bankroll, which was virtually nonexistent, for a drink of ice-cold water. In later years he'd sometimes pause before taking a drink of water and say, "I'm remembering that day on the boxcar, dreaming of a drink just like this. It makes it taste so much better."

Despite his poor living conditions on the road, the Colonel always prided himself on being clean. Many times, he'd slip into restrooms at service stations, hoping to find a bar of soap large enough to take with him so he could wash regularly during his travels.

"I promised myself then, that when I became successful, I would never have to use a sliver of soap again," he later recalled.

As he rode through the flatlands of the Midwest, he was reminded of his native Holland, where you could look for miles in any direction and never see a mountain or even a small hill. He was enthralled by the miles and miles of grain fields, so he decided to jump off the train in a small western Kansas town. He found work handling bags of grain in a flour mill and rented a room in a nearby boardinghouse. He often flirted with the the owner's daughter, who dished out the food during mealtimes. This usually resulted in an extra portion for the handsome young man. One Sunday, Andreas spent the afternoon sitting in the parlor with the young lady. The next Sunday another young boarder would have to take over the duties because, when the daughter became a bit too serious for his comfort, Andreas moved on to another town and another job.

While traveling across the plains, he was caught unprepared by an early spring snowstorm that suddenly sent temperatures below freezing. His only pair of shoes had huge holes in the soles. He wrapped his feet in newspaper, and then stuffed them in his shoes to keep them warm. He also huddled in the corner of the boxcar, trying to keep his tall and slender frame from the cold breeze. The only thing he could do was try to keep warm and search for a better climate. He later recalled how those wintery days and nights in the Midwest, hungry and shivering in the cold, made him so thankful to be able to live in Palm Springs.

Andreas had been on the road for several months without any hassles from immigration regarding his citizenship. Police and citizens were tolerant of hobos during the Depression, especially in railroad towns. However, he did get a bit jumpy when he saw anyone in authority and did his best to remain inconspicuous. He was headed south when another major change occurred. He met his new parents.

2

The High Seas

It's long been rumored that the Colonel killed someone before he left Holland. It's true. He did. He killed Andreas van Kuijk and gave birth to Tom Parker. (More on that in a bit.)

But that's not all. Rumors persist to this day that he murdered the twenty-three-year-old wife of a greengrocer in Breda, Holland, in a botched robbery and then ransacked the home for cash. Police reports still exist, though they never pointed to him as a suspect or, for that matter, even a person of interest. The only "evidence" to emerge was in the late 1970s when Albert Goldman was assembling his salacious book *Elvis,* and he collected some ragtag quotes from Lamar Fike, a disgruntled member of the Elvis's Memphis Mafia, about Parker's occasional violent temper.

It's true: there was no love lost between Colonel Parker and Lamar. The two went at it like cats and dogs, but those were verbal spars and usually brought on by Lamar, who tended to run his mouth and stick his nose where it didn't belong. Lamar was Elvis's friend and felt safe under his protection, but whenever he said something the Colonel didn't like or questioned something about how things were being run, the Colonel let him have it. And trust me, it was warranted.

In the late 1990s, another rumor emerged from a British tabloid that Parker had knifed a man to death in a fairgrounds brawl, but no proof was ever offered. Again, mere speculation.

This I can tell you with great certainty: Colonel Parker wasn't a criminal—he wasn't even a hustler. Crime wasn't in his blood; hard work was. If he needed money, all he had to do was work, which he did in abundance in Holland. As a child, he learned to get jobs by working hard for free, such as watering the animals at a traveling circus. There was nothing in his background that jibed with his becoming a criminal. Some people might argue that he was a con artist. I think of him as a man who saw angles that no one else did.

Killing defenseless housewives and knifing people in brawls? From a man who loved every animal he ever saw? Not likely.

The more likely answer is that his hasty and mysterious departures were interpreted as suspicious but were just due to Andreas not being much for goodbyes. The Dutch are extremely private people. They don't like to draw attention to themselves, they don't discuss their accomplishments or property, and they are reserved and formal when dealing with outsiders. They don't ask personal questions and definitely don't answer them. They don't even discuss personal matters with close friends. Sentimentality was a wasted emotion as far as Andreas was concerned. He told me many stories about his past over the years, but it was because he might offer it up as a life lesson or get a good laugh out of it. There was never much nostalgia attached to his stories.

When Andreas jumped the train in Huntington, West Virginia, he was looking for work and came across a small carnival. He was fascinated by American horses because they were much smaller compared to the huge animals he had known back in Holland. Andreas introduced himself to the owners of Parker Pony Rides and told them about his experience in handling animals. He must have made an impression because he was hired on the spot. Soon he was on the road with the owners, traveling from city to city throughout the South, setting up their small concession in any location they could find. Self-service grocery stores, the precursors to the supermarket, introduced around 1915, were ideal locations, since many parents took their children with them while they went shopping.

The Parkers took a strong liking to the hardworking, personable

Dutchman and decided to legally adopt him. They ventured to the courthouse in the small town in Georgia where they were working and filled out the necessary paperwork. Andreas felt that since he was enjoying a new life, in a new country, with a new family, it was only appropriate that he should have a new name as well.

He chose his first name after his distant cousin, the clown. The middle name was the Americanization of his own given first name, and he took on the surname of his new parents.

Andreas Cornelius van Kuijk was dead. Thomas Andrew Parker was born—a man in the New World. He would go on to create much more in his life, but his promotional legerdemain was the result of seeing opportunities no one else saw. Elvis Presley and the other entertainers he propelled to stardom had natural talent.

However, Tom Parker was his greatest creation, and would always remain so.

Shortly after the adoption proceedings, the Parker family realized their new son should also be baptized. Catholic-born Andreas Cornelius van Kuijk was now, in the eyes of the Lord, Thomas Andrew Parker, Protestant. People leave the Catholic Church for many reasons—better music, better sermons, fewer rules, a spouse of another faith. In Tom's case, he left the church for a new family.

That, however, didn't last long. The ocean beckoned. Tom traveled with Parker Pony Rides for a few more months until his wanderlust kicked in again. No one who has ridden the rails can stay tethered to one spot on the Earth for long. (In the 1980s, one octogenarian ex-hobo took off and rode the rails again because he missed his peripatetic life as a young man so much.)

But this time Tom was getting homesick too. His mother's birthday was coming up in September, and he wanted to surprise her. He reluctantly told the Parkers of his plans and promised he would rejoin them upon his return to America.

Tom quickly found deckhand work on a freighter bound for Europe, and on September 2, 1927, nearly eighteen months after leaving

Holland, he showed up on his mother's doorstep in Breda, bearing gifts for her as well as his brothers and sisters.

His return also coincided with the celebration of his sister Adriana's engagement. The eighteen-year-old drifter was warmly greeted and was soon the center of attention at the party. He adamantly refused to tell them what he had been doing in the United States, and he certainly wasn't going to tell them he had a new American name and had switched religions. Everything was on a need-to-know basis.

It wasn't long before the merriment of the moment began to wear off. Breda had changed considerably after his departure and, from his perspective, not for the better. The city was growing and becoming more industrial. Breda had always been a center of food and drink production. Hero conserves and lemonade, Mentos mints, licorice, and chocolate were all made there, and the factories were growing bigger, attracting more workers. The once-sleepy town of thirty thousand was booming now.

Not one for idle time, Tom took a menial job on the waterfront loading and unloading barges while keeping his eyes open for a position on one of the larger boats. The Dutch were the leading European sea power for more than a hundred years, beginning in the late sixteenth century when they dominated the Baltic trade. Around the same time, the Dutch East India Company was born, quickly tossing the Portuguese out of the East Indies (now Indonesia) and monopolizing the rich spice trade. Whether dragging for cod or sailing to the far side of the world for cinnamon and pepper, every Dutch boy felt as comfortable at the helm as he did at the plow.

Luck was with Tom, and he found a deckhand position on a ship that traveled between Breda and Rotterdam. Since the company had small dormitory-style rooms above their offices in the larger city, Tom moved his trunk and meager belongings there. With some seniority under his belt, he got better jobs, first on short trips to nearby ports, and then to exotic ports in China, Japan, and the South Seas. In later years, when he might make a mention of a foreign city or country to me,

Colonel Parker would comment, "I was there in nineteen-whatever," and spoke knowledgeably about the country or region. It seemed as if there wasn't any place in this world he hadn't visited.

Life aboard the freighters was not easy. Ships were half the size they are now but had twice the crew—living conditions were extremely crowded (the seamen slept in stacked canvas hammocks) and fresh water was limited. Personal hygiene was not a priority. One sailor working on a tramp steamer during the same period said his berth smelled like wet chickens, a high school locker room, and diesel fuel. They put in long hours, and there was little to do when off duty other than gamble, sleep, or pursue a hobby like macramé or shell art. Tom often went to sleep serenaded by a variety of night sounds that he had never heard around the lakes in Breda.

He spent many off-duty hours on the top deck by himself just to collect his thoughts and breathe in the fresh sea air. Standing nearly six feet tall, he was quickly accepted by his older and much shorter shipmates. He felt, at last, that he was a member of a family that cared about him. His hands grew strong and calloused. When he had blisters, he rubbed fat and salt into his palms, making them strong as elephant hide. He learned how to tie a variety of knots and how to use a knife.

Despite the living conditions, Tom loved the water and was mostly happy aboard these ships. He was eating regularly and traveling the world. He signed on with any vessel that had a destination he had yet to experience. He mastered many trades about the ship and was a quick study. Steamers were coal powered, which meant the "black gang" (because they were covered in coal dust) shoveled coal to keep the steam up. Temperatures could get up to 120 degrees in the fire room. One man's job was to break up big chunks of coal in the boiler with a fourteen-foot-long steel bar, all the while trying not to get thrown against the hot boiler in pitching seas. After spending a short time below deck, Tom had learned how to take an engine apart like a seasoned mechanic. These engines were not like car engines. They had personalities and quirks. He told me one ship's engineer started a pair

The High Seas

of Fairbanks Morse diesel engines by dropping a lit cigarette into the cylinder. He didn't know why it worked, but it did.

Tom especially liked helping the ship's cook because it meant he ate well. After a few days at sea, their supply of fresh meat would be quickly depleted, so they'd switch to fish and more fish, sometimes replaced with salt pork. He discovered there were only so many ways to cook fish, and his taste for salt pork waned after a few days at sea.

On many of his sojourns he'd leave the ship for a while and take odd jobs on shore just to eat something different. Tom was not only cheerful but could do the work of several grown men and was a welcome employee no matter what job was at hand. He would return to his room in Rotterdam from time to time to stay rooted in Dutch culture but did not return to Breda. By now, he was a citizen of the world. Going back to the draft horses was not an option.

One of his favorite memories was of the captain serving every member of the crew a loaf of bread and a liter of wine on Friday evenings. It was always good for morale, because any form of alcohol was strictly forbidden, although most of his seasoned mates smuggled aboard a bottle of wine or rum. It was on these ships he developed his lifelong habit of dipping a piece of bread into a glass of wine during his meal.

On a trip to Spain, he disembarked in Madrid specifically to take on local supplies. He soon fell in with a band of wandering gypsies because of his ability to handle horses. They accepted him as one of their own, and he joined their nomadic travels around Spain. His reluctance to eat leftover foods most likely stemmed from this short period in his life, as the band of gypsies had no refrigeration, and anything not eaten at a meal had to be tossed. Although he enjoyed his new "family," Tom overheard two of the elders discussing plans for him to marry one of their tribe's beautiful women. He pondered it for a minute but decided he didn't need marriage to weigh him down. He quietly slipped away in the night and returned to the docks.

While snaking up the Rhine River valley in Germany on another trip ashore, Tom visited the town of Cologne. It was in this city where he came across "4711 cologne." He felt it was much more than just a nice-smelling men's cologne and thought it actually held therapeutic properties. He often recommended it to anyone who had a headache or sinus issues and gave away many bottles over the years.

During his early travels, Tom got a taste of dialects and languages and could mimic just about any foreign accent. His mind was like a sponge, soaking up information from every person and place he'd ever encountered. There wasn't anything in the world he wasn't interested in, and he spoke with great authority on many topics.

His learning wasn't limited to the differences in cultures. On many of their trips ashore, crew members would gather in the sleazy dockside taverns and drink. To no one's surprise, all that testosterone and alcohol resulted in many fistfights between the seamen and the locals. Tom didn't enjoy these ugly confrontations, but he quickly learned that if there was going to be a brawl, it was best to get in the first punch. He didn't always win, but it did swing things in his favor. He later admitted to being a fair boxer when he joined the military, but soon gave it up because he wasn't a fan of getting hit.

While his travels took him to many ports throughout the world, Tom especially grew to love the Far East. However, he never found a city or country that impressed him enough to leave the ship and find a permanent job ashore.

After the First World War, many European countries needed help in becoming self-sustaining, and the United States supplied much of that assistance. Tom quickly surmised the United States offered not only lots of variety, but the best quality of life. He yearned to return there, this time legally. However, he learned from his shipmates that his chances of immigrating to the country were slim.

Following World War I, immigrants poured into the United States from Europe as their lives were upended from the brutality. These immigrants were looking for a gentler, more prosperous way of life. In 1921, Congress passed its strongest immigration laws to date. It established a quota system for all aliens throughout the world. The cap was set at 3 percent of current foreign-born residents from each country.

The High Seas

For example, if there were already a thousand Dutch living in the US in 1910, no more than thirty new immigrants from Holland would be admitted that year. Immigrants also had to find an American sponsor who had the financial resources to guarantee they would not become a burden on the state. The chances of an eighteen-year-old runaway from a small country being granted permanent resident status were almost nil.

A decade before, tens of thousands of poverty-stricken families abandoned their farms in the Dust Bowl and poured into California. By 1936, losses hit the equivalent of approximately $500 million per day in 2022 dollars. Animosity toward the "Okies" and "Arkies" was high. Many were turned away or beaten by police at the California state line.

The famed Ellis Island immigration center in New York had been the portal for most starry-eyed immigrants, but that door was now slammed to almost everyone. Canada, also suffering from depression and drought, enacted policies like its southern neighbor.

On one of his final voyages, in 1929, Tom and his shipmates found themselves stranded on a small island in the Dutch West Indies. Rather than paying the crew, the captain of their ship simply sailed off to another location. Without funds, many men were forced to sign aboard the first ship available. Tom had severe misgivings but really had no choice. The captain of this new ship was roguish. The new crew members were not permitted to go near the cargo area. Tom's instincts proved correct, as the ship was carrying illegal rum to the Prohibition-controlled United States. As the ship entered the Gulf of Mexico and approached the shores of Alabama, they were greeted by the US Coast Guard. The captain was ordered to sail into Mobile, where he was arrested. Thankfully, the crew was released without having any of their papers checked.

Tom wasn't on Easy Street just yet. He was without papers and had very little money in his pocket. The only clothes he possessed were those he was wearing. Doing what came naturally to him, Tom hopped the first freight train he could catch and jumped off in Atlanta, Georgia.

When he reached the Peach City, it was time for another life-changing decision. Did he want to continue traversing the world, living hand to mouth, scrounging for meals and shelter, or was it time to find some stability? He obviously chose the latter, because he did one of the most unlikely things expected of him. He joined the United States Army on June 20, 1929, (six days before his twentieth birthday) and did so under his American name: Thomas A. Parker. However, he acknowledged his Dutch birth and told military authorities he had immigrated to the US four years prior—a fact that is inconvenient to some in the Elvis World who want to sling mud at Colonel Parker for hiding his true identity.

World War I had been as unpopular as the Vietnam War later was. Immediately afterward, and into the 1930s, the American people, congressional representatives, and presidents pursued a policy of avoiding future wars with major European powers. The orders of the day: maintain a minimum army for defense, avoid embroilment with the Old World, and promote international peace.

Defense budgets were slashed. Rifles were outmoded. Mounted cavalry were still in use. One active officer had fought the Sioux.

Regular army life was devoted to nonmilitary tasks only the army had the resources and organization to tackle. These were the same types of jobs FEMA and other federal agencies take on today—showing up to floods, blizzards, and hurricanes with cots, blankets, and food, improving navigation and flood control by working on rivers and harbors. For a short time in 1934, the Army Air Corps carried air mail. The biggest job began in 1933 when President Franklin Roosevelt created the Civilian Conservation Corps (CCC) and ordered the army to administer it.

The CCC was a voluntary work relief program that employed millions of young men on environmental projects during the Great Depression. They received housing, food, clothing, medical care, and $30 per month (equivalent to about $650 in 2022 dollars), with $25 required to be sent home to their families. About 300,000 young men joined the CCC, many becoming soldiers and sailors in World War II.

The High Seas

The CCC provided "three hots and a cot" and a job in a nation where employment was hard to come by. Many veterans swear the military gave them discipline and focus. Tom already had that, plus a strong will, a sharp mind, and the work ethic of twenty mules. But he needed food, a paycheck, and a place to lie low until times got better. All that spelled army.

Tom's timing was fortuitous. On June 20, 1929, a few months before the bottom fell out of the stock market and plunged the nation into the Great Depression, Thomas A. Parker signed up for a two-year enlistment with the 64th Coast Artillery, and six days before his twentieth birthday, the future "Colonel" became a buck private, serial number 6363948.

Uncle Sam was taking just about anyone who didn't have a contagious disease, wasn't missing a limb, or didn't have a felony on their record. Germany had been roundly defeated with American help, but the war had been extremely unpopular. The army had been slashed to the point that it was the size of the Portuguese army (about 12,000 officers and 125,000 enlisted men). Cavalry patrolled the Mexican border. Except for a dozen experimental models, they had no armored vehicles.

The army recruited heavily for men to send to the bases in Hawaii—officers like General Douglas MacArthur believed the next war would be with Japan, and it would be mainly naval. Shoring up a forward base like Hawaii was a priority. The Japanese invaded Manchuria in 1931, then thumbed their nose at pressure from the US and the League of Nations to make them leave. It was a harbinger of things to come.

Because of Hawaii's distance from the mainland, most married men didn't want to leave their families in the States. Tom figured it was just another 4,300 miles between Holland and Hawaii and told his recruiter he'd be happy to go.

The same year Parker was inducted into the army, Inter-Island Airways began offering the first scheduled air service in six of the largest

Hawaiian Islands, but large parts of the territory were still remote and uninhabitable except to natives. Many Hawaiians existed as they always had: casting nets in the surf for mullet, spearfishing at night with torches, tending small taro patches, and living in grass huts. Japanese immigrants worked on the vast pineapple and sugar plantations.

Tourism was growing. About twelve thousand people vacationed in Hawaii annually. (Today, approximately fifty thousand people arrive *daily* at Honolulu International Airport.) The iconic pink Royal Hawaiian Hotel was built on Waikiki Beach in 1925. The most popular—and the most expensive—rooms overlooked the gardens because no one wanted to look at the ocean after a long voyage. Waitresses wore kimonos (that practice ended overnight on December 7, 1941). Luxury liners began arriving in Honolulu, which now boasted paved streets. Because Hawaii was so remote, island vacations were long. Some tourists brought their cars on the ships with them. "Beach boys" taught them how to surf and paddle outrigger canoes.

After basic training, Tom Parker was shipped to Fort DeRussy near Waikiki, arriving on October 19, 1929. Once there, he received a week of instruction before being transferred to Fort Shafter. Built in 1905, it is the oldest fort on the island of Oahu, sitting three miles north of Honolulu at the base of the Koolau Mountains on former Hawaiian crown lands that were turned over to the United States after annexation.

Tom was one of several thousand soldiers who helped protect the naval base at Pearl Harbor, manning three giant sixty-inch searchlights in defense against attack by sea. Beyond that, they didn't do much. A posting to the "Paradise of the Pacific" was prized in the army. Senior officers vied to serve their sunset tours there. The weather was balmy, the beaches spotless, food exotic, and scenery spectacular. There was so little to do one department commander in the early 1920s assigned soldiers to scrub oil stains from the pavement. Life in the "Pineapple Army" was as laid back as the military gets.

The only opportunity the troops had to go anywhere was on Sundays, when they were permitted to attend chapel service. It was there that Tom first noticed a young woman in the choir. She was quite plump but popular. Then again, she lived on an island full of GIs.

Tom discovered the singer was the daughter of the base commander. Most soldiers wouldn't dare to make an approach, but Tom sought her out after the service to compliment her on her singing voice. She was easily charmed by his manner and tall good looks. He casually asked if she had a manager. She did not, she replied.

"The only places I have ever sung are in school and church," she said.

That left an opening, and Tom offered to become her manager, citing his "many years of experience" in the entertainment business and the fact that he had a famous aunt in Europe who traveled with the opera. Impressed, she readily agreed.

A few days later Tom was called before his first sergeant and was told the base commander wanted to see him right away. The sergeant was not happy; he didn't want any of his soldiers rocking the boat and undermining his authority or making him look bad.

"Private Parker!" he barked. "What kind of trouble could you possibly get into at church?!" Tom simply shrugged his shoulders and grinned.

A military staff car arrived and drove him to the base headquarters where the general's daughter was waiting. They talked briefly and made plans for him to visit her at home with her parents. The base commander and his wife took an instant liking to the personable young man who had given their daughter confidence. They quickly approved of her "business" relationship with this soldier.

Once a week the general's staff car would pick Tom up and drive him to their home so he could advise her while she practiced running through the scales. He remembered that his opera-singing aunt had used a metronome, so he suggested she obtain one, although he wasn't quite sure what it was used for. Sitting in the parlor he would start the metronome and smile encouragingly as she sang. Unfortunately, her only "bookings" in Hawaii were the chapel service and the base Officers' or NCO Club.

She did make sure that Tom accompanied her to each event, which meant he was able to meet many important people, both military and civilian, and enjoy a much better lifestyle than other privates. Whenever he saw his name posted for KP duty, he quickly added an extra rehearsal with his prized client, managing to avoid KP on a regular basis, much to the chagrin of his sergeant. He did get called up unavoidably for nighttime guard duty and ended up protecting the base cemetery for an eight-hour shift. America was at peace during this period and things were still fairly calm in Europe and Asia. For Tom Parker, life was mostly good.

Back in Breda, no one knew of his American military service or, for that matter, if he was even alive. In late spring, his family received a trunk containing all his personal possessions. The shipping company needed his room and could no longer store his items. His mother had no idea what was going on until some time later when she received a letter, written in English and signed by a "Tom Parker." Subsequent letters were accompanied by small photos and just enough information to let her know that he was alive. There was never a return address. Maria also received small payments from her son's payroll deduction that came out of Washington, D.C.

Of course, sending money home left Tom short on cash. What he did have was "invested" in craps games. He had learned to gamble while working on the freighters. Between sending money to Maria and the dollars he made and lost from craps, he was broke most of the time. He did, however, always have enough for regular trips to the base barber shop. The barber's wife baked the most delicious pies, and soldiers could sign up for a haircut and take a pie with them. It wasn't necessary to get a haircut to obtain a pie; you just had to pay for it. One might think the troops were almost bald, based on the number of haircuts shown on their books.

Near the end of every month, Tom's money was depleted, and he'd have to obtain a loan from one of his army buddies to get by until the next paycheck. He entered the army broke and exited the same way.

Throughout his young life, Tom was routinely being "adopted" by a family, and the same thing happened in Hawaii. Tom's friend Arnold Kufferath recalled: "My father was walking our Russian wolfhound in the park one day when a slender young man began asking questions about the dog and petting it adoringly. It was obvious he loved animals." The senior Kufferath invited Private Parker home for a Sunday afternoon dinner.

Arnold took an instant liking to Tom, as did his sister, Louise, and her husband, Sonny Cortes. He was invited to the Cortes home often for backyard barbeques and was told he could bring an army buddy or two with him if he liked. All his life he took pleasure in sharing with others the good things that came his way, so he jumped at the chance and loaded the car with friends the next time he went.

He was, even during his army days, an organizer. Arnold recalled that after the cookout, Tom's friends couldn't get everything they'd brought with them to fit back in the trunk, so he showed them how to reload it before heading back to the base.

"Tom Parker was one of the most intelligent men I ever met," Arnold said, who remembered that he had lost all traces of his Dutch accent. "No one could pull the wool over his eyes."

Arnold Kufferath remained friendly with Tom over the years, and he and his family were always invited to visit Elvis and the Colonel on a movie set or in their hotel room when they visited Hawaii.

"Once, when they arrived by ship, my daughter Gale and I were permitted to board the ship before it docked," he fondly remembered. "Tom took us to Elvis's cabin, where Gale had her picture taken with him. She was certainly the star at her school the next day."

In 1931, Tom Parker was shipped back to the Coast Artillery Training Center at Fort Barrancas in Pensacola, Florida. Situated on bluffs overlooking the entrance to Pensacola Bay, the fort dominates the deep harbor. When Tom was stationed there, the army used the fort as a signal station, small arms range, and storage area.

This was a spit-and-polish military operation and not as relaxed as Hawaii. The Florida Panhandle was not the land of aloha 'oe. Consequently, Tom couldn't get away with the stunts he had pulled in Hawaii. He had few if any stories to relate about his duties there.

"The Colonel never spoke too much of his army days," Loanne Parker once told me. "We discovered that his military records were destroyed[2] in a fire, though he did obtain his honorable discharge certificate in 1982."

While at Fort Barrancas, Tom befriended three men from Louisiana and maintained a lifelong friendship with them. They were Leonard Speaks, Roscoe Van Ander, and Conway Baker. Baker went on to play pro football with the Chicago Cardinals and later landed a job with the Shreveport Police Department.

On June 19, 1932, Thomas Parker was discharged with the same rank he held when he entered the army: buck private. Three years in the army and discharged without a single stripe! It's obvious that he still questioned authority at the most inappropriate times. He was doing things his way despite what price he might pay for that privilege.

He must have been a glutton for punishment or realized that the security of the army in the throes of the Great Depression was not to be underestimated. He reenlisted for duty the very next day and, a month later, on July 18, was promoted to private first class. He stayed on for another year. On August 19, 1933, Thomas Parker was given an honorable discharge and a final paycheck of $117.57.

Now a civilian once again, Tom Parker was ready to start anew and take steps to finally fulfill his destiny.

---

2 On July 12, 1972, a devastating fire at the National Personnel Records Center in St. Louis, Missouri, destroyed an estimated 16 to 18 million Official Military Personnel Files documenting the service history of former military personnel discharged between 1912 and 1965. It's a pretty good guess that Parker's files were destroyed in what historians deem an unparalleled disaster.

3

The Road to Success

Tom Parker had had his fill of army life. But, if he'd taken a long look around the country, he might have reenlisted for a few more years. When he enlisted in 1929, unemployment was around 3 percent. By the time he was discharged in 1933, more than 20 percent of the population was unemployed. Nearly one out of every four people was out of work. The average family income dropped by 40 percent during the Great Depression.

The Great Depression held a stranglehold on the country. President Herbert Hoover didn't believe it was the government's job to "meddle" with the economy. Between 1930 and 1935, nearly 750,000 farms were lost through bankruptcy or sheriff sales. Banks—eleven thousand of them—failed, and the stock market would not recover for another quarter century. In the cities, soup lines stretched for blocks. Shantytowns popped up everywhere, especially along railroad tracks, and were nicknamed "Hoovervilles" in honor of Hoover's "let it run its course" policy. People lost their homes. Those who could find work were paid starvation wages. Parents turned teenagers out of the house and onto the road because they couldn't feed the whole family. A 1940 poll revealed that since the start of the Depression 1.5 million married women were abandoned by their husbands. Nutrition was so poor that children developed rickets—a disease rarely seen even in Third World countries today. America was not a pretty sight in 1933. (Infrequently noted is that 40 percent of the country felt no effects at all.)

The country did have a brand-new president named Franklin Delano Roosevelt who spoke to the nation on the radio about something called the New Deal to alleviate the pain Americans were feeling and to reshape government policy.

In Roosevelt's first hundred days (a yardstick against which every subsequent president is judged), he signed a host of banking reform laws, emergency relief programs, work relief programs, and agricultural programs. A raft of new federal agencies was created that to this day are known by their acronyms: the Federal Deposit Insurance Corporation (FDIC) to increase public confidence in banks by initially insuring deposits of up to $2,500 per person; the Social Security Administration, inspired by European models, to administer economic assistance to retirees who paid for their own future economic security by contributing a portion of their income; the Public Works Administration (PWA) for constructing government buildings, airports, hospitals, schools, roads, bridges, and dams; the Works Progress Administration (WPA) to help the unemployed return to the workforce through public works projects such as the Lincoln Tunnel, the Triborough Bridge, LaGuardia Airport, and the San Francisco–Oakland Bay Bridge.

One very popular move by FDR was repealing Prohibition, which gave Americans a brighter outlook on life, if nothing else. With the legalization of drinking, the beer gardens at carnivals soon became one of the most popular attractions.

It would have been a perfect time for the seasoned and hard-bodied twenty-four-year-old Tom Parker to hit the rails again. Instead, he headed back to the world of show business he had left behind four years before with the Parker Pony Rides. This time, it would be on a much grander scale. He decided to join the carnival.

Tom worked for several carnivals and circuses through the 1930s, including the Detrich Shows, Johnny J. Jones Exposition, Royal American Shows, L. J. Heth Shows, Travers Chautauqua Shows, and the Hoxie Bros. Circus. The latter was founded by Hoxie Tucker, the only man I ever heard Colonel Parker call "sir." Tucker opened his first show in 1943 and played mountainous towns in the southern states where other shows dared not to go.

As the Colonel related to me, Tucker was his most important mentor in the carnival business, and he was deeply appreciative. Later, when Elvis came to the Las Vegas Hilton, Colonel Parker made sure that Hoxie and his wife, Betty, got the best seat in the house—a large leather booth facing center stage.[3] The Colonel valued his friendships and never forgot those who took him under their wing.

While Hoxie Bros. Circus was the most influential, the Johnny J. Jones Exposition had been one of the country's largest carnivals. However, it fell on hard times when its founder died. A new owner took over, and the show was soon back on the road with Tom Parker firmly aboard. The show traveled from town to town by train with the carnival trucks strapped down on flatbed cars. Once they reached their destination, the trucks were removed from the train and driven to the carnival site. They even had dining cars, such as they were, and sleeping cars for many of the specialty acts and management. Depending on how many rides and sideshow attractions the carnival had, the trains could run from twenty to thirty cars in length and were usually brightly painted with the name of the company printed on the sides.

About three hundred carnivals toured the United States during the Great Depression. For many in small towns and rural areas, the carnival came only once a year. Exotic animals, freaks, rides, live music, and tasty food were a gateway to the wider world. Prizes weren't limited to stuffed animals in 1930s carnivals; far more valued were smoked hams, cans of coffee, and pound bags of sugar.

For workers like Tom Parker, the carnival was still a difficult and hardscrabble life. They labored long hours doing difficult tasks. Setting up the entire site and breaking it down a few days later was no

---

3 Hoxie Tucker's former son-in-law, David Siegel, whom I have known since the age of nineteen, now owns the Las Vegas Hilton. He has installed Jim Gissy, who is also a good friend, as the hotel president.

easy feat. It was not unlike building a small village in an open field or parking lot every week. As soon as the trucks were unloaded, mechanics began bolting together the thousands of pieces of equipment that formed the Ferris wheel, merry-go-round, and other rides. Tents began popping up everywhere and were quickly filled with games of chance and their inexpensive prizes. Other larger tents were erected to hold the many sideshow attractions. Electricians had to lay miles of cable to light it all. And this was usually done in blistering summer heat, since that was prime time for the carnivals.

Here again, Tom's many talents came into play. He did everything from repairing trucks and other equipment to selling candy apples and acting as a barker for various sideshow acts, as well as serving as pitchman for many of the games. Tom soon became an expert at one of the most important jobs with any carnival: laying out the grounds.

Since the layout would vary with every city they visited, the object was to pack as many tents and rides into a given space as possible. Sometimes it was a high school football field, a town square, or just an open field. More tents meant increased income for the carnival owners and a good layout man was well respected.

Tom also became quite proficient at loading and unloading the big carnival trucks. Many times, he recalled to me his first attempt at reloading. Tom and his co-workers had no trouble unloading the first truck, but when it came time to put it all back, they had many pieces of equipment that wouldn't fit. His boss simply said, "Everything came off that truck, and it will fit back in. Now unload and do it right because you will be here until everything is on board." The crew then loaded and unloaded that truck three times before they got it right. The next town required only two attempts, and after that Tom and his friends got it right every time. (In later years, he prided himself on being able to fit a maximum amount into the most minimal space.)

"I remember helping load a station wagon with all the remaining souvenirs, luggage, and other items following an engagement in Vegas," said Bruce Banke, former publicity director for the Las Vegas

Hilton. "I looked at the pile . . . to be loaded, and then the interior of the wagon. I told him, 'No way is it all going to fit in, Colonel.' He said, 'I'll show you' and quickly took over. Fifteen minutes later, after everything was in place, he gave us one of those, 'So you doubted the Colonel?' looks and left."

Carnival workers led a rough life. The carnies slept wherever there was space—laying out their bedrolls on the ground, on the merry-go-round platform, or in any tent that happened to be open. At the time, Tom owned only one pair of pants. At night, he placed them between two boards and slept on top of them, thus creating his own overnight pressing service.

Carnival workers were a tight-knit unit and often became each other's adopted family. Tom very much felt he belonged in this setting and with these people. This was a running theme throughout his life, and he often looked for a new "family" to replace the one he had left behind in Holland.

Despite the promises coming out of Washington, D.C., the country continued to struggle during the Great Depression, and many people still could not afford the luxury of attending the carnival. However, the difficult times didn't keep the hardworking carnies from eating, and that soon became one of Tom's primary responsibilities. When they arrived in a new town, it was his job to decide how to purchase groceries on credit because they usually couldn't afford to pay until some money came in. On one stop in Jackson, Mississippi, it rained for five straight days and business was nonexistent. Consequently, the carnival bosses couldn't afford to pay their grocery tab and other local bills. Tom went to see the owner of the grocery store, with whom he had established some credit.

"We have decided to stay another week to give more of the townsfolk a chance to enjoy the carnival," he said. "Now, we can give you a check for the groceries we have already received and go to another store for the coming week, or we can just continue the credit tab that we have already running and then pay you for everything at the end of next week." Of course, the grocer was delighted with another week of lucrative business (those carnies could eat!) and agreed to extend the carnival's credit.

The carnival posted a sign reading HELD OVER BY POPULAR DEMAND and hoped for improved weather and enough business to at least pay their food bill. Tom found out the grocer was a widower and invited him to enjoy the carnival as his guest.

"We have a little lady with the show I'm sure you will enjoy meeting," he informed the widower. The tent where the beautiful exotic dancer Little Egypt was going through her routines was their first stop. The lonely grocer thoroughly enjoyed the performance. Tom then invited him to have dinner in the cookhouse where the sultry and well-endowed hooch dancer and her mother were conveniently seated at his table. Of course, the grocer was instantly smitten and continued to visit the cookhouse on a regular basis.

The weather remained miserable, and the show made little money in Jackson. They stayed a full three weeks, running up a considerable grocery bill. But credit was not hard to come by with the lovestruck grocer. When it came time to move on to Meridian, Mississippi, the grocer was invited to come along. By this time the grocer was so hooked on Little Egypt he would have followed her to the real Egypt. Meridian was a stone's throw for this guy, who was happy to make the ninety-minute drive.

Fortunately, the weather cleared, and business improved in Meridian, so they were able to pay him in full. At this point, Little Egypt suddenly remembered a fiancé back in Tampa, which dashed the romantic hopes of the grocer, who returned home alone to the Mississippi Delta.

Tom's imaginative thinking led the carnival bosses to put more and more responsibilities on his shoulders. He was especially good at thinking up business-building promotions. One of Tom's most successful promotions involved carnies catching sparrows in nets and painting (or dying) them yellow, labeling them "singing" canaries, and giving them away as prizes at many of their games of chance. Of course, they always had a real singing canary on display that would sing up a storm. If a customer brought his canary back and complained that it couldn't sing a peep, it was carefully explained to him that canaries seldom sing for a time after relocating. By the time it was discovered these birds were never going to serenade their new owners, the carnival had moved on.

Tom even improved on the old P.T. Barnum "egress" stunt. To help improve turnover and expedite customers leaving a tent so more could come in, he posted a huge sign over the exit door that read EGRESS THIS WAY. People assumed it was another freak show or strange animal and would head through the door, not knowing egress was simply another word for exit. They suddenly found themselves outside, unable to get back in (unless they wanted to pay admission again, which many did).

Another winning promotion was called "Wedding on the Wheel" and was successful in just about every town they visited. When they arrived at a new location, Tom headed to the local courthouse and collected the names and addresses of couples who had recently applied for marriage licenses. One lucky couple would be invited to be wed on the Ferris wheel, and usually accepted.

When they did, Tom would drop by a local bridal store and obtain a wedding dress in trade for all the free publicity the event would generate. He did the same for the man's suit (sometimes even getting an extra suit for the best man: himself!), a wedding cake, bridal bouquet, groceries, and even a suite in a local hotel. Of course, the businesses that offered the promotional items would mention the carnival and the unique wedding in their local advertising. Family and friends of the newlyweds attended the event and afterward spent money on the many rides and games on the midway. It was a win-win promotion for everyone concerned, especially the carnival.

Tom's promotions did so well he was soon given the added responsibility of advertising manager for the carnival, although he didn't even know how to type or lay out an ad. Tom quickly learned that by approaching a secretary at the local paper and sweet-talking her he could get her to type the ad for him, and even go so far as to lay out the ad for him. He was a fast learner and was soon quite a pro at it himself.

Carnival bosses had an unusual way of keeping employees on the job through the entire season. Workers were often paid with "show scrip," also known as "Duke" or "company money." A portion of their regular weekly pay would be held back and paid to them at the end of the tour. This would keep them from wandering off halfway through a residency. The Duke currency could be used in the carnival's cookhouse or on laundry and other carnival-related services. It could also be exchanged between carnival employees and was as good as real money when it came to gambling.

According to Gene Autry's autobiography, *Back in the Saddle Again*, character actor Pat Buttram first met and befriended Tom Parker at a carnival in Du Quoin, Illinois, sometime in the mid-1930s. Years later when Buttram played Mr. Haney on the popular TV series *Green Acres*, he told Autry he patterned the role after his well-known friend.

On the show, Haney was the country wheeler-dealer. There's usually one in every small town in America. They own the auto dealership, the hardware store, and a real estate agency. His wife owns a beauty parlor. Haney's trademark on the show was always showing up with what Oliver Douglas needed.

"How is it you always show up with what I need?" Douglas asked.

"How is it you always need what I show up with?" Haney replied.

It's a question Elvis Presley may have asked himself once or twice.

Carnies were fond of animals, most of them thinking they somehow brought good luck. When the show first started in the spring, they'd head to an animal shelter and pick up a new mutt or two to accompany them on the road. The dogs soon established their territorial rights and woe to any "town" dog that ventured too close to the carnival.

Tom had his own dog, Teddy, a sandy-colored half-Labrador/half-husky male, which he became very fond of. Tom taught the animal to "smile" by raising his flews and showing his teeth. Whenever he drove anywhere, Teddy was there right by his side and remained in the car. If someone approached his vehicle, Teddy would flash his smile, which resembled an angry snarl, and the person would quickly retreat. Tom fondly recalled to me what a great companion Teddy was all those years on the road.

The Road to Success

When Tom joined the Sells-Floto Circus (which started in 1902 and was one of a handful of shows owned by the American Circus Corporation), as it traveled through the South, he had to start over at the bottom of the ladder. The good news was they traveled mostly by train.

One of his first assignments was making sandwiches and lemonade for circus workers while en route to a stop. When the train stopped to take on water during their long trips between locations, Tom sprang into action and fed the hungry laborers.

One day Tom's boss had extra duties for him, so he asked a coworker to load the refreshments at the next stop. Unknown to Tom, he placed the barrel under the wrong box car—the one containing the big cats. By the time Tom discovered it was in the wrong location, it was too late to make a change.

The roustabouts were gathering around the food site, and these were not the type of individuals you want to disappoint. So, Tom did the only thing he could do—he sold them his sandwiches and lemonade. Several of the burly workers came back and complained about the taste of their drinks. He assured them they were simply trying out a new recipe and would be happy to go back to the old flavor by the next stop. He was not about to tell this rowdy bunch that the lions had relieved themselves over the lemonade barrel.

Tom was crazy about all circus animals, but he especially liked a huge Indian elephant named Meena, who became good friends with a German Shepherd named Sam who had also joined the circus. The dog stayed near Meena at night and, now and then, she would gently touch him with her trunk to make sure he was still there. As the elephant walked through the streets on her way from the train to the circus grounds, Sam was right at her side. They became inseparable. One day as the train was being loaded to leave for the next town, the dog wandered off. Workers searched everywhere for Sam but finally had to give up and leave. Meena was distraught. She constantly moved her trunk from side to side, searching for her little friend. She refused to eat or sleep and began getting unruly, even surly with her trainers. They were worried she would become dangerous and difficult to handle. At night she cried. Tom was so concerned about Meena's well-being he decided to sleep next to her.

Fortunately, their next stop was not that far away, and they were scheduled for a five-day run. Shortly after their final performance, Sam showed up, tail wagging and looking very thin and road weary. When Meena's trunk touched her old friend, she let out a resounding trumpet, and everyone connected with the circus shared her joy. They had one happy elephant once again and Tom could return to his normal sleeping habits.

Tom soon found a new outlet for his promotional abilities and began coming up with gimmicks to keep the circus going. At one point, during a run of bad business, the bosses were thinking of lowering the price of admission from fifty cents to a quarter.

"I have a better idea," Tom told them. "We'll raise our price to one dollar and offer customers half their money back if they aren't completely satisfied." It worked. Business improved, and even though just about everyone said they were "dissatisfied" and asked for half their money back, the circus didn't experience a loss.

While wintering with the circus in Tampa, Florida, during the off season, Tom Parker met and fell in love with Marie Frances Mott, a pretty, petite, and vivacious twenty-six-year-old divorcée with a great sense of humor and a young son named Bobby. They met in 1935 at the South Florida State Fair where she worked at the Hav-A-Tampa Cigar stand. She later went to work as a waitress at a coffee shop in Tampa. Tom was very attracted to her, and she showed her interest by serving him extra-large helpings whenever he would drop by the coffee shop.

Tampa was the winter headquarters for most of America's carnivals and circuses. Tom took a series of odd jobs in the area to make ends meet between seasons. Several of his gigs involved playing a department store Santa Claus. (He continued to play Santa for the next half century or so, even entertaining my children during the holidays.) From Santa's throne near the entrance, he discovered he could see most of the store and scan for shoplifters. When there were no children to sit on his lap, he strolled around the store, keeping an eye out for potential thieves. He had reason.

One day, Tom went to the store manager and offered to work as a security guard in addition to his duties as Santa. Shortly after he picked up the security job, he was walking through the appliance department when he noticed a man slipping a small radio into his pocket. He stopped the thief, not immediately recognizing him from the carnival.

"Santa would like to know what you just did," Parker said in an intimidating tone.

"Tommy, if you rat me out, I'll just tell them you were in it with me," the man said. For once, Tom Parker was speechless and watched his co-worker walk out the door with the radio.

Another Santa gig was at a Walgreen Drug Store for three dollars a day. Tom was constantly hungry and rarely got breaks. One day, a little girl who was sitting on his lap asked her mother if she could have a hamburger. Tom's eyes lit up, and he quickly asked the young girl if she wanted Santa to eat with her. He ate well that day, thanks to the little girl and her generous parents who certainly couldn't say no to Santa Claus.

When the circus went back on the road in the spring, Marie joined them, first as a ticket seller and later handling the candy apple concession. She was very outgoing, and Tom's friends took an instant liking to her. Everyone began referring to her as "Mrs. Parker," thinking that they were, indeed, hitched. However, it wasn't until June 1, 1945—a good decade after they first met—that they were married while touring with singer Eddy Arnold in Hancock County, Mississippi.

When the carnival returned to Tampa in the winter, Marie went back to waitressing or playing the piano at a retail music store. She never studied music but could play by ear. She could memorize a song just by hearing it a few times. Tom was forever grateful that Marie was willing to work when money was scarce.

It was in Tampa, during the winter of 1939, when they met a handsome singer named Gene Austin. He was touring with a major production titled *Models and Melodies*, which featured a cast of almost sixty people.

Austin had shot to fame with a series of recording hits such as "My Blue Heaven," "Ramona," and "Girl of My Dreams," all of which sold very well. The show traveled to locations throughout the South in a fleet of trucks. Tom's dynamic personality quickly won him a new friend. Tom asked Austin if he needed a good man to work with him, but was told he already had a partner who handled the bookings and publicity and was doing a bang-up job.

"Leave your name and number with me, and if I can use you, I will certainly give you a call," Austin promised.

As fate would have it, Austin and his partner had a falling out. Austin immediately placed a call to Tom in Florida to join him in Atlanta. By the time Tom hung up the phone, his carnival and circus days were over.

Models and Melodies performed in a huge tent that could accommodate crowds of up to five thousand people. After Tom took over the promotional duties, there was seldom an empty seat in the tent. Austin was delighted with his new road manager and his unique abilities.

Even the name-brand, product-promoting stars of today could take a lesson or two from Tom Parker when it came to the art of product endorsement. He was a master at obtaining free advertising for Austin in every city he played. The format was simple and straightforward. He would usually write a letter, supposedly from Gene Austin himself, such as the following letter he wrote to Tom Chin, manager of the Sam Choy Cleaners in Mobile, Alabama:

> Dear Mr. Chin:
> My business manager informs me that his investigation shows your services to be the best in Mobile. For that reason, we are awarding you the contract for all our cleaning and laundry when we appear in your fair city. Congratulations.
>
> Gene Austin

The Road to Success

The proud Chin would then take out a large ad in the local newspaper proclaiming the addition of his famous new client, showing the letter and, of course, announcing the dates and location of the next Gene Austin show in Mobile.

Tom did the same thing for hotel rooms, restaurants, grocery stores, gasoline and motor oil, Ford trucks, and other products in every town where they appeared. In one town, Coke would be Austin's favorite drink, and in the next it would be 7UP. One newspaper clipping showed both soft drinks being his favorites.

Tom was constantly looking for ways to cut expenses for Gene Austin. While traveling ahead of the show, he'd call back to his assistant, who remained with Austin, to relay the details of the next booking. Long distance calls, which were a major expense in those days, always had to be placed through an operator. Tom would call collect and ask for "Charlie." His assistant told the operator he was on the lot someplace and that it would take a couple of minutes to find him. He would remain on the line while Tom struck up a conversation with the operator. Then he laid the trap.

"Say, miss, did you know the Gene Austin Show is coming to town?" he'd ask.

"No, sir, I didn't," the operator would reply.

"Yep, next Tuesday. It will be in a big tent on Farmer Jones' lot right next to the Texaco station on the south edge of town," Tom would inform her. "He has a big lot that will handle both the tent and the parking. The tent will be facing east in case you are interested."

His assistant would write it all down and then announced in panting voice as if he'd been running around the lot, "I understand Charlie went into town for supplies. He'll have to call you back." Since Tom hadn't connected with his party, there was no charge for the call. But all the pertinent information had been passed along.

Another way they saved money was to print Gene Austin's photo on all his checks. When they paid the small bills, they used these checks, and about 60 percent of them were uncashed as the people who received them kept them as souvenirs. Over time, this amounted to a considerable amount of money. Unfortunately, it wasn't enough to keep the show running smoothly.

The world was starting to look like a very dangerous place in 1939, and this didn't go unnoticed by many Americans. Threats of another war were rumbling across Europe, and the American government was cracking down on travel. Tires and gasoline were tough to come by. The US officially declared itself neutral in the war, in September. But that all changed with the December 7, 1941, attack on Pearl Harbor. Days later, Roosevelt had decided to initiate the Manhattan Project after being urged to do so by Albert Einstein. The war lapped at America's shores. A Nazi rally at Madison Square Garden in February drew twenty thousand people. In June, the SS *St. Louis,* a ship carrying a cargo of more than nine hundred Jewish refugees, was denied permission to land in Florida after already having been turned away from Cuba. It was forced to return to Europe. Many of the passengers later died in Nazi death camps. In November, Roosevelt signed into law the Neutrality Act of 1939, allowing for arms trade with belligerent nations (Great Britain and France) on a cash-and-carry basis. Isolationists in Congress fought it tooth and nail, despite Nazi armies sweeping across Poland in only twenty-seven days two months earlier.

Attendance at the carnivals and other entertainment attractions soon started dropping off. (In 1941, however, the government decreed that carnivals and circuses were essential to the morale of the people on the home front, and they were urged to stay on the road, as difficult as it might be. But that came with its own set of problems.)

The tires on the trucks transporting the *Gene Austin Show* finally got so bad they would drive a couple of their trucks to the next site, remove the tires from one, and return to the last town to put them on another vehicle. To impress people with the size of the show, Tom had one truck with a sign that read GENE AUSTIN SHOW TRUCK #5. The second would have a sign GENE AUSTIN SHOW TRUCK #16. They had only six trucks, but it looked like a fleet of thirty. And they were lucky to keep any of them on the road.

To compound their troubles, Austin's previous partner had left him in tax trouble with Uncle Sam. Storms, tornadoes, and hurricanes added to their financial woes. Austin finally called Tom into his office and explained that he was going to close the show.

"I just can't pay eighty-five people and the tax man," he confessed. "We close the show Saturday night." After their final performance, Tom drove Austin to the train depot in the pouring rain and saw him off for New York, where he would continue to perform as a solo act. Austin later moved to Nevada and ran for governor.

In later years, the Colonel spoke fondly of Gene, and many times he would say, "I learned that from Gene Austin." A good example of this was when a stranger approached him and asked, "Hi there, Colonel, remember me?" The Colonel would invariably reply: "Of course I do, good buddy. How are you, anyway?" Then the Colonel would turn to Loanne and say, "Gene Austin taught me to say I remembered someone, even when I didn't. And, most of all, if a man was with his wife or friends, it is important that he not be embarrassed by denying that I know him."

Near the end of Gene Austin's life, I would go with the Colonel to visit him once a month at his Palm Desert home. He was one of the Colonel's first mentors, and the Colonel never forgot it. These visits were warm, and the two men reminisced, often over a nice meal, laughing about the old days. I know these visits cheered up Gene and lifted the Colonel's spirits. Gene always took credit for the Colonel's success—and the Colonel didn't disagree.

From childhood, the Colonel wandered the face of the earth with tough people—seamen, gypsies, carnies—who had to be tough to survive. And yet, he was very sensitive to the feelings and plight of others. It was that deep sensitivity that made the shell he created around himself.

No doubt about it—Tom Parker's life was on the ascent, he was making big professional strides, and a man of Tom's stature and character was certainly worthy of a title. Before 1776, the Virginia Company recognized colonels as heads of the colony. Everyone else was a colonist or colonial. The only person above the colonial colonel was the governor.

"Colonel" today connotes a Southern gentleman, and the honor is largely a Southern tradition. Everyone knows the most famous colonel—Harland Sanders—who was made an honorary Kentucky colonel in 1935 in recognition of bringing amazing fried chicken to the nation and the world. Tom Parker is undoubtedly the second-most famous colonel.

Louisiana Governor Jimmie Davis issued a certificate in 1948 making Tom Parker an honorary "Colonel" in his home state. From that time on, he was known as Colonel Tom Parker to his friends, enemies, and business associates.

But in 1940, the world around Tom was in turmoil. Holland had fallen to the Germans in May of that year. Naturally, that had Tom concerned. Although he had chosen a new life in a new country and had no intention of ever returning to his native land, his family was always on his mind. Tom's memories of the living conditions in Holland during World War I were still sharp and painful to him. He didn't want his family experiencing those same hardships again. In America, it was doubtful that the carnivals would be in business if the United States became involved in the conflict, so Tom decided it was time to look for other work.

He read in the Tampa newspaper that the Hillsborough County Humane Society was looking for a field agent. He felt his longtime love of animals and his talent with horses uniquely qualified him for the job. But, he decided, this might not be enough. He needed some "credentials" that would push him to the front of the potential line of applicants.

He had an army of friends in Tampa from his carny days, one of whom worked at a service station. He asked his friend if he could borrow a long white smock.

"You want to be a mechanic?" he was asked as he tried it on. "No, a veterinarian," Tom replied. A doctor friend who treated the carnies provided a stethoscope to complete the picture. He may not have been a veterinarian, but sure was going to look the part.

"Doctor Parker," complete with his beyond-reproach credentials, applied for the job, sat through a short interview, and thoroughly impressed the hiring committee with his wit and electric charisma. In fact, they were so delighted to have such a distinguished professional applying for the position, that they didn't even ask to see anything that would remotely resemble a veterinarian's license.

Doctor Parker went on the payroll on November 16, 1940, with Marie as his secretary. They moved into a small furnished apartment on the second floor above the Humane Society's offices and animal holding area. The apartment was the first permanent roof over Tom's head since he left Breda nearly seventeen years earlier.

Tom hit the ground running and had many ideas for making the Humane Society successful. Cleanliness had always been important to him, and he immediately set about making the entire area spotless. He needed help and put some of his unemployed carny pals to work, including a few of his dwarf friends, some of whom he'd publicized as his "dog catcher in charge of animals."

Tom also realized that the Humane Society needed to increase its fundraising efforts to stay in business. Shortly after he was hired, "Dr. Parker," as he was called by his co-workers and subordinates, discovered that one woman sitting on the board of directors was an avid cat lover and often spoke of her many pets with great enthusiasm. While they had a separate area for expectant dogs to stay until their litters were born, there was no such facility for cats. At the next monthly board meeting, Tom made a plea for a new maternity ward for expectant felines housed at the Humane Society. He directed his remarks toward the board member, explaining how important it was that these poor defenseless future mothers have peace and quiet.

"They must be kept away from the mean, barking dogs, until it is time for them to deliver their cuddly little bundles of love," he pleaded. The board member thanked him for his sensitivity and understanding of the animals, especially cats, and immediately wrote out a generous check for their new "feline maternity ward." Later, after she saw the nice care facility he had built with her donation and dedicated in her name, she told the rest of the board they were lucky to have such a prized employee who was so caring about the needs of the animals. She also recommended that Dr. Parker receive a substantial raise.

Tom turned in monthly reports to the board listing everything they did at the Humane Society during the prior thirty days, from the number of miles they put on the truck and cans of food used to the number of calls received.

His carnival-born skills for promoting and obtaining free publicity once again came into play for the Humane Society. In December 1940, the shelter had an abundance of puppies and kittens on its hands. Tom, dressed as Santa, threw a Sunday afternoon party at the shelter complete with entertainment and refreshments. Guests were awarded lottery numbers to win a free prize. Thirty-eight happy families went home with pets thanks to Dr. Parker.

He applied his brilliant mind to fundraising efforts and instituted a donation policy that helped the Humane Society tremendously. His first effort in that direction was the installation of small empty wooden barrels around the grounds and inside the offices. Each keg had a large padlock attached to it, a slot cut in the top, and bore a sign that read: YOUR DONATIONS FOR THE HUMANE SOCIETY ARE APPRECIATED. Whenever customers received an animal from the Humane Society, they were encouraged to leave a donation in one of the barrels. One day a customer told Tom, "I appreciate my new puppy and want to leave a three dollar donation, but all I have is a five dollar bill." Tom smiled and said, "No problem," and lifted the keg. To the customer's surprise, the keg had no bottom, and the money was lying on the ground. Tom counted out the correct change and replaced the keg over the money. During Tom's entire time at the Society, that customer was the only one other than Tom who knew the secret of the kegs.

Very rarely did people pull the wool over Tom Parker's eyes, but it happened at the Humane Society when a heavyset Cuban man came in to see if they had a young goat that he could take home as a pet for his children. He explained that, as a child in his native Cuba, he had a pet goat of his own that he loved very much. At that time, they did

The Road to Success

have a goat that had been abandoned, and Dr. Parker arranged for the adoption. He asked the man if he knew how to care for and feed the animal, and was assured he did.

"I have raised many goats, señor, and this one will receive the best of care," he said with a little too much confidence.

Within two weeks, the Cuban gentleman returned and had another request.

"Dr. Parker," he said, "all my children's little friends have fallen in love with our new pet goat and now they want one of their own. Do you have more?" The man was in luck, as another goat had just been brought into the Humane Society. As he departed with the animal, he left a nice donation in a keg and gave Tom his card.

"If you get any more, please call me at this number because all my children's little friends now want their own goats," he said. A routine was established, and each time an abandoned goat was brought in, the Cuban customer was called. He was so grateful and told Dr. Parker repeatedly how happy he was making all the children with their new pets. And he wasn't just a taker; he always left behind a nice donation.

A few months later, Tom and Marie went on a date to a Cuban restaurant with some friends. Tom was surprised to learn his customer was the owner of the place. The Cuban man appeared a bit nervous as he greeted Dr. Parker and presented the couple with restaurant menus. As Tom shortly discovered, the house specialty was goat. He wasted no time telling him that there would be no more free pets for his children and their friends to enjoy.

From winning free publicity, to creatively slashing expenses, to charming everyone within earshot, Tom was learning everything he would need to know to handle the biggest star in the world. *Under promise, over deliver, and do it all with a smile, all the while working hours which would flatten most people, often on an empty stomach.* This was the Parker formula. He applied it to everything from running a carnival to being Santa.

But the real test was about to come.

4

Pulling Rank

World War II was in full swing, and America was on the ropes. There was a big demand for almost all essentials, especially metal, rubber, chocolate, sugar, meat, and gasoline. "Make It Do or Do Without" was the order of the day at home. Pennies were made of steel. Speed limits were lowered to reduce wear on rubber tires. Scrap drives were held to drum up old cars, bed frames, radiators, pots, and pipes. People planted "Victory gardens" in backyards and vacant lots, producing a billion tons of food. Recycling made its first appearance, dwarfing any modern effort. Rags, paper, silk, and string were all reused. Silk wasn't for stockings anymore; it was for parachutes (more than a few paratroopers brought their parachutes home from the front to be remade into wedding dresses). Unemployment was a thing of the past and the Gross National Product more than doubled. The US wasn't just supplying its own forces; Britain and the Soviet Union were being supplied as well.

Instead of living off the land, American soldiers brought their own canned food. When a truck broke down, the Americans just pushed it in a ditch and ordered another one brought up. While injured German troops sat in hospitals repairing broken rifles, Americans just asked for a new one. There was no way the Reich could compete. American industry truly won the war.

More difficult to produce than metal and chocolate, however, were people. By late 1942 all men aged eighteen to sixty-four were required to register for the draft. Eventually thirty-six million men registered. The country was so desperate, they even called the thirty-six-year-old Tom Parker back for duty. He was told to report to Camp Blanding, outside of Jacksonville, for a pre-induction physical. And he was fully prepared to go, but a persistent back problem that had plagued him from his early days working on the barges in Holland was compounded by his new girth and earned him a deferment. Parker, however, vowed to do his part to help America whenever he saw fit. Later, he demonstrated his patriotism time and again when he managed Elvis Presley.

The war effort continued to hamper travel in America, and fans could no longer afford to buy enough rationed gasoline with their coupons to travel any distance to see their favorite stars. The highways were filled with long military convoys carrying troops from training centers to military bases for transfer overseas. Americans were stuck in their homes listening to war news on the radio and trying to figure out how they were to survive with little gasoline, meat, coal for heat, and other necessities of life. And especially, no entertainment.

Tom Parker was about to make his mark where the latter was concerned. In 1943, he left the Hillsborough County Humane Society and became the road manager for Pee Wee King, a songwriter, bandleader, and country recording artist. He also managed Gene Austin and Eddy Arnold and booked personal appearances for Ernest Tubb. When Tom was booking entertainment he not only liked rubbing elbows with the famous but realized he did promotion very well. The marketing concept Tom developed during his carnival days translated well with promoting country stars. He'd strike a deal with a major department store where fans could clip a coupon out of the paper and buy discount tickets at the retail outlet (hopefully along with a few other items). The chain store naturally paid for these ads, and a few complimentary passes for the store manager also went a long way and greased the wheels.

As he did with carnivals and circuses, Tom traveled ahead of the show, arranging publicity, putting up posters, setting up ticket sales and radio interviews. When entering a new town, he took note of the various fraternal organizations that met weekly. This information was usually posted on the welcome sign at the city limits. He'd then attend the meeting of the Lions Club or Kiwanis and offer to sell them rolls of tickets at a discount. It was a great fundraising opportunity for the organization and Tom enthusiastically explained how much money they could raise for their favorite cause. He'd remain there for the show and, as soon as it was over, he was off to the next location.

Tom regularly looked for ways to tie in his artist with a product, just as he had done with Gene Austin. One of his early clients, actor/singer Roy Acuff, represented a flour company. At any location where Acuff was booked, Tom would hire a cook and have her bake fresh biscuits with Roy Acuff Flour for the patrons. Fans waiting to purchase tickets were given a delicious hot buttered biscuit to enjoy while in line. And, once inside, they bought a big soft drink to wash it all down.

Religious shows were usually exempt from paying any taxes in the mid-1940s, so Tom always made sure one of the acts he was booking sang gospel music. Whenever one of his outside people spotted someone resembling a tax man approaching (they were usually easy to identify—glasses, bow ties, battered briefcases) they'd immediately alert Tom. The show would stop in mid-song, if necessary, and he'd bring on the gospel act. As soon as the tax man was satisfied that it was, indeed, a religious gathering, he'd depart. Then the show would start up once more, much to the bewilderment of the patrons.

Another way to get around paying additional taxes was to be part of the agricultural exemption and put up a livestock exhibit of some type. It didn't matter how large an exhibit was if it had live animals on display. Tom would usually use a pig or several chickens, which he could easily obtain at any location.

Probably the biggest Tom Parker myth of them all evolved from the chickens he had on display. A rumor made the rounds that when one of the acts could not perform, Tom brought out his "dancing chickens." According to such illustrious publications as *LIFE* and other magazines, he'd place the chickens on a hot plate covered with sawdust and they would dance to music. The story was preposterous on its face, but the Colonel often used the story to check the gullibility of people. As absurd as it was, more people believed it than not.

"I have a deep love for animals and would never intentionally hurt one," he said more than once in passing.

Traveling with the *Grand Ole Opry* stars in the war days was not easy. There were no luxury buses yet, and certainly no airline travel. It was all done by car. Many times, acts performed matinees and evening shows in two different cities. When the first act was finished, the entertainers departed quickly for the next town, where they would begin the evening show. As soon as the second act finished, they jumped into their cars and rushed to the next location and, hopefully, arrived in time to slip into their spot on the show. The other acts followed suit. Car trouble was always an issue, especially since they were driving on tires that were usually worn down to their inner tubes.

Tom recalled to me how some of the hotel rooms he stayed in on the road were flat-out dives. It was important to save expense money wherever possible. As an advance man for the show, he didn't rate a better room and usually got the cheapest rate he could find. One night he checked into a real fleabag after a long drive. He was tired and just wanted to shower and get into bed, but the room was a mess, the bed was lumpy, the window shade was missing, and there were no towels available. Experience had taught him that in a place like this, it would do no good to complain. That's all the clerk at the front desk heard. So, he tried an alternative tack and went the reverse psychology route.

He wearily walked back to the front desk and told a white lie.

"I just wanted to tell you that I have stayed in many hotels," he said to the bored clerk, who was expecting another gripe. Then he paused for a moment. "But the room you gave me tonight is very nice. I think I'm really going to enjoy my stay."

The man was speechless.

"You're the first person to say anything nice about this hotel since I have worked here," the clerk said. "Is there anything I can do to make your stay even better?"

Tom then ticked off a list of things from turning out the VACANCY sign to requesting extra towels, and the clerk did it with a smile on his face. Tom Parker knew that understanding the predicament of people and giving them the benefit of the doubt would ultimately pay off. He understood the psychology of the fan (or the desk clerk), which can help create good feelings. And good feelings, of course, open wallets. The Colonel also respected hardworking people and felt that the lowliest job is as important as the highest. He quickly grew irritated when people who considered themselves important used their influence to impress others. He often made it a point to let people at every level know that he respected their importance. God knows, he had been there himself.

Of all the country entertainers Tom worked with in those days, his favorite was Eddy Arnold, whom he considered an extremely intelligent and personable man and, more important, an emerging country star.

They first met in late 1944 during a Saturday night airing of the *Opry* at Nashville's Ryman Auditorium. Arnold had been a member of Pee Wee King's band for several years—Tom booked King's band—but felt it was time to break out on his own. Arnold asked Tom if he would be interested in serving as his personal manager after his contract with Dean Upson lapsed. The timing couldn't have been better. At the time, Tom had under contract a wide variety of artists and wanted to concentrate on one performer only. I believe the Colonel was a perfectionist and wanted to put all of his energy behind one act rather than twenty different ones. He was a detail-oriented manager and felt the artist was best served in this capacity when he could give them his full attention. He felt Arnold had the potential to become a superstar, and he later proved his theory to be correct when serving just one client.

They signed a contract, and Tom handled Arnold exclusively for almost a decade. All of his energy and promotional talents were directed solely to the management of Eddy Arnold, which, I believe, set him up perfectly to handle Elvis Presley later on. The two men also established an instant friendship that lasted for well over half a century.

Arnold, a handsome twenty-five-year-old with a beautiful voice, was a solid choice. He had a tenor that was not only mellow but went beyond hillbilly. He had fans outside the country genre and had strong potential as a crossover artist. When the two men decided to team up, they were both still relatively young and hungry. They had left secure jobs that guaranteed food on the table and were moving into a higher, relatively unknown level of show business. Each felt confident in their respective abilities to handle the challenge and knew they were a solid team. It turns out, they were both right. Eddy had the ability to charm audiences, and Tom knew how to promote and obtain the best deals possible. His friends told him repeatedly that he was making a big mistake to give up everything to become Eddy's exclusive manager. Tom and Eddy proved them all wrong.

Soon, Tom was on the road full-time with Eddy, and Marie was not pleased. While she had been known as "Mrs. Parker" for several years by the carnies, and later by the townsfolk in Tampa, she became increasingly insistent that they get legally married. Perhaps it was Tom's draft notice that made her aware that if something happened to him, she had nothing to fall back on. Living together out of wedlock was not as accepted back in the 1940s as it is today, and Marie was not getting any younger. She had already told her parents they had gotten hitched in the prior decade during their carny days. They finally got married on June 1, 1945, at the Hancock County Courthouse in the southern Mississippi town of Bay St. Louis while Tom was on tour with Arnold. To her delight, they were now a real family, although Tom never did adopt her son, Bobby Ross, Jr.

Arnold was already under contract as a spokesman for the Ralston Purina feed company when Tom took over his management. However, he expanded Eddy's involvement with the company. At every Purina event held for its dealers, guests received samples of several

Purina products, a boxed lunch, a walking cane,[4] and entertainment by Arnold. This arrangement worked exceedingly well for everyone. The guests were fed, given swag, entertained, and encouraged to buy and sell more Purina products. And they got to watch a great show, which led to more record sales and an increased radio audience.

During this period, two gentlemen who became extremely important in Tom's life were teaming up. Al Dvorin and Tom Diskin had gone to school together in the Chicago, Illinois, area. They played in the same bands together before Tom joined the navy and Al enlisted in the air corps. When the war ended, Al returned to the Windy City and opened a theatrical agency. He did his booking through a mail-order talent catalogue. He soon represented singers, dancers, acrobats, high-wire acts, little people, and just about every all-girl band in the Midwest. He was booking strip joints, hotels, nightclubs, fairs, and any venue with a chair that needed an act.

He soon realized that he needed a reliable office manager and hired his old friend, Tom Diskin. The two men were complete opposites. Al was big and blustery with a thick black mustache and a perpetual cigar sticking out from under it. Tom, on the other hand, was quiet but well organized—so organized in fact that he even sorted out Al's paper clips. They were like the Odd Couple but good for each other.

Diskin had three singing sisters who went by the stage name of the Diskin Sisters. They were appearing with Pee Wee King in Chicago when Eddy Arnold saw them and suggested to Tom Parker that they would sound good on his Purina radio show in Nashville. Not wanting his sisters to travel alone out of state, Diskin asked his boss for a leave

---

[4] An interesting note from this period: The gentleman selling the walking canes to Tom Parker was Arkansas businessman William Jefferson Blythe III. Three months after his death in an automobile accident, his wife, Virginia, gave birth to a son christened William Jefferson Blythe IV. At age sixteen, William Blythe took on his stepfather's last name, which was Clinton. On the last day of his life, in 1997, Tom Parker proudly watched on television Bill Clinton's second inauguration as president of the United States. By then, Bill Clinton had been a card-carrying member of the Snowmen's League for years.

of absence from the agency so he could accompany them south. Diskin met Parker on his first visit to Nashville, but there was little conversation between them.

However, nothing and no one missed Parker's attention. He was always observing what was happening and was totally aware of everything and everyone going on around him. On their second meeting, he approached Diskin and asked, "Are you involved in anything now that you can't get out of?" Diskin said he wasn't and was hired by Tom Parker on the spot.

The same traits that had made Diskin so valuable to Dvorin's operation became evident to Parker. He was a cheerful young man, intelligent, with a good sense of humor and an amazing talent for details. He fit into the Parker operation perfectly. Tom Parker was ingenious at taking on a major project and creating the big picture. Diskin had the patience and understanding to work out the minute details that were necessary to fulfilling Parker's grand vision. He became a most important part of All Star Shows and was the liaison between Parker and everyone else. Parker seemed overpowering to most people, those who didn't know how exactly to respond to his boundless energy and active mind. When a situation would arise, it was Diskin who smoothed everything out. He had the utmost respect for his boss, and his loyalty to him is legend. Just like that, Tom Diskin's life changed forever. One minute he was living in Chicago, helping his sisters break into show business, and the next thing he knew he was in Madison, Tennessee, working for a man who was destined to change show business forever.

With Tom Parker's guidance and Tom Diskin's execution, Eddy Arnold's career began to soar. Parker worked an extraordinary number of hours and needed only a few hours of sleep each night. His mind was constantly working overtime. Soon after he took over as Arnold's manager, he negotiated a recording contract with RCA Victor, and it put them in the big leagues. Arnold's recordings were becoming huge hits on the charts. His songs "Anytime," "What a Fool I Was," "Don't Ever Take the Ribbons from Your Hair," and "There's Been a Change in Me" were all in heavy rotation and selling extremely well.

By 1946, Arnold was playing major engagements throughout the South, and Tom had him hosting a portion of the *Grand Ole Opry* on network radio. His easy charm and big talent, along with Tom's business savvy, were a winning combination.

After weeks of trying, Tom finally convinced Arnold to give up the steady but confining *Opry* gig to host his own coast-to-coast show sponsored by the Ralston Purina Company. It went over so well it soon became a daily show called *Checkerboard Jamboree*, originating live from WMAK radio in Nashville.

The daily show limited Arnold's availability for personal appearances outside of Tennessee. To get around this, Tom had him record several shows in advance. Radio technology was progressing rapidly after the war, and they were soon able to do remote broadcasts from several stations while out on the road. They both saw the potential in syndicating their radio shows and soon had the fifteen-minute *Eddy Arnold Show* recorded and sent out to radio stations across the country. By the end of 1947, more than three hundred radio stations aired the prerecorded shows.

The Arnold skyrocket ride, with Tom Parker at the controls, continued with one chart-topping hit after another. "Make the World Go Away," "Just a Little Lovin'," "Tennessee Stud," and his trademark "Cattle Call" helped make Arnold the nation's number one country recording artist.

As Arnold's stock continued to rise, Tom Parker's fortunes also took a turn for the better. Because Arnold made his home in Madison, Tennessee, Tom and Marie made the move from Tampa to be closer to his star. In August 1949, he plunked down $20,000 on a beautiful three-bedroom, two-bath home on Gallatin Road in rural Madison. It was built of stone, boasted a large fireplace in the living room, and was surrounded by acres of rolling farmland. He converted a garage in the back of the house into an office and later added another small building to hold his files and other memorabilia.[5]

---

5 When Parker finally sold the property in 1992, the area was entirely zoned for commercial business.

Marie loved her new home and quickly made friends. She had them over for frequent visits, dinners, and card games. She was also a member of the local garden club and was very active in her Baptist church on Gallatin Road. She would later recall this period as the best time of her life.

Tom's Madison offices had many innovative additions that he used to his advantage. One was a phony stock market ticker-tape machine like the kind that brokers used to print out stock market quotations. When an important meeting was taking place, and he wanted to pause it, he surreptitiously pushed a button that set the machine off with a ringing bell. He would politely excuse himself and say, "I have a stock that I am watching very closely." He'd then look at the tape with great interest, which gave him a chance to collect his thoughts for the next portion of the meeting.

Another device he used to his advantage was a recording machine with the sounds of cows, chickens, pigs, horses, and a barking dog. When an important call came in from New York, Los Angeles, Chicago, or some other large metropolitan area, Tom punched up the machine and advised the caller that they caught him out in the barn tending to the animals. He'd then apologize and ask them to speak up so that they could be heard over the livestock. This inevitably brought up questions about the size of his farm. That was Tom's cue to go into greater detail about his herd of cattle, the hundreds of chickens, and his many horses. Sometimes he'd even brag about his racing stable.

It was from this home office that Parker commenced a lifetime relationship with the William Morris Agency in Los Angeles. He negotiated Arnold's first two movies, *Feudin' Rhythm* (1949) and *Hoedown* (1950). While they were never Academy Award contenders, both films did good business at the box office.

Parker also made inroads to Las Vegas when he booked Arnold into the plush El Rancho Hotel, the first resort hotel, built in 1941, at the north end of the Las Vegas Strip. It was the first of many very successful headline engagements in Vegas that Arnold would enjoy for years. At the time, the desert city was still a small gambling center but was emerging as a tourist destination.

Las Vegas has always been a strange place, but Vegas in the 1950s was beyond surreal. Nuclear testing was going on sixty-five miles north of the Strip. The Chamber of Commerce published a map showing the best places to see nukes exploding. There were Miss Atomic Blast beauty contests. Casinos began installing carpeting. The electric cowboy "Vegas Vic" sign appeared in 1951. He said, "Howdy, pardner" every fifteen minutes around the clock until people complained about his relentless voice. In 1954, the county sheriff was busted for owning a brothel and the governor had to resign. The Rat Pack (Frank Sinatra, Dean Martin, Sammy Davis Jr., Joey Bishop, and Peter Lawford) ran over the town like a wolf pack; the 1950s was their heyday.

Almost all the big hotel casinos—the Riviera, the Sands, and the Dunes—were built in that decade. Eastern Jewish and Italian mobsters financed the hotels and installed their own front men. The tourists, gamblers, and vacationers financed all of this, and they weren't the young things in bikinis and muscle shirts you see by the pool at the Hard Rock today. That demographic couldn't afford Vegas in the 1950s. This was the American postwar boom, and a lot of people who were making good money (and had just survived World War II) wanted to have a good time, cost be damned. They had grown up during the Great Depression, working full-time jobs when they were nine; they froze or roasted their asses off fighting Germans and Japanese, and now had good-paying jobs. The one week a year they took off happened in Vegas, and their wives had a fur coat or stole to show off in the desert while they took in the top acts in the country, swam in immense pools, and dined on buffets of roast beef, shrimp, and potatoes au gratin.

"They were great, great audiences," said comedian Red Buttons. "You'd look forward to working, and the money was enormous. Four weeks in Las Vegas could buy you a Third World country."

For entertainers, it was paradise. The joints fought over talent and paid them handsomely. For people who were used to touring by train or car, Vegas was a place to earn a great paycheck but still come home to the missus each night. And then along came Elvis.

"Like a jug of corn liquor at a champagne party" is the way *Newsweek* magazine described Elvis's Las Vegas debut.

Tom Parker not only helped to bring top acts to Sin City but changed the face of Las Vegas–style entertainment forever when Elvis began appearing live again in 1969. As far as I'm concerned, a bronze statue of Colonel Tom Parker should stand alongside Elvis outside the Hilton on Las Vegas Boulevard.

The hobo turned carnie turned music manager was finally living the American dream. He often went head-to-head with the top executives in the entertainment field and rarely drew the short straw. His word was his bond and was as ironclad as one of his contracts, and so was his friendship.

While Colonel Parker was very adept at promoting Eddy Arnold, he was promoting himself at the same time. He was not a quiet behind-the-scenes player who made discreet moves on behalf of a client. No, he wasn't that guy. He was *never* gonna be that guy. Tom Parker may not have been *the* star, but he was definitely *a* star, even if only in his own mind.

For example, newspaper ads for Arnold would contain large copy reading, "Under the exclusive management of Thomas A. Parker." He also made sure his name and logo (a red covered wagon that read WE COVER THE NATION) appeared in all news releases that went out promoting Arnold's concerts and other appearances. He easily justified this self-promotion by saying, "Anyone interested in booking Eddy Arnold certainly knew who they had to contact to get it done."

Arnold was not always happy with the antics of his blustery manager, however. While he trusted him completely, he didn't care for his flamboyant approach to business or how his promotional attempts came with a carny flair. He was oblivious to fashion, would break out straw hats and checkered shirts at press parties, or would personally hawk programs, photos, and buttons to fans waiting in line to get into a venue.

He wasn't always tactful in his dealings either. He worked Arnold and his band relentlessly and browbeat the crew members in public when they didn't follow his exact orders. Other times he'd con people at a radio station out of a free lunch or threaten a record store if they didn't properly promote an Eddy Arnold record release. Parker got unbelievable results for his client, but he was obnoxious and not so gracious, which didn't go unnoticed by Arnold.

"Tom's a dear man, a good manager, but a completely different person than me," Arnold was quoted in Michael Streissguth's 2009 biography *Eddy Arnold—Pioneer of the Nashville Sound*. "I'm very laid back, very quiet, not flamboyant at all. Tom is."

Their two vastly different personalities began to clash more and more. Arnold, who was the consummate gentleman and professional, was not used to these confrontations, nor did he find them pleasant. It finally came to a head during Arnold's second Las Vegas appearance at the Sahara hotel in May 1953. Arnold had intercepted a phone call meant for Parker. It was a promoter confirming a show that Parker had booked for Canadian crooner and RCA Victor recording artist Hank Snow. That came as a shock to Arnold, who had signed an exclusivity deal with Parker for 25 percent on everything that he made. (The deal worked both ways—the manager managed only one client, and the client had only one handler.) Most managers received 15 percent, but Parker got an extra 10 percent for that exclusivity clause. And Arnold was happy to give it to him because he knew the Colonel was worth every penny. Everybody knew Colonel Parker's work ethic, which was that he essentially spent every waking hour thinking about how to make his client richer and more famous. Who wouldn't want a guy like that in your corner?

Yet Arnold felt Parker had outright breached their contract. And yes, he had. After he finished the Vegas engagement, Arnold had his attorney reach out to notify Parker his services were no longer required. It would cost Arnold $50,000 (more than half a million in 2022 dollars) if he wanted his independence that badly. This was a downright shame, as the two men had worked so well together, enriching each other during one of America's more robust periods.

The two worked out an undisclosed but amicable separation agreement and had only nice words to say about each other in the press when they made a joint announcement in an August 1953 issue of *Billboard* magazine.

"I have nothing but praise for Tom. He's been a great manager," Arnold told the *Billboard* reporter. "It is my desire that we remain friends."

And they most certainly did. Eddy Arnold and Colonel Parker remained close friends until the end, exchanging phone calls and visiting on a regular basis. In fact, Colonel Parker was instrumental in getting Arnold booked into the International Hotel in 1970 where Elvis had a residency when he resumed his concert career. He also booked a two-week engagement for Arnold at the Sahara in the late 1970s, which was a big deal back then. Arnold was also a key speaker at Colonel Parker's tribute service in January 1997. Whatever disagreement the two men had decades before, I can assure you it passed quickly. I was with the Colonel in Las Vegas a lot in the 1970s, and the two men made a point of seeing each other whenever possible. There was great mutual respect between these two men.

Their parting turned out to be fortuitous for Colonel Parker. Arnold's career had peaked and never again reached the heights that it had under Parker's management. I can tell you from personal experience that Eddy Arnold regretted parting ways with the Colonel. However, he was still in a very good place financially. Arnold's record royalties, publishing, and personal appearance income, along with solid long-term investments had made him a wealthy man. He became one of the few country artists of his generation to make and keep his fortune. When he died in 2008 at the age of eighty-nine, he was worth about $40 million. And a former carny with a catchy name put a good portion of that fortune in Arnold's pockets.

Colonel Parker found no problem rounding up more clients after his split with Arnold. He was soon back booking several country stars, rather than just one. He had much more prestige in the industry than ever before. His roster included Webb Pierce, Carl Smith, Cowboy Copas, Roy Acuff, Mother Maybelle and the Carter Sisters, Bashful Brother Oswald, Pap and His Jug Band, and Hank Snow.

During the same period, he organized the famed Hadacol Tour for the company's owner, Louisiana Senator Dudley J. LeBlanc. LeBlanc, whose nickname was "Dud," was a wily Cajun huckster and he was the key to the Cajun vote in Louisiana. Democrat or Republican, it didn't matter: if you had the money, he'd endorse you to win the bayou vote.

"Hell, you can't buy LeBlanc," said Louisiana Governor Earl Long. "You can only rent him."

Hadacol was promoted as a vitamin supplement but it was actually a potent spirit that contained 12 percent alcohol. It was usually consumed by elders, though its popularity soared in dry counties and with teenagers. One consumer wrote to LeBlanc in 1950: "I was disable [sic] to get over a fence. After I took eight bottles of Hadacol . . . I feel like jumping over a six-foot fence and am getting very sassy." Country and Cajun performers often sang about it: "Drinkin' Hadacol" by "Little Willie" Littlefield, "Everybody Loves That Hadacol" by Tiny Hill and His Orchestra, and "What Put the Pep in Grandma" performed by Audrey Williams with the Drifting Cowboys. LeBlanc, neither a doctor nor a pharmacist, created the name "Hadacol" from his former business, the Happy Day Company, maker of Happy Day Headache Powders. (The company folded when the Food and Drug Administration seized it.) The American Medical Association condemned Hadacol in 1951. That same year LeBlanc sold Hadacol to Northern investors. It turned out the brand was crushed by millions in debt LeBlanc hadn't disclosed and gave them a major hangover. It also killed his chances for reelection in Louisiana.

The Hadacol Tour throughout the South featured Hank Snow as the star and showcased several older Opry stars who performed and then gave thinly veiled testimonials onstage about how Hadacol had improved their energy level, even hinting that their sexual prowess was pleasing to their spouses and put new pep into their marriages. These shows sold Hadacol by the boatload[6] under the auspices of wellness, which made the sponsors and consumers very happy. Even better, the cost of admission to the show was a Hadacol box top. It was a win-win scenario for everyone involved, and the kind of happy outcome that was Colonel Parker's trademark. On the last tour in 1950, LeBlanc netted $3 million.

But the most impressive thing about that tour was Snow, who was the most successful music star to come out of Canada during country and western's formative years. He was also a distinctive stylist, a talented songwriter and guitarist, and would demonstrate over time to be one of the most prolific recording artists of all time. He also proved to be a masterful businessman and recognized the same in Colonel Parker.

Snow grew up dirt poor, was sent off to live with a grandmother when his parents divorced, was beaten by her, ran away often to his mother, and was beaten like a rented mule again when she remarried. But cotton fields and sharecropping were not his lot. Snow was from a seaside town in Nova Scotia. As a teenager he worked on cod draggers (until his schooner almost went down in a gale and he swore off the sea forever), sold fish door-to-door, cut firewood, and unloaded ships. Christened Clarence Eugene, he started out playing for free on a radio station. The announcer suggested he change his name to "Hank" because it sounded better with cowboy songs.

His career didn't age well. In later years, when country music started becoming slick and heavily produced, Snow helped form the Association of Country Entertainers. He and the other founders decided (with good reason) that moves like welcoming Olivia Newton-John to country radio while dropping folks like Roy Acuff were not headed in the right direction. He relented three years later, saying, "Judging from my record sales of the past three years, I've been doing something wrong. If you can't beat them, join them." His career was effectively over when Garth Brooks soared over audiences on a wire

---

6 Boatload is an understatement. No fewer than a hundred trucks made up the tour—most of them loaded with cases of Hadacol.

and Tim McGraw got buff, married a hot country superstar wife, and began starring in movies and television.

But long before that, in the spring of 1954, Parker booked Snow on a record promotional tour for RCA Victor that was extremely successful. Snow wrote him a letter from the *Grand Old Opry* offices in Nashville that read, in part:

> *Dear Tom,*
> *Now that the Victor Tour is over and I feel somewhat rested, I thought I would drop you a line to let you know just what I thought of the complete tour. First, I want to say I think it was one of the greatest record promotions I have ever been connected with. Second, it was the great job you and members of Jamboree Attractions did that made this so outstanding. Really, if every promotion was handled as this one was, this business would be Christmas Day all year 'round. I noticed all the things you did when I went out on stage to do my bit, you were always down in front giving me a hand. Thanks, pal.*
>
> *Your friend always,*
> *Hank Snow*

Throughout 1954, Hank Snow was so pleased with Parker's handling of his bookings that on November 20, 1954, he and Colonel Parker entered into a three-year agreement that would commence on January 1, 1955. The terms of their contract read that personal expenses would be paid out by each, but business expenses would be shared. The Colonel was to receive 15 percent of all gross receipts of Snow (except for personal appearances for which he would receive 25 percent and for any existing contracts renewed for a better rate he was to receive 25 percent of the increase; if Colonel Parker renegotiated a personal appearance fee, anything over the original amount would be split 50/50). Their working relationship must have been satisfactory to both because a month later they entered into a partnership agreement

Pulling Rank 81

forming a booking/promotion agency known as Jamboree Attractions/Hank Snow Attractions. It proved to be a successful promotional outfit and booking agency in the South, especially for young country singers.

Things only improved when Snow's RCA Victor recording of "I Don't Hurt Anymore" became that year's number one country/western recording. The Colonel once again was managing the country's top artists. His reputation in management at the time was stellar, and it was only getting bigger.

The next chapter in Colonel Tom Parker's life was unfolding. His experience and ability was about to be put to the test when he and a young history-making singer joined forces. America—and the world—was about to be turned on its ear.

5

Artist of the Century

The first time Colonel Parker had an opportunity to see Elvis Presley live in concert was on November 24, 1954, when Elvis was appearing at the Municipal Auditorium in Texarkana, Texas. The nineteen-year-old swivel-hipped singer with the pouty good looks and combed-back and slicked-down ducktail had been making a lot of noise in the Deep South that year, which saw the Sun Records release of "That's All Right," "Good Rockin' Tonight," and "Milkcow Blues Boogie."

"That's All Right" caught the attention of Memphis disc jockey Dewey Phillips, who played the single in constant rotation on his top-rated show, *Red, Hot & Blue,* on WHBQ radio. It was one of the first programs in the Memphis area to play rhythm and blues and rock 'n' roll during the 1950s. All the kids listened to *Red, Hot & Blue*. It played their music, not their parents'. It was considered a big deal for a local like Presley to be featured on the radio. He was about to break out of his Deep South base (mostly screaming teenage girls and male rockers who weren't jealous of Elvis) to become an international phenomenon, but he needed a little time and a big push from the right kind of power.

Enter Colonel Tom Parker.

By now Tom had enough experience in the music business to master it. At least that's what someone like Elvis saw—a businessman who knew what he was doing. He'd have had no idea of the crow-and-beetle circus in Holland, the carny years, or the Hillsborough County Humane Society in Tampa., Florida. The Parker formula—under promise, over deliver, scrutinize every tiny detail, and work mule-killing hours—worked for every act.

It might seem as though Parker constantly bumped into good luck, but luck really had nothing to do with it. Ever since he was a child, staying alert and keeping an eye out for opportunity was how he got work and, once he'd secured that work, became invaluable.

So, it wasn't a coincidence that Colonel Parker was in Texarkana that night. He had received a field report from Nashville promoter Oscar Davis, who was doing advance work for an Eddy Arnold appearance in Memphis's Ellis Auditorium in October 1954. Parker's eyebrows raised when Davis described a live appearance Elvis made at a club called the Eagles Nest, which packed the joint nightly.

Davis eventually managed to meet Elvis backstage through Bob Neal, Elvis's manager, who knew Colonel Parker through his business dealings. Neal was more of a friend than a manager, though.

Neal was a local disc jockey for WMPS—a country station in Memphis—when he first met Elvis in 1954. He liked Elvis and, at the time, felt the two could benefit each other as Neal was looking to expand his reach in the entertainment industry.

"I was thinking one day, and asked Elvis, had he got a manager," Neal recalled to a Nashville reporter in 1973. "He said 'No' and, well, I said, 'I've never been a manager, but let's try it.'"

And try it they did for about eighteen months. They even had a contract. However, Neal could only do so much for his client. He had no established network outside of the South and Elvis's bookings were mostly relegated to nightclubs, dive bars, and rodeo grounds. Elvis wanted better bookings and felt it wasn't an unreasonable ask. That was problematic for Neal, who, in addition to his duties as a disc jockey, ran a music store, and his new role often required him to be away from his wife and children. He did not have the vision nor the time to take Elvis to the top, but he knew someone who did.

That man was Colonel Tom Parker.

Neal knew firsthand of Parker's connections in the entertainment business, so he had no doubt Parker could take Elvis's career to the next level and wanted the two to meet. Neal was not territorial when it came to Elvis and wanted only the best for him. The best meant having Colonel Parker represent him, which is exactly what Davis told Elvis that night. So now the Colonel and Elvis knew about each other, but the Colonel needed to see this young man with his own eyes and do it in a way that didn't tip his hand that he might be interested in signing him to a personal management contract.

When Parker entered the Municipal Auditorium that night in Texarkana, a seven-hour drive from his home in Madison, Tennessee, he didn't know what to expect, but he liked what he saw.

"They [the audience] were going crazy, especially the young girls," the Colonel told me one night in his Palm Springs office. "They were screaming and fainting and throwing their clothes on stage."

He added that every female on the premises lost control of her heart, senses, tear ducts, and in some cases, bladder, to the heartthrob with the ball-bearing hip joints.

Nothing like this happened at a country performance, no matter who was playing. This was something entirely new. And it was very powerful.

The Colonel remained in the back of the room that night and left before the show was over, making no contact with Elvis. But the memory of the spectacle that took place remained etched in his memory, and when the time was right, he would act.

That moment came to pass on February 6, in between Elvis's two sets at the Ellis Auditorium in Memphis. Parker, Bob Neal, Tom Diskin, Oscar Davis, and Sun Records' Sam Phillips met across the street from the venue at a café called Palumbo's, a nondescript eatery in a brick building on Poplar Avenue. Elvis and some of his bandmates sat in for a portion of the meeting.

Phillips recognized there was something bubbling underneath the surface with rock and roll and helped advance the genre. A former owner and operator of three radio stations in the Deep South, he was also an early investor in the Holiday Inn chain of hotels and an advocate for racial equality. He put his heart, soul, and sweat into Sun Records and Sun Studios, and Elvis was his prized artist. At that gathering, Colonel Parker ruffled a few feathers, most of them belonging to Phillips. Parker explained to Elvis that Sun didn't have the connections to get him in front of a national audience. Naturally, Phillips got his dander up. Not only did he give Elvis a big break by recording him, but he poured a lot of work into Elvis's career.

Neal stepped in and wisely eased tensions by bringing up Elvis's upcoming tour. Davis mentioned that working with Parker could get more of Phillips's records into more stores, which he liked hearing.

For Elvis, it was not so painful. Everyone seated at the table wanted him to succeed (and all of them played a part in his eventual success). He was most especially impressed with the cigar-smoking Colonel Parker, who agreed to work with Bob Neal until his contract with Elvis expired. Elvis also joined the Jamboree Attractions tour, although he didn't exactly start on the right foot with Hank Snow.

The Colonel told me that at one of Elvis's first Jamboree shows, he went on right before Snow, who was the headliner. Elvis did his thing, shaking his hips, as his twinkling eyes, a half smile that pinched his cheek into a dimple, and those pouty lips made for a combustible combination, causing the young girls in the audience to go mad. And when he left the stage after a few songs, he took pretty much the entire audience with him. When Snow finished his set, he cussed Elvis out.

"This is a family show, young man!" Snow lectured. "What you did out there was extremely lewd, and I don't ever wanna see you do that again, or you're gone from this tour."

Elvis was stunned, but he bit his lip. He was an extremely polite young man and had been taught to respect his elders. He let Snow—who was a complete jerk—speak his piece, but he wasn't going to stop being who he was or hold back on his performances. He knew what audiences responded to, and he wasn't about to deliver a flat show to appease Snow, whom he probably thought was past his prime. Keep in mind, Snow was a small man who stood no taller than five foot four. He had a little man's complex and a big chip.

Colonel Parker wasn't that crazy about him either, but he never let on how he felt. Snow could be abrasive and talked down to a lot of people on tour because they were beholden to him. But that didn't mean they respected or liked the man.

In the meantime, Colonel Parker still needed Snow to do his bidding, especially where it concerned Elvis's parents. Snow was Gladys Presley's favorite singer, and the Colonel planned to cash in that chip when he needed it.

While appearing with Webb Pierce at the Robinson Auditorium in Little Rock, Arkansas, on August 3, 1955, Elvis invited his parents, Gladys and Vernon Presley, to see him perform and to meet Colonel Parker for the first time. Prior to 1971, the age of majority—when one was considered an adult—was twenty-one, and at the time Elvis was still twenty years old, so his parents were legally his guardians and were central to all negotiations. It's been said that Vernon and the Colonel got along just fine, but Gladys didn't walk away with a favorable impression. And I get that. Privately, the Colonel was a hoot and a lot of fun, but to outsiders and the media, he came off as glib or flippant. He wasn't a "glad-handing" type of guy who worked a room. He operated on a need-to-know basis with people and usually played his cards close to the vest. He was a hard-boiled man and was all business, all the time. What you saw was what you got, and not everyone liked that approach.

There were other subsequent meetings and a few failed attempts by Colonel Parker to sign Elvis, and it was Gladys who did the rebuffing. She sensed the Colonel was pushing too hard and told her son to wait. People like Gladys have a word for people like Colonel Parker: slick.

That meant Colonel Parker needed Hank Snow more than ever. He asked Snow, who professed to be a clean-living Christian (despite his foul mouth, bad temperament, and cruel treatment of people), to put in a good word for him whenever he spent time with Elvis's parents.

Bob Neal, who was in the middle, was certainly pushing for the Colonel. He wasn't getting the type of major bookings he knew Elvis deserved. Plus, he was getting deeper into debt, and Elvis was already in the habit of spending money faster than it was coming in. Neal even offered the Sun Records masters of Elvis's early recordings to RCA Victor in New York City. Joe Delaney, a friend of the Colonel's, was with RCA Victor at the time. He recalled this incident in vivid detail.

"Neal offered the masters to Manie Sacks, who was VP of recording at the studio," Delaney said. "Manie's reaction was, 'I don't know if *it's* a man or a woman. I don't know if *it's* Black or White. I can't understand a damn word *it* is saying. Send it all back, but with a nice letter.'" According to Delaney, Sacks was hardly a visionary. He had also just turned down Frank Sinatra on behalf of the label, feeling his music was on the way out.

The Colonel was highly respected in the business and was certainly better known than Elvis at the time. In his field, Colonel Parker was an established star and Elvis was only beginning. Neal explained to his young star that there wasn't a better promoter around than Colonel Parker, and not just in the music business but in Hollywood as well. Elvis needed someone with the Colonel's connections and skills to get his career off the ground because up to that point, no one north of the Mason-Dixon Line had really heard of him.

Elvis alternated working on the Jamboree Tour with Hank Snow and playing separate dates with Bill Black and Scotty Moore that were arranged by Neal. He was still under contract to the *Louisiana Hayride* and couldn't venture very far from the northern Louisiana area on most weekends. All the while, Neal was attempting to get the Colonel more involved in the bookings. One of the reasons Gladys was such a big stumbling block was that she constantly worried about her son when he was on the road. She was concerned about accidents and the way fans were reacting to his shows. They shared a deep bond after the stillborn death of Elvis's twin brother, Jesse Garon, and she worried about him day and night. Some say needlessly. The wild stories coming out of some of the local media weren't helping matters either. She knew that bigger bookings meant more time away from home for Elvis.

However, Bob Neal persisted, and on August 15, 1955, he, Vernon Presley, and Elvis Presley signed an agreement that would make Colonel Tom Parker Elvis's special advisor for a period of one year. The Colonel added his signature and his assistant, Tom Diskin, was there to witness the signing.

The agreement also contained several concessions Neal made to the Colonel, including one that would have Elvis playing one hundred personal appearances within one year for the special sum of $200 each. Another stipulation provided that if future negotiations broke down and Neal decided to "freelance" with Elvis, the Colonel would be reimbursed for time and expenses and would have first call on several cities at the special rate of $175 for his first appearance, $250 for the second, and $350 for Elvis's third appearance in each city. Under this clause, the Colonel received exclusive rights to book Elvis in a total of forty-seven major cities from coast to coast, including New York, Chicago, Las Vegas, and Los Angeles.

Everything seemed to work itself out and go smoothly, because a few months later, on October 21, 1955, the Colonel received a telegram from Vernon and Gladys Presley, indicating they were fine with his representation of their son when it came to any and all recording, television or motion picture contracts. They fully authorized Colonel Parker to execute these deals exclusively on behalf of their son.

A few days later, a telegram arrived at Colonel Parker's Madison, Tennessee, offices from his new client, Elvis Presley, thanking him on behalf of himself and his parents. In the telegram Elvis states that Colonel Parker was the best and most wonderful person he could ever hope to work for. He also promised his undying loyalty—a vow he kept to the end of their partnership—and that he loved Colonel Parker like a father.

Elvis continued to tour with Jamboree Attractions under the direction of Colonel Parker. Hank Snow wasn't happy with the arrangement, feeling income generated from Elvis should go directly into the company. The Colonel argued that if that were the case, all expenses for Elvis should come out of the company as well. Snow did not agree. He did not believe Elvis had star quality and that his popularity would not last. Therefore, when the Colonel signed on as "advisor" to Elvis Presley, he was signed under the Colonel's own All Star Shows and not Jamboree Attractions / Hank Snow Attractions. Parker contended that Snow did not want Elvis in his company. The Colonel continued to book both men—Snow under the Jamboree Show banner while Elvis was booked under All Star Shows.

One of the final blows came in late 1955 when Snow came out after one of the shows to sign autographs. He was busy signing for fans when Elvis came out to do the same. The line of fans quickly shifted from Snow to Presley. It was palpable to everyone, including both stars. One of Snow's fans, to pacify him, only made matters worse.

"They don't love you 'cause you're old, Hank," he said. "But I love you."

Which wasn't true. They didn't love him because he didn't shake it like Elvis did.

This was rock 'n' roll's Big Bang. As John Lennon later said, "Before Elvis there was nothing."

Elvis was a multiple threat. First off, there was his music. This was a young white boy playing Black music at a time in the South when white disc jockeys wouldn't touch a Black record (and Black DJs wouldn't touch a white one). In a 1956 interview with a newspaper journalist, Elvis said, "The colored folks been singing it and playing it just like I'm doin' now, man, for more years than I know. They played it like that in their shanties and in their juke joints and nobody paid it no mind 'til I goosed it up." The young people were listening to Black music. In the South in the 1950s, that was like a second sun rising in the morning. What in the heck was going on in the world?

And just as shocking was his act. The one Snow decreed "lewd"—that hip-shaking, pelvis-thrusting, quivering, gyrating, ass-grinding series of moves that screamed, "I'm taking Sally behind the barn and when we get back, she ain't going to be your little girl no more." *Time* magazine called Elvis a "sexhibitionist." FBI psychologists laid out parents' fears about Elvis: that teenagers could easily be "aroused to sexual indulgence and perversion by certain types of motions and hysteria—the type that was exhibited at the Presley show." Pentecostal preachers went into orbit a year before Sputnik over Elvis. TV talent shows wouldn't broadcast him below the waist lest the youth of the day begin rutting in the streets like hogs in heat.

Riots broke out at his concerts. At two shows he performed at the 1956 Mississippi-Alabama Fair and Dairy Show, one hundred National Guardsmen were on hand to prevent crowd trouble. In August 1956, in Jacksonville, Florida, a local juvenile court judge called Presley a "savage" and threatened to arrest him if he shook his body while performing at Jacksonville's Florida Theatre. His Honor was sure Elvis was "undermining" the youth of America. (Presley stood still at the show as ordered but poked fun by wiggling a finger.) Local officials started denying permits for Presley appearances. Teens just piled into cars and drove elsewhere to see him. Most radio stations wouldn't play him. The ones that did suffered repercussions from advertisers. His former wife, Priscilla Presley, stated in her 1983 memoir that "his performances were labeled obscene. My mother stated emphatically that he was 'a bad influence for teenage girls. He arouses things in them that shouldn't be aroused.'"

Colonel Parker hadn't just signed a deal with the Next Big Thing. He was present at the formation of the entire rock 'n' roll universe.

One of the very first things Colonel Parker did on his new client's behalf was to spring him from his Sun Records deal. Not only did the Colonel recognize the limited reach of Sun Records but also that Sam Phillips wasn't very generous to his artists. He was giving a 3 percent royalty rate when 5 percent was the going rate. No one even discussed an advance; it was simply out of the question. And he knew they knew it. He admitted it in a 1986 *Rolling Stone* interview.

"When they left me, I didn't blame them personally because I knew the stories they had heard," Phillips said. "And the stories were simply—no matter if I had been giving them 10 percent—'Man, is that all you're getting?' These people were unsuspecting. It was their first contract. Their first adventure into the world of business and a little money. When they got a damned check for $50,000—can you imagine? They hadn't seen that much money in their lifetime or in their daddy's lifetime." He added he didn't bear them any ill will.

When Johnny Cash eventually left Sun Records in 1961, he suspected that Phillips was shorting him on royalties. Cash's first royalty check under Phillips was a whopping $3.30, and that was with a couple of hits under his belt.

To be fair, Phillips ran a much smaller operation than most record labels. Elvis never complained about his royalties under Sam Phillips because he was grateful for the opportunity to do what he loved. Phillips also put about sixty thousand miles on his car driving to radio stations and distributors to promote his artists. He had skin in the game, and often the business aspects of running a label drove him to drink. He even checked into a mental hospital at one point. As far as Colonel Parker was concerned, none of that mattered. All he was concerned about was who could offer his client the best deal and give him the long-term support needed to build and sustain a career.

The only label that met those criteria from Colonel Parker's point of view was RCA Victor. They had history, after all. Parker got Eddy Arnold one of the largest royalty rates ever for a recording star at that time, and Hank Snow's contract wasn't too shabby either. The relationship with RCA was stellar and pretty much smooth sailing. Once a contact was signed, sealed, and delivered, Colonel Parker never pulled any funny stuff—no renegotiation tactics, no sudden dramatics, no stunts involving his stars. He lived up to every word on the written contract, and didn't talk to the label again until the contract lapsed and it was time to strike a new one. He also made sure never to leak to the press what the deal was or brag about how much his client received. He was professional and discreet. For that, the Colonel was greatly respected by music, film, touring, and promotional executives, or anyone who conducted business with him.

As far as Sun Records went, Phillips knew he didn't have the means to send Elvis where everyone knew he was headed. Southern banks wouldn't touch the music business, and Phillips refused to go public and lose control. He was painted into a corner.

"I had looked at everything for how I could take a little extra money and get myself out of a real bind," he told *Rolling Stone*. "I mean, I wasn't broke, but man, it was hand-to-mouth. I made an offer to Tom Parker, but the whole thing was that I made an offer I didn't think they'd even consider—$35,000, plus I owed Elvis $4,000 or $5,000."

He didn't necessarily want them not to take it, he added.

RCA Victor would buy out Elvis's masters from Sun, a deal that Bob Neal could not put together a few months earlier. The negotiations started at $5,000 and finally hit the $25,000 mark. Phillips wanted $30,000, including a $5,000 deposit or he announced he would be shopping the masters himself.

On October 25, 1955, the Colonel received a telegram from W. W. Bullock, vice president at RCA Victor, tendering a recording contract to Elvis Presley. The $25,000 agreement was for three years at a royalty rate of 5 percent of retail price plus two one-year options. RCA would recoup $20,000 from one-half of the royalties.

Phillips had given them until November 14, 1955, to make the deal. The Colonel waited until 7:25 A.M. on the 14th to send this wire to Bullock from his offices in Madison:

Dear Bill,
Your wire received. The option to pick up the Presley contract expires at midnight today. Since Sun Records wants a cash deposit of five thousand dollars ($5,000) to pick up the option by today,

time is short. As I have to wire this money from here or you can wire it from up there, either way I am pressed for time. I am very happy to handle everything from here and advise you when the lawyer should meet me. But if for some reason your people rather deal direct this is OK with me.

I have nothing to gain by handling this deal other than to protect all of us. I only want to go on record that today is the last day to get this deal as per Sun Record agreement. Tomorrow he may go up again. Personally, I believe the price too high, however, the talent is there, and we should make money. The deal involves forty thousand dollars ($40,000). Thirty-five thousand ($35,000) to Sun Records. Five ($5,000) to Presley. Three television guest appearances and complete promotion coverage. I did manage to stop the release till we know what we are going to do today so hurry as the banks close here at two p.m.

Regards, Colonel Tom Parker

That afternoon the Colonel received a short wire from Bullock in New York. It didn't sound promising: *Cannot wire your request. Will call you Tuesday morning.*

The lights must have been on late Monday night in the RCA Victor offices in the Big Apple. At 9:56 the next morning, the Colonel received another telegram from Bullock. It authorized Parker to exercise the option for the Sun Record-Presley, instructing him to advance $5,000 to Sun Contracts (Phillips) immediately and masters to be transferred to RCA for an additional $35,000 and a $5,000 bonus to Elvis Presley to be executed on or before December 1, 1955.

With that authorization, the Colonel called Sam Phillips to tell him they had a deal. He even took $5,000 out of his personal account and sent it on its short trip to Memphis with a personal note:

Enclosed is my cashier's check as promised by me on the phone a few minutes ago, for $5,000 as per agreement between your company,

Bob Neal, and myself. Regarding Elvis Presley's contract, I will work out the rest of the details as soon as possible and will wind everything up. Thanking you for your help and with best wishes.

Sincerely, Colonel Tom Parker

At 4:43 the same afternoon, the Colonel received a telegram from Sam Phillips stating that upon his receipt of the $5,000 certified check, their deal would be legal and valid.

The Colonel continued to fire off correspondence to New York. Later the same evening he wrote to RCA Victor's lead attorney, H. Coleman Tily III. The second sentence in his letter had to be the understatement of the year:

It was good talking to you today. I have been busy.

After receiving your wire, or rather the wire from Bullock, I went down to the bank and had a cashier's check made out for five thousand dollars. I called Sam Phillips and asked him if I should wire the money or mail the check airmail. He said mailing the check was OK with him. This I did this afternoon. Now we will have to get the time and dates worked out when you should come down here to Nashville and go with me to Memphis to close everything off properly. The sooner the better.

You did not mention the three guest shots on TV in the wire. They must be part of the contract with the Presleys or I will be in the middle. There are many details to be worked out to protect this setup and it would be best for you to plan to come here first and we go on to Memphis from here. Let me know when to set this up so we can get it over with. We should move fast to catch some of the fall business for RCA.

When you make out the check for my refund on the five thousand, be sure and mark the check as a refund to me so it does not look like I am being paid by RCA. I am very proud to advance the money for RCA as I am a stockholder anyway.

Enclosed is the option agreement. It should be okay. Did the best I could to handle this without you being here to help me.

Sincerely, Colonel Tom Parker

The next morning the Colonel wrote another letter to RCA executives in New York, this one directed to Steve Sholes, who headed up RCA's Country and Western recording division, with a copy to Bullock:

As you know, I have deposited the escrow money with Sun Records out of my bank account for your company until we can get together next week. May I suggest for your consideration that it may not be a bad idea after all the negotiations have been completed, that you take the master to "I Forgot to Remember to Forget" and make a special nationwide release on this. This is one of the strongest numbers on the market present with hardly any coverage, but it is number 7 on the best-sellers. I am not trying to tell you what to do, of course, but I know that you are open for suggestions.

It will take a great deal of coordination and mutual understanding to get the most out of this new contract. I will support this with all my ability as long as I feel that the association is mutually beneficial.

I know you will be happy to know that radio, television, motion pictures, endorsements, publishing, and theaters will be handled on an exclusive basis by me with no interference from Elvis's manager. Bob Neal will be associated with us in a capacity as manager and he will be in charge of personal appearances pertaining to one-nighters but will work closely with us. However, at the same time, I will have final decision pertaining to the above-mentioned details with the exceptions of the one-nighters, which are part of Bob's contract with the Presley family. This will enable me to be more available to pursue the television, radio, and motion picture possibilities for Elvis.

I am now waiting for word from Memphis so Mr. Tily can meet with me and we will go to finish up all the details. Until that time, nothing should be released. I am planning to have Hank Snow in a picture with Elvis Presley for a publicity release—Hank welcoming Elvis to the RCA Victor family, which, of course, I will inject Sam Phillips, Bob Neal, and Tily in, fitting in with the situations in Memphis, when they are completed.

We are to receive three guest appearances on television coast-to-coast—the first one within 60 days after the signing of the contract. This has been a hard job for me for the past month to negotiate. It was a pleasure to do this for RCA and I know we will all benefit by it in the long run.

Colonel Tom Parker had just negotiated what would be one of the biggest deals in the history of the recording business—one that would eventually yield RCA Victor over a billion dollars over the course of several decades—and give Elvis a flagship record label that would cater to his artistic output until his untimely death. During Elvis's first year with the label, RCA sold 12.5 million singles and 2.75 million albums. The powerhouse label had its first real superstar.

On November 21, 1955, Elvis Presley officially became the newest and brightest member of the RCA Victor recording family when he signed the contract authorizing the release of his Sun master recordings and naming RCA as his new recording company. The contract was also signed by Vernon Presley (Elvis was still underage at twenty), Bob Neal, the Colonel, and H. Coleman Tily III for the company.

Elvis took his RCA bonus money and went on the first of his many spending sprees, buying presents for everyone. He bought his parents a new pink Ford and, for his mom, some expensive jewelry. He also bought her two Mixmasters so she could have one at each end of her kitchen counter. Finally, he went out and bought himself some new clothes. Things were looking up, thanks to Colonel Parker.

After signing Elvis to his new contract, an RCA spokesman was quoted as saying, "We got pretty excited around here. We hadn't seen anything that weird in a long time."

Although some of the RCA executives may have thought Elvis a bit strange, they quickly discovered his manager was not one to be trifled with. Early in the agreement, an RCA executive strongly expressed his disappointment that Elvis had failed to show up at a cocktail reception in San Antonio, Texas, for many of their selected dealers.

"You'll be hearing from New York," the executive warned Colonel Parker. "We have to have cooperation on these things."

As predicted, Colonel Parker did get a call the next day from the main office, wanting to know why Elvis was a no-show.

"Well, I don't recall any clause in our contract that says Elvis has to appear at a cocktail party for dealers," the Colonel replied with great aplomb. "However, if you would like to talk about a separate agreement that covers all of this subject, just let me know."

That not only ended that conversation quickly but let RCA Victor know that anything outside their contract would cost them extra where it concerned Elvis Presley. The Colonel saw everything in black and white. The i's had to be dotted and the t's crossed. He had lived on bread and water, and sometimes lived without bread or water. The world was not paved with free money. There were no free rides and no mercy. That extended to corporate record labels, movie studios, and television networks.

Colonel Parker's relationship with RCA was long, esteemed, and very cordial. Every time a new executive joined the company, the Colonel was among the first to call and welcome that person into the "family." The only RCA executive he had frequent disagreements with was Steve Sholes, who wanted to tell Elvis and the Colonel how and what to record. This unsolicited advice truly bugged Elvis. Doing what any respectable manager would do, the Colonel picked up the phone, called Sholes directly, and in no uncertain terms told him to back off. I can tell you from being in the same room with the Colonel when he made those calls, you did not want to be on the other end. He "took care of business" and then some.

On the same day Elvis signed his RCA Victor contract, the Colonel and Bob Neal renegotiated the terms of their personal financial agreement. Hereafter, the Colonel would receive one half of Neal's commission after deducting 5 percent for expenses from gross receipts. If Neal were making a 25 percent commission, 5 percent would be deducted for expenses and they would equally divide the remaining 20 percent. This agreement worked both ways for contracts negotiated for Elvis by Neal and for contracts negotiated by the Colonel. Exempt from this latest commission-sharing agreement, however, were any contracts signed by the Colonel for appearances in any of the forty-seven cities covered in the August 15 agreement.

Elvis had agreed to the above arrangement but was still only twenty at the time. On January 25, 1956, just two weeks after turning twenty-one, he appeared before V. H. Ellis, a Nashville notary, to confirm that the agreement signed on November 21, 1955, remained legal and binding.

Because of Hank Snow's unwillingness to have Elvis permanently on his show, agreements between Snow and Colonel Parker were dissolved. Elvis's popularity was soaring and Snow's prediction that he would fade into the sunset quickly came back to haunt him. Any future Hank Snow bookings by the Colonel as an independent agent through his All Star Shows would be as follows:

Weekdays—Bookings up to $750, Parker would receive 15 percent commission. Bookings over $750, Parker would receive 50 percent commission.
Weekends—Bookings up to $1,000, Parker would receive 15 percent commission. Bookings over $1,000, Parker would receive 25 percent commission.

Snow requested that Colonel Parker produce a detailed breakdown of all receipts of payouts, along with gross and net earnings. The Colonel quickly replied that since all matters between them had been settled, he could see no purpose an audit would serve.

"Of course," the Colonel wrote to Snow, "I would expect you to bear the cost of it and would also have to be made at my convenience.

If an audit is made, I would also want you to furnish hotel bills, car expenses, plane tickets, and other expenses for which you have refunded out of our business, and which bills and receipts you did not turn over."

Snow quickly dropped the matter but advised the Colonel that his new manager, Mae Axton,[7] would handle all his future bookings. Despite their business differences, Colonel Parker and Hank Snow stayed in close contact and several letters in my files indicate they remained friends for several decades. In December 1957, Colonel Parker wrote a letter to Snow suggesting he get in touch with a Mr. Philpott of Ralston Purina, as he had recommended him to open a new mill in Canada the following spring. This was strictly a friendly gesture, and he made it clear he wanted no payment or commission for it. Snow later sent the Colonel a box of cigars as a gift of appreciation for the tip.

On March 15, 1956, Bob Neal's contract with Elvis ran out, and he was officially out of the picture, though they remained friendly. This cleared the way for the first of several exclusive contracts between Elvis Presley and the Colonel. This contract, created by Colonel Parker and signed by both parties on March 26, 1956, modified and expanded the November 21 agreement between the Colonel and Neal. It gave Colonel Parker sole and exclusive authority to operate as Elvis's "Advisor, Personal Representative, or Manager" in any and all fields of public and private entertainment.

Elvis's concert earnings multiplied as soon as the Colonel took over management full-time. Through much of 1955, records show he was making between $175 and $250 for each performance. On November 22, one day after Neal signed a new agreement with the Colonel, it shot up to $1,000 a performance. In July 1956, Elvis received $2,500 against a

---

7 Mae Axton was known as "The Queen of Nashville" and the mother of singer-songwriter Hoyt Axton. She co-wrote "Heartbreak Hotel," which was Elvis Presley's first national hit, with Tommy Durden.

percentage. By the end of the year, Elvis's asking price per performance had shot up past the $10,000 mark and was climbing rapidly.

On Elvis's twenty-first birthday, the Colonel and Marie Parker invited him to their house for dinner. The Colonel had placed a $100 bill under his plate as a birthday gift. Elvis was delighted.

It was the first $100 bill Elvis had ever seen.

I wasn't there that night, but I can almost hear the Colonel assure Elvis there would be many more of those Benjamins in his future. And there would be. Some of them were spent on a twenty-three-room mansion, pink Cadillacs, guns, jets, luxury vacations, jewelry, and feeding and watering an entourage . . . among other things.

6

Elvis Presley Inc.

Colonel Parker didn't know much about the movie business. His only experience was the two low-budget films that Eddy Arnold made, and he'd had few dealings with Hollywood executives and producers. Here he would be going up against the big boys, some of the fastest-talking and -thinking dealmakers in the entertainment industry. These boys were slick, smart, and every ounce the actors as the stars they put in their movies, and they were quite used to getting their way.

The Colonel figured he knew just about all he had to know about recordings, tours, endorsements, and peddling souvenirs. But this was going to be a different ball game and the Colonel had never taken a swing, much less got up to the batter's box. But he had three things going for him: a sharp mind, a pair of brass balls, and a longtime friendship with Abe Lastfogel, president of the powerful William Morris Agency in Los Angeles, California.

Lastfogel, referred to as "The Pope" at the agency, was a Hollywood legend and the ultimate wheeler-dealer. Born in New York in 1898, Abe was one of eight children raised in a cold-water tenement. His father worked in the meatpacking industry and spoke no English. Abe started work at the age of fourteen as an office boy for William Morris when the agency had a staff of four. By 1932, he ran William Morris. He was a short, stocky man who wore bow ties and smoked cigars. He was famous, not for the stereotype of a Hollywood agent, screaming, cursing, and throwing phones, but for being calm. When the US entered World War II in 1941, Lastfogel was chosen to head the USO's overseas entertainment efforts, Camp Shows.

Within a year after Pearl Harbor, Camp Shows put on professional entertainment in 1,500 camps and installations every two weeks. Camp Shows units landed in France only forty-three days after D-Day. The Allies were still bogged down in Normandy. By V-J Day, Lastfogel's singers, dancers, and comedians provided 428,000 performances.

After the war, his client list included Jimmy Durante, Spencer Tracy, Katharine Hepburn, Mae West, Al Jolson, Edward G. Robinson, Lana Turner, Rita Hayworth, James Cagney, David Niven, Jack Lemmon, Walter Matthau, George Burns, Will Rogers, and Danny Thomas.

Lastfogel and Parker first met in the 1940s, and the Colonel made a deep impression on both Abe and his wife, Frances.

"That Tom Parker is a winner," Frances Lastfogel, a former vaudeville singer, told her husband. "You should keep your eye on him."

He did, and they remained in touch throughout the years. No doubt the Colonel thought Lastfogel would be a great ally, and he planned to use that relationship capital strategically. With Elvis as his prized client, it was time to call in that favor.

Hal Wallis, one of the most successful producers in Hollywood, had been hounding Colonel Parker for a few months ever since he saw Elvis on *Stage Show*. It wasn't like Wallis to tip his hand. As production chief at Warner Bros., the fifty-six-year-old Wallis had produced such classics as *The Adventures of Robin Hood, Sergeant York, Casablanca, High Sierra,* and *The Maltese Falcon* with Humphrey Bogart. As far as producers and studios went, it didn't get any bigger or better.

Wallis also had a hand in catering to the youth market. He produced many films with Dean Martin and Jerry Lewis, but by early 1956, sensed the famed comedy duo wanted to go their separate ways and was looking for someone to fill that void.

Colonel Parker was intimately familiar with the law of attraction. The more somebody wanted something or someone, the more you kept them at bay. Wallis sensed great potential with Elvis but wanted him to do a formal screen test before he invested his time and a studio's money. Parker felt Elvis was a proven commodity and didn't want anyone "test-driving" his client. If Wallis wanted him, he'd have to pay, and pay through the nose, just like everyone else. Wallis wasn't going to budge on that matter, but he still let it be known that he wanted Elvis badly. He started a telephone and letter-writing campaign that lasted for several months, to the point where Colonel Parker was vexed and worn down. He finally agreed that Elvis would take a screen test for Wallis at the cost of a round-trip ticket, hotel, and fifty dollars a day in expenses, which would be paid by Paramount Studios, which was eager to see what the singing sensation could do.

On March 25, the day after his final appearance on the Dorsey Brothers' *Stage Show*, Elvis flew from New York to Los Angeles, where he was met at LAX by Colonel Parker, his assistant Tom Diskin, and William Morris agent Leonard Hirshan.

From his discussions with Colonel Parker, Wallis knew that Elvis wanted to become a dramatic actor in the mold of James Dean, Marlon Brando, Rod Steiger, and Karl Malden. However, Wallis saw Elvis as a media celebrity who could easily fill in as a movie star. That move, in fact, had become a Paramount staple. The producer set up the screen test to judge how both Elvis's dramatic and musical talents would come across on film.

Presley's screen test consisted of two parts. First, using a toy guitar, Elvis would lip-sync a performance to his recording of "Blue Suede Shoes." It was intended to see if the energy and sex appeal that came across in Presley's TV appearances could be transferred to film. Following would be two dramatic scenes from *The Rainmaker* to assess Elvis's acting potential.

If Elvis was nervous, he certainly didn't show it. His natural charisma took over, and not only did it take over the screen, it leapt off it. Wallis was extremely pleased. With the test out of the way, Colonel Parker was in a better bargaining position than ever before.

In April 1956, Colonel Parker flew to Los Angeles, where Lastfogel whisked him to the exclusive Hillcrest Country Club on Pico Boulevard to meet Wallis. They were there to negotiate a deal for Elvis's first feature film, *Love Me Tender*, for 20th Century Fox,[8] starring Debra Paget and Richard Egan, who grew sideburns to play Elvis's older brother. At first, the studio wanted to sign Elvis as a contract star for around $700 a week. The Colonel rejected that idea immediately. Not only did he want a $15,000 salary[9] for Elvis for four weeks of work, but he also demanded a percentage of the gross profits.

Lastfogel could not believe his ears. A percentage deal was virtually unheard of at that time, especially for someone who had never acted before—not even in a high school play. Wallis was aghast. The Colonel quietly pointed out that they wanted Elvis in the movies because they knew his millions of fans would buy tickets.

"It's as simple as that," the Colonel said. Lastfogel wasn't sold. He leaned over and whispered to Parker that he was overreaching.

"Colonel, you're losing this deal for us," he said.

Colonel Parker looked Lastfogel dead in the eye and said, "Abe, you can't lose something you don't have."

"It's just not done this way," Lastfogel said. With that, the Colonel got up from the table and walked out of the meeting. A few hours later he received a call in his room at the Beverly Wilshire Hotel.

"Okay," conceded Wallis. "You have a piece of the action."

Although Elvis received third billing in the film, the various posters, one-sheets, lobby cards, publicity stills, and advertising featured a full-length shot of Elvis standing, with guitar in hand, proclaiming, Mr. Rock 'n' Roll in the Story He Was Born to Play! On October 28, 1956, at the Paramount Theatre in New York City's Times Square, a large cutout figure of a mystery man holding a guitar with a question mark teased the next film that would appear there.

---

8 Paramount Studios "loaned out" Elvis Presley to 20th Century Fox for his debut film.

9 Wallis offered Elvis Presley a contract for one movie with options for six more. That contract was totally rewritten in 1958.

Elvis Presley Inc.

Love Me Tender[10] debuted on November 16, 1956, while hundreds of young girls gathered outside the Paramount Theatre screamed Elvis's name as the large cutout was unveiled. This welcome, of course, was all arranged by Colonel Parker. Actor Richard Egan's contract called for him to receive top billing; the Colonel got around that by getting the studio to place a huge fifteen-foot blowup of Elvis in front of major theaters.

Love Me Tender was so successful that film costs were covered in the first three days of its release. It was the first of thirty-three films Elvis made, all non-exclusive as the Colonel would never tie him down to one studio. Hal Wallis turned out to be their favorite producer, involved in nine Presley pictures in all. He reluctantly had to loan Elvis out to Fox for *Love Me Tender* as he was busy working on *Gunfight at the O.K. Corral* (1957) at the time.

In between recording sessions, movies, and television, Elvis continued making concert appearances. But not without problems. While he may have been the heartthrob of young ladies around the country, that certainly wasn't the case with their boyfriends and many of their parents. Rock 'n' roll was under constant attack in most of the puritan press. Many radio stations refused to play Elvis's music, and some even smashed his records on the air.

Threats of bodily harm and even death forced Colonel Parker to resort to different methods of sneaking Elvis into hotels and venues. One way was to have Elvis lie on a couch, cover him with a piece of canvas, and have it "delivered" to his suite. Another method was to have him hide in a laundry truck if he was headed to a concert.

On one date in Iowa, word spread that he would be pelted with eggs, tomatoes, and other assorted produce if he took to the stage, so police searched every young man as he entered the building. To demonstrate how civic attitudes changed toward Elvis from community to community, when he arrived in New Orleans, the Colonel ar-

---

10 *Love Me Tender* was originally titled *The Reno Brothers*, but the name was changed to take advantage of the Elvis Presley single from the soundtrack, which became another number one hit.

ranged for him to receive the keys to the city. In Oklahoma City, police and members of the board of censorship attended his afternoon performance to see if they would permit a second show that evening. The chief of police not only saw nothing wrong with his act but asked the Colonel if he could bring his young daughter backstage after the next show to meet Elvis. (Of course, the Colonel took full advantage of the wide disparity in Elvis's popularity. While his female fans were buying all the "I Love Elvis" buttons, their boyfriends were spending their allowances on "I Hate Elvis" buttons. The Colonel loved it whenever he could cover the spread and sell to both sides.)

Elvis seemed bewildered by all the animosity directed at him. It appeared as if every ill in the country from juvenile delinquency to a complete breakdown of the nation's morality was being blamed on him and his music. And it was coming from everywhere, from the press to the pulpit. An irate preacher in Des Moines, Iowa, blasted him: "Elvis Presley is morally insane! The spirit of Presleyism has taken down all the bars and standards. Because of this man we are living in a day of jellyfish morality."

Opposition was especially heavy in the Catholic community. In Canada, eight girls from Ottawa's Notre Dame Convent School were expelled after attending one of his shows. In St. Louis, girls from Notre Dame High burned him in effigy and destroyed mounds of Elvis souvenirs while praying for forgiveness for their excesses. Many Catholic schools posted "off-limits" notices on their bulletin boards whenever Elvis appeared in their town or city.

All of this weighed heavily on an ailing Gladys Presley. She and Vernon were beginning to receive hate mail at their Memphis home, accusing them of inciting juvenile delinquency through their son. Marie Parker was also receiving criticism from her friends in Madison, Tennessee. Her Garden Glove members told her that she should be ashamed of her husband because his star client was corrupting youth. Church members also began to shun her. This was the period when she began an intense dislike for her husband's world of show business and would tell anyone within earshot about her hatred of the industry. It

Elvis Presley Inc.

was quite a change from the days when her husband had represented "respectable acts" like Eddy Arnold and Hank Snow. Back then, Marie was one of the social leaders of the community. Now, she was a pariah. And she didn't like it one bit.

The Colonel never really took any of it seriously. He knew that controversy was good for business. A reporter once asked him what he thought of Elvis's suggestive moves onstage. His response was classic Colonel.

"I'm thinking of putting a wiggle meter on him to see how many wiggles he gets per minute," he quipped. "I wonder if there's a world wiggle wecord, er record, out there somewhere."

Despite the adverse press, the demand to see Elvis in concert, in films, and on television ran high. Ed Sullivan said Elvis would never appear on his popular Sunday night variety show, which broke out many entertainment acts.

If you appeared on *The Ed Sullivan Show,* it meant you'd arrived in show business. For Mr. and Mrs. America, if Ed Sullivan had someone on his show, that person was *Someone*.

"He's just not my cup of tea," Sullivan said dismissively of Elvis. That cup of tea must have boiled over when he finally caved into the public pressure. When he got around to calling Colonel Parker, he was told the price was $50,000, nearly ten times more than any previous act.

Even though Sullivan was one of the most influential people in entertainment at the time, and that people would have killed to appear on his TV show, the host relented and paid the fee. But it was well worth it: he enjoyed his highest ratings ever. More than 80 percent of the country's TV sets—60 million viewers—were tuned in for the first of Elvis's three greatly hyped appearances on his show. (Sullivan's viewing audience at that time averaged about 14 million). In fact, the other networks threw in the towel rather than face the competition. NBC-TV preempted *The Steve Allen Show* with local movies, something they would also do for Elvis's second Sullivan appearance six weeks later. The first Sullivan show aired on September 9, 1956, and was hosted by the distinguished British actor Charles Laughton, another "stoneface," as Sullivan was recovering from an auto accident. Sullivan's show originated in New York City but, because Elvis was still in Hollywood filming *Love Me Tender*, his four numbers were performed live at the CBS Television City Studios in Los Angeles, which showed him in full view. It was during his third Sullivan appearance—by popular demand—that the cameras were not permitted to film Elvis from the waist down, a publicity stunt that the Colonel confessed was entirely Sullivan's idea.

At the end of that run, Sullivan did an about-face and told his national audience, "This is a real decent, fine boy. We've never had a more pleasant experience with a big star."

What a shock this must have been to moral America!

Back in Madison, Tennessee, record amounts of fan mail poured into Colonel Parker's home office. He insisted that every letter be answered. Fan clubs were popping up all over the world, which meant more marketing opportunities for Elvis, an area of expertise on which the Colonel could have written several books and taught a master class to executives.

One of the first things Colonel Parker did after signing Elvis was to incorporate and form Elvis Presley Enterprises. In 1956, he hired Hank Saperstein, a highly successful film producer, distributor, and promoter to work with him on marketing his star. Manufacturers were selected to produce every kind of collectable merchandise imaginable. By the end of their first year together, Parker and Saperstein came up with more than sixty different pieces of Elvis merchandise, grossing approximately $20 million in sales. The items ranged from shoes, clothing, school supplies, jewelry, buttons, dolls, stuffed animals, wallets, bolo ties, lipstick, hot plate holders, and even dog tags. The "I Love Elvis!" and "I Hate Elvis!" buttons were hot sellers and printed in several languages.

The Colonel was always thinking of new and unusual ways to promote Elvis. To ramp up sales of a new RCA album, the Colonel came up with the idea of giving away a small piece of Elvis's clothing with each album sale. His parents were asked to collect everything that Elvis no longer wore and ship it to MGM Studios in Hollywood where shirts and pants were cut up into one-inch squares and placed in envelopes that went inside every album cover.

Years later, someone mentioned to the Colonel that the flower beds around Graceland were buzzing with an above normal number of bees.

"Bees?!" exclaimed the Colonel. "Elvis bees! Why, I bet we could get about 25 cents a sting!" The Colonel blazed a trail that set the stage for the marketing of celebrities for generations to come. A writer for the now defunct *Look* magazine, in its November 13, 1956, issue wrote when referring to the twenty-million-plus teenagers who were dishing out money for Elvis items: "Perhaps it is to lighten our burdens that the Lord sends us from time to time, imaginative men like Colonel Parker who realizes that life is a great hilarious fruitcake loaded with potential profits. It was Parker who founded the Great Elvis Presley Industry."

Now manager of America's hottest young superstar, as well as its most controversial, the Colonel arranged for the mayor of Tupelo, Mississippi, Elvis's birthplace, to proclaim September 26, 1956, as "Elvis Presley Day." His parents and grandmother and an endless procession of relatives he really didn't know that well joined him in a triumphant return home as friends and fans turned out by the thousands. He did two shows at the Mississippi-Alabama Fair and Dairy Show, the same arena in which he had appeared as a ten-year-old, performing the country classic "Old Shep." It was his first public performance. Now, over twenty thousand screaming fans showed up and turned the event into pure bedlam. It was later reported that more than fifty thousand people were turned away at the gate. Fortunately, the Colonel anticipated what the reaction would be to Elvis's homecoming and augmented the hundred members of the Tupelo City Police Department and the Mississippi State Highway Patrol with troops from the local National Guard. Still, some crazed teenagers made it through the police line and ended up onstage where they managed to rip buttons from Elvis's shirt. Of course, this horrified his mother Gladys and grandmother Minnie Mae, who were sitting in the audience.

By the end of their first mind-boggling year together, Colonel Parker had taken a hip-swinging, singing Memphis truck driver under his direction and changed the entertainment and music industries forever. *The Wall Street Journal* reported that since the Colonel had started marketing Elvis merchandise, they had grossed some $22 million in sales. His records and albums were selling in the millions, and his first movie established him as the next big male film superstar. He was firmly entrenched in the then 90 percent top tax bracket.

With the phenomenal success of *Love Me Tender* and the resulting hit single and album, the film studios were quick to spot a formula that would work to perfection for the next several years. In Elvis Presley's case, that meant finding a good working script, recording several songs (including, possibly, a title tune), filming the movie quickly, and lining up the movie to coincide with the release of (hopefully) a number one song. This would be followed shortly thereafter by a quality soundtrack album.

The Colonel was the first manager to conceive of a synergy to cross-promote all these entertainment products. The movie ads would promote the RCA single and album, and the album cover in turn would promote the movie. The system functioned like a well-oiled machine.

Vernon Presley handled all his son's personal finances. Having survived the Great Depression, Vernon was known to be extremely tight with a dollar. Many times, the Colonel would divert money directly to Elvis without Vernon being aware. A letter he sent to Elvis around this time was written in code (he addressed it to Private First Class Faron Presley) that read like gibberish. But it included a check for $1,000 and was signed "The Admiral." That, I'm sure, Elvis understood.

In January, 1957, Elvis started work at Paramount on his second film, *Loving You*, the first of nine movies he made with producer Hal Wallis. Colonel Parker negotiated another incredible deal, including top billing over established stars Lizbeth Scott and Wendell Corey. In addition to a $20,000 salary, Elvis received 50 percent of the film's net profits. The deal had the potential of making Elvis the highest-paid movie star in history. Vernon and Gladys Presley made a cameo appearance in a concert segment near the end of the film, much to the delight of Elvis. His mother passed away a year later, and it was said that Elvis never viewed the movie again.

The film was another musical drama that could have passed for an Elvis biography—a truck driver who could sing, named Deke Rivers, was discovered by a music publicist. That's because the script was tailored to Elvis's life at the time by screenwriters Herbert Baker and Hal Kanter, who also directed the picture. Kanter traveled to Memphis to meet with Elvis and to shadow him for a few weeks. He went to Shreveport, Louisiana, to witness Elvis's last performance on the *Louisiana Hayride*. He saw firsthand the reaction from the fans, as well as Colonel Parker's handling of his client, all of which ended up in the script.

Elvis received his first screen kiss from not one, but three starlets. Not a bad way to earn a paycheck. The results from the film were the same as before: *Loving You* became a top-grossing motion picture for Paramount Studios, and its lead single, "(Let Me Be Your) Teddy Bear," backed with "Loving You," became a million-selling single. The album, which was loaded with hits and famous cover songs, spent ten weeks at number 1 on the *Billboard* Top Pop Album chart. It was later certified gold by the Recording Industry Association of America (RIAA).

The film premiered on July 9, 1957, at the Strand Theatre in Memphis, and opened nationally on July 30. The single-screen theater wasn't as grand as some of Memphis's other movie cathedrals, but it sat approximately a thousand people and could accommodate large crowds on a date night. To cash in on Elvis's massive appeal, for the first time ever, Paramount made a conscious decision to bypass the established first-run theater system. Instead, they opted for a wide release, placing the movie in neighborhood theaters across the nation. This new structure, which the studio called the "Presley Pattern," delivered the product straight to its market by cutting the expenses of splashy premieres in downtown theaters, choosing to place the film directly in suburban theaters for a wider and more profitable release.

Shortly after the movie wrapped, Colonel Parker received a letter from famed Hollywood director, Cecil B. DeMille, whose works included *The Ten Commandments*, *Union Pacific*, and *The Greatest Show on Earth*. DeMille praised Parker as a "deep nick in Elvis Presley's wheel—and certainly to his good." The Colonel wasn't starstruck by any man or woman, but I can assure you this telegram was one of the Colonel's prized possessions.

Elvis had barely completed *Loving You* before he was on the set of *Jailhouse Rock* in May 1957, utilizing the same successful formula as before. The film co-starred former child star Judy Tyler, who died in a tragic Wyoming traffic accident just a week after filming was completed.

Jailhouse Rock would long be considered one of Elvis's best films, with the title song becoming a number one smash hit. The main production number from *Jailhouse Rock* was choreographed by noted dancer and choreographer Alex Romero, from films taken of Elvis performing onstage, and is recognized as the forerunner to today's pop music videos.

Stars like Paul Newman, Russ Tamblyn, Jean Simmons, and Gene Kelly dropped by the set to watch Elvis perform, applauding when a scene was completed. These were people Elvis grew up watching and admiring, and it must have felt surreal that these celebrities were now coming to his place of work to fête him. Elvis, of course, was gracious and polite, and his reputation for impeccable Southern manners resonated throughout Hollywood. Word of mouth was that he was a good guy and there was no diva-like behavior with him.

Colonel Parker went the extra mile in his job duties by keeping in constant contact with Vernon and Gladys Presley to let them know everything was going well. When the Colonel couldn't call or write, he had Tom Diskin handle it. On May 21, 1957, just after filming began on *Jailhouse Rock*, Diskin wrote a letter to Vernon and Gladys Presley informing them that Elvis was happy, well, and enthusiastic. He also apprised them of Elvis's condition after an emergency operation. Lastly, Diskin informs Elvis's parents that his El Dorado could

Elvis Presley Inc.

no longer accommodate all of his staff ("The Memphis Mafia") and that he needed to buy a limousine.

Diskin's mention of the Presleys' new home was a reminder of Colonel Parker's largesse. On April 19, 1957, the Colonel co-signed a loan for $29,250 with the bank so the Presleys could purchase a home at 1034 Audubon Drive in a well-to-do Memphis neighborhood. While Elvis was making good money, the Presley family had absolutely no credit rating on their own. With Vernon's prison background and the state of their finances, Vernon and Gladys had been unable to obtain a loan. The Colonel came through for them. Thanks to him, the Presleys had a nice home and every monthly payment of $160.61 was made on time, thanks to Elvis's royalties from "Heartbreak Hotel."

The Presleys loved their new four-bedroom ranch-style home with a carport and backyard swimming pool. However, the postwar suburban abode failed to provide privacy from an increasing army of fans who congregated there, some of whom began camping on the Presleys' front lawn. The neighbors even complained they couldn't park their cars and could not cross the street without a police escort for most of the thirteen months Elvis lived there.

Elvis later found and fell in love with a beautiful colonial estate set in an oak grove in Whitehaven, Tennessee, just eight miles south of Memphis off Highway 51, later renamed Elvis Presley Boulevard. He christened the estate "Graceland." Today Graceland is the second-most-visited home in the United States, after the White House, and millions know it by name and image.

Ruth Brown Moore, then separated from her husband, sold the property, which included a four-car garage and its fourteen surrounding acres, to Elvis on March 19, 1957, for $100,000. A month later, his parents moved into the enchanting mansion. Elvis wasted no time making the place his own, erecting a stone wall and installing the famous music-themed gates. Elvis, who was filming *Jailhouse Rock* at the time, didn't spend his first night at Graceland until June 26, 1957, but he visited while the work was in progress.

With the movie and recording career taking up most of Elvis's time, Colonel Parker booked Elvis on only four short concert tours during all of 1957. In March, he played four dates in major Midwest cities. That September he toured the Pacific Northwest and British Columbia with five shows in four days. It was the only time Elvis ever played outside the United States. The following month, he was booked for shows in Los Angeles, San Francisco, and Oakland. During the California excursion, he once again came under increased police scrutiny. The Los Angeles chief of police sent word to Elvis through an emissary to "clean up his act" and dispatched several officers from the LAPD vice squad to film his stage antics from the back of the Pan-Pacific Auditorium. Elvis, who was usually very respectful of authority, made an imaginary halo with his fingers over his head and offered his wrists up for handcuffs.

"I'm glad to see I have so many fans in the police department," he joked. Nothing came of it, but the Colonel told the press afterward that their next concerts would be in Hawaii, "where everyone wiggles!"

At a party in his suite at the Knickerbocker Hotel after the show, Elvis met Ricky Nelson while hosting entertainers Sammy Davis Jr., Tommy Sands, Nick Adams, and Carol Channing. Ricky revealed to me years later that the two of them had a private get-together. He said Elvis, who had watched him for years on *The Adventures of Ozzie & Harriet*, took note that Ricky was now touring and gave him some special advice.

"When you are being led through a crowd of girls by your bodyguards, make sure never to hook your arms with them, just put your hands on their shoulders and let them pull you," Elvis said. "One time a girl grabbed onto my crotch from behind and I was dragged for a long way before I could get the bodyguards' attention!"

Ricky howled, thinking that was the funniest thing he had ever heard. But he also knew how treacherous running a gauntlet of crazed teenage girls could be.

Even though Ricky Nelson, who I managed for several years, was competing with Elvis for the title of King of Rock 'n' Roll, the two men got along well and genuinely liked each other. They played football, baseball, and softball together when Elvis lived in Los Angeles during the "movie years." They also hung out together in Palm Springs in the 1960s and 1970s. I remember one night we all went to the Howard Manor to see Jody Reynolds and Bobby Craig perform a set. Jody was a friend of mine, but Elvis knew about him. Bobby was Ricky's keyboard player. The two performed songs by Elvis and Ricky Nelson, and the crowd ate it up. It was a fun evening for all, and the audience went nuts.

Ricky was especially close with Colonel Parker and thought the world of him. Truth be told, there were many times when he was much closer to the Colonel than Elvis. However, Ricky was the rare performer who did not want Colonel to manage him.

"Rick, you should go see Bill Belew. He makes all of Elvis's jumpsuits," the Colonel told him once. What the Colonel didn't know was that Ricky was not fond of the jumpsuit years and left it at that.

Elvis closed out the 1957 tour by sailing to Hawaii on the USS *Matsonia* for three shows, one of which was before ten thousand servicemen and -women and their dependents at Pearl Harbor. The Colonel and his staff flew over but sailed back on the USS *Lurline* with Elvis.

By this time, Al Dvorin not only assisted the Colonel and Tom Diskin on tour but he was also booking the opening acts and conducting the orchestra. For the two Hawaii shows, Al figured he could find plenty of good opening acts from the mainland who were appearing there. He was surprised to find there were none. He took in every show on the island before he came across a Polynesian revue performing at the Queen's Surf Hotel on Waikiki Beach. Al signed the entire group to open both performances and announced it as "Elvis's special tribute to the beautiful people of Hawaii." The audience loved it.

For those three shows (two at the Honolulu Stadium and one at the Schofield Barracks), Elvis wore his famous gold lamé jacket. These were some of his greatest shows ever, and his last concerts of the 1950s.

After arriving back on the mainland, Elvis returned to Graceland, where he would spend Christmas of 1957 with his family. His most important holiday greeting came from Dwight D. Eisenhower on December 20.

It wasn't a card with a tree and Santa on it. It was a standard draft letter signed by the president of the United States.

Elvis was told he had a month to report to Kennedy Veterans Hospital in Memphis for his physical on January 20, 1958. Once he passed, he was the possession of the United States government for the next two years.

The King of Rock 'n' Roll was being busted down to Private E-1 Elvis A. Presley.

7

G.I. Blues

Getting drafted into military service is probably one of the most dramatic events that can take place in a young man's life. In Elvis Presley's case, it was also one of the most important career decisions he ever had to make.

It took a while for the news to sink in, and everyone in the Presley camp was devastated. Some of his closest buddies couldn't believe it and tried to apply reason to the situation, thinking it was what Elvis probably wanted to hear.

"Man, they won't take you . . . you're too big a star!" one said. Another piped in, "You're paying too much in taxes for them to take you for two years." One acolyte offered: "The fans will never permit it!"

Guess they didn't know Uncle Sam that well. He did as he damn well pleased and took many a movie star at the start of World War II. Jimmy Stewart and Clark Gable were established stars who fought in the air war over Europe during WWII. Gable was ostensibly in the Army Air Corps to make a movie about the air war. Stewart was a squadron leader with enormous responsibilities. He flew missions during Big Week, the biggest air battle of the war.

Both Gable and Stewart were nearly killed over Germany. A piece of flak blew through the floor of Stewart's cockpit, ripping open a two-foot-wide hole. If he hadn't been wearing his harness, he would have been hurled out of his seat. He ended up flying twenty missions in all.

Gable served twice as a reserve gunner. On one mission, a 20 mm shell punched through the floor of the plane, tore off the heel of Gable's boot, and went out through the roof inches above the star's head.

To be fair, the government offered them the options of staying at home, working on propaganda, and similar roles, but both—for their own reasons—played the movie star card not to stay out of combat, but to get into it.

Everyone affiliated with Elvis was truly in shock—that is, everyone but Colonel Parker. He zigged when everyone else zagged. The Colonel saw this scenario as a golden opportunity to improve Elvis's image around the world.

"Elvis, you're going to serve and serve proudly," he said with a knowing smile.

One of the rumors circulating at the time was that the Colonel had "arranged" for Elvis to be drafted because he was having trouble controlling him. When I asked about it later, the Colonel laughed at the insinuation.

"Now why would a manager who has millions invested in a client want to have that client drafted? That would be crazy," he asked. "First, you never know how his career would be affected being out of the public's view for two years. If the public forgets about him, it's the end of his career."

Elvis could easily have gone into the Special Services and breezed through his two years as an entertainer like many before him, singing for the troops at military bases around the world. He could have even served as a recruiter, but Colonel Parker knew he would be ripped apart by the media and the highly critical Middle America establishment. His reputation, which wasn't perfect to start with among adults and the media, would be tarnished beyond repair. The press was ready to nail him if it looked like he was getting any preferential treatment. Or worse, tried to finagle his way out of the draft.

So, Elvis joined the US Army. What better way to show the world that Elvis Presley was an all-American boy than doing his duty for the country he loved?

"It can only enhance your career," the Colonel advised him. Elvis ultimately agreed with his assessment of the situation.

Another major factor was that the world was at peace. The Korean conflict had been over for nearly five years. There was trouble brewing in some place called Vietnam, but America wasn't involved. Yet.

The draft certainly did put a crimp on things. Elvis was about to shoot *King Creole* for Paramount Pictures. But the studio seemed more worried than Elvis. At the request of Y. Frank Freeman, who was head of Paramount at the time, looking at millions of dollars in production losses, Uncle Sam gave Elvis a deferment to finish the motion picture.

Elvis arrived in Hollywood on January 13, 1958, for several days of soundtrack recording prior to the beginning of principal photography for *King Creole* on January 20. Shooting continued on the Paramount lot in Hollywood through the end of February.

Hal Wallis, who was producing his second film starring Presley, had selected Michael Curtiz (*Casablanca*) to direct. The Hungarian–born Curtiz started during the silent film era and was one of the most prolific directors in cinematic history. He had worked with Wallis on many movies at Warner Bros., but this was the first time the two teamed up at Paramount.

King Creole co-starred Carolyn Jones and Dean Jagger and was filmed entirely in black and white. While the film's soundtrack album only made it to the number two spot, "Hard Headed Woman" soared to number 1 on the singles charts. As for the movie, *King Creole* is widely considered the best of Elvis Presley's thirty-one theatrical movies, and he received the best reviews for his dramatic acting up to that point.

Everyone wanted a shot at a final Elvis appearance before he began his two-year hitch with the army, even the boxing world. The TelePrompTer Corporation was the promoter of the big Sugar Ray Robinson–Carmen Basilio rematch for the world middleweight championship. They offered the Colonel $200,000 for Elvis to serve as a narrator. And this was four years before *Kid Galahad*, his first and only fight movie. Unfortunately, the Colonel had to turn it down as there wasn't enough time to put it all together and finish the film before Elvis entered the military.

On March 24, 1958, the US Army welcomed the most famous recruit in military history, and the Colonel was not about to let the event go unnoticed. When asked what he was going to do while Elvis was in the army, the Colonel replied with a sly grin, "I consider it my patriotic duty to keep Elvis in the ninety percent tax bracket."

The army was going to pay Elvis $99.37 a month. The Colonel bit down on his cigar and got to work. He helped his star client earn about $2 million during the two years he served in the military.

After a follow-up physical at Kennedy Veterans Hospital in Memphis, Elvis was sworn in with a dozen other nervous, young recruits and boarded a chartered Greyhound bus bound for Fort Chaffee, Arkansas. A three-day media circus was about to unfold with the Colonel serving as ringmaster.

The caravan escorting the bus consisted of several automobiles filled with family, friends, several dozen writers and photographers, and, of course, the Colonel and his staff. By the time the bus stopped for lunch at Earl's Hot Biscuits in West Memphis, there were more than two hundred people waiting. Someone had done his homework and knew that the bus carrying new recruits from Memphis always stopped for lunch at this restaurant. It's very probable the Colonel was the person assisting with that homework because he was there that day in the crowd, handing out 8x10s of his boy. The recruits went inside to eat, but Elvis had to stay behind because of the fracas that had unfolded. He was provided a sandwich and soft drink that he had to eat on the bus.

When all the recruits were finished, they boarded the bus and headed down Highway 70 and drove for another ninety miles. Their next stop was in North Little Rock at a family-owned place called Fisher's Steak House on 1919 E. Broadway.

While the rest of the soldiers went in through the front of the restaurant, Elvis was escorted through the back door and met up with his fellow recruits in a private dining room. The food was all homemade and tasty as could be. Uncle Sam picked up the check.

The last leg of the trip was about 115 miles, and they arrived at Fort Chaffee Military Base around 11:15 P.M. Amazingly, there were still a few cars filled with loyal, hard-core fans who had tailed them from Kennedy Hospital that morning.

Upon arriving at camp, Elvis had to pose for pictures and conduct interviews in a separate reception room. The rest of the recruits hit the sack and went instantly to sleep once their quarters were sorted out. Personnel had been anticipating Elvis's arrival since his draft announcement, but even with that head start they weren't fully prepared.

The Colonel was busy passing out balloons promoting *King Creole* and giving his own one-on-one interviews, telling any reporter who was interested what a great soldier Elvis would be. Every move of recruit 53310761 was being photographed by a horde of nearly fifty newsmen. Vernon was grim-faced and Gladys appeared on the brink of tears as the press went crazy.

Elvis never lost his smile as he made his cot repeatedly at the request of the cameramen. One photographer even hid in the barracks to get a photo of a sleeping Private Presley, but they were soon discovered and escorted off base by the Military Police. *Life* magazine ran a full-page photo of Elvis in his underwear being weighed, a clipping that undoubtedly appeared on the bedroom walls of millions of young girls around the world.

The next morning, Colonel Parker and Elvis had breakfast together in the enlisted men's hall with dozens of photographers in attendance, recording every bite of his meal. Afterward, Elvis took a battery of written and oral aptitude tests, received several inoculations, and sat through presentations on how to be a soldier. The recruits were also handed their first military paycheck. Elvis received seven dollars for that day. A reporter asked what he was going to do with his new infusion of cash.

"Start a loan company," Elvis quipped.

The number of photographers nearly tripled when Elvis received his army regulation buzz cut. As his famous dark duck tail was turned into a shave tail, Elvis famously joked, "Hair today, gone tomorrow!"

The Colonel also got into the act, commenting as Elvis's hair hit the floor, "Would you look at that? There must be a million dollars' worth of hair on the floor. We could make souvenirs out of it and sell one hair at a time!" He might have been joking when he said it, but in the Colonel's mind, he could see a small fortune being quickly swept up. Elvis forgot to pay the barber for his 65-cent shearing and, to his embarrassment, had to be called back for payment.

When Elvis tried on his new uniform with dozens of other new recruits in the huge supply depot, the Colonel tried to persuade him to wear one of his trademark string ties, much to the delight of the media.

"Thanks, Admiral, for trying to get me in trouble with the army on my second day," Elvis laughed.

Elvis spotted a telephone booth against the wall and went over to call his mother. The press started to follow him until the Colonel stepped in front, held up his hands and stopped them.

"I think a boy is entitled to talk to his mother alone," he said. They got the hint. (Sadly, Gladys Presley wasn't long for this world. She died of hepatitis a few weeks later on August 14, 1958, while Elvis was in basic training. Elvis was shattered.)

From Fort Chaffee, the entire Presley/Parker roadshow proceeded to Fort Hood just outside Killeen, Texas, for basic and advanced tank training. Elvis would soon join up with twenty thousand other recruits. Again, the Colonel was orchestrating the show, but this time the army was better prepared. Lieutenant Colonel Marjorie Schulten, the base public information officer, decided that it was time for Private Presley to begin his training.

"One day," she told the Colonel. "You have one day to deal with the press and tomorrow it's over." The Colonel, who had reaped more publicity in three days than most stars receive in a lifetime, said simply, "Well, Colonel, from one Colonel to another, you're the boss."

On the first day Elvis was drafted into the army, Colonel Parker gave Elvis the boost he needed. "You will soon be a soldier in the

United States Army," he said. "I have every confidence that you will be a great one."

Elvis fully applied himself in training, neither asking for nor receiving any special treatment. He also purchased a hi-fi stereo set for each service club at Fort Hood, as Special Services could not afford them.

A short time later, the Colonel received a phone call at his hotel room in Killeen from Lieutenant Colonel Schulten, who wanted to meet with him to make sure he understood Elvis was not going to receive any special attention or treatment during his stay at Fort Hood.

"Why don't you explain it to him [Elvis] in person?" he asked. "You tell him what you want with him in your office and Elvis will be there."

The Colonel accompanied Elvis to the public information officer's headquarters and waited outside while the private met with the female lieutenant colonel. He could, however, see what was going on inside, through the glassed partition. Lieutenant Colonel Schulten was gruff and all business when she started in on the humble recruit who was sitting in front of her, cap in hand and looking very nervous.

Colonel Parker had a hard time containing his laughter because the longer Elvis was in the room, the more animated and relaxed she became. The frown slowly gave way to a huge smile. He had totally charmed her. As they walked out to see the Colonel, she had her hand on his shoulder and said, "Elvis, if there is anything special you want to eat, just let me know. And you come back and talk to me if you have any problems. You just tell me about it." Elvis worked his magic.

After the three-day madhouse was over, the Colonel and his staff returned to their offices in Madison, Tennessee, with one purpose in mind: keep the Presley name front and center with the public for the next two years. Easier said than done. This was uncharted territory for any artist of Elvis's stature, but the Colonel not only managed to pull it off, he made it look easy.

One primary device was telegrams. The Colonel fired off telegrams for almost every occasion, covering everything from movie premieres, appearances, gala events, births, and anniversaries. In the two years Elvis was in the army, the Colonel's records show a total of 1,084 telegrams burned up the wires.

The Colonel sent a telegram to talk show host Steve Allen at NBC Studios, wishing him a happy Father's Day. He sent a similar one to Abe Lastfogel at the William Morris Agency. Telegrams also went to entertainers' openings. When Ricky Nelson opened at the Royal Hawaiian Hotel in Honolulu, he received a "best wishes" telegram. Similar telegrams were sent to Sophie Tucker, Milton Berle, Ed Sullivan, and Arnold Stang when they had Las Vegas openings. These telegrams were also sent to record and movie studio executives, radio stations, magazine editors and writers, and newspapers. When celebrities had children, birthdays, or celebrated an anniversary, they could expect a telegram. Even politicians received telegrams wishing them a happy New Year!

And each one of them was signed, "Elvis and the Colonel."

Sometime after Elvis was discharged from the army, he winked at the Colonel and said, "I didn't know I had written to so many people while I was in Germany."

The Colonel flew to Texas twice to see Elvis in basic training to have some papers signed and to report on how his career was progressing without him. They had already recorded several songs to be released during his army stint, and *King Creole* was out and hailed by the critics as Elvis's best film to date. It quickly became one of the top five films of the year.

When the army announced that Elvis would be shipped out on September 22, 1958, for an eighteen-month tour of duty in Germany, Colonel Parker and his staff sprang into action once more. With the army's full cooperation, again knowing how positive the publicity would be, a press conference was set up at the aged Brooklyn Army Terminal in New York City where Elvis would be able to tell his fans and the media farewell. A military band was brought in and nearly a hundred and fifty reporters and photographers were on hand, along with a host of RCA executives, the Colonel and his staff, and Elvis's father and grandmother.

G.I. Blues

The media wanted the usual photo of Elvis walking up the gangplank with a duffel bag on his shoulder. His own duffel bag had already been loaded aboard, so a substitute bag had to be quickly located. The entire sendoff was arranged by the army brass right down to the traditional farewell kiss from a pretty WAC. Even though thousands of celebrities had shipped out of the Brooklyn facility since it was built during World War I, this was the first press conference ever held there.

The conference went exactly as planned and Elvis came across as confident, well-spoken, and extremely well-mannered.

"I'm looking forward to Germany," Elvis told the crowd of assembled reporters. "I would like to tell my fans that in spite of the fact I'm going away and will be out of their sight for some time, I hope I'm not out of their minds and look forward to my return and entertaining again."

With the well-rehearsed military musicians playing "Hound Dog," "Don't Be Cruel," and "All Shook Up," Private Elvis Presley walked up the gangplank of the USS *Randall* with his phony duffel bag to set sail for Columbus Quay, Bremerhaven, Germany. The Colonel was all smiles as Elvis turned around to wave goodbye, rotated his shoulder, snapped his fingers, and buckled his knee, all caught on film for the entire world to enjoy.

At the Colonel's suggestion, RCA later released a record titled *Elvis Sails*[11] covering the entire event, ending with the long blast of a ship's horn. Of course, the Colonel sold the label a photo of his boy in uniform for an *Elvis Sails* calendar for $13,000.

Elvis arrived in the German port of Bremerhaven almost two weeks later and the event was considerably less organized without the Colonel's expertise. Captain Allan W. Galfund was in charge as public information officer. He had already been advised by his superiors that there would be no "hullabaloo like there was in the United States when Elvis departed." Galfund was already swamped with requests

---

11 *Elvis Sails* is a songless EP containing three interviews with Elvis shortly before he left for Germany.

for interviews. The army quickly instituted new rules. No one would be permitted to interview Private Presley.

He may have been sleeping in a barracks with twenty-nine other young men and gagging down creamed chipped beef on toast, but Elvis was certainly the only private earning $1 million a year. His records were constantly spinning on the radio; his movies were playing in the theaters; memorabilia and albums were flying off the shelves; and his story dominated the newspapers (as he was the number one story in the country).

RCA producers were well prepared for their star's absence. They had stockpiled a ton of unreleased material. Between his induction and discharge, Presley had ten Top 40 hits, including "Wear My Ring Around Your Neck," the best-selling "Hard Headed Woman," and "One Night" in 1958, and in 1959, "(Now and Then There's) A Fool Such as I" and the number one "A Big Hunk o' Love." Not bad for a private whose military job was driving a tank around.

In Germany, Elvis received more mail in a single day than the entire thousand-man armored division stationed in Friedberg. Colonel Parker was also receiving "army mail." Lots of it. Fans around the world evidently thought the Colonel would be by Elvis's side during his entire tour of duty and would personally hand-deliver letters to the singer. By coincidence, there was a Colonel Parker stationed at the Pentagon. One day he called the other Colonel Parker begging for mercy.

"My office is being inundated with mail for you. We can't handle it!" he cried. "What do you want me to do?"

The Colonel gave the most natural reply, "Mail it to me."

A few days later two mail trucks pulled up at his Madison, Tennessee, office and unloaded about twenty huge bags of mail.

The Colonel corresponded with Elvis on a regular basis during his year-and-a-half stay overseas. His letters were usually typed by himself, and a typical letter—all of which are still in his files—would run three or four pages, single spaced, never indented, and with very little punctuation. He kept Elvis up to date on every aspect of his career—what movies were in release and how they were doing, current record sales, and, most important, what was in the works upon his discharge. He included a lot of personal news as well.

The letters also contained words of advice, much of it crucial where it concerned Elvis's career.

"Never have your photo taken out of uniform because people will think you are goofing off," he wrote. "You are getting a better reaction every day for just being a soldier and nothing else."

Elvis did exactly as Colonel Parker suggested and was just another army "grunt." One of his army buddies was quoted in a magazine article that must have pleased the Colonel: "He [Elvis] sat on his butt in the snow just like the rest of us and ate the same crummy food. He was a real Joe."

Well, almost. He donated his army pay to charity, purchased TV sets for the post, and bought an extra set of fatigues for everyone in his outfit. In June 1959, with fifteen days of leave, Elvis and his friends traveled to Munich and Paris. In Paris they partied for a week. On several nights, Elvis invited the whole chorus line of girls from the 4 O'Clock club back to his hotel. The next day the club couldn't start the show because the girls were still in his suite.

"It reminds me so much of the life I used to lead before I went into the service," Elvis told a reporter.

But he never lorded it over his fellow soldiers. He also partially paid for the mess hall to be renovated. (It was later named after him.) When his tour of duty was over, his commanding officer said, "He fooled us all. We had our stomachs up to here with all these celebrities, singers and actors, and we figured Presley for just another lightweight. But he never angled himself into anything easy and he shows some exceptionally good judgment for a kid worth a few million dollars. This guy Elvis has made it popular to be a good soldier. It was great for us."

The army held a press conference before Elvis was discharged. A reporter asked Elvis about his decision to serve as a regular soldier instead of as part of the service club.

"I was in a funny position," Elvis said. "Actually, that's the only way it could be. People were expecting me to mess up, to goof up in one way or another. They thought I couldn't take it and so forth, and I was determined to go to any limits to prove otherwise, not only to the people who were wondering, but to myself."

At one point while Elvis was in the army, Eddy Arnold called the Colonel and asked if he would go with him to Lyndon Johnson's sprawling ranch in Gillespie County, Texas, about fifty miles west of Austin. Arnold had been requested to perform at a party that Senator Johnson was hosting for the president of Mexico. Colonel Parker agreed, and it was a memorable experience for both men. For the Colonel, it led to a lifelong friendship with Lyndon Johnson. During his term as the US senator from Texas, Johnson confided in the Colonel that the Democratic Party wanted to nominate him for vice president, but he was reluctant about committing because he had his sights set on the presidency. He then asked Colonel Parker what he thought he should do.

"I really believe you should accept the nomination for the vice presidency. At least it would bring you closer to your goal, and we never know what surprises life will bring." Little did the Colonel realize that he was prophesying the outcome of a world-shattering event.

It was also the Colonel who proposed the Lyndon B. Johnson campaign slogan, "All the Way With LBJ." Johnson loved it.

"I think it is a great theme and we are going to use it all the way," he told Colonel Parker.

In October 1959, the Colonel's letters began containing more information regarding Elvis's homecoming just five months away. While the city of Memphis wanted to host a big parade and celebration, the Colonel had other thoughts as expressed in a telegram around that time. He told Elvis that it would be better for his public image if he came home as a regular soldier without any fanfare. He pointed out that many heroic soldiers come home from wars without parades. It was an excellent point.

While Elvis was in Germany, the Colonel routinely saw to it that fresh flowers were placed on his mother's grave and sent photos. This was the side of Colonel Parker that many rarely saw.

In early January of both 1959 and 1960, Colonel Parker flooded major radio stations across the country with reminders that Elvis's birthday was January 8, and most responded by playing his music all day long. Dick Clark received a petition with well over three thousand signatures asking him to remember Elvis's birthday on his network TV show.

The Colonel directed the entire two-year battle plan from his Madison offices with frequent business trips to both coasts. In that time, he was making sure Elvis stayed on everyone's minds until March 5, 1960—the date of Elvis Presley's official discharge.

I look at it this way: if someone is hooked on Coca-Cola and it is taken away from them for two years, they are going to crave it even more. Especially if they continue to hear it advertised and other people talking about it. That is what happened with Elvis. The army took him away from his fans for two years. The Colonel continued to keep them "thirsty" for more. By the time Elvis was discharged, they were parched.

The Colonel never missed an opportunity to get publicity for his star soldier. The prestigious Music Operators of America organization was holding its annual convention at the Morrison Hotel in Chicago in 1959. He called his friend Al Dvorin, who had returned to his booking agency while Elvis was away, and told him to sign up a dozen of his best little people. Al responded by booking fifteen, including Eddie Gaedel, who was the only little person to ever appear in a major league baseball game. Chicago White Sox owner Bill Veeck had signed him for one at bat as a stunt. He took four straight balls and walked.

Al put all fifteen of these little people into a cab and sent them to the hotel where the large convention was taking place. He led the parade into the hotel as his followers carried a large banner that read, ELVIS PRESLEY FAN CLUB OF CHICAGO. The Colonel, of course, had alerted the media in advance and stole the publicity spotlight away from the rest of the convention and diverted the attention to his star.

He pulled a different stunt at the second annual Disc Jockey Convention in Miami, Florida. Armed with two thousand autographed photographs of Elvis in two sizes—a large tousle-haired portrait and a small full-color version—Colonel Parker plastered the Americana Hotel with mementos of his celebrated artist.

The media asked how Elvis was doing in Germany and whether the Colonel thought his client would still have a career when he returned. He assured them that Elvis was in a good place.

"I've had offers worth over a half million dollars," Colonel Parker said, "for Elvis's appearances on weekends throughout Europe." He added that he had Elvis booked on a major network show and his next three movies picked out—one for Paramount and two for 20th Century Fox—once he finished his military service.

It was obvious the Colonel was feeling good. Elvis was in the homestretch of his tour of duty and was about to return to the States, as a sergeant no less. The Colonel was very careful to let Elvis make all the artistic choices in their partnership, which is why it worked so well. However, there was a onetime exception: the selection of "Are You Lonesome Tonight?" as the first single upon his discharge. The Colonel made a special case for this song; he felt it was exceptional and sensed its crossover appeal.

Colonel Parker's sense of humor was no more evident than in an incident that occurred shortly before Elvis's discharge. Producer Hal Wallis was desperately trying to get the Colonel to commit his returning star to a movie immediately upon his release. Several phone calls from Wallis resulted in the same answer from the Colonel: no one knew what Elvis wanted to do when he got back.

"I'm certainly not going to pressure him," the Colonel said. "And besides, I'm sure he will want to spend some time relaxing at Graceland."

Wallis was not pleased with that reply and told the Colonel so. This time, however, he had pushed too hard. The Colonel arranged for a novelty newspaper to be printed, and then arranged for the phony front page to be substituted for Wallis's regular Sunday paper early in the morning before he got up.

When Wallis sat down at the kitchen table and opened his paper, he almost fainted. The headline blared: "Elvis Enlists for Two More Years!"

It wasn't until his heart stopped pounding that he realized that the Colonel had, indeed, been pushed too far, and this was his way of letting Wallis know it.

Had Wallis known about a spirited teenage girl that Elvis befriended while in Germany, he might have done more than faint. Priscilla Beaulieu was the fourteen-year-old stepdaughter of an air force captain who had been transferred to Wiesbaden, Germany, in August 1959. She met Elvis a month later at his house at Goethestrasse 14, courtesy of Currie and Carole Grant, who escorted her there to meet her idol. (Fans congregated outside the house to see Presley as he came and went to work at the base. A sign was put up stating that autographs would be given between 7:30 and 8:00 P.M.) Priscilla's China doll–like beauty left him breathless. For a man who could have any woman in the world, this was quite a strong reaction. She was petite, demure, and polite. He thought she looked like an angel. And best of all, from Elvis's point of view, her age was not a deterrent.

"And she's young enough that I can train her anyway I want," Elvis declared to his friend Rex Mansfield, who was there that night.

Elvis sent for Priscilla a few days after their initial meeting. Her parents, particularly Captain Beaulieu, were hesitant about their teenage daughter seeing a famous rock 'n' roller whose image oozed sexuality. But Elvis was not a man to give up so easily and coddled them with "yes, ma'ams" and "yes, sirs," laying on his thickest charm and pulling out all the stops to placate the Beaulieus. He assured them that he would treat their daughter with the utmost respect, and that there would always be a chaperone along when they were together. They cautiously granted permission if a set curfew was observed. In no time Elvis violated it, always offering a plethora of excuses.

Priscilla had a series of drivers who ferried her back and forth during the week, as well as almost every weekend starting on Friday nights. She and Elvis spent as much time together as they could, and Priscilla's grades at school suffered as a result. I imagine it wasn't easy being a ninth grader, dating the world's most famous singer and getting only a few hours of sleep at night.

Their "special friendship" didn't go unnoticed by reporters. But it was an era when the press corps even turned a blind eye to President John F. Kennedy's many Oval Office dalliances. I seriously doubt that Elvis's secret relationship with Priscilla would have remained a secret in today's era of 24-7 news, "gotcha" journalism, and paparazzi ambushes, not to mention fans with smartphones. It was a different time.

Priscilla was photographed by the press at the airport when Elvis left for America, and some of those photos ended up in *Life* magazine, labeling her "the girl he left behind." Beyond this, there was surprisingly little publicity about their relationship. The Colonel encouraged Elvis to remain tight-lipped about Priscilla, or any other relationship for that matter.

For the time being, Elvis went along with Colonel Parker's belief that an all-consuming relationship would hurt his image and be bad for his career. Priscilla patiently waited for their reunion when she got back to the States. Elvis had more pressing matters at hand.

On March 3, Presley's plane arrived at McGuire Air Force Base near Fort Dix, New Jersey. Nancy Sinatra, RCA representatives, and Parker were there to welcome him home, as well as a huge crowd of fans. Two days later, on March 5, Sergeant Presley was officially discharged from active duty with his service officially noted as honorable. He was awarded the Army Good Conduct Medal. To his delight, the military qualified him as an expert marksman with several weapons.[12]

---

12 There is an interesting footnote to Elvis Presley's service. In 2007, the army shut down the Ray Barracks, where Elvis had been stationed, and handed it over

Elvis had been out of the public spotlight for two years and would soon be a civilian. But, the big question was, how would he be accepted? And most important to Colonel Parker, would he still be perceived as a star by an adoring public?

---

to the German government. Immediately before turning off the main power to the post equipment, the commander of the signal battalion played "Hound Dog" over the loudspeakers.

8

Fame and Fortune

As requested by Colonel Parker, there was no big welcoming party or a parade down Main Street for Elvis Presley when he returned to the US after being discharged, though there were thousands of fans on hand to greet him at the Memphis train depot, as well as lots of family and friends. The Colonel arranged a press conference following his arrival at Graceland, but that was the extent of the hoopla. One Memphis radio station did play his records twenty-four hours a day to mark his homecoming. He spent a fun-filled two weeks with his father and friends in Memphis before he was back in Nashville recording at RCA Studios.

RCA Victor knew the public was eagerly awaiting Elvis's first new recording and promised to have it in release within seventy-two hours. They had advance orders from distributors for almost 1.5 million copies of "Stuck on You"—the first of four number one singles Elvis scored in 1960. The others were "It's Now or Never," "Are You Lonesome Tonight?" and "Surrender."

"It's Now or Never," written by Aaron Schroeder and Wally Gold, was an instant smash and ultimately became Elvis's biggest hit, with total international sales, according to *The Guinness Book of World Records*, of twenty million records. The song shot straight to number one in America and the United Kingdom, opening new doors for Elvis with adult listeners. Many easy-listening stations with more mature audiences found the song disarming and gave it regular play.

Artistically, Elvis broke new ground with "Are You Lonesome Tonight?," a song he grew to love so much (the one that the Colonel pushed hard to release as a single). It knocked everyone out, even though Elvis was afraid to release it. He thought fans might not like it because of the narrative in the middle of the song, quoting William Shakespeare's sentiments that "all the world's a stage."

It took a lot of lobbying by Colonel Parker and Elvis's inner circle, seven months to be exact, but Elvis did finally relent, and the song's takeoff was nothing short of astronomical. The single shot straight to number one and stayed there for six weeks, boosted by airplay on easy-listening stations across the country. In Britain, it topped the charts for four weeks and was his sixth number one single in the United Kingdom.

After the two-day session at RCA, Elvis returned to Memphis, and the entire entourage, including its newest member, army buddy Joe Esposito, boarded the train for a twenty-four-hour ride to Miami, Florida. The Colonel turned the trip into a presidential-like campaign tour with Elvis appearing on the train's rear platform at every stop. There were large crowds of fans and press at every station. The latter didn't just magically appear; they had received copies of the itinerary in advance, courtesy of the Colonel.

Elvis's first major television appearance as a civilian was for the Timex-sponsored *Frank Sinatra's Welcome Home Party for Elvis Presley* on NBC. It was taped in Miami in the Grand Ballroom of the world-famous Fontainebleau Hotel on March 26, and later aired on May 8, 1960. Elvis received a record $100,000[13] net plus an additional $25,000 for travel and other expenses. No doubt a large portion of those expenses went to Elvis's accommodations. He and his entourage, later

---

13 Timex was able to raise a portion of the record-breaking amount offered to Elvis Presley by charging admission to the six hundred people who paid a premium to attend the taping of the show—an idea given to them by Colonel Parker.

known to the world as the "Memphis Mafia," stayed in the penthouse of the Fontainebleau Hotel and had a ball.

Sinatra serving as the host to welcome Elvis back from the army was a surprising selection given his past comments on Elvis. He was on the record as saying Elvis's music emitted a foul odor and even hurt his ears.

"His music is deplorable, a rancid-smelling aphrodisiac," Sinatra told reporters when Elvis first hit it big. "It's the most brutal, ugly, degenerate, vicious form of expression it has been my displeasure to hear." Even though Sinatra's vitriolic comment had been made years before, in the 1950s, Elvis never forgot the remark. And perhaps in a way, he was making him pay through the nose.

The Colonel had originally offered first dibs to Jackie Gleason because of Elvis's earlier performances before being drafted. When told the price was $125,000, Gleason went ballistic.

"Are you nuts?!," he screamed at the Colonel. "No one has ever received that much money for a single TV performance!" He looked at the Colonel and said, "Colonel, you're asking way too much money."

"I don't know what you are talking about," the Colonel calmly replied. "If I was your manager, I'd still be asking $125,000 for you." Gleason followed the logic but refused to pay. So the Colonel took the deal to Frank Sinatra, who paid without even so much as a counter offer.

Elvis sang "Fame and Fortune" and "Stuck on You," two of the songs he had recorded just days before in Nashville. He then teamed up with Sinatra and they sang each other's songs: Elvis sang Sinatra's "Witchcraft" while the Chairman of the Board gave "Love Me Tender" a shot.

Ed Sullivan, in his nationally syndicated newspaper column, wrote, "Youthful fans will never forgive Sinatra for restricting Elvis to just two songs. The truth of the matter is that Presley's astute manager, Colonel Tom Parker, flatly insisted Presley would sing only two songs! Colonel Tom, using the logic of a farmer, was a firm believer in not giving a hungry horse an entire bale of hay."

Elvis and Colonel Parker were the hottest property in show business. A rider to the contract the Colonel negotiated with Sinatra's representatives stated Elvis was to be credited as a "special guest" performer on the show, followed by his name being printed at 100 percent the size of the title of the program. Sinatra insisted that Elvis appear in a tuxedo, just as he was, after doing the first number in his army uniform. The Colonel protested.

"He just got out of the army, Frank," he said. "He doesn't have a tuxedo that fits. You'll have to have one made for him. And all the boys (Scotty Moore, D. J. Fontana, and the Jordanaires) backing him will look out of place if he's in a tux and they aren't. And I don't own one either. How am I going to look if all my boys are dressed up and I'm not?" Frank had everyone fitted for tuxedos, including the Colonel, and they all looked great, except you can see all the boys on stage were wearing boots.

The show was taped before hundreds of screaming young fans. In fact, they screamed so loudly that plaster fell from the ceiling. The Colonel had guaranteed just such a homecoming welcome by distributing over half of the free tickets to local Elvis fan clubs. The fans received such preferential treatment at the show that the media covering the event was relegated to the back of the room to watch the taping on one of thirty TV monitors. With Sammy Davis Jr. (a big Elvis fan), Peter Lawford, Joey Bishop, and Nancy Sinatra as special guests, the show had a national viewing audience of 41.5 percent.

Following the success of the show, Elvis recorded the soundtrack for his fifth movie, *G.I. Blues,* which would begin production the first week in May. They were heading west once again.

Since Elvis still did not like to fly (though he later overcame that fear and owned several jets and planes), the Colonel rented two special railroad cars for the trip west from Memphis to Los Angeles—a lounge car with couches, table games, and special sound equipment, plus a sleeping car with private staterooms. The eighteen one-way fares ran $80.54 each! The entire tab for the two-day trip, as arranged by the Colonel through the Louisville & Nashville Railroad Company, including buffet service for two days plus security, cost $2,424.41. It included a total of ninety-nine stops along the way from Memphis, down through Arkansas, across Texas, into New Mexico and Arizona, and finally through Southern California's desert into Los Angeles.

Following their train ride from Memphis, the Colonel and company set up semi-permanent residency in the plush Beverly Wilshire Hotel, and Elvis recorded the eleven-song soundtrack for the movie in late April and early May, 1960, at RCA Studio C and Radio Recorders in Hollywood. It rocketed to the number one position and stayed there for eleven weeks and remained on *Billboard*'s album charts for nearly two years. It was also nominated for two Grammy Awards. It seemed as if Elvis could do no wrong in the immediate aftermath of his military service.

Principal photography on *G.I. Blues* commenced on May 2, 1960, and was shot on the Paramount Studios lot. The film, co-starring beautiful South African actress Juliet Prowse, was loosely based on Elvis's military stint in Germany. It was a different Elvis than fans had seen in his pre-army films; he cut down on his famous moves dramatically and didn't sneer once.

The film was hugely successful and was welcomed by fans around the world, who were thrilled to have their idol back. They cheered a little too hard in Mexico City, however, where riots broke out at the theaters and the Mexican government said no to all future Elvis Presley films.

There was more to the story than that. They said no to Elvis himself. In his book *Refried Elvis: The Rise of the Mexican Counterculture*, author Eric Zolov learned from a Mexico City record executive that a powerful Mexican political figure wanted to contract Elvis for a private party for his teenage daughter. He sent Elvis a blank check to fill in as he wished. Presley (read: the Colonel) returned the blank check. The politician was livid. He invented a quote, which ran in a Tijuana tabloid gossip column and was attributed to Elvis. It read as follows: "I'd rather kiss three black girls than a Mexican." A national radio station read the quote over the air and reaction was swift. A student group held record burnings. Elvis was declared persona non grata by the

Mexican government. His 1963 movie *Fun in Acapulco* was filmed on a Hollywood lot and at a California hotel rather than on location to avoid any unpleasantness.

The rules were always the same whether Elvis was on the movie set or in a recording studio: visitors were kept to an absolute minimum. The studio and Colonel Parker didn't want any outside distractions. The exceptions to this rule were top film and TV stars such as John Wayne, Steve McQueen, Dean Martin, Jerry Lewis, Ricky Nelson, Vince Edwards, and Warren Beatty, who were regular visitors to the *G.I. Blues* set.

Scriptwriters and songsmiths were delighted that Elvis was back, and screenplays began pouring in. The proven "formula" not only still worked after a two-year hiatus but was stronger than ever.

Colonel Parker never told Elvis what movies to make. Elvis also had final script approval, which the Colonel negotiated for him. That said, some of the scripts that were offered to Elvis were so bad they never got past the Colonel. A few of the rejected titles include *Big Mike, The Sweetheart of Sigma Chi,* and *Mock Trail.* The owners of singing mules and tow-headed kids with snub noses were crushed.

The Colonel and his staff worked closely with the studio's publicity people as well as RCA Records executives to promote every film and soundtrack. His promotional strategy was basically the same for every film. They would broadly cross-promote the opening of the film with the release of the title song and album in record stores across the country. Every piece of mail that went out of the studios would carry promotional material on the latest film, including calendars. Elvis took photos with any celebrity who showed up on the set. The all-important fan clubs were supplied with weekly updates, and members were asked to call their favorite disc jockeys and request Elvis's songs from the latest soundtrack. And finally, elaborate press kits were mailed to radio, television, and newspaper people around the country.

With the Colonel's careful and nuanced guidance, Elvis received incredible publicity with every project he undertook. However, Rogers & Cowan, a major Hollywood public relations firm, thought they could do a better job promoting and publicizing Elvis. They told the Colonel that no other manager in the business personally handled the publicity for their clients. Instead, they all employed outside agencies, usually for huge fees. Rogers & Cowan representatives made a short presentation and, at the end of it, the Colonel asked, "Just how much money are we talking about here?" The agency representatives, sensing they had a toehold, quoted him a minimum fee of $10,000 a year (nearly $100,000 in 2022 dollars).

"That sounds about right," the Colonel quickly replied. They were having financial struggles due to the extremely high tax rate, so he turned the tables on them and proposed the agency pay them instead—$5,000 the first year and $15,000 the next year. He may have been joking, but it is important to note that every major star had outside publicity representation that could cost several thousand dollars a month extra. The Colonel considered publicity just another of his managerial responsibilities.

Soon after the final scene was finished on *G.I. Blues,* everyone shuffled over to 20th Century Fox to begin *Flaming Star,* a western that was originally written for Marlon Brando. Elvis, with heavy makeup, played a half-breed Indian named Pacer Burton. It was his first film without a title song and is ranked as one of Elvis's best movies. Film editors were still splicing together that picture when Fox opened production on *Wild in the Country* on November 11, 1960. It was shredded by the critics. Elvis cut five songs for this picture, although only three made it to the screen. Preview audiences were given a choice of two endings. In the original cut, co-star Hope Lange died, but viewers decided to give her a reprieve and let her live in the final version. Though she survived, the movie died the death of a dog in a doorway.

Bosley Crowther, the highly influential film critic for *The New York Times* wrote, "Nonsense, that's all it is—sheer nonsense—and Mr. Presley, who did appear to be improving as an actor in his last picture, is as callow as ever in this. The few times he sings are painful—at least they are to our ears—and his appearance is waxy and flabby. Elvis has retrogressed."

Sure, there were hits and misses, but mostly hits. Colonel Parker and Elvis never forgot where they came from, and this was evident when some thirty-seven charities benefited from the Colonel's promotional genius on February 25, 1961. That's when he called upon many of his show business friends to participate with Elvis in two charitable shows. First, he had Governor Buford Ellington declare it "Elvis Presley Day" in Tennessee. Colonel and Elvis hosted a $100-a-plate luncheon at the Claridge Hotel in downtown Memphis where he arranged for Elvis to receive a special plaque from RCA Records for having sold seventy-five million records.

With entertainer George Jessel as emcee and comedian Dave Gardner heading up an all-star lineup, the Colonel and Elvis raised $51,607 for needy Memphis charities. Elvis was joined onstage by Scotty Moore on guitar, D. J. Fontana on drums, Boots Randolph on sax, and Floyd Cramer on piano, four of the best musicians in the business. A few months earlier, the Colonel had read in the *Los Angeles Herald Examiner* of the plight of the USS *Arizona* Memorial on the 19th anniversary of the Japanese attack on Pearl Harbor in Hawaii. The *Arizona* was one of the battleships sunk by the Japanese on December 7, 1941, taking 1,177 American sailors to a watery grave.

A full ten years after the fatal attack, the only sign that indicated the *Arizona* ever existed was an American flag attached to its rusting smokestack sticking out of the water. In 1951, Congress formally drafted a bill calling for a shrine to be built, but they did not appropriate any federal funds. After years of governmental boondoggling, President Dwight D. Eisenhower finally signed legislation authorizing construction of the memorial in 1958. But it had to be built with private funds only and then maintained by the US Navy. An estimated $500,000 was needed to complete a memorial, and only about half was in the commission's coffers. Organizers wanted to start construction on the twentieth anniversary of Pearl Harbor but needed about $50,000 to get the ball rolling. The public funds were not forthcoming according to the article. A journalist called the whole thing a "national disgrace."

Elvis was scheduled to begin filming *Blue Hawaii* in the islands on

March 26, 1961. The Colonel made a quick call to Elvis and explained the situation. He wholeheartedly agreed with the Colonel's idea of a benefit show. Elvis himself was not only charitable but also had a patriotic streak a mile wide. He believed strongly in his country and was proud to be an American.

With Elvis on board, the Colonel then phoned his friend George Chaplin, editor of the *Honolulu Advertiser*. The newspaper was spearheading the fundraising campaign and frankly, they had hit a wall. They needed a miracle.

"We'll help build that memorial," the Colonel said. "Elvis will do a benefit concert in Honolulu." And then, in true Parker fashion, he added a few stipulations.

The biggest stipulation was that everything would have to be donated, including the four-thousand-seat Bloch Stadium, stagehands, lighting, ushers, sound, musicians . . . and yes, even Elvis! Also, everyone would have to buy a ticket to the show, no exceptions. The Colonel bought the first two tickets as a gesture of goodwill. Chaplin was delighted to help put the Colonel's plan—no small undertaking—into action. Everything was donated for the benefit and every ticket was sold. When an aide to an admiral inquired about the commanding officer's seating arrangements, the Colonel asked, "What kind of tickets did he buy?" When told the admiral "Doesn't buy tickets," the Colonel replied, "Well, maybe someone will buy him one because everyone pays." The admiral got the message and even bought ten $100 VIP tickets.

The Colonel had booked his old friend, *Grand Ole Opry* comedienne Minnie Pearl,[14] as a guest star on the show, as well as comic Sterling Mossman. The show staff thought Pearl was a little long in the

---

[14] Minnie Pearl, the stage character of comedienne Sarah Colley, was one of the Colonel's biggest boosters and got onto both of our cases about him writing a book. After Albert Goldman penned his 1981 book *Elvis,* she wanted Colonel Parker's name cleared. "Don't you listen to Tom," she said to me backstage at a Leon Russell concert in Nashville. "You write that book and clear this up. He [Parker] won't do it, but you need to."

tooth, but it turned out she still had the comedic goods and was a big hit with the audience.

Outfitted in a $10,000 gold lamé jacket with silver sequined lapels and cuffs, black slacks, a guitar with inlaid mother-of-pearl slung around his shoulder, and a lei of fragrant orchids around his neck, Elvis was ready to rock the house.

The hysteria that greeted his entrance was staggering. More than five minutes passed before the crowd settled down enough for him to launch into a nineteen-song set that included "Heartbreak Hotel," "Don't Be Cruel," and "All Shook Up."

Backed by the Jordanaires and several Nashville musicians he had recorded with a month before, Elvis gave an inspired and playfully uninhibited performance that wasn't anything like his '50s concerts, but wasn't as polished as his later Vegas shows either.

The concert was a resounding success on all fronts. The fans got their money's worth, and Elvis regained his confidence in front of a live audience. The show raised approximately $62,000 for the memorial fund.

The spotlight that the concert shone on the memorial effort helped revive public interest in the project. That September, Congress donated $150,000, and the Hawaiian legislature added another $50,000 contribution to the pot. With the $250,000 already collected from the federal and state sources combined with the $275,000 in donations, construction on the memorial began in March 1962.

After everything was over, there was $54,000 in expenses that had to be paid from the benefit. Elvis and the Colonel each wrote personal checks for $27,000.

The Colonel and Elvis finally saw the *Arizona* Memorial they helped get off the ground and onto the water on May 30, 1962. While there, they laid a wreath in the water containing more than one thousand carnations with an inscription. It read: "Gone, but not forgotten. Elvis and the Colonel."

9

We Are Family

Up to this point, I've pretty much kept myself out of the picture. Now you'll hear where I came into the story, how Colonel Parker and Elvis entered my life, and the role they played in shaping it.

I met the two men on the same day in the early sixties. It was summer in Palm Springs, and I was barely in my teens.

I grew up on a grape ranch in the San Joaquin Valley in Central California. Dad was Thomas McDonald, a World War II veteran who was wounded in the Battle of the Bulge. He was big and sturdy at six feet two but walked with a limp for the rest of his life after his injury. Once grounded, the army still wasn't done with him. They made him an air-conditioning and refrigeration mechanic, which is how he earned his living. Serving as an Evangelical minister fed my father's soul, but it didn't put food on the table.

Mom, whose first name was Zella, was a homemaker who hailed from Missouri. She was a sweet and loving mom and a dutiful preacher's wife. She had to be, because she kept going into church with poisonous snakes. I'll explain in a second. . . .

My father held several jobs for a reason: times were hard, and I learned from an early age that nothing in this life is ever given to you; no meal was going to magically appear on our table come suppertime and no clothes were suddenly going to appear on our backs. We worked hard, we worked long, and we took whatever work we could to earn extra money, including cutting grapes.

And we gave thanks to our maker on Sundays. Sunday church service was something else. It was filled with lots of poor and working-class people who made sure to wear their Sunday best, and it was filled with rattlesnakes.

Snake handling was a religious rite observed in a small number of isolated churches during the "Holiness movement." Its roots were firmly planted in Appalachia in the early part of the twentieth century and wended its way through evangelical and charismatic churches in rural America. The snakes were front and center in our church, and that's exactly where my dad wanted his wife and son to sit. When the snakes were pulled from their cages, they were brought down the aisles. We didn't want to be anywhere near them because they scared the crap out of me and my mom. And if the snake reached out for you, it meant you were a sinner.

My mother died from complications of kidney disease when I was fifteen years old. Dad was forced to raise me on his own. He wasn't much of a disciplinarian because he treated me like a little man. Not that there was much time for coddling; work was the priority. Times were so hard that schooling wasn't a priority either. I went to about sixty schools in my youth. But mostly, I'd start and stop or not go altogether. My father lived nomadically, bouncing around from town to town for Oral Roberts, helping him set up his tent revivals.

They used an old Ringling Brothers tent that had the capacity for ten thousand people, and my brother, Gary, and I helped pitch it when the revival hit town. The entire process of raising the tent usually took a few hours and many people.

On those trips we'd drive down in my dad's white Thames (an English Ford van) and pitch a small tent on the grounds. When it was over, he went back to fixing air-conditioning and refrigeration units, and I tagged along. We were very close.

Most of California was built without air-conditioning, but the same does not hold true for the Mojave Desert. My dad recognized this. What was once a luxury was now a necessity, especially in a place like Palm Springs. With cheap air-conditioning, builders could cool affordable houses without the thick walls and deep porches of historic homes. Living in the desert became possible for millions because of air-conditioning.

Starting in the 1950s, we rented an apartment and spent our summers in Palm Springs, tending to business. My father worked for HA Simsarian Heating & Air Conditioning, a very large company that had a firm foothold in California at the time. They developed a nice clientele, maintaining heating and air-conditioning units for the who's who of Palm Springs. I had a bicycle with a wagon containing tools, parts, and air filters.

Back then, Palm Springs was the size of a village and the playground of the rich and famous. We had the keys to many celebrities' homes, including Liberace, Kirk Douglas, Carole Lombard, Clark Gable, William Randolph Hearst, Samuel Goldwyn, Howard Hughes,[15] Bob Hope, and Lucille Ball. But they were there only on weekends and extended stays in the winter and spring. The place was dead in the summer, thanks to triple-digit heat, which often resembled the feeling of a convection oven. But for us, that's when we got about 85 percent of our business.

It was on one of those hot summer days when I walked into the home of Jack L. Warner, in Old Las Palmas, a historic neighborhood that drew celebrities and film industry leaders. I was there to change out the air filter and check on the AC unit and make sure it was running smoothly. No big deal. And no big deal because usually no one was in the house. I was in and out of each home in fifteen minutes, tops.

But on that summer day I met Elvis, so I was a little delayed.

Elvis was staying at the Warner estate and was lying poolside with a female companion, a beautiful blond woman who was sunbathing

---

15 I personally never met Howard Hughes, but he was friendly with Colonel Parker. They routinely played cards at his Las Palmas home when the business mogul was in town, before he became a hermit.

without a stitch of clothing. They were outside when I let myself in. I didn't hear them, and they didn't see me. I made my way to the air-conditioning unit to change the air filter. I had to open a trapdoor to get inside and was lying on the floor, which got the attention of a small white poodle. The dog began barking and then nipped at my pant leg. I was cursing at him when someone walked over, picked the animal up and held it in his hands. Then the person addressed me.

"Boy, come on out from under there," the voice commanded. "What are you doing?"

When I crawled out from underneath the unit, I spoke my mind.

"Well, I'm trying to change out your air filter, but your dog's trying to eat me up," I said, very matter-of-fact. He almost fell over laughing.

"Well, this isn't my dog. It belongs to that girl out there," Elvis said, pointing to his nude companion through the sliding glass doors. Suddenly he realized his faux pas and gently walked over to shut the curtains, shielding me from getting a better look. Like any normal teen, I was more interested in the naked lady outside than the rock star inside.

Elvis asked me why I was changing out the air filter. I explained who I was and why I was there. I told him how Jack Warner's house, which he was renting for a period, was part of my monthly routine. He asked me to take a seat so we could talk some more. I knew who he was. My mother loved Elvis, and we'd go see his movies whenever we could. In those days, the movie theater was one of the few places that offered air-conditioning in the San Joaquin Valley. And if it was an Elvis movie, even better. I was also familiar with his music because radio stations played his records almost nonstop in the 1950s and early 1960s. You'd have to be living under a rock to not know who Elvis Presley was.

Elvis asked me where I was from, who were my parents, and the usual "getting to know you" questions. He was sincere and inquisitive and gave me his undivided attention. When I got to the part about my father being a follower and later an evangelist in the Assembly of God church, Elvis was hooked.

"You're an Assembly of God kid," Elvis said. "So am I."

Elvis then asked if they spoke in tongues. For those of you who don't know, speaking in tongues is regarded as one of the "gifts of the Holy Spirit" once someone receives Jesus Christ as their savior and Lord. It's a form of communication to God but in a language that is unrecognizable to the unindoctrinated.

"Yes, they did speak in tongues," I answered. Elvis kept firing away.

"And did you guys have the snakes in your church?" he asked. Yes, we had snakes at our services, I told him. He nodded with a knowing smile. I can't say with great certainty that his church used them in their services, but he asked leading questions, and I just assumed he knew the answers. From the look on his face, at least, he was no stranger to the practice.

When I got to the part about working for Oral Roberts and setting up the big top, he became even more engaged. Elvis said one of his favorite musicians was Buford Dowell, an organist for the Roberts organization who whipped the crowds into a frenzy and brought thousands to Christ during the altar call. He asked if I knew who he was.

"Of course, I do," I said. "I help lug that big organ of his onto the stage whenever he plays," I said. Elvis looked at me almost not believing what I said, so he decided to test me.

"Well, what type of organ does he play?" Elvis asked, quizzing me.

"He plays a Hammond B3," I answered. "And he has a Leslie speaker cabinet." That nearly blew Elvis's mind.

"Whoa, little man!" he nearly shouted. "You really know your stuff!"

Elvis was starting to get a real kick out of me. He asked if ushers still used the velveteen offering bags (the old version of the collection plate). I confirmed they did and usually played a song called "Meeting Tonight (On the Old Campground)" for the collection. Elvis sang a couple of the verses of the song right on the spot.

Now I was starting to gain a little credibility with Elvis. He then asked me about setting up the big top tent with my dad and how it was done. I laid out the procedure, how many people it took to assemble, and how long it took from start to finish. The stakes were about four to five feet long, and they needed to be two-thirds in the ground. The big tent used about three hundred stakes, each needing two hundred to three hundred blows. An experienced team of seven roustabouts could pound them all in in an hour. Elvis was also under the impression that elephants were used to pull the canvas to the top. I laughed.

"Naw, that was in the old circus days," I said, chuckling a bit. "We use the winch power on a diesel truck."

Elvis exploded with laughter, nearly falling out of the chair. He couldn't believe the things coming out of my mouth or how much our backgrounds aligned, especially where it concerned church, spirituality, and revivals. That coincidence, I believe, bonded us that day and again in the future.

I think we talked for about a good hour straight—the blond bombshell sunbathing in the backyard be damned! Seriously, though, what I appreciated most about Elvis was that he didn't talk down to me or treat me as lesser than, but like an equal or peer instead. And oddly enough, I didn't feel intimidated by the biggest star in the world. Just two people chatting about the things they knew best. Home to Elvis was show business and old-fashioned churchgoing. Naked blondes were old hat, but he never gave them up either.

Our conversation was interrupted when Colonel Parker called. Elvis picked up the phone and Parker must have asked him what he was up to that day.

"I'm talking to this really funny kid over here," Elvis laughed. "And get this . . . he's a preacher's kid!" That was a form of shorthand between the two.

As I got to know them much better later, Colonel Parker and Elvis Presley were endlessly fascinated by television evangelists and stopped whatever they were doing to watch them when channel surfing. They each watched for very different reasons. Elvis was a deeply spiritual man and was reverential toward men of faith. He listened for the message to see if it resonated with his soul. For the Colonel, he was looking for the con. What was the evangelist's angle? How did he rope them in at the altar? What was the take on the collection? I don't think the Colonel had a spiritual bone in his body, but that's not to say he wasn't a moral or decent man. He was both. He just had a different way of looking at things. He was a born showman in every sense of the word. Like a watchmaker, the Colonel wanted to take apart every production he ever saw to see how it worked.

When Elvis finished explaining who I was, the Colonel was intrigued as well.

"Send that kid over here," he said to Elvis.

Colonel Parker lived a few blocks away, and Elvis told me that his manager wanted to see me and gave me his address and directions on a piece of paper. I didn't think anything of it. After all, I was just a kid. After he gave me the paper, he bid me farewell.

"Hey, stay in touch, kid," he said, not knowing how much I would be in later years.

It didn't take but a minute or so to find Colonel Parker's house. It was nice but not over-the-top. As I would come to discover, the home was owned by the William Morris Agency, and they allowed the Colonel to live there rent-free—an arrangement he made with them to keep his costs down.

The Colonel kept a low profile when it came to his life and spending habits. Given where he came from and how hard he scrambled to survive in his early adulthood, this was a palace, and he certainly didn't need any more space. I didn't know then how hard he had lived when he was younger.

I knocked on the door, thinking it was going to be someone in the military. Out stepped a pear-shaped man, wearing a terry-cloth robe, with a cigar dangling out of the side of his mouth. It was Colonel Parker. He said hello, spotted the bike and wagon hauling all my air filters, and asked if I would change his out. I said I'd be happy to.

"Well, come on in," he said, then took me to his heating and air unit. I looked at his vent, determined the size of the filter and installed it for him. When I finished, he asked me the cost.

"Twenty-five dollars," I said, pulling out my pad and writing out the invoice as he fished out a bill in his pants pockets. He finally found one: it was a fifty-dollar bill. He handed it over and told me to keep the change. It was the best tip I ever received.

He then asked me to come into his drawing room so he and his wife, Marie, could talk to me.

"So, what's this I hear about you and revivals?" he asked.

He practically asked me the same questions as Elvis, and I went through the whole discussion. We talked about setting up the big top—something he did probably hundreds if not thousands of times with the circus. Mostly, he wanted to know about the legitimacy of the revivals.

"What's the real deal with those people that want to get healed?" he asked. "The ones in the wheelchairs . . . do you push them up the ramps?"

"Well, sometimes they walk up to the chairs and sit down in them, and then I push them up the ramp, right to the stage, right to the preacher," I said. "Then he lays hands on them. They'd either shout or start speaking in tongues and then walk down the ramp all by themselves." At this point, the Colonel convulsed with laughter. He suspected it was a con; I had just confirmed it for him, and he loved getting the inside scoop.

He compared the altar call (or a call to action) to a carnival "midway pitch," which he confessed he did many times to get people into the tent to see Madam Zinga and get their fortunes told. Later, when I started promoting concerts, he told me that when he put together copy for Elvis's radio spots, it had to say, "Hurry, hurry, hurry . . . don't you dare miss it!" It was another trick he learned from his carny days. Then he imparted some of his wisdom to me.

"People do things cuz you tell them to do it," he said. "You have to pull them in and tell them three times."

We spoke for three hours straight, and my best guess is the Colonel liked how I represented myself. He could tell I was a hard worker who had taken on a lot of responsibility at a very young age, qualities he had as well. His admiration then morphed into concern.

"If you live near Fresno and travel on the road with your dad, and spend time in Palm Springs, where do you go to school?" he asked.

"I'm really not in school," I confessed. "I haven't been for a couple of months now." Marie finally piped up, and she wasn't too happy with that reply.

"Well, your daddy can't do that," she said loudly and firmly. "You gotta go to school, boy!"

Throughout the summers, I'd see the Parkers, who would invite me over for barbeques and stay-overs. Elvis would even attend some of these barbeques with a few of his guys. Over time, I became a member of the Parker household and didn't even need to knock on the door. I'd just show up and announce myself. This went on for years. One day the Colonel asked me to come visit him the next day for a barbeque.

I did as he asked and swung by the house. He greeted me at the door, but this time he was wearing an apron. He was cooking in the backyard and asked me to join him and Marie there. He was an excellent cook from his merchant marine days and was making hobo stew, which was his specialty.

It didn't take long before he got down to what he really wanted to talk about. And it knocked me for a loop.

"Greg, Marie and I have discussed this at length," he said. "We think you should come here and stay with us in Palm Springs and go to school."

"And do what?" I asked.

"You don't have to do anything but go to school," the Colonel said. They not only had the means but the time and the desire to make sure I was properly cared for and received a proper education.

It was a magnanimous gesture, but it took some convincing to get my dad on board. These were two strangers, but the times were different back then. I was considered a man in my father's eyes, but in reality, I was still a lad. My dad checked around, found out who Colonel Parker was, and finally relented.

And that was how life started with my second family. Plenty of people had taken the Colonel in when he was younger and treated him like family. It was only natural for him to do the same when he had the opportunity. I had no idea, but I was about to learn the ropes of show business and promotion from the man who was the best in the world at that time. For now, though, the Parkers offered me a steady homelife, a solid education, and loving care. Later, when I got married to Sherry and started a family of my own (Gregory, Tom, and Suzanne Marie), the Parkers treated them as their daughter-in-law and grandkids.

We were family to the very end.

10

Lucky Streak

Elvis's lucky streak from 1960 extended well into 1961. He dovetailed the triumph of the concert for the USS *Arizona* into the filming of *Blue Hawaii*, the biggest box-office success of his film career, raking in more than $14 million. The Paramount film, which co-starred Joan Blackman and Angela Lansbury, also spawned a soundtrack that became the country's number one album, stayed on *Billboard*'s album charts for seventy-nine weeks, and sold five million copies.

Directed by Norman Taurog, the film was a return to the formulaic, lighthearted musical comedies the public had come to know and expect from Elvis and included seventeen songs. No doubt that was at the prompting of producer Hal Wallis.

Wallis was, bar none, the top producer in the movie industry, but he wasn't the easiest man to get along with despite enjoying a strong friendship with Colonel Parker over the years. The Colonel recalled the following anecdote to me:

"One day Hal and I were talking together on the *Blue Hawaii* set," the Colonel said. "I said to him, 'Hal, why don't people like you? I don't have any problem getting along with you, but everyone else says you give them problems, and they don't like it.' He thought about it for a moment and replied, 'Colonel, I don't know what their problems are.'" The Colonel surmised that the only reason Wallis liked him was because the famed producer needed to have at least one friend in his corner. Wallis was a lucky man because Tom Parker was a good friend to have.

Speaking of problems, Colonel Parker began viewing Elvis's ever-growing entourage as a nuisance. They accompanied him everywhere and many lived with him. They were on his movie sets, washed his cars, acted as his valets, and started to screen his phone calls. Many of the Colonel's messages to Elvis were not getting through, much to his annoyance. Some of the guys like Joe Esposito, Red West, Sonny West, Charlie Hodge, Jerry Schilling, and a few of the others became friends of mine over the years, but it was a revolving-door membership with some strange and flaky dudes insinuating themselves into Elvis's life. Hanging with the King was the highlight of their lives, and that was as good as it was going to get for some of them. Also understand that these boys were in their early twenties, living in Tinseltown in an era after the invention of the pill and before AIDS, and just letting off some steam. However, the Colonel didn't see it that way. He was trying to run an enterprise, and the things they did were public and were a reflection on Elvis. Colonel Parker was very old-fashioned when it concerned discretion. Whatever one did behind closed doors was none of his business. But if you were with Elvis and did something stupid that besmirched his name, it wasn't a pretty picture.

Elvis and the boys were staying at the Beverly Wilshire Hotel when they first came to Los Angeles. Apparently, it was a round-the-clock rodeo, which included impromptu karate demonstrations, music blaring at all hours of the night, numerous pratfalls, food fights, football games in the hallway, water and shaving cream fights, and a constant parade of friends, starlets, and dates in and out of their suites. The wealthy patrons of the hotel who lived there year-round weren't exactly in tune with their sophomoric brand of humor. They started turning the screws on management to crack down on these wild-eyed Southern boys. They eventually got an eviction notice, and the Colonel had to scramble and find them a place to rent. "The Beverly Hillbillies" were now residents of Bel Air.

One message a member of his entourage forgot to pass along to

Elvis was a dinner party invitation from Marilyn Monroe. Since Elvis was never told about it, he missed out meeting the greatest sex symbol of the twentieth century.

"I know people forget," the Colonel wrote to Elvis. "But I also notice they don't forget to eat on time."

After that missed opportunity with Miss Monroe, every memo concerning Elvis attending a social function ended with two lines at the bottom: "Yes, I will attend" or "No, I will not attend."

Sometimes the memos got heated, especially where it concerned Elvis's entourage. In a piece of correspondence from Colonel Parker to Elvis in the early 1960s, he wrote that he found it amazing that out of the five people in his employ, none of them were doing much to alleviate his stress or take on any responsibilities. The Colonel noted that while Elvis is working on a film, he employs someone to wake him up, get him to the studio, and inform him of his work schedule. He found it incredulous that Elvis was paying these people simply to hang out with him and nothing more. He ended the letter with a not-so-paternal pat on the back: "I am not angry at your friends. I like them all, but I am too old to start raising another family."

I'm sure part of Colonel Parker's frustration stemmed from the fact that he worked twenty-four hours a day, seven days a week on behalf of Elvis. He rarely, if ever, took vacations. He enjoyed working so much that it was certainly more pleasurable to him than sitting on a beach sipping on a mai tai. The Colonel simply wasn't built that way. He was a thoroughbred when it came to work and could go on and on forever.

But every man has his limits. When a bunch of boys are so out of control that a dinner invitation from a highly important and influential person is lost in the shuffle, that's a problem. A big one.

The Colonel was negotiating new movie contracts so fast it seemed everyone in Hollywood had a script that was reported to be Elvis's next project. Some of the high-concept titles pushed the boundaries of good taste: *Fastest Guitar Alive*, *Never Say Yes*, *Gumbo Ya*, *You're Killing Me*, *The Kiss That Set the World on Fire* (opposite Brigitte Bardot), and *That Jack Valentine* with Elvis playing a James Bond type.

Follow That Dream was next up under a contract the Colonel had negotiated with United Artists. The film was originally titled *Pioneer Go Home*, and probably would have done better under that name. While filming on location in Crystal River, Florida, on the Gulf of Mexico in July 1961, the Colonel visited the set and noticed that Elvis's twenty-one-foot trailer was the same size as the supporting actors' trailers. That just wouldn't do. He ordered a twenty-seven-foot model and had it billed to the production company. The Colonel knew there would be problems with the company when the unauthorized trailer arrived, so he needed a diversion. The assistant producer had told one of Elvis's staff they were going to break for lunch. "Please advise the Colonel," he asked.

When the Colonel was told, he exploded. "That does it. No one talks to the Colonel around here anymore. Just forget the Colonel. From now on you're in complete charge of this operation," he roared at the startled staffer. "I'm out of here!"

The assistant producer told his boss that the Colonel was mad. They were frantic, thinking he might take Elvis and walk off the set. When the new trailer arrived, no one would dare bring it up. Some of the Colonel's contrived temper tantrums were spectacular to watch, most usually motivated by money.

The Colonel did have a trigger temper, which he referred to as his "volcano." When he went into one of his rages, it wasn't a pretty sight. To his credit, most of the time there was good reason for the volcano to erupt. He would use a temper tantrum as a small child does, which was to get his own way in a situation. They were usually very loud and almost always very effective.

One of the key sets for the movie was a rustic house the studio had constructed. It was also completely functional. Once the filming was completed the production company began to dismantle the building, but the Colonel stepped in; no doubt his Great Depression instincts kicked in.

"Why waste a perfectly good home?" he asked. "I'm sure we can find a suitable place for it." The entire house was donated to the Florida

Boys Ranch and was moved to their acreage near Yankeetown where it was tabbed "The Elvis Presley Canteen." The Colonel also donated two miniature ponies and a small covered wagon that were used in parades all over the state and helped raise funds for the place. The Colonel supported many charities over the years, but he had an especially soft spot for those involving children and animals.

The Colonel remained on the United Artist set through the end of the year for *Kid Galahad*. The fight film received favorable reviews, and Elvis developed a pretty good left hook. A young tough guy named Charles Bronson received fifth billing. Elvis knocked out several opponents and six songs.

In March of 1962, it was back to Paramount to make *Girls! Girls! Girls!* whose title left no doubt what terrain the film would cover.

The Colonel's offices at MGM were reopened in August for *It Happened at the World's Fair*. The Seattle Chamber of Commerce should have paid production costs on this 1963 movie, which generated substantial positive exposure for the city.

Over the years, the studios had assigned numerous publicists to work on Elvis's films, but they never lasted. One lasted only a day. Another was left on an island in Hawaii after getting into trouble with the Colonel. Most managers pushed the studio publicity staffs to do more and more. The Colonel believed less was more.

The head of publicity at Metro-Goldwyn-Mayer was the highly respected Howard Strickling, who had handled the press for such superstars as Greta Garbo, Spencer Tracy, Katharine Hepburn, Elizabeth Taylor, and Jean Harlow. He and the Colonel had great mutual respect. However, when Elvis returned to MGM, Strickling was faced with the responsibility of assigning another publicist to work with the Colonel and his staff. He knew it was a difficult assignment and one few of his people relished.

Stan Brossette was in his early twenties when he joined the MGM staff as an office boy in the publicity department. He had recently been promoted to the position of apprentice publicist. After a few years of on-the-job training, his next step was as a junior publicist and, if he was lucky, some ten years later he would possibly become a senior member of the staff. He was called into Strickling's office one day and told he was the next in line to work with Elvis and the Colonel.

"Howard asked me if I was up to it," recalled Brossette, who eventually became one of Hollywood's top freelance publicists. "What else could I say but, 'OK, whatever.' All I knew was the Colonel's reputation. I had never even met the man."

The Colonel was the only manager in Hollywood who had his own studio offices. When Brossette walked in there for the first time, he was scared to death.

"Studio people used to walk past them and whisper, 'That's Colonel Parker's office.' No one knew what went on inside. My heart was pounding. I really don't remember too much about that first meeting. Little did I know at the time how much fun they could all be and how nice they were."

Strickling had made it very clear to Brossette that his number one duty was to keep the Colonel happy because of his penchant for rolling over the studio flaks.

"If the Colonel wants to take you out of town for a month—two months—just do it. You don't even have to call in. Just go," Strickling told him.

Brossette remembered his early days with the Colonel as nothing but good times.

He recalled: "Colonel Parker kind of took me under his wing. Not only did I not know how to do anything right, but I also didn't know how to do anything! It was obvious to me that family was important to him, and I soon became a part of that family.

"Early on I learned so many important things from the Colonel, and one of the biggest was 'boundaries.' There were many boundaries that no one crossed over. So, many people to this day believe the Colonel woke Elvis up in the morning, helped get him dressed, picked his music, and did everything else for him. I learned very early that the Colonel never crossed these boundaries. The Colonel would tell Tom

Diskin, who would tell Joe Esposito, who would tell Elvis. Those were the boundaries."

Hollywood was hit by a major strike during Brossette's first years with Elvis and the Colonel. People who had worked at the studios for thirty years were suddenly out of work, including the studio's entire publicity department.

"About two weeks into the strike I received an envelope from the William Morris Agency," Brossette remembered. "I had no idea why they would be sending anything to me. I opened it and found a check in my name for $100. At the time, that was about a week's pay, and I couldn't understand why they would be sending it to me. I called their accounting department and was told I was on their payroll. For the entire length of the strike, I was paid by William Morris for doing nothing, thanks to the Colonel. Colonel Parker would rather promote a free hamburger from a greasy spoon than have a steak and lobster dinner given to him."

Irv Schechter, on assignment from William Morris, remembers how the Colonel used his sense of humor to get his point across to Elvis. The studio had called and complained that Elvis had arrived late on the set three days in a row. It was costing them money for every minute he was late. The Colonel immediately called Joe Esposito and asked him to be sure to drive Elvis past his MGM offices before taking him to the set the next morning. About the time Elvis was to arrive, the Colonel grabbed a sponge and bucket of water and began washing windows. Elvis and Joe soon drove by. Elvis spotted the Colonel and told Joe to stop.

"Admiral, what in the world are you doing washing those windows?" Elvis asked incredulously.

"Well, Elvis, if you arrive late on the set a couple of more times, we will both be back doing the jobs we had before the movies and concerts started. I thought I might as well start practicing manual labor again."

Elvis busted out laughing and got the full picture. He was on time for the rest of the shoot.

Before fame arrived, the Colonel's life had been much, much harder than Elvis's. But he knew Elvis was still just a kid at twenty-six, and losing his temper wasn't going to get either one of them anywhere. He could guide his star through any situation with unerring wisdom, but if Elvis didn't stick to the path, they were sunk. There was the criticism over Elvis's dancing; they weathered that. There was the army. Elvis enlisted as a regular Joe, completed his full enlistment, and came home without fanfare. That was three bullets dodged. Becoming famous is one thing; avoiding becoming infamous, entirely another. Once you're at the top, you're walking across a lagoon on the backs of alligators. Get off a plane exhausted and snap at a fan once, and you've gone from being America's Sweetheart to "that S.O.B." The press loves a fall as much as it loves a rise, and they're happy to send you in either direction. Chuck Berry, Jerry Lee Lewis, Bill Haley, and Carl Perkins all had huge hits, and by the end of the 1950s and early 1960s, they were all playing state fairs and honky-tonks. There were no guarantees. The Colonel was not about to go back to riding the rails with an empty belly.

With the success of *Blue Hawaii*, I think the die was cast on Elvis's movie career. If it didn't contain songs, sizzle, and sexy women, the public really wasn't interested. Many people are under the impression this was a dictate of Colonel Parker's, but I was around plenty of times when the Colonel told him, "Elvis, you don't always have to sing."

It's no secret that Elvis aspired to have a serious acting career. But other actors, such as James Dean, Paul Newman, Montgomery Clift, Rod Steiger, and Steve McQueen, got most of the plum dramatic roles that appealed to Elvis. *Cat on a Hot Tin Roof*, *Thunder Road*, *Rio Bravo*, *The Defiant Ones*, and *Baby, the Rain Must Fall* come to mind. One enterprising producer, Jerry Wald, who made a tidy sum on Elvis for *Wild in the Country*, told the Colonel that he had a script for his client that practically assured him the Oscar. But there was a catch; Elvis had to lower his fee because the script was so expensive, Wald said. The Colonel seemed to do his best thinking when asked for a discount from someone who wanted to do business with Elvis.

"Tell you what, Jerry," the Colonel proposed. "If you pay us the money we want and Elvis wins the Oscar, we'll refund you your money."

Wald put his head down and walked out of the room. The Colonel never heard from him again.

The Wald anecdote is perhaps one of the reasons the Colonel formed the Official Snowmen's League of America, Ltd. It was an unofficial club with no meetings or bylaws. It was a send-up of the Showmen's League of America, a jab at the movie industry, because once the Colonel and Elvis got to Hollywood, they had to constantly be on guard for "snow jobs"—slick lies told to them by movie executives and producers looking to curry favor or gain an advantage. Some of the biggest names in show business, politics, and commerce were members, and clamored to get in, including presidents,[16] captains of industry and some very powerful people.

I remember billionaire Kirk Kerkorian wanting to get a membership when Elvis started playing live again in Las Vegas, but he knew the rules were that he couldn't ask to join. He had to wait for an invitation from Colonel Parker. So, he tried a different tactic: he came to the Colonel's office at the MGM Studios lot—the lot he owned—to circumvent the Colonel. Instead, he asked Ed Bonja and me to ask the Colonel for a card. He did this three times. The Colonel finally had one made after his third attempt and gave him the card.

Businessmen and philanthropists Walter Annenberg and Barron Hilton waged a mock war in a letter-writing campaign to Colonel Parker for a position as "vice potentate." I have two binders of these craftily worded letters, in which these two billionaires jockeyed for position in a make-believe club.

Entertainer Pat Boone had not one but two cards—a regular and a deluxe edition. The Colonel really liked him, and so did Elvis. Years later, producer Chris Christian, my sons, and I were taping Pat for a TV segment in his Beverly Hills office when we started talking about Elvis

---

[16] Presidents Lyndon B. Johnson, Ronald Reagan, and Bill Clinton were all card-carrying members of the Snowmen's League of America, Ltd.

and the Colonel. Pat happened to mention that he was a proud member of the Snowmen's League and had a card.

"Show me!" I almost demanded, but with a laugh. He looked around his office, located the card, and held it up in the air.

"Found it!" he said with a huge smile.

"It should have been in your wallet," I replied. We all had a big laugh. Then Pat told us a great story of how he earned his special deluxe card.

"In 1963, I released an album called *Pat Boone Sings Guess Who?*, which was a tribute album to Elvis on Dot Records," Boone recalled in September 2022. "I was originally going to use Elvis's name in the title, but Colonel Parker put a stop to that. I said, 'Colonel, this is a tribute to Elvis . . . what else can we call it?' He said, 'Pat, we're friends, but bidness is bidness. You put Elvis's name on that record and it's going to sell more copies, so you have to pay a royalty for that.'"

Pat said once Dot Records founder Randy Wood heard about the request, he was furious and wanted to scrap the album. Pat told him he was almost finished with the album, which contained some of his best work and was being backed by great jazz musicians. Pat said he'd rather just pay the royalty for the use of Elvis's name and settle the issue before it got out of hand, but Wood wasn't having it.

"I'm not paying Tom Parker a royalty when you're doing a tribute album to Elvis, which is really just promoting him," Wood said. "No way."

"Well, let's just call it something else," Pat suggested.

"What else could we call it?" Wood asked.

Pat came up with the name *Pat Boone Sings Guess Who?* He also paid an artist from Holland to paint the cover, which was Pat in a gold lamé suit, holding an acoustic guitar, and striking an Elvis-like pose, with song titles from some of Elvis's biggest hits on each side.

"We didn't use Elvis's name at all, but it couldn't have been about anybody else," Pat said. "Elvis saw it, heard it, and called me to tell me that he thought it was great, thanked me, and said that he had no issues with the album."

Shortly after its release, Pat received a letter in the mail from Colonel Parker, congratulating him on getting around him. Also tucked in the envelope was a tin super-deluxe Snowmen's card.

"It's one of my proudest possessions," Pat said with a big smile. Colonel Parker served as the club's "First High Potentate Snower"—the head honcho. In order to join, the person being inducted had to prove themselves worthy, and then recite a special poem in the presence of other snowmen. If they were successful, they received their Snowmen's League card, which was signed by Colonel Parker and read: "This will certify that (name) is a Genuine Snower in good standing. This card is only valid if the Snower snows to do good." The card came with a booklet containing a special poem written by the Colonel:

Welcome To Our New Snow Members
Now you are like one of us
In fair and snowy weather.
You will know from day to day
How SNOWMEN live together.
You know how CLOSE we are,
Like snowflakes on the window.
But never let your snow befall
On some unworthy fellow.
We cling like peaches on the vine
And drink our snow like it was wine.
We always do the things we do,
And now YOU are included too
Potentate

Although there was no admission to join, it cost members $10,000 to leave the Snowmen's League of America, Ltd. It was a gag, an inside joke. But if you didn't have a card, it meant you weren't that close to Colonel Parker or Elvis.

By January 1963, Elvis was back at Paramount Studios for *Fun in Acapulco*. Elvis's karate workouts proved as helpful in this film, as they did in *Kid Galahad*, since he was cast as a footloose trapeze artist. Elvis was as at home with a Latin beat as he was with rock 'n' roll, which bore out on the album soundtrack.

Although he was making an average of three movies a year and selling millions of records, Elvis was experiencing financial problems. Elvis lived above his means, and he and the Colonel were in the highest possible income tax bracket at the time, paying Uncle Sam some 90 percent of their gross earnings. This maximum tax would begin falling in 1964 thanks to legislation signed by President John F. Kennedy the year before.

One time, a friend of the Colonel's was sitting in his living room in Palm Springs, bitterly complaining about the high taxes he had to pay that year.

"You know, John, I don't mind paying my taxes because I can remember the good ol' days when I did not have to pay income tax because I had no income," the Colonel said, bringing a sense of levity to the room. "I can remember the days when a $200 IRS refund check was like a major inheritance."

I never forgot that remark, not because I never had any income, but because I could also remember the days when a $200 IRS refund check was like a major inheritance.

Money, or lack thereof, was a running theme in Elvis Presley's life. He was always in need of it because he had no respect for it. He was always giving extravagant gifts and loans to everyone. He couldn't be faulted for his kindness and thoughtfulness, but there was no limit to his gift giving. He gave away cars, homes, motorhomes, and motorcycles to friends and complete strangers—and in bulk! Graceland also took a lot of money to run, with its staff, upkeep, maintenance, and property and payroll taxes. And here's the thing: when you've been on top of the world for so long and are still relatively young, you never think about the other shoe dropping or that one day your earning capacity might diminish. Many of Elvis's projects were dictated by how much money he could make, not necessarily for artistic reasons. A July 7, 1963, letter from Vernon Presley underscored their money woes, outlining the fact that even though he had invested in tax-free bonds on behalf of Elvis, they were in debt, overdrawn, and not able to meet payroll. He asked for a loan of $150,000 to see them through.

And people wondered why Colonel Parker made movie deal after movie deal for Elvis. Part of the problem was that Elvis would not perform in outdoor stadiums (mostly because of the inferior sound) and there were limited large indoor venues at the time. Concert ticket prices were still very low, so movies were the only conceivable way Elvis could make the kind of money he needed to maintain the lifestyle to which he had become accustomed.

MGM once again welcomed the Colonel and company in July for the classic *Viva Las Vegas* with Ann-Margret in a featured role both on and off camera.

From her breakout role in the film version of *Bye Bye Birdie* (loosely based on Elvis's induction into the army), the sultry Swede was the biggest female star in Hollywood. Dubbed "the female Elvis" by the media because of her high energy, vivacious personality, and mesmerizing effect on members of the opposite sex, Ann-Margret was considered the perfect woman by every man with eyes in his head. Certainly, George Sidney thought so.

Elvis couldn't help but notice the *Viva Las Vegas* director spent more time on her production numbers during rehearsals than his. He suspected that Sidney was infatuated with his co-star. When Elvis saw in the dailies that she was getting plenty of flattering close-ups while he was relegated to window dressing, he suspected something was up. Also, a lot of effort was expended on her song-and-dance numbers per Sidney's direction. Elvis's scenes were simpler, with hardly any production. There was also a rumor going around that Sidney once had a cameraman shoot a four-minute close-up of her prized derrière.

Elvis didn't mind that Ann was getting some face time on camera, but he did object to the underhanded diminution of his role. So, he put in a call to Colonel Parker to do some serious damage control.

The Colonel came down like a ton of bricks on producer Jack Cummings, the nephew of legendary Louis B. Mayer, the studio's former ironfisted boss.

"Ann-Margret may be a big star right now," the Colonel bellowed at Cummings, "but Elvis pays the freight!"

When the smoke cleared, the close-ups were divided equally between the two stars, and Sidney was ordered to delete a duet on "You're the Boss" in which Ann really vamped it up for the cameras.

The movie proved to be as colorful and exciting as the city itself with ten rocking musical numbers and more energy generated in the accompanying dance routines than that produced by the nearby Hoover Dam. It is ironic that both stars would end up performing on the same stage at the Las Vegas Hilton in the early 1970s when the movie offers dried up. Despite its mid-July start, the final product wasn't released until the following June, after the release of *Kissin' Cousins*, which started filming in October 1963 and was completed in November.

Elvis and Ann-Margret romance headlines were everywhere. While her career was going well, she was nowhere near the star he was.[17] Elvis decided he wanted the Colonel to manage Ann, as well as himself, to boost her career.

"I'll even pay you extra," Elvis pleaded. The crafty Colonel immediately went into his "negotiating" mode. He calmly took the cigar out of his mouth, looked at it, stuck it back in, and lit it. It bought him time to formulate a response.

"No problem. I'll be happy to do it," he said. "But the only way it can happen is for me to spend half of my time managing her and the other half with you." Elvis's eyes widened, and he thought for a moment. That arrangement wasn't going to work for him.

"You know, Colonel, it wouldn't be fair to expect you to work as hard as you would have to do if you managed her too," Elvis said. "Let's just forget it."

---

17 For *Viva Las Vegas*, Elvis was paid $500,000 and 50 percent of the profits after the studio recouped its initial investment. Ann-Margret received $150,000.

Early 1964 found Colonel Parker and his nomadic followers back on the Paramount lot for *Roustabout,* a film that was very close to the Colonel's heart because it was about the carnival. It carried an all-star lineup including Barbara Stanwyck, Joan Freeman, and Leif Erickson, and featured eleven new songs (the soundtrack went to number 1 on the *Billboard* Top 200 album charts). It was also the first movie set on which Elvis was injured.

A fight scene proved a little too realistic. Elvis knocked down a stuntman with a karate slash, but as he went down, the stuntman's foot caught Elvis in the head. He was rushed to the hospital, treated, and released.

While on the Paramount set one day, the Colonel read in the paper that President Roosevelt's private yacht, the USS *Potomac,* was about to be destroyed. This bothered him greatly, and he suggested that Elvis purchase the vessel for $55,000 and added another $20,000 of his own money. A press conference was arranged for February 3, 1964, where Elvis would turn the ship over to Danny Thomas, who would auction it off and raise funds for the St. Jude Children's Research Hospital in Memphis. St. Jude had long been a favorite charity of both Elvis and Colonel Parker.

Wanting to see his latest project, the Colonel and his staff visited the Long Beach docks at 7:00 A.M. the day before the ceremony and found the craft to be in deplorable condition. He immediately contacted the Long Beach Port Authority to see how much it would cost to clean and repaint it. He was quoted a price of $18,000 and was told it would take at least three days. The media had already been alerted and the press conference was scheduled for the next day.

"There's no way we can repaint the entire ship in that little time," they said. The Colonel surveyed the situation and calmly replied, "Then just paint the side facing the dock," which they did, for $8,000. The unpainted part of the ship was roped off and could not be seen by the public or the press, and no one was the wiser.

The presentation of the *Potomac* to St. Jude received worldwide publicity and earned Elvis even more goodwill with the public, thanks to Colonel Parker.

Of course, goodwill can be tendered when things are going well. And they were going extraordinarily well. *Girl Happy*, which featured a dozen new tunes, brought the Colonel back to MGM that June. While it did decent business in America, it caught fire in major foreign markets, including Hong Kong, and did 20 percent better than *Viva Las Vegas*. No one could figure out the exact reason, but no one was complaining either.

Colonel Parker and Abe Lastfogel were negotiating another contract with a major agency when the term "force majeure" came up. The Colonel questioned what it meant. Of course, he knew that an actor's strike was a distinct possibility, and the term meant that, in the event of a strike, the actors would not be paid. Translation: Elvis would not be paid. The lead attorney for the studio assured the Colonel that it was a nebulous term.

"Colonel, it doesn't really mean anything," he said.

"Since it doesn't mean anything, suppose you just remove it from the contract?" The attorney hesitated, and then agreed to the Colonel's request rather than lose face.

Again, the Colonel's offices remained open at the home of the roaring lion while work started on *Tickle Me* in October. It was the only Elvis film to date that had no new songs written for it, just nine previously written numbers. As a promotional gimmick for this film, the Colonel had packages consisting of nothing more than feathers made up. Pretty clever if you think about it.

MGM also produced *Harum Scarum* in early 1965. It could possibly go down as Elvis's worst film ever. The sets and costumes were leftovers from other movies, and it even went through four title changes. When I asked the Colonel about the film years after it was made, he came up with a classic response.

"I don't read the scripts, and if those studios aren't smart enough to come up with a good story, I can't help 'em," he said. "For the kind of money they are paying us, we can leave the problem of making pictures to them."

When the movie was released in the fall of '65, the Colonel suggested the studio take out ads saying, "Here's a real turkey for your Thanksgiving!"

Even though Elvis's films weren't considered high art or Oscar contenders, they always made money. That's why the Colonel could secure Elvis incredible deals—six- and seven-figure salaries, a piece of the profits, and all expenses paid. One time a producer asked the Colonel how much it would cost for Elvis to film a cameo appearance in one of his movies. The Colonel gave his standard reply: $100,000. The producer was in shock.

"Why, even Jack Lemmon doesn't even get $100,000!" the producer said incredulously.

"Maybe Mr. Lemmon needs a new manager," came the reply.

The Colonel was just as famous as Elvis in Hollywood circles and amid the New York elite. Truman Capote, author of *In Cold Blood*, was a friend of Colonel Parker's, who referred to him as "Mr. Truman." One day, the Colonel asked him if he had heard Elvis's latest release. Capote confessed he had never heard Elvis sing any song (what planet did this guy live on?!), let alone his latest. The Colonel called his office and had a dozen Elvis albums delivered right away. A few days later, he saw Capote and asked how he liked Elvis's music. He hesitated for a while, then answered.

"You know, Colonel, I think something is wrong with my record player," Capote offered.

The elfin literary giant claimed in an interview two years before he died that the two had dinner once.

"Elvis Presley gave me the only dinner party I've ever heard of his giving in Las Vegas," Capote said. "He lived very near me (in Palm Springs), and he was going to open at this big hotel in Las Vegas . . . and he invited me to come up to see it, 'cause I had never seen him. . . . He was nice, I sort of liked him."

It's plausible, given that Capote frequented Palm Springs and was a friend of the Colonel's. It's also true that Capote, who dropped more names than a Beverly Hills real estate agent, routinely claimed to be friends with anyone who was anyone.

By that time, not as many people were spinning Elvis's records. His last number one record was 1962's "Good Luck Charm" and it seemed as if the teen market was pining for something else. One of the big reasons the Colonel pointed Elvis toward movies instead of concerts was an upcoming invasion from abroad.

A few years before, four young lads in England had formed a band. They started with the name the Quarrymen, and eventually changed it to the Beatles.

When Elvis got out of the army, they were still getting their musical footing and paying their dues in Hamburg, Germany. Soon they would be warming up in their native England and, after that, ready to take on the colonies.

"The Beatles?" Elvis asked. "Never heard of them. Sounds like an act that belongs in a flea circus."

But they would also change everything else in entertainment, turning everything upside down, in about a year's time. And, when they finally reached our shores and were introduced to American audiences on *The Ed Sullivan Show* and shattered all prior TV ratings—including his own—Elvis wouldn't be so flippant.

11

Elvis in the Age of Aquarius

Their relationship started with a simple welcoming telegraph. On their first trip to New York City to appear on *The Ed Sullivan Show*, in February 1964, the Beatles were thrilled to receive the following telegram, which the host read on the show to approximately seventy-three million people (38 percent of the entire population):

> *Congratulations on your appearance on The Ed Sullivan Show and your visit to America. We hope your engagement will be successful and your visit pleasant.*
>
> Elvis and the Colonel

A short time later the Fab Four returned to America for a major North American concert tour, and another telegram from the Colonel greeted them (the Colonel was one of Western Union's best customers) before the start of the tour. It read:

> To Brian Epstein and The Beatles,
> *If there is anything I can be of service with as a friend do not hesitate to call. If you have time, give me a call when you come to town.*
>
> Elvis and the Colonel

Many now might think that Colonel Parker was riding on the Beatles' coattails to get some cheap publicity for Elvis, but that was not the case at all. The Colonel was extending good old-fashioned American hospitality to the Beatles, and their manager, Brian Epstein, who came to look on the Colonel as a friend and mentor. There were many times that Epstein called the house in Palm Springs seeking advice from the Colonel. The Beatles were blazing a path at the speed of light, and the only person that had ever been in Epstein's shoes was Colonel Parker. The two men liked each other immensely, but they could not have been more different.

Epstein grew up the son of upper-middle-class Jewish retailers in Liverpool and flailed between acting and working in the family business. After he became the Beatles' manager, he signed away 90 percent of their merchandising rights—a mistake the Colonel never would have made. He also got them thrown out of the Philippines after inadvertently snubbing that country's first lady. Epstein lost thousands of pounds playing baccarat or chemin de fer at London gambling clubs. He also enjoyed uppers and weed.

The Beatles had many musical inspirations, but always went out of their way to credit Elvis as the artist who inspired them to pick up their instruments and begin their rock 'n' roll odyssey.

"Before Elvis, there was nothing," John Lennon once said. How Elvis felt about the Beatles . . . well, that was another story. He thought Lennon and McCartney were excellent songwriters, and he especially liked "Hey Jude," "Get Back," "Lady Madonna," and "Yesterday" (he also enjoyed performing "Something" by George Harrison). According to my friend Sonny West, Elvis's bodyguard, he owned "well-worn copies" of their albums *Rubber Soul* (1965) and *Revolver* (1966).

As the Beatles prepared for their US invasion, they hinted in the press that Elvis Presley and Paul Newman were the only people they really wanted to meet. Brian Epstein contacted the Colonel in hopes of gathering everyone together, but the Beatles' recording and touring schedule and Elvis's movie obligations made it impossible.

Paramount Studios executives wanted to have the Fab Four

appear in Elvis's movie, *Paradise, Hawaiian Style*, which started principal photography on July 27, 1965. But that was pie in the sky and would have been a contractual nightmare for Colonel Parker and Brian Epstein to pull off. While on location in Honolulu at the Ilikai Hotel, Elvis received a telegram from Alan Livingston, president of Capitol Records, which was the Beatles' label. He was invited to the August 24 reception for the group in Los Angeles at the Capitol Records Tower on Hollywood and Vine. Elvis balked on the grounds that the wrong party was being asked to make the effort.

"Hell, if they want to meet me, they're going to have to come and see me," he said.

Was he touchy about the fact that the Beatles were beginning to eclipse his popularity? I'd say that was probably a good guess. In the eighteen months since they invaded the United States, the Beatles registered an amazing sixteen Top 10 hits, nine of which zoomed straight to the top of the singles charts. Album sales weren't too shabby either: they dinged the Top Ten nine times, six of them in the number one slot.

They also managed to conquer Hollywood their first time out of the gate with the inimitable *A Hard Day's Night*. The viewing public loved it, and so did Elvis, who watched it at the Memphian Theater many times, enjoying the zany British humor. *Help!*, their second offering by United Artists, was a musical comedy-adventure (shot in color this time around); it outperformed its predecessor by $1 million. The single and soundtrack album of the same name raced up the charts, eventually reaching the number one spot. Everything they touched seemed to turn to gold (or multi-platinum).

So, the negotiations continued, as delicately and intensely as if an arms pact instead of a rock 'n' roll summit were being hammered out. Finally, Colonel Parker and Brian Epstein agreed on a date for the grand event—Friday, August 27, 1965.

At around 10:00 P.M. that night, three Cadillac limousines pulled up to Elvis's Bel Air house at 525 Perugia Way. The Beatles had to work their way through hordes of screaming fans at the gates. Despite the secrecy both Parker and Epstein insisted on, the meeting was somehow leaked.

The Beatles later spoke of how nervous they were to meet Elvis; they got stoned on the drive over to his place, and their longtime driver, Alf Bicknell, got lost thanks to the haze of smoke. Elvis was also a little apprehensive but was determined to play it cool. When the doorbell rang, he remained in the den while one of his buddies went to answer the door.

Elvis's red shirt with high Napoleonic collar contrasted nicely with his Hawaiian tan. He also sported black slacks and a black windbreaker. When the boys arrived, he was sitting in the middle of the horseshoe couch with his feet up, smoking a cigar and channel surfing via remote control—the essence of cool. Also, in the room were Sonny West, Red West, Jerry Schilling, Joe Esposito, Richard Davis, Larry Geller, Patti Parry, Billy and Jo Smith, Alan and Jo Fortas, Marty and Patsy Lacker—members of the Memphis Mafia and their wives—Priscilla, and Colonel Parker.

Accompanying the Beatles were Brian Epstein, road managers Mal Evans and Neil Aspinall, driver Alf Bicknell, press chief Tony Barrow, and British journalists Chris Hutchins and Ivor Davis, who covered the Beatles' first 1964 tour of America for London's *Daily Express*. Later, Davis wrote an award-winning memoir called *The Beatles and Me On Tour* in 2014.

Even though Hutchins and Davis tagged along, the agreement was they could not write anything about that night. More than fifty-five years later, Davis broke his silence by giving me his recollection of that musical summit:

"The story really starts in 1964 when The Beatles were playing the Hollywood Bowl and were staying in Bel Air. Colonel Parker went to their house and brought them sets of cowboy hats and garb, and said hello and got to visit with Brian Epstein," Davis recalled. "That's when they first started talking about bringing their 'boys' together. Now, The

Beatles were very keen about this, particularly John, who really wanted to meet Elvis."[18]

Davis said he shared conversations with Lennon about when he first heard Elvis on Radio Luxembourg. He said Lennon told him about lying in bed late at night in his room at his Aunt Mimi's home in Liverpool listening to rock music on his transistor radio.

"Britain did not have any rock 'n' roll stations in the late 1950s and early 1960s, and Radio Luxembourg you could get on shortwave late at night," Davis said. "John told me he'd be in bed listening to this guy named Elvis, singing a song called 'Heartbreak Hotel,' and 'Blue Suede Shoes' and other songs, and he was enchanted by his music."

"I actually saw this handwritten letter that Brian sent to Colonel Parker," Davis said. "And in that letter, Brian said, 'Let's not make this a media event. Let's make this a private meeting.' By that, Brian meant no press, no media, no cameras, no tape recorders. Just the two parties meeting casually and enjoying each other's company. Parker agreed, but when we arrived at the house, there were about a hundred girls outside, so I'm of the belief that Parker tipped off the Elvis fan club and all these girls showed up."

So why was Davis invited in the first place given Epstein's dictate that there were to be no media present at their meeting?

"My only guess is that they wanted a witness as to what went down that night," he said. "Maybe they understood that history was going to be made, and they needed someone to vouch that it actually happened."

Davis said after the cars parked, Lennon, who was stoned, was the first out of the car and "led the charge" to Presley's front door. As the

---

18 Colonel Parker met with Brian Epstein in 1964 at the Beverly Hills Hotel, where the latter stayed while in Los Angeles. They wanted to bring the two parties together, but between the Beatles' hectic tour dates and Elvis's insane shooting schedule, their timetables were simply incompatible. They vowed the following year they'd make it happen. They did and even laid out some ground rules on a sheet of paper.

Beatles approached the den, John Lennon launched into an Inspector Clouseau routine.

"Oh, zere you are, Elvis!" he said as they entered the room.

"That was pure John," Davis said. "Even though he was desperate to meet Elvis, he was inclined to be irreverent. That was just his way . . . to downplay this whole thing."

Luckily, Elvis got the bit. He thought Peter Sellers was the greatest comedic actor around, smiled and said, "It's nice to meet you boys." He shook hands with everyone, and John and Paul took seats on his right and George and Ringo to his left. The Colonel and Epstein retreated to the corner to leave their artists alone to talk.

Once everyone was settled, the oxygen suddenly left the room. Nobody had a thing to say. The obviously starstruck Beatles sat there staring at Elvis, possibly because they were stoned or were just in awe (or both). While Elvis waited for someone to get the conversation ball rolling, he again started clicking on the remote control. Later, Paul McCartney remarked it was the first time he'd ever seen a remote control television.

"No one tried to intermediate; no one said a word, and The Beatles just watched him turn channels. It was very odd," said Davis, who watched from the corner of the room. "It was quite a spectacle in and of itself because they didn't have remotes in England, and they didn't have color TV in England. Elvis had both, and it was a large-screen TV for that time."

About thirty seconds passed that way, and finally Elvis tossed the remote on the coffee table and announced, "Hell, if you guys are just gonna sit there and stare at me, I might as well go to bed. I didn't mean for this to be like the subjects calling on the King. I thought we might sit and talk and jam a little."

"For whatever reason, that word 'jam' broke the ice," Davis said. "All of a sudden the four of them came alive."

Some of Elvis's guys left the room and returned with electric guitars. Elvis began fiddling around with a bass plugged into an amplifier near the television. Looking at Ringo, Elvis said, "Sorry, there's no drum kit. We left that in Memphis." So, Ringo played with his hands against the back of the chair. Later, he got a pair of bongos.

Elvis had the jukebox turned on, and they proceeded to jam to Cilla Black's "You're My World," Charlie Rich's "Mohair Sam," Chuck Berry's "Johnny B. Goode," and the Beatles' "I Feel Fine." The last song had a tricky bass part, but Elvis had no problem with it, and Paul made the mock announcement, "And coming along quite promisingly on the bass . . . Elvis!"

Some of the songs Elvis stopped after three or four lines, saying, "Let's do something else." Ivor Davis noticed that the Beatles deferred to Elvis on the playlist.

While they jammed, Colonel Parker and Epstein got busy when Parker opened a coffee table that converted into a roulette wheel and declared, "The casino is open!"

Parker and Epstein spent the night gambling, with Joe Esposito serving as their professional pit boss. The Colonel bragged to me years later, when recounting that story, he won a nice sum of money from his British counterpart.

When Elvis and the Beatles stopped jamming, they entered a freewheeling conversation that included discussions on stardom, crazy fans, their mutual dislike of flying, and of course, music. Davis overheard John ask why Elvis no longer made rock 'n' roll records like the ones he did in the 1950s. It was like hearing a record player screech.

"In a way, it was a criticism and an insinuation that the stuff Elvis was doing as of late was crap," Davis said.

Ever the Southern gentleman, Elvis answered the question in his most diplomatic tone.

"It's my movie schedule," Elvis said evenhandedly. "It's so tight. But maybe I'll do one just for kicks."

"Then we'll buy it," John said with a smile, instantly defusing the situation.

Then Elvis sprang up from the couch and invited the group on a tour of the property. The first thing he wanted to show them was his brand-new black Rolls-Royce Phantom Five in the garage. The car was longer than the standard four-door Rolls Royce, and it had extended leg room in the back. The car cost around $50,000, which was a small fortune back then (and the equivalent in purchasing power to about $475,000 today). George Harrison, who later became a real racing and car enthusiast, especially admired the vehicle.

It was around 2:00 A.M. when the Beatles and their entourage headed for the door. John went back into Inspector Clouseau mode.

"Sanks for ze muzik," he said, pumping a fist in the air, "and long live ze King!"

Before they left, Colonel Parker stepped up and handed each Beatle a gift bag containing a box of Elvis records and souvenir table lamps shaped like covered wagons (the logo on Parker's official letterhead).

Epstein invited everyone to return the visit the very next night at the Beatles' rented home in Benedict Canyon, just a few miles away. Elvis felt one visit was plenty.

"Well, we'll see," he said, shifting uncomfortably. "I don't know if I'll be able to make it or not." He walked them out to the driveway and said, "If you ever get to Memphis, make sure you come and see us." And with that, the rock 'n' roll meeting of the century was over.

The two parties never saw each other again (Ringo did see Elvis backstage in Las Vegas in 1970), and sadly, didn't develop a closer relationship.

As the sixties wound down, Elvis came to personally disapprove of the Beatles' public image, as some of them openly used and discussed their drug use. He also bristled at some of the anti-Americanism that attended their particularly strident criticism of the war in Vietnam on their last tour, and later, when John Lennon began using his platform to protest the war. Elvis had put his own career on hold for two years to serve his country, and he didn't like it when foreigners badmouthed Uncle Sam. And, like many others, Elvis was offended when Lennon offhandedly said in 1966 that the Beatles were "more popular than Jesus."

The times were a-changin', but not so much in Elvis Presley's world. Politically and culturally, by the mid-1960s the country was going through a seismic shift. The civil rights movement was in full swing, with Martin Luther King Jr. marching through the Deep South. America's journey to the moon reached Earth's orbit with the first manned crew. The first American troops arrived in South Vietnam in March 1965, and the first antiwar protestors marched in Berkeley, California. Both efforts would escalate rapidly through the year, with the ferocious Battle of Ia Drang taking place in November 1965. That same month, Quaker Norman Morrison set himself on fire outside the Pentagon to protest the war.

Music was changing too. With Bob Dylan going electric at the Newport Folk Festival and Jefferson Airplane making their debut in August 1965 in San Francisco, psychedelic rock was introduced to the scene. It wasn't a good look for Elvis, who increasingly began to resemble a relic from the days of sock hops.

Somehow, the Age of Aquarius had finally arrived on our doorstep, and Elvis and the Colonel weren't prepared for it. Sure, Elvis was still loved by millions, but his demographic was getting older. His original fans had graduated high school, moved on to college, entered the workforce, and started their own families.

As for the Beatles, well, they were just beginning to hit their stride as Elvis was entering his career slide.

12

Reel to Real

Elvis was fortunate enough to have a second act when he came back from the army and safely landed in the movies, but many of his 1950s peers weren't so lucky. Pop music was a youth phenomenon, and many fans grew out of it or moved on with their lives or their listening habits changed. Fifties artists such as Bill Haley, Little Richard, Chuck Berry, Jerry Lee Lewis, the Everly Brothers, Frankie Avalon, Fabian, and Ricky Nelson all gave way in the 1960s to the Beatles, the Rolling Stones, the Byrds, Simon & Garfunkel, Buffalo Springfield, Jefferson Airplane, and the Doors.

Colonel Parker's philosophy was, "If it ain't broke, don't fix it." And if there was a studio willing to shell out big bucks for Elvis to star in movies, the system wasn't broke. They found a willing taker in MGM Studios. And Elvis returned to their lot in February 1966 for *Spinout*. They remained at the studio for *Double Trouble*, starting in June. Elvis played twins in this film, and carried this one by himself with no "name" co-stars. However, they paid him handsomely: $750,000 plus 40 percent of the film's profits. Only thing was, there wasn't much profit to be had. *Double Trouble* was a real turkey and wasn't released until the following April, two weeks after his next film project, *Clambake*.

Irv Schechter, a talent representative from the William Morris Agency, recalled one meeting the Colonel had with Hal Wallis and his partner, Joe Hazen. They were in heavy movie negotiations and putting strong pressure on the Colonel. At one point in the debate, Hazen used the word "conjecture." The Colonel stood up and said, "You know, I'm just a Tennessee country boy. I don't understand words like that. I've got to check with my staff." With that he turned and walked out the door, much to the shock of Wallis and Hazen. Schechter was in the outer office waiting to drive him back to his office.

"Irv, 'conjecture' is a form of a guess, right?" he asked.

"Right, Colonel. But if you knew that, why did you come out here and ask me?"

The Colonel slowly smiled.

"Those two were ganging up on me in there," he said. "I needed a few minutes to gather my thoughts so I can go back in and get the best possible deal."

It sure beat relighting a cigar.

The Colonel recalled to me another deal he negotiated. He and a studio head were haggling over a contract that the Colonel had drawn up.

"I was in pretty heavy negotiations and the fella across the table was arguing about the contract," the Colonel said. "I told him, 'You know, the first time I made a contract with a promoter I got taken. So, I went home, found the clause in the contract that did the damage and cut it out. Then the next time it happened, I did it again. And again. And again. Then, one day I put all those smart-assed clauses together and that's the one you're holding there!"

In time, he stopped getting taken and did the taking. Part of the reason for his success was that, by then, the Colonel had perfected "the look," which was a prolonged and icy stare. I can assure you it was most effective. Grown men would quake when he turned "the look" their way. Most of the time he had a purpose when he used "the look," it but occasionally it happened spontaneously. No one wanted to be on the receiving end. Several times, during filming, he would arrive on the set and just stand off to the side with "the look." He would say nothing and then turn and walk away. Regardless of what was happening, those present would try to figure out why they had been gifted with that icy stare. Usually, there was no reason, he simply wanted to shake things up. He also knew that if there were any guilty parties around, they would probably mend their ways, believing he knew what was going on.

Easy Come, Easy Go ended up at Paramount in September 1966, as Elvis continued his blistering pace of making one movie every four months. The critics were very positive about the film, perhaps because it had something of a plot and only six songs. (Colonel Parker had pushed Freddy Bienstock to come up with better tunes.) Since this was Hal Wallis's last movie with Elvis, he was no longer anxious to please him and demanded that Elvis record at Paramount Studio's cavernous soundstage, even going so far as to set up daytime sessions. That didn't suit Elvis at all, who preferred the intimacy of a recording studio and recording in the evening.

But Elvis still got his name above the title. That alone made it a moneymaker. And that was good because, once again, Elvis needed to bring in more money.

On January 2, 1967, Elvis Presley wrote two very important letters—the first to Harry Jenkins at RCA Victor Record Division in New York City and the second to Lou Goldberg in the accounting division at the William Morris Agency in Beverly Hills, California—that, in essence, made the relationship between Elvis and the Colonel a joint venture partnership as opposed to a standard artist management deal. But the Colonel never collected on the 50 percent contract with All Star Shows because Elvis wasn't touring yet. In the latter part of the 1970s he did, but even that really wasn't truly 50 percent because all the show expenses were taken off the top before the Colonel received his share.

This was more of a legal matter and kept their management contract up to date. Many writers, biographers, and a few select members of the Memphis Mafia have chosen to use this contract to point out that it was drafted by the Colonel in haste after Elvis fell and hit his head after ingesting too many drugs. The rumor was that Colonel Parker didn't have much faith that Elvis was going to live much longer and served up a contract that enriched himself at the expense of his partner. But if you follow the chronology, that simply isn't true. The contract was dated January 2, 1967; Elvis took his spill in March 1967.

People seem to think that Elvis was a hayseed and brainwashed by Colonel Parker. I'd say that's an insult to Elvis's intelligence. He had in Ed Hookstratten an unapologetically aggressive attorney—truly one of the finest in Los Angeles. He also had a cadre of agents and attorneys at his disposal at the William Morris Agency. Elvis was surrounded by top-notch people looking out for his business interests. If a contract was alarming or suspect—or just wasn't to their liking—it would not have been signed. But facts are pesky things and it's sometimes not convenient to apply logic when a narrative has been established and rarely challenged. The only financial aspect of life Elvis was unwise about were his spending and saving habits; though he was warned by Vernon, Priscilla, and others. It didn't matter what was coming in—and it was a lot—it was never enough. Elvis continually found ways to spend more than what he made. He was even creative about it. Case in point: the purchase of the Circle G Ranch.

When Elvis decided Graceland wasn't big enough to handle the eighteen horses he had accumulated (Elvis bought a horse for almost everyone who was close to him) plus the stable staff of nine, he decided it was time to purchase a ranch. While riding his Harley-Davidson, he discovered a 163-acre working cattle ranch for sale about twelve miles from Graceland in Horn Lake, Mississippi. The spread included a small white-arched bridge across a lake, a barn with horse stalls, and a herd of Santa Gertrudis cattle. But what really sealed the deal for Elvis was a concrete cross that stood out in the pasture by itself. Elvis saw it as a message from the Almighty that the land was blessed. No one had the heart (or courage) to tell him the cross was a landmark for a nearby airport.

Vernon Presley was vehemently opposed to the new expense—a whopping $437,000—and had to put up Graceland as collateral. Elvis renamed the place, formerly known as Twinkletown Farms, "The Circle G" in his mother Gladys's honor.

The Colonel probably didn't think the ranch was a good idea either, but didn't say a word. If that's what Elvis wanted to do with his money, that was his business. He just knew it was a distraction, which seemed to be a more frequent necessity these days.

Elvis saw the ranch as the perfect commune where all his buddies and their ladies could live. He was going to give each member of his inner circle half an acre of land and a down payment to build a home. He even was going to insert a provision in the ranch deed that if anybody stopped working for him or was fired, he would have the option of buying back the land at current market value. He decided to bring in trailers for everyone to stay in until the homes were built. In addition to the cost of developing the land, Elvis spent another $100,000 in a week's time for twenty-five new trucks, mostly Ford Rancheros and Chevy El Caminos, for all his "ranch hands."

The horses were all trucked in from Graceland, including Mare Ingram, named after Memphis mayor William Ingram. The Memphis Mafia were all having a ball, riding horses, skeet shooting, picnicking, and partying. In the meantime, it put a dent in the Presley bankroll to the tune of nearly a million dollars. Elvis needed some temporary cash flow to finance his latest spending spree. Enter: *Clambake*, another beach-and-bikini romp with United Artists.

Elvis had put on about twenty-five pounds since his last film and teetered around two hundred. While he got plenty of exercise on the ranch, he ate as he pleased—lots of fried Southern cuisine, cheeseburgers, steak, as well as ice cream, cookies, and other desserts. A week before the cameras rolled, Elvis reported to the set in a foul mood because he was heavier and the script was the usual silly movie fare. Director Arthur Nadel was upset to find his star in less than stellar shape, and he had the wardrobe department work overtime to fit Elvis with clothes that concealed his new spare tire.

Colonel Parker enlisted the services of Joe Esposito and Charlie Hodge to keep an eye on Elvis and report back to him if there was any suspicious activity. When some of the guys found out about it, there was major infighting in the ranks.

Elvis's way of combating his weight problem was popping diet pills given to him by Dr. Max Jacobson, the notorious Beverly Hills dentist known around town as "Dr. Feelgood," dispensing his "miracle tissue regenerator" shots—a cocktail of amphetamines, animal hormones, bone marrow, enzymes, human placenta, painkillers, steroids, and multivitamins.[19]

Elvis received industrial-sized jars of pills from Jacobson in every color, shape, and size that could send someone in any direction they wanted to go: up, down, or out of your mind. It was all heavy-duty stuff that could only be obtained by prescription.

He didn't lack for anything when he was back in Tennessee. Elvis's personal physician was Dr. George Nichopoulos, a Memphis-based doctor who was the son of Greek immigrants. He was introduced to Elvis through George Klein's[20] then-girlfriend, Barbara Little, who worked as his secretary. He became known to everyone as "Dr. Nick." A decade later, that name would become known to the world.

The night before *Clambake* started principal photography in the second week of March, Elvis tripped over a television cord in the bathroom of his house, fell, and hit the back of his head. Priscilla found him unconscious. A private doctor was summoned who came over with a portable X-ray machine. Except for a lump on his head the size of a golf ball, Elvis was fine.

Colonel Parker was most definitely not fine. After calling the studio

---

19 Jacobson's medical license was revoked in 1975.
20 George Klein met Elvis Presley in 1948 in an eighth grade music class at Memphis's Humes High School. They remained buddies all the way to their senior year. Many people gave Elvis a hard time about his flashy clothes, especially athletes, but Klein accepted Elvis for who he was. After high school, Elvis pursued his musical career and Klein went to radio school and eventually became a prominent Memphis DJ. When Elvis first hit, Klein played his music nonstop. The station, thinking rock 'n' roll wouldn't last, fired Klein. That's when Elvis hired Klein in 1957 as a travel companion on tour, the year before Elvis went into the army. He is considered one of the original members of the Memphis Mafia. He remained friendly with Elvis until Presley's death in 1977.

to explain that his star was going to be two weeks late in reporting to the set, the Colonel gathered Elvis and his troops and laid down the law.

"You wouldn't be in this condition if your head was on straight," Colonel admonished Elvis. "There are going to be major changes taking place around here. United Artists could tear up the contract they have on Elvis for this delay, and this could cost us millions!"

The Colonel added that it was time to "scale things back" because Elvis was spending a lot of money and was living way beyond his means. One of the solutions was for everyone to take a pay cut and to stop bringing their problems to Elvis.

"Elvis is an entertainer, and he shouldn't be distanced from what he is supposed to do," the Colonel said. "You're all lucky to be here. If you don't like it, there's the door."

As the Colonel spoke, Elvis sat in a chair looking dejected and didn't say anything. He wasn't used to being dressed down, especially in front of his guys. Things had to change.

The first to go was the cornucopia in the medicine cabinet. Ironically, Elvis was vocally anti-drug. He disapproved of everything those dirty rude hippies were doing. He rarely drank and didn't even keep alcohol in the house. But the pressure to crank out three to four movies a year and keep the money flowing was intense. As the Colonel demanded, he would straighten up. For a time.

For seven years Priscilla had been Elvis's lady-in-waiting. He had her safely ensconced in Graceland while he shot movies and cavorted around in Hollywood. In the summers he'd go back and they'd play house. But that all changed when she turned twenty-one. That's when Elvis sent two first-class plane tickets to Los Angeles; she traveled with her stepfather for the visit.

The Beaulieus lodged at the tony Bel-Air Sands hotel while Elvis issued a stunning edict to his buddies: no more raucous parties at his Bellagio Road home. He did, however, encourage the guys who were married to bring their spouses around to his suddenly family-friendly abode to make a good show for Priscilla's father. Elvis poured the hospitality on thick, making sure Priscilla and Captain Beaulieu were taken in his Rolls-Royce to all the famous sightseeing spots in Los Angeles and on scenic oceanside drives in Malibu.

He had vowed to Captain Beaulieu he would see that Priscilla received the best education available, and he did. Elvis had enrolled her at Immaculate Conception High School, an all-girls Catholic school in Memphis. He'd openly expressed his desire to Captain Beaulieu to marry Priscilla, but only when she was old enough. With Priscilla ensconced at Graceland, Elvis could continue living a double life—nine months a year in Los Angeles dating co-stars, starlets, and models, and the summer months in Memphis with his steady girl. It was the best of both worlds; Elvis was living the dream. But now that she was of legal age, Captain Beaulieu had expected Elvis to live up to his promise. And that was a hard thing to do as Elvis was living the good life in California.

I remember one time the Colonel and I were driving around in Beverly Hills and pulled up next to Elvis at a stoplight at Sunset Boulevard and Beverly Drive. He was on his motorcycle with a sumptuous looking Natalie Wood holding on to him from behind. Elvis looked over at the Colonel and winked.

"Well, it looks like Elvis is doing pretty good," the Colonel said to me deadpan, then we both cracked up. Indeed, he was doing very well with the ladies.

Elvis's career was based entirely on his sexy image, and he needed to maintain the illusion that he was available to the public, he told Priscilla. And for a while, she bought it.

When Priscilla turned twenty-one in 1966, Elvis ran out of excuses. When the time finally came, he got a touch of "cold feet." That's not a knock against Priscilla but merely a statement about where Elvis was at that time in his life. He was the cock of the roost, and he wanted to strut his stuff. Young, handsome, and sexy, Elvis was on top of the world. He was the world's biggest celebrity, and with that came a go-go lifestyle that he had become accustomed to. The world was one big, tasty smorgasbord of opportunities for Elvis, and he wanted to sample it all. He didn't want to settle down in the prime of his life, if ever, and did not want Priscilla living with him in Los Angeles and cramping his freewheeling bachelor lifestyle. He wanted his princess tucked safely away in the castle at Graceland so he could continue his no-strings-attached lifestyle in LA. It was a double standard he freely embraced, and if the shoe had been on the other foot, Priscilla would have been out of the picture with the snap of a finger. When she first moved into Graceland, he curtailed a lot of her after-school activities. She had to be escorted wherever she went, couldn't even bring female classmates over to the house. God forbid if she even thought of talking to a single male.

For nearly three years, Elvis kept Priscilla at more than arm's length. In fact, it was about two thousand miles most of the time, while he was making movies and doing what he liked in California. But she read the gossip rags and the scandal sheets' salacious coverage of Elvis's exploits in La-La Land. The stream of photos of him with other women and reports of his torrid affairs naturally bothered Priscilla. And eventually, she was no longer too timid to confront him about it. He blithely dismissed the photos as phonies or movie stills of love scenes. She bought it at first, but she grew less gullible and more cynical. Priscilla suspected he was engaging in wild, carefree behavior with other women while she was pining away at Graceland, waiting for him to pop the question. She wasn't wrong either.

He did finally agree to let Priscilla move to California with him. In February 1966, they settled into a ranch-style home at 10550 Rocca Place in Bel Air. The four-bedroom home in the hills offered them plenty of seclusion from the outside world, but with members of his entourage and their wives installed in the other bedrooms, they didn't have much privacy. Still, if Elvis wanted privacy, he could have told everyone to scram—and they would have. Even though Elvis was extremely polite, he wasn't shy about letting anyone know his true feelings. The truth of the matter is, he liked having lots of people around. But Priscilla was willing to make that sacrifice if Elvis was willing to slip a ring on her finger. With *Clambake* in the can and two months until his next movie, the timing was good. He finally popped the question in December 1966.

The planning of Elvis's wedding went on for two weeks in Palm Springs with the Colonel in full command. Priscilla even flew to San Francisco to buy her wedding gown under an assumed name. Room reservations were made in nearby Yuma, Arizona, to throw off the media.

Private jets were chartered with no destinations indicated. Close friends were told to make sure they were free to travel at a moment's notice, but no reason was given. The media knew something was up but couldn't figure out what it was. There weren't any leaks simply because no one knew what to leak.

The Colonel's cloak-and-dagger operation was going full blast. He did everything but put out the wedding invitations in disappearing ink. On April 30, 1967, the phone calls began. Close friends and family chosen by Elvis were told to fly into Las Vegas and check into various hotels. Still, no one knew why. Milton Prell, the Colonel's friend, and owner of the Aladdin Hotel on the Las Vegas Strip, was notified, as was Frank Sinatra.

At 4:00 A.M. on May 1, the Colonel's "invasion" plan went into effect.

Fans and the media had gotten wind that something was in the works and planted themselves outside Elvis's leased home in Palm Springs. The wedding party of the Colonel and Marie, Elvis, Priscilla, Joe and Joan Esposito, and George Klein slipped out the back door and ducked into a waiting limo. At the airport, Sinatra's private jet, the *Christina*, was ready to taxi for takeoff. Its destination was the private Hughes VIP terminal at McCarran Field in Las Vegas.

Another limo met them at the airport and whisked them downtown to the Clark County Courthouse where the marriage license bureau was open twenty-four hours a day. Joe Esposito paid the fifteen-dollar fee, and they quickly returned to the Aladdin, where they entered through the loading docks behind the hotel.

A huge five-foot-high wedding cake sat in the Aladdin's bake shop, decorated with everything but the names of the bride and groom, which would be added at the last minute. Champagne was chilling, but waiters and waitresses had no idea who would be drinking it so early in the morning. Milton Prell's private suite was decorated, but employees didn't know why.

At 11:45 A.M., Nevada Supreme Court Justice David Zenoff performed the ceremony with Priscilla's sister, Michelle, serving as maid of honor, and Joan Esposito as a bridesmaid. Joe Esposito and Marty Lacker served as best men. Some sixty people attended the reception following the ceremony, most of them not even knowing why they were in Las Vegas until earlier that morning when they gathered in the Aladdin's lobby and were quickly escorted to Prell's suite.

Red West and his wife, Pat, and a few other members of the Memphis Mafia all flew to Las Vegas thinking they were on the list to be present during the wedding, but when they got there they learned that they could only attend the reception. Red didn't feel that was right. He had been friends with Elvis since high school and was understandably hurt about being excluded from the wedding. His wife Pat cried. They didn't stick around for the reception and returned to LA. This caused a serious rift between Elvis and Red that lasted a couple of years.

While the Colonel didn't want the ceremony open to the media, he naturally wanted it photographed. He had called MGM publicist Stan Brossette and asked him to bring two of the best studio photographers available with him to Las Vegas, but wouldn't tell him why.

"One of my photographers speculated that Elvis was going to get married," Brossette recalled. "I remember telling him he was way off base—that the Colonel would never let Elvis get married in Las Vegas. It wasn't the right image. 'If Elvis gets married, it will be in the Baptist Church in Memphis,' I predicted." Before the ceremony the Colonel took Stan and the two photographers aside and told them exactly where the cameramen were to stand.

"You don't move an inch from those two spots," he told them emphatically. He didn't want anything to distract from the ceremony, especially roaming photographers.

The Colonel placed Stan in the doorway where he could see what was going on and no one could get past him into the room. As the ceremony began, Stan noticed that one of the photographers was in a position where he could not get a clear shot of Priscilla's face. He glanced around the room but couldn't find the Colonel to ask to change the location. He then noticed the photographer slowly inching his way to a better position. Stan knew that the Colonel had given strict orders to remain in one location but hoped the Colonel wouldn't notice the movement. Suddenly he saw a cane come down on top of the photographer's head with a gentle thump. The photographer quickly returned to his assigned position. However, Stan noticed that the Colonel didn't use his cane until he was sure the photographer had taken several good shots showing Priscilla's face.

After the ceremony, the newlyweds boarded the *Christina* and were jetted to Palm Springs. When they landed, Elvis and Priscilla were picked up in a new Lincoln Continental Executive Limousine by Lehmann-Peterson, a $27,000 wedding gift courtesy of Colonel Parker. (That's about $250,000 in today's purchasing dollars.) The Colonel would have never bought something so extravagant for himself.

The Colonel had pulled off the wedding of the decade in complete secrecy. As Dick Kleiner, a nationally syndicated entertainment columnist, would write the next day, "I'd like to see Colonel Tom Parker head up the CIA."

After two days in Palm Springs, Elvis and Priscilla headed back to Graceland, where they held a reception for family, friends, and relatives. They even dressed up in their wedding attire for all to see. The newlyweds spent a month alone at the Circle G, taking walks, riding horses, and enjoying romantic sunsets. They also ventured into the city where Elvis watched screenings of the latest movies at the newly refurbished Memphian Theater.

In June they headed out to Hollywood for his next film, *Speedway*. It featured fast cars and crashes, dozens of go-go dancers in miniskirts during the musical numbers, and a fistfight or two. Elvis packed up members of his entourage and their wives—a first. And it was the final trip in Elvis's private Greyhound bus, which was later sold to cut expenses. The following year the Circle G Ranch was sold, after all the Santa Gertrudis cattle had been auctioned off.

Speedway found Elvis back in the driver's seat in a racing picture, co-starring with a new marquee name to help him boost the film: Nancy Sinatra. She was his only female co-star to ever receive equal billing. The soundtrack featured seven songs, one of them by Nancy Sinatra.

The eldest daughter of Frank Sinatra had made a big splash in late 1965 with "These Boots Are Made for Walkin'," followed by a slew of other Top 40 singles. The song made her an instant household name and sex symbol. She was also recently divorced after her marriage to entertainer Tommy Sands imploded. It was said that Nancy adored Elvis, and the two flirted like crazy on the set. She has claimed over the decades that despite her attraction to Elvis, they never became intimate because she didn't want to get involved with a married man. And soon-to-be father to boot.

In anticipation of their new arrival, Elvis and Priscilla purchased a home at 1147 Hillcrest Drive in the Bel Air section of Beverly Hills for $400,000. Priscilla redecorated every inch of the house, including a pink nursery.

Lisa Marie Presley finally made her debut on February 1, 1968, weighing in at nearly seven pounds. Her middle name came from the Colonel's wife, Marie Parker. On her departure from Memphis's Baptist Memorial Hospital four days later, she was met by thousands of cheering fans. Other than his new baby girl, there wasn't much to cheer about in Elvis's life.

His movies were as predictable as superhero flicks are now. Renata Adler of *The New York Times* wrote that *Speedway* was "just another Presley movie—which makes no great use at all of one of the most talented, important, and durable performers of our time. Music, youth, and customs were much changed by Elvis Presley twelve years ago; from the twenty-six movies he has made since he sang 'Heartbreak Hotel' you would never guess it." In the *Los Angeles Times* Kevin Thomas wrote, "Presley pictures can be unpretentious fun, but this one is both uninspired and too much of an imitation of too many of his previous movies. . . . There aren't even very many songs to break up developments too predictable to outline here."

That last line summed up what fans could expect from the King at this point in his career. Married, a father, and without a hit record for so long it was embarrassing, he might as well have taken up driving a station wagon and playing golf. He was a living relic adrift in a cultural landscape of hippie psychedelia. Everything around him was changing while he stayed the same.

By the time 1967 rolled around, the best he could do was "Indescribably Blue," which peaked at number 33 on the *Billboard* singles charts. A couple of his singles hadn't even charted that year, which would have been unheard of a decade before. The same went for his movies.

Spinout (1966) marked the end of Elvis's reign as a Top Ten box-office draw in the annual movie exhibitor's poll. Movie audiences were becoming more sophisticated in their tastes and moving in another direction. Audiences were getting hipper and more discerning, feasting on rich offerings such as *Bonnie and Clyde, The Graduate, Cool Hand Luke*, and *In the Heat of the Night*. As much as Elvis's movies were beloved, they now belonged to a different generation.

Producer Hal Wallis, who had once been Elvis's most enthusiastic booster in Hollywood, began to lose faith in Presley's star power and his commitment to film work. Both Elvis and the Colonel had come to consider the Paramount lot as sort of a second home, but the uninspired nature of Wallis's last two Presley films, *Paradise, Hawaiian Style* (1966) and *Easy Come, Easy Go* (1967), revealed the legendary producer had lost interest in Elvis and was just fulfilling the obligations of their contract. He went on to greener pastures while Elvis was cinematically put out to pasture.

Stay Away, Joe was Elvis's next film project, again at MGM. In their reviews, the critics suggested the public do the same thing. Elvis starred as a Native American rodeo rider named Joe who was given some cows and a bull named Dominic to start a cattle ranch. To celebrate their good fortune, they throw a big barbeque and roast a bull!

(Not Dominic, though.) Six new songs were recorded, and nobody really cared. For the first time since *Wild in the Country*, neither an LP record nor an extended-play single was planned for the soundtrack. It was just as well. No one came to see the movie—it grossed just $1.5 million. A *Variety* review called the film a "generally flat comedy" with "many forced slapstick situations." Kevin Thomas of the *Los Angeles Times* wrote that *Stay Away, Joe* was ". . . out of touch with latter day appreciation of some basic dignity in all human beings. . . . At best, the film is a dim accomplishment; at worst, it caters to outdated prejudice. Custer himself might be embarrassed—for the Indians."

Perhaps the best thing I can say for *Stay Away, Joe* is that the Colonel negotiated a stellar deal for Elvis: $850,000 and 40 percent of the profits. Given the paltry box-office receipts, Elvis did not see much of the back end.

The people who wrote film titles at MGM were working overtime when they came up with *Live a Little, Love a Little*, for Elvis's next movie in March. The comedy, directed by Norman Taurog, his ninth and final collaboration with Elvis, was shot in and around Los Angeles over a six-week period. It contained only four new songs but did have singing idol Rudy Vallee in the supporting cast. The highlight of the movie was the screen debut of Brutus, Elvis's own Great Dane. That seemed fitting given that the film was a glorified dog with fleas.

By this time, Elvis was signaling a time-out to the Colonel.

"I really miss the fans, Colonel," he confessed. "I'd like to go back to live performances again." The Colonel didn't disagree. But he also didn't want to set up Elvis for failure. He knew the musical landscape had changed, and "them Beatle boys" and other long-haired rock bands were the ones selling out concert tours.

"Elvis, if you go back out on the road and you don't sell out, you're no longer the King of Rock 'n' Roll," the Colonel said. That must have hurt the Colonel to say—and hurt for Elvis to hear—but at the time it was true. It was a necessary but painful caution to protect his partner.

The Colonel knew that at some point Elvis would have to make a return to the stage, and when he did, it would have to be triumphant. He felt a major TV show in front of a live audience would be the best tryout. Some eight years after his Sinatra television appearance, Elvis went back on TV after the Colonel negotiated with NBC for the one-hour "Singer Presents . . . Elvis" special (later widely known as "The Comeback Special").

In October 1967, the Colonel approached Tom Sarnoff, the West Coast vice president of the National Broadcasting Company, about a possible Christmas television special. The Colonel must have been inspired, because he negotiated a $1.25 million package that included $850,000 for the financing of a future motion picture (*Charro!*), as well as funds for a television soundtrack.

Colonel Parker negotiated a deal with Singer to purchase the first 100,000 copies of the soundtrack. In return, they received an exclusive to sell the albums in their stores for a six-week period before a wider release to the public.

The show aired on Tuesday, December 3, 1968, and featured only Elvis, with no other acts or guest stars, although he was backed by sixteen singers and forty musicians. The shows had been taped in June before a live audience at NBC Studios in Burbank, California, with very tight security. The show received excellent ratings—a whopping 42 percent of the US viewing audience was tuned in. The program boasted a higher audience share of women between the ages of eighteen and forty-nine than any other program that year and was NBC's highest-rated program of the week. The album soundtrack, *Elvis*, cracked the Top 10 and eventually went platinum. Decades later, *TV Guide* named it as one of the hundred greatest moments in television history.

At the end of the show, the Colonel burst onto the backstage, his eyes shining with emotion.

"Where's my boy?" he yelled. Elvis came out of his dressing room, and the Colonel gave him a big hug.

It was a good thing the special was a smash, because Colonel Parker originally pitched it to NBC as a Christmas special. Had it not been a huge success, either a lawsuit or a refund was at hand because the contract was certainly violated. Colonel Parker was extremely nervous that NBC was going to demand their money back, and neither Elvis nor the Colonel had the cash to return. That notwithstanding, the show firmly put Elvis back in the driver's seat.

In October, Elvis was back at MGM to do *The Trouble with Girls*. It was a return to the musical comedies that had become his stock in trade, but audiences were no longer interested in this type of passé fare. Oddly, the movie did perform well at the drive-in circuit. The best thing about the film was the introduction of the song "A Little Less Conversation," which would form the basis of a remix that returned Elvis to the international music sales charts in 2002.

In his next movie outing, Elvis grew a beard, hung up his guitar, and stifled his wiggle for *Charro!* The only song in the film was performed over the opening credits. The film was financed by National General Pictures, and had a supporting cast that could be best described as "Who?"

Universal had the honor of backing Elvis's final scripted movie with *Change of Habit*. This would seem to have been the appropriate title for his final movie, co-starring Mary Tyler Moore, since that was what the Colonel was about to accomplish—a change of habit.

By 1969, Elvis had ground out thirty-one movies over thirteen years. He was ready for something else. After the incredible success of the "Comeback Special," Elvis wanted to go back to performing before live audiences. Elvis and the Colonel went into one of their many closed-door meetings, and the result was that the Colonel was only too happy to accommodate him. Let me underscore this again: it was Elvis leading the Colonel on an artistic endeavor, not the other way around.

Proof was in the 1969 recording session for *From Elvis in Memphis*. It's been written time and again that Elvis's career was at a low ebb and that he "bucked the Colonel" to record at Memphis's American Sound Studio. To me, this is another blatant falsehood. Colonel Parker couldn't have cared less where Elvis recorded because that fell on the artistic side of their relationship. That had nothing to do with the Colonel, as far as he was concerned. In fact, he felt Elvis chose wisely because it was hard to argue with the results.

Producer Chips Moman and the American Sound Studio's house band, the Memphis Boys, cut more than a hundred singles in the span of a few years (1964–1972). Aretha Franklin, Neil Diamond, Dusty Springfield, B. J. Thomas, and Petula Clark all recorded there, and many of those recordings became classic rock and pop staples. It was in a less than desirable part of town—an armed security guard and a not-so-friendly dog watched the parking lot. Elvis entered through the back door and stepped inside and looked around the place.

"What a funky, funky place," he said. "Good Lord, what have I gotten myself into?"

He needn't have worried. He was in great hands with Moman, and they recorded perhaps the best-received album of Elvis's career, which included "Kentucky Rain," a Top 20 single, and "In The Ghetto," Elvis's first Top 10 single since 1964, selling more than a million copies. Also cut during that session, but not included on the album, was Mark James's "Suspicious Minds."

In November 1969, "Suspicious Minds" became Elvis's first number one song in seven years, and was the centerpiece of his Las Vegas shows. Decades later, it was overwhelmingly voted by fans around the world as their favorite Elvis Presley song of all time.

For the Colonel, it was all about timing. To his credit, he never approached anyone with hat in hand. Others would have to do the approaching, and if they did, they'd better come prepared to pay the fair market value for his boy. That wasn't a problem for multi-millionaire Kirk Kerkorian.

13

Viva Las Vegas

Kirk Kerkorian, the airline, real estate, and hotel tycoon, had just built the International Hotel, two blocks off the famed Las Vegas Strip on Paradise Road. The International was to be the largest convention-oriented hotel in the world.

In early 1967, Kerkorian purchased the Las Vegas Downs horse track, which was located on eight acres of prime real estate directly adjacent to the mammoth, county-owned Las Vegas Convention Center. Critics thought he was crazy to build a major gaming property that far off the Strip. Las Vegas had been built on high rollers, nickel slot players, top-name entertainment, and $1.95 dinner buffets. The days of huge conventions of fifty thousand to seventy-five thousand conventioneers were far in the future, but Kerkorian saw them coming.

He quickly put together an expert staff to operate his $60-million, thirty-story hotel, which would open in less than two years. (By contrast, Kerkorian's 5,000-room MGM Grand Hotel in Las Vegas that opened in the early '90s and cost $1.85 billion.) His first step was to hire Alex Shoofey, the very successful executive vice president of Del Webb's Sahara hotel to run the hotel side of the 1,519-room project. Jimmy Newman, a longtime, highly respected gaming executive, was named vice president of casino operations.

Shoofey then raided his own staff and hired seventy-three Sahara executives and key staff members to form the nucleus of the

International's staff. Kerkorian's next move was a masterpiece in pre-planning. He bought Bugsy Siegel's pride and joy, the rundown 777-room Flamingo hotel located in the middle of the Strip, directly across from glitzy Caesars Palace, to use as a training site for his entire International staff.

The plan at that point was to sell the Flamingo in 1969 and move all its employees into the International just prior to opening. However, the innovative team of Shoofey and Newman spent about $2 million remodeling and turned the twenty-year-old property around, making it into a big moneymaker. Kerkorian decided to keep the Flamingo, causing considerable problems for the staff. Instead of picking up and moving into the International a month before opening, the entire executive staff had to find replacements for themselves and their staffs to continue running the Flamingo. Recruiting offices were opened from Miami to San Francisco. The Las Vegas market was not large enough at that time to handle so many new jobs.

One of the key features at the International Hotel would be its main showroom—the largest room of its kind in the world, with 1,500 seats, including a balcony. It would also feature the finest light and sound systems. The mammoth stage was sixty feet wide and more than two hundred feet deep, and it was designed to handle both superstars and major production shows. Even the doors leading into the huge dressing rooms in the basement were ten feet high to permit showgirls through with their large, feathered headpieces.

"I want to headline only the biggest names in the business in the showroom," Kerkorian told Shoofey. "And I mean new faces in Las Vegas!" Shoofey, a demanding taskmaster, knew there was only one person in the world capable of handling that type of assignment: the legendary Bill Miller.

The former owner of the famed Bill Miller's Riviera nightclub, located just over the George Washington Bridge in Fort Lee, New Jersey, sixty-five-year-old, gray-haired, and perpetually suntanned Miller was enjoying semi-retirement in the Caribbean. He was immediately hired by Shoofey and took over the entertainment duties at the

Flamingo while looking ahead at the monumental job of finding fresh new faces to open the International. Kerkorian was adamant when he said, "Sinatra, Sammy, and Dean Martin are great, established Las Vegas entertainers. But I want exciting new faces at the International!"

Miller told Shoofey there were only two names out there big enough to open the International: Elvis Presley and Barbra Streisand.

Streisand was a proven commodity, having just won an Academy Award for *Funny Girl*. Elvis was still soaring after his '68 "Comeback Special," but he had not done another major concert in several years. Ironically, both had played Las Vegas earlier in their careers—Streisand in 1963 as an opening act for Liberace at the Riviera, and Elvis in 1956 for Shecky Greene at the New Frontier.

Miller was leaning toward Elvis to open the property. He put in a call to his old friend, Colonel Tom Parker, and flew in to meet him in Los Angeles. Even though they still had to negotiate, the Colonel felt strongly about one thing: Elvis would not open the new property.

"You let Miss Streisand do that," he told Miller. "We'll come in a month later after you get all the kinks worked out." Of course, with any project that large, there were problems with the stage equipment and the sound system, but they were quickly corrected. (On opening night, a heavy sandbag fell from the fly loft, hitting the stage a few feet from Barbra. She never missed a beat. "See what happens when you build places this big with a G.I. loan?" she told the audience. The quip got big laughs.)

Shortly after the agreement was OK'd, the Colonel arranged for Elvis to fly into Las Vegas on February 26, 1969, for a "contract signing" media event. Miller and Shoofey decided to hold it on the showroom stage at the unfinished International.

Bruce Banke, then director of publicity for both the Flamingo and International hotels, drove Elvis, Joe Esposito, and some of the boys over to the new hotel to sign the initial contract. The unfinished showroom still showed bare steel beams, but no one was about to tell Elvis to put on a heavy construction hat, even in a hard-hat construction area.

"On the way back to the Flamingo, Elvis was in the passenger seat next to me," Bruce recalled later. "We were on Desert Inn Road waiting to make a left turn at a traffic light onto Paradise Road when an attractive woman in a new Mercedes pulled up beside us. She glanced over and gave us a condescending look. Elvis smiled and waved. She returned her focus to the traffic light and suddenly realized what she had just seen. Her head snapped back to the left and her mouth dropped open. Just then the light changed, and I hit the gas. I glanced in the rearview mirror and saw she was still sitting there, mouth agape. Joe and the guys were howling all the way back to the Flamingo."

Loanne Miller, who later would become the second Mrs. Colonel Parker, had just moved to Las Vegas in December 1968 and was looking for a job. Friends had told the tall, attractive divorcée that in Las Vegas it wasn't *what* you knew but *who* you knew. Although she didn't know anyone, in mid-March she answered a newspaper ad and was hired as secretary to Nick Naff, the International's executive director of publicity and advertising.

Nick was a highly charged, fast-paced executive who had previously worked in local advertising agencies and at the Las Vegas News Bureau, the publicity arm of the Chamber of Commerce. Bruce had joined him at the Sahara in February 1967, when Del Webb sold the old Thunderbird Hotel where he was the publicist. On August 9, 1967, they walked out of the Sahara and into the Flamingo with the other members of Shoofey's team to begin an incredible ten-year roller-coaster ride together.

"Nick was extremely talented," Bruce remembered, "which was good because we were charged with creating every piece of collateral material for the new hotel from matchbooks to menus to marquees. Fifteen-hour workdays were common, seven days a week."

One afternoon in early April, Nick received a call from the Colonel's office in Los Angeles notifying him there would be a meeting next week between Parker's staff and key International executives. He was asked to have his entire staff present. Nick was beside himself.

"What staff? All I have is Bruce [Banke] and Patrick [O'Neal]!" he exclaimed. "This is going to be embarrassing," Loanne recalled to me. "He looked at me and said, 'You will have to attend the meeting, too. I have to show up with more than just two people. Bring your pad and pen, but if you take any notes, you're fired.'"

The stage had been set for one of the most important events in Loanne's life.

The luncheon meeting was set up in Kerkorian's private villa at the Flamingo, although he was not present. The Colonel arrived with his entire staff plus George Parkhill and Harry Jenkins from RCA and Freddy Bienstock from Hill & Range, Elvis's music publishing company. He also came carrying a four-foot-tall teddy bear for Shoofey's young daughter, Teri Lynn Shoofey. Miller represented the hotel, along with Nick and his staff. Everyone in the room was wearing suits except the Colonel, who was dressed casually and wore a cap. He was smoking a large cigar and walked in with a cane, although he didn't appear to use it for support. He was an imposing figure, standing over six feet tall, somewhat overweight, and deeply tanned.

Loanne Miller wasn't much of an Elvis fan. While she respected his rise to fame and his standing in the entertainment world, her real curiosity was "the man behind the man." She hadn't even met Alex Shoofey, the president of the hotel, or any of his key executives. She had seen him and knew about his reputation for having only the best people work for him, although he would not tolerate any mistakes, even from them.

Nick introduced his entire staff, and it quickly became apparent that the two key players—the Colonel and Shoofey—were used to being solely in charge. The rest of those attending were truly supporting acts. The two were jockeying for position, and everyone else melted into the background. At one point reference was made to "goodies" for Elvis and the Colonel, while motions were made indicating these goodies were going to be "under the table." The Colonel was adamantly opposed to the idea.

"Everything we do is on top of the table or forget it," he said. "We don't do business that way."

Loanne couldn't believe someone would talk to an executive of the hotel in that manner, and she was truly impressed.

"I realized then that Colonel Tom Parker was one of the most special people I had ever met," she later told me.

After everyone was introduced and had chatted for a few minutes, Shoofey suggested they adjourn to the adjacent dining room for lunch. Because Loanne didn't want to take a seat above her position, she waited until everyone else was seated around the large circular conference table. She was shocked to discover the only seat vacant was the one located between the Colonel and Shoofey! Loanne loved food, but that was one meal she barely touched. She was afraid she would drop a utensil or spill her coffee.

Of course, the two superpowers kept talking around her; she was fascinated. Neither of them said a word to her, but her life would soon be changed by both.

"By August of that year, I would be working in the office of the president, and, by the next year, I would start a working relationship with the Colonel," she recalled. (In later years, Colonel would tease her about eating so little at that first meal. He always claimed to be shocked when he finally discovered her hearty appetite.)

Bruce sat on the opposite side of the table to stay out of any possible line of fire between the two strong-willed heavyweight players. He had known Loanne only a month, but he knew neither one of them needed that kind of pressure and felt sorry for her. He remembered it as one of the longest meals of his entire life.

"I don't know who was more nervous: Nick, who thought Patrick or I would pull a major goof-up, or Loanne, who must have rearranged the food on her plate about a hundred times," Bruce said. "I figured she must have been getting an earful from both sides as she sat there, staring straight ahead, pretending to be deaf, but taking it all in."

Loanne recalled that later that evening, after her nerves returned to some semblance of normalcy, she told a friend she had met the most amazing man ever.

"He's definitely a genius," she said.

The following day, a formal contract was signed, calling for Elvis to perform two shows a night for four weeks in 1969, and then two four-week engagements a year starting in 1970 at $125,000 per week, or a half million dollars per engagement, putting him at the top of Las Vegas's entertainment scale, even above Frank Sinatra, Dean Martin, and Barbra Streisand. Sure, it's nice being the Chairman of the Board, but it's better to be the King.

Every time Elvis arrived in town, a fleet of limousines transported him and his entourage from the Howard Hughes Charter Terminal and whisked them to the hotel's north laundry entrance. They occupied the penthouse—the thirtieth floor Imperial Suite—which came to be known as "the Elvis Suite."

The unfinished International Hotel officially opened at 10:00 A.M. on July 2, 1969, an extremely hot day. The interiors of the rooms on the upper fifteen floors weren't even completed at that point, compounding the problems faced by the brand-new property. Barbra Streisand's opening performance was well-received, with suave actor Cary Grant, a close friend of Kerkorian's, serving as master of ceremonies before an invitation-only audience. Peggy Lee was also very successful as the opening headliner in the hotel's showroom-sized five-hundred-seat lounge. But the hotel's opening with Streisand was nothing compared with what took place twenty-nine days later.

Elvis quietly rehearsed his band at the Riviera Hotel in Palm Springs. It was the perfect place for such an undertaking—it was quiet, low-key, and away from the glare of the media spotlight. The TCB Band[21] consisted of Ronnie Tutt, Jerry Scheff, James Burton, and Larry Muhoberac (who was replaced by Glen D. Hardin in February 1970). Burton and Hardin were nabbed from Ricky Nelson's group, and he was none too happy about losing them. James Burton had played with him since the "Ozzie & Harriet" days and even lived with the Nelson

---

21 While Elvis rehearsed the TCB band in Palm Springs, the International's musical director, Joe Guercio, prepared the horn section in Las Vegas.

family for a time. It caused some hard feelings between Ricky and James, though they eventually got over it.

Those guys had worked together a lot on other projects and recording sessions throughout the years. Elvis also knew them, and there was a looseness and familiarity with these musicians. They bonded quickly and had a lot of fun.

Elvis came to love Palm Springs: it was a place where he truly felt safe, and his privacy was respected. He ventured out into public more there than anywhere else. He enjoyed hopping on his Harley and cruising Palm Canyon Drive, browsing the books and magazines at Bookland, eating bacon and eggs at the counter of Milton F. Kreis Drugstore and Patio, and shopping at the Mayfair Market.

Alan Ladd Hardware was another place Elvis liked to venture, or should I say, was forced to venture. Elvis's fans stole his mailbox several times, and we would have to make a trip to the hardware store to replace it. Their good-natured manager, Bill Bachwick, would come in after hours and open the store up for us. Then, in the middle of the night, we'd switch it out. I know of at least three times we did that.

While Elvis was preparing for his show, the Hilton's publicity department was completely unprepared for the onslaught from the hundreds of writers who wanted to cover Elvis's return to live performing. The phones had been ringing all month with requests from Europe, Japan, Australia, Great Britain, and every major entertainment publication in the US to get press seating for opening night. Kerkorian made his private DC-9 available to fly in key writers from New York, Chicago, and the Southern California area. They eventually had to spread the press out over several nights to accommodate it all. Avid fans from around the world tied up hotel phone lines requesting show and room reservations. The entire engagement was almost sold out before it started. Las Vegas had never seen an opening like it.

As soon as the audience was seated for Streisand's final midnight performance, the Colonel turned the hotel into an Elvis fantasyland. He plastered custom-made banners, pennants, posters, oversized cardboard records, and pictures on every pillar and wall, both inside and outside the hotel. He augmented his own staff with counselors hired from the International's Youth Hotel. (The International was the first Las Vegas hotel to build separate facilities just for children.) Every night, fans would tear down anything they could reach, and the next morning the Colonel would have it all replaced. This became standard operating procedure for the next seven years.

"It's the best kind of advertising we could possibly do," he claimed.

At the conclusion of every four-week engagement, the fans were encouraged to take everything down. By the next morning, the only things remaining to indicate that an Elvis appearance had just concluded were a few pieces of Scotch tape on the walls and a couple of dangling strings.

Early in the morning of July 31, 1969, with the temperature already over 100 degrees, Ad Art Sign Company crews began lifting ten-foot-high ELVIS letters designed by the Colonel into place on both faces of the mammoth International marquee in front of the hotel. They were larger than any letters ever used on a Vegas marquee—sixteen separate pieces—and had to be wired down instead of clipped on so they wouldn't blow off and injure someone.

Elvis's opening performance on July 31 was by invitation only, with most of the prime seats reserved for casino VIP players and the press. Comic Sammy Shore was Elvis's opening act, which had to be one of his most difficult gigs ever. The capacity crowd, while sophisticated for the most part, wanted to see the King, and expressed their feelings to this veteran comic.

The audience for the opening engagement was jammed with celebrities.[22]

As the houselights went down and the 10,000-pound gold lamé,

---

22 Opening night included Ann-Margret, Angie Dickinson, Burt Bacharach, Dick Clark, George Hamilton, Carol Channing, Wayne Newton, Paul Anka, Shirley Bassey, Pat Boone, Cary Grant, Fats Domino, Henry Mancini, and Sammy Davis Jr., who led a long standing ovation for Elvis.

Austrian-made draped curtain slowly rose, Elvis walked out onstage completely unannounced. Stars were usually introduced by an off-stage announcer, but the Colonel said, "When the audience comes to see a show, they know who they are there to see. If someone has to tell them who you are, you are definitely not a star."

Elvis grabbed the microphone, and hit his signature spread-legged stance from the '50s. His knees started to twitch. Before he could sing a note, the audience exploded, giving him a rousing standing ovation—led by Sammy Davis Jr.—even climbing on chairs and screaming so loud the enormous chandeliers rattled.

His voice sounded much deeper and richer than it had been before. Elvis later admitted being nervous at first, but as soon as he got into "Love Me Tender," he quickly hit his groove and gave a performance that had the critics raving. The Colonel advised Elvis not to do any encores.

"Always leave them wanting more," was a Colonel Parker proverb.

A headline in *Billboard* magazine read, "Elvis Retains Touch in Return to Stage." A *Rolling Stone* reporter wrote, "Elvis was supernatural, his own resurrection." *Newsweek* observed, "There are several unbelievable things about Elvis, but the most incredible is his staying power in a world where meteoric careers fade like shooting stars." Around the world, the reviews were glowing. One would have thought the Colonel wrote them himself.

During the show, the Colonel stood backstage and was grinning from ear to ear.

Midway through Elvis's single opening night performance, the Colonel asked the International's publicity department to set up a press conference. This was a surprise that had the hotel's catering staff scurrying to set up a press interview area in the hotel's 70,000 square-foot Grand Ballroom. They expected some two hundred writers and photographers to attend. Members of the press were thrilled with the opportunity to talk to Elvis and thanked the Colonel profusely. The Colonel's real reason for the opportunity was that he knew many of them were headed out to midnight shows featuring other headliners.

He kept them tied up with Elvis so they couldn't write about any entertainer other than Elvis the next day.

The press conference was classic Colonel Parker. He wore his traditional white, floor-length smock emblazoned with "Elvis! In Person! International Hotel!" all over it. The mood was very relaxed as Elvis stood in front of the podium, one foot planted on an adjacent chair and surrounded by his father and friends. He knew the show had been a resounding success, and he was enjoying every minute of it, as were the reporters and photographers who were eating it all up. Flashbulbs were popping everywhere, and the Colonel stood on the sidelines, smoking his cigar and smiling contentedly. The Colonel always kept out of the way and let Elvis run the show at these events. If Elvis directed a question to the Colonel, he would oblige and answer, but it was usually all about Elvis. The only time he interjected was when someone asked Elvis a loaded question. The Colonel would cough, warning Elvis to choose his words carefully. The press eventually caught on. One New York City writer told him, "You know, Colonel, you really should do something about your cold."

Twenty-eight days after opening night, Elvis had broken every Las Vegas attendance record. Over 102,000 fans had an opportunity to see him. His single show record of 2,200 in the International showroom will stand forever, thanks to fire department seating limitations that went into effect in the mid-'70s restricting it to 1,500. Seats were so hard to come by that Elvis fans happily squeezed six or seven people into a booth meant for four. A chair in the aisle was as good as a ringside seat. They would have been willing to hang from the chandeliers to see their hero sing.

During Elvis's opening week, several RCA executives came in at various times to see their top-selling artist in person. The Colonel had arranged for RCA to record the final six nights of the International engagement, resulting in Elvis's first double album, *From Memphis to Vegas / From Vegas to Memphis*. It went platinum.

Shoofey and the International staff were delighted with the business Elvis generated during his initial appearance. The showroom had grossed well over $3 million during Elvis's run. Casino revenues and food and beverage profits soared. The hotel wanted Elvis back as soon as possible and would have played him 365 days a year if they could.

Elvis was probably one of a handful of Las Vegas superstars who could draw people to Las Vegas simply because he was appearing there. Most visitors come for the casinos, and the shows are a bonus. In Presley's case, it was "Honey, Elvis is in Las Vegas. Let's go to Nevada!"

One local entertainment columnist erroneously wrote that Elvis was coming back to Vegas for three days over Thanksgiving weekend. It was picked up by the wire services, but no one confirmed the information. The switchboard got jammed for several days and people couldn't even get through to make room or restaurant reservations.

Again, the Colonel knew the value of not overexposing Elvis and agreed to a return engagement at the end of January 1970. Elvis spent the remainder of 1969 at Graceland with Priscilla, Lisa Marie, and, of course, his entourage.

Shortly after Elvis closed his first Vegas engagement, Loanne transferred into the International's executive offices as a secretary for hotel president Alex Shoofey. Although she had worked closely with Herb Heiman, a vice president at RCA Records, handling the press for Elvis's opening, she had not seen the Colonel since the day they first met at the April luncheon. He was not forgotten, however, as the entire town was talking about the impact Elvis and the Colonel had on Las Vegas. It wasn't until January 8, 1970, when the Colonel came in for a meeting with Shoofey, that she saw him again. He spoke politely to her on the way out.

A pattern soon developed that would remain in effect for the next six years. The Colonel and his staff would come in a week to ten days before opening night and set up headquarters in what had become his permanent offices in the south wing of the fourth floor. The rooms and suite were all rather nondescript, nice, and comfortable, but nothing you would write home about. They certainly didn't compare to the accommodations on the twenty-eighth and twenty-ninth floors reserved for the casino high rollers. However, the Colonel and his staff were quite comfortable in their new surroundings.

They still needed a large room in which to store the many boxes of Elvis souvenirs, programs, and other items that were sold in the lobby. While on an exploratory tour of the second floor of the hotel, near the housekeeping department, the Colonel found a space full of hundreds of cases of toilet tissue and Kleenex.

"Now, wouldn't it make more sense to keep these supplies closer to the area where the maids pick up their sheets and pillowcases, soap, and other supplies every day?" he asked.

It made sense and the Colonel soon had himself a huge storage room. (Although, even if it hadn't made sense, he would still have had it.)

Elvis, on the other hand, took over the thirtieth-floor Imperial Suite, a lavish five-thousand-square-foot master suite that occupied nearly one half of the top floor of the hotel. It contained four bedrooms, including a master bedroom suite, five bathrooms, a sunken tub, a living room furnished with a grand piano, a sauna and steam room, a private elevator, and a fully equipped kitchen. The piano was so large that, in order to get it inside, it had to be lifted by a crane to the thirtieth floor before the suite was even completed. The dining room featured an enormous glass dining table that seated a dozen people. The entire suite had been decorated by designer Phyllis Morris in two colors—yellow and black.

The view from each of the huge picture windows was magnificent. To the east sprawled the city of Las Vegas, right up to the side of distant Sunrise Mountain. The view looking south at that time revealed mostly desert. About a mile away was the tiny campus of Nevada Southern University, later to become UNLV, which is not so tiny. Farther to the south was busy McCarran International Airport, already planning major expansions as officials attempted to keep up with the city's phenomenal growth. To the west was the Las Vegas Strip. By day it was drab, with the big hotels and their lavish landscaping and crystal-clear swimming pools surrounded by acres of barren desert that would someday become the sites of some of the most magnificent resort hotels the world would ever see. At night the millions of glittering lights would come on, transforming it all into a dazzling adult Disneyland. And finally, looking north, there were the lights of a more subdued downtown Casino Center where many of the locals would go for their evening's entertainment. Beyond that was North Las Vegas and the ever-growing Nellis Air Force Base. On most days, Elvis and his buddies sat on the balcony and watched the air force's top fighter pilots fly over the Nellis bombing range.

Before every engagement, the Colonel would contract up to half of the available forty-eight-foot billboards in Southern Nevada, sometimes as many as two hundred. Every engagement carried a different theme. He also ran full-page ads and sometimes double-page ads in both local newspapers, the *Las Vegas Sun* and the *Las Vegas Review-Journal*, hailing the return of the King. In many ads, the Colonel promoted the acts appearing in other areas of the hotel. One ad advertised the fact that Elvis was appearing in the main showroom in very small type and announced in huge letters that Ike and Tina Turner and Redd Foxx were co-starring in the lounge, and the rock musical *Hair* was appearing in the hotel's theater. The ads also contained the name of the act following Elvis in the showroom a few weeks later.

One of the Colonel's favorite activities prior to every opening was his "Breakfast with the Radio Reps." This stemmed from his carny days when the best way to reach customers was by radio. He would invite the sales managers of every radio station in Las Vegas to his suite. After plying them with food and alcohol and regaling them with his favorite stories, he'd take each one individually into his office and make a deal. Nine times out of ten he bought radio airtime well below the going rate. Nobody treated the sales managers so well.

With the billboards, hundreds of radio commercials, newspaper and entertainment trade ads, cab tops, bus stop benches, and the hotel's own publicity efforts, the Colonel said, "even the prairie dogs in the desert knew Elvis was in town."

Elvis was the star, and the Colonel was his manager. Their roles were clearly defined.

"All I can do is let the world know you are here," the Colonel told him.

The world heard, and the world came. It's estimated that during the years Elvis was a headliner in Las Vegas, 50 percent of the city's visitors saw his show. Of the eight biggest headliners in Vegas history with seven years of residency or less, Elvis still beat them all, both in total revenue and number of shows performed. Diana Ross, Celine Dion, Rod Stewart, Barry Manilow, Elton John, and Adele are eating Elvis's dust almost five decades after his death.

The King remains the King to this day.

14

20,000,000 Elvis Fans Can't Be Wrong

After Elvis Presley's second engagement at the International, the Colonel met with a young promoter from New York named Jerry Weintraub. He wanted to talk about booking Elvis's concert tours and taking him out on the road. Weintraub, a tall, handsome jeweler's son from the Bronx, had been trying to set up a meeting since late 1968, shortly after Elvis's successful "Comeback Special."

Weintraub had a very small operation. It was so small, in fact, he had no staff and little money. But he did have confidence in his ability to promote, and then some. At the time he was managing Pat Boone, Paul Anka, Shelley Berman, Joey Bishop, the Four Seasons, Jane Morgan, (whom he later married), and a relatively unknown singer named John Denver. His main goal was to reach the Colonel and convince him he could spearhead a successful touring operation.

Weintraub used every method possible to set up a meeting with the man. One of his contacts was Harry Jenkins, a vice president with RCA Records. Jenkins had become the liaison between the Colonel and RCA, so he had the Colonel's ear. Even though Colonel Parker ducked Jerry's calls for almost an entire year, his persistence won out. The Colonel admired Jerry's doggedness and finally took his call. He knew this was one of the major factors for his own success. When the Colonel had a goal in sight, as Jerry did, he let nothing interfere with reaching it. After several meetings and countless phone calls, the Colonel and Jerry finally reached an understanding.

"I called every day for months and months," Weintraub recalled in his 2010 memoir. "I did not flip him in the course of one of those calls, but I had planted my name so deep in his [Parker's] brain he would never forget it. Whenever he thought of taking Elvis on tour, he thought of Jerry Weintraub."

The Colonel deemed that Jerry could have the rights to promote Elvis's tours if he could produce a check in the amount of a million dollars. Financing a concert tour with a superstar of Elvis's caliber was a major undertaking. Financial guarantees were needed to book stadiums, hire musicians, charter private aircraft, and cover the myriad other financial arrangements that had to be made.

Weintraub talked to Steven H. Weiss, an attorney who had worked with Led Zeppelin and Jimi Hendrix, who told him about a company in Seattle, Washington, that was highly experienced in tour management. More important, they had financing.

The company was Kaye-Smith Enterprises. One of the key owners was actor Danny Kaye, who just happened to have made his last Las Vegas appearance at the International Hotel in the winter of 1969, just a few months after Elvis's debut. The company owned a dozen radio stations, a Muzak franchise, and recording studios. They also had a successful promotional division called Concerts West, run by Terry Bassett, Pat O'Day, and Tom Hulett. Kaye-Smith had been very successful in booking rock 'n' roll concerts throughout the United States. Concerts West provided the tour personnel to service the entertainers. It was highly regarded in the business.

Weintraub brought the Elvis tour deal to Kaye-Smith Enterprises, and they put up the initial money. With a million-dollar check in hand, the Colonel agreed to get the tours started but insisted that tickets were priced at $5, $7.50, and $10, but no more.

The Elvis tour group was spearheaded by Weintraub, who formed Management III Productions. Hulett and Concerts West provided the tour working crew, and Bill McKenzie of Kaye-Smith handled the accounting responsibilities. These gentlemen were presented to the Colonel as working for Weintraub in Management III.

Jerry was so anxious to have the Colonel believe they were his employees that during the early tours, Bill McKenzie did not stay at the International but went back and forth from the Riviera for the meetings. In fact, many times Weintraub would talk to Tom Hulett as though he were the boss at Management III, and Tom responded as if he were.

Their initial six-day, seven-show Elvis tour kicked off on September 9, 1970, at Veterans Memorial Coliseum in Phoenix, Arizona, two days after he closed at the International. The show was not without incident. Minutes before Elvis was supposed to go on, Colonel Parker was approached by the city fire marshal, who informed him there was a bomb threat. He immediately stood up and said, "Tell Elvis not to come to the building. . . . Come on boys, let's get out of here."

The fire marshal was taken aback and asked the Colonel where he was going.

"If there is a bomb in the building we don't want to get blown up," the Colonel politely told the fire marshal. "You go up on the stage and tell this audience of ten thousand people that there's not going to be an Elvis concert and that everyone has to leave the building without seeing him."

Realizing the bigger threat was the ten thousand angry fans who might tear down the venue with their bare hands, the fire marshal allowed the show to go on.

At the concert, Elvis was wearing a green scarf around his neck and threw it to a fan in the front row who screamed like she was giving birth. It played so well that Elvis incorporated the scarf throw into his act, doling out multiple scarves at every show. According to tour manager Charlie Stone, this created havoc with Elvis's security team and the police detail working the concerts.

"Before the show began, I always gave the officers instructions as to what took place onstage while Elvis was performing, that under no circumstance were they to take their eyes off the audience," Charlie said. "I cautioned them that if they looked away even for a moment, a crowd of women would likely trample them in their attempt to get closer to Elvis or to get a coveted scarf."

Officers new to the security team often grinned or rolled their eyes, thinking they could handle a few enthusiastic fans. Eventually, they learned the hard way. Charlie certainly did.

One night in Cleveland, Ohio, he was guarding the stage when a group of women came running from the wings of the stage, and he had to intercept them. He was bruised and battered. He ended up with a cut on his eye and was bleeding profusely, requiring four stitches. He learned from this incident never to underestimate the strength of a woman.

"Elvis fans are not typical fans. They have resources and strength beyond any imagination," Charlie said. "They seemed to acquire superpowers when they were in Elvis's presence and would break through any barrier."

At a concert in Hollywood, Florida, Charlie got it from both ends. When he wouldn't allow a female fan to go to the front and get a scarf from Elvis, she told him her husband was a cop. That didn't fly with Charlie.

"If I let you go to the stage, I'd have to let every other woman in the building go up as well," he said. That didn't sit well with her, and she angrily huffed off. A minute later, a plainclothes police officer approached Charlie and showed him his badge.

"My wife wants to get a scarf, and I want you to let her go to the stage," he said. Charlie held his ground and explained that simply wasn't possible. The cop then pressed a gun against Charlie and he had a sudden change of heart.

"Impossible means nothing to an Elvis fan," Charlie said. "They are very persistent; and, if a husband wants to keep his wife happy, he'll resort to desperate means."

Following Elvis's second Las Vegas run, two Los Angeles concert promoters offered a $1 million guarantee for Elvis to perform a concert at the eight-thousand-seat Rotunda of the Las Vegas Convention

Center adjacent to the hotel in August, just prior to opening his third engagement at the International. The Colonel politely declined out of loyalty to Kerkorian and Shoofey.

"Fellas, that just wouldn't be fair to the folks at the International," he told them. They countered with a concert date at the forty-five-thousand-seat California Angels' baseball stadium in Anaheim. Again, the Colonel nixed the idea, pointing out its proximity to Las Vegas.

The Colonel did take Elvis into the fifty-thousand-seat Astrodome in Houston, Texas, for a three-day engagement that he had already arranged. He had met with Buddy Bray of the Houston Livestock Show in August 1969 and signed Elvis for six shows in the Astrodome (February 27–March 1, 1970) where he broke every attendance record by drawing 207,494 people. The contract price was $150,000; the Colonel received a 25 percent commission.

For Elvis's August 1970 Las Vegas engagement, the Colonel proclaimed it the "Elvis Summer Festival" and outdid even himself with decorations. Even front-of-the-house employees got involved in the fun, wearing Elvis scarves and white Styrofoam skimmers.[23] Every day the Colonel had to replace a number of the dealers' hats and scarves, either because they were "lost" or were "left at home." Actually, they were usually given away to big tippers, which didn't bother the Colonel in the least. "Everyone has to make a buck," he'd say.

As usual, the Colonel arrived a week early to put his colorful show together. What made this engagement even more enjoyable for him was the fact that his old pal Eddy Arnold was preceding Elvis in the showroom. Of course, the Colonel's influence with the International's management had a great deal to do with the signing of Eddy, and the star did excellent business.

Despite a slowdown in the nation's economy in the early '70s, the hotel was sold out in advance for all twenty-eight days. School was on summer recess and fan clubs were flying in from around the

---

23 A skimmer is a 1920s-style straw hat. Think Shakey's Pizza or Farrell's Ice Cream Parlor.

world. Guests attending the opening night performance received complimentary copies of Elvis's latest album, *On Stage,* recorded at the hotel in February. Presenting gift packages to everyone on opening night became another tradition.

The Colonel was also thinking beyond the vinyl grooves. He brought in a forty-man production crew from MGM studios to film *Elvis: That's the Way It Is,* a documentary showing Presley in both rehearsals and onstage at the hotel. Elvis didn't have to memorize a script or be on set at 6:00 A.M.; he just had to be himself and was rewarded with a $500,000 salary and $150,000 in expenses.

The eight huge Panavision cameras were everywhere, filming interviews with everyone from the president of the hotel to fans in the casino, who were included per the direction of Colonel Parker. They loved every minute of it.

The movie was also a coup for the International Hotel, which gained major exposure, as well as Las Vegas itself. Oscar-winning Denis Sanders helmed the project, which the Colonel wanted finished, edited, and ready to be shown in theaters by Thanksgiving. Denis delivered a great film, and on time.

During the dinner show on August 12, the Colonel was sitting in his usual booth, located on the aisle. With him were Jim O'Brien, Tom Diskin, and Loanne. The MGM crew was filming the show and had set up a makeshift barricade on stage. Elvis was not aware of the structure and strolled close to the audience. He suddenly found himself blocked by the barricade and unable to move back from the edge of the stage. Screaming female fans in the ringside area stormed the stage. The Colonel was out of the booth in a flash. He was beside Elvis before anyone knew what was happening. Despite his bad back at age sixty-one, he grabbed the stunned star and boosted him over the barricade, away from the hundreds of frantic hands reaching out for him.

It was also during the August engagement at the hotel that Elvis received his first death threat. Joe Esposito's wife, Joanie, took an early morning phone call at their Los Angeles apartment since the caller couldn't get through to Joe at the hotel. He told her a man was on his way to Las Vegas to kill Elvis. He would disclose the name of the assassin for $50,000. Joe contacted the FBI and his phone was tapped, but the shakedown artist never called back. The same afternoon Joe picked up the mail at the front desk, which included a large white envelope without any postage. Inside was a showroom menu that featured a picture of Elvis. Someone had drawn a gun pointed at Elvis's head and had scribbled in the word "Die!"

The Colonel and his staff met with hotel security, agents from the local FBI offices, and Elvis's own boys in his fourth-floor offices. Elvis had sent word with Joe that he was not about to cancel any shows because of "some nut." Rather than intimidated, he was angry. With FBI agents at the door, plainclothes officers roaming the showroom, the hotel's 125-man security force on high alert, and Elvis's own security team (headed up by Red and Sonny West) onstage and in the audience, the show went off without a hitch. An ambulance was on call in the back of the rear stage doors, just in case. After a few more uneventful performances, the alert was called off.

Following Elvis's final 3:00 A.M. Summer Festival show on September 6, 1970, the Colonel and Jerry Weintraub began making last-minute plans for Elvis's first tour under the Management III Productions banner. The hotel wanted Elvis back as soon as possible. The Colonel agreed on January and August dates in 1971, a pattern that he would follow for the next two years.

He told Shoofey, "Elvis wants to play some concert dates in California, and you know we won't do that if it is too close to our Las Vegas dates." And Elvis did tour the entire West Coast from Seattle to San Diego in mid-November. Concert tours would provide the biggest security test for Elvis and his boys. Under the Colonel's direction, security was tight from the moment he left Graceland until the moment he slipped back through its front doors at the completion of the tour. The Colonel personally made a pre-show tour of every facility where Elvis was scheduled to appear. He met with key building personnel, the security people hired for the event, and the local police to cover their participation.

Most tours involved a different city every evening. To maintain order, Tom Diskin provided the musicians with a detailed schedule covering every move from initial takeoff to the final landing.

In November 1970, Elvis was back on tour, opening in Oakland on the 10th and closing on the 17th in Denver. Elvis looked and sounded great and enjoyed the touring and live performances again. They all traveled in style as Colonel Parker contracted private jets for each tour. Because most of the dates involved a series of one-night stands, using commercial air travel would have been nearly impossible.

With private planes there was no need to pass through public terminals, decreasing security issues. The Colonel and his advance staff traveled in a smaller jet to check out all hotel accommodations and assign rooms, then inspect the building's facilities and personnel, especially the concessions people, and plan all of Elvis's security measures to ensure his safety and privacy. The musicians and merchandising people traveled separately in a larger plane.

There were no passes or free tickets given out for any of the concerts. In one city during the November tour, a newspaper reporter became angry when he could not obtain free passes and threatened to write a bad review of the show. The Colonel puffed on his cigar, looked him right in the eye and said, "Do whatever you want. By the time your review is printed the show will be over and we will be gone."

One of the Colonel's other primary rules was that no visitors were allowed backstage before the show. Elvis dressed in his hotel room and arrived at the venue during the intermission and spent a minimal amount of time in a dressing room. After the show, Elvis went directly from the stage to a limousine with its engine running.

After each tour, the Colonel and his staff and Management III personnel returned to the Las Vegas Hilton and made tour settlements. This tour had also been very successful. Elvis got rave reviews and the tour crews were establishing successful patterns of operation. The Management III / Concerts West personnel had top-notch people who were experienced in handling ticket sales, stage operations, and all the many jobs necessary behind the scenes to make a concert tour a success. Weintraub's enthusiasm and sharp mind made him a quick study of the Colonel's special promotional techniques. They also had a good rapport on the road.

The Colonel often gave pointers to promising young men, and Jerry had what it took to understand the Colonel's techniques. In fact, he'd use these same techniques in the coming years to his advantage in promoting John Denver and other artists, as well as a very successful career producing movies. But when it came to Elvis Presley tours, the Colonel was the final authority, and Jerry reported directly to him.

Ever since his 1968 "Comeback Special," his 1969 Vegas residency, and his return to touring in 1970, there was a spark and artistic rejuvenation to Elvis's work. His confidence was soaring and he was willing to try some new things—even a new Christmas album, albeit reluctantly. With the lame and uninspired movie years behind him, he was sucking up energy from live performances and the contact with his fans. They inspired him and invigorated him as an artist. He was a new man.

Elvis' Christmas Album, released in October 1957, was a deluxe double LP comprised of six popular holiday songs, two Christmas carols, and four gospel tunes. It reached number 3 on *Billboard*'s album charts and was reissued two years later when Elvis was on duty in Germany. It was a perennial seller and the album remained on the charts for several years, eventually selling more than three million copies in the United States alone. Every holiday season, those songs were played on the radio, garnering him nice-sized royalty checks and mechanicals[24] from airplay. For years there had been demand by the fans (and the Colonel) to do another Christmas album, but Elvis kept putting it off. By 1971, there was no more delaying.

Colonel Parker had booked Nashville's Studio B for a week in May 1971, so that Elvis could cut a Christmas album, a gospel album, and a couple of singles for release in the summer and fall. With Elvis's

---

24 Mechanical royalties are generated each time an artist's copyrighted musical recording is reproduced in a digital or physical format.

upcoming concert activities increasing, future studio time would be limited. The goal of these sessions was to generate perhaps a year's worth of new songs.

The new Christmas album, which was already announced to the public by RCA, was undoubtedly the top priority for the Colonel and the label. As we would eventually discover with Elvis, the feeling was not mutual.

The Colonel asked me to accompany him on this trip to Tennessee. Even though I had my own thing going—and a new family, to boot—it was hard to say no to him when he asked for something. For some strange reason, I sensed that Colonel Parker needed a companion. Turned out, I was right.

Ever since the Colonel brought Elvis to Hollywood and took him away from Tennessee, there was some resentment from the Nashville recording industry toward both men. Specifically, their gripe was that by taking Elvis to the West Coast and changing his sound, it almost put country music on life support. And that's just not supposition; thousands of country radio stations changed their formats to rock 'n' roll because of Elvis's arrival on the music scene. It may sound stupid or trivial, but there truly were some hard feelings. But as far as the studio went, it was homecoming week for Colonel Parker. He welcomed several visitors in the RCA lounge, including Johnny Cash and June Carter Cash, Minnie Pearl, Eddy Arnold, and Ernest Tubb.

Built in 1957, RCA Studio B became known as the birthplace for the "Nashville Sound,"[25] a style characterized by background vocals and strings that helped establish Nashville as an international recording center. And of course, Elvis had his own history there. He cut approximately two hundred songs in Studio B, including many classics such as "Heartbreak Hotel," "Stuck on You," "It's Now or Never," "Good Luck Charm," and "Are You Lonesome Tonight?"

For many years, Country Music Hall of Fame inductee Chet Atkins

---

25 In addition to Elvis, Studio B's other hitmakers included Eddy Arnold, Waylon Jennings, Dolly Parton, Jim Reeves, Willie Nelson, and Floyd Cramer.

managed RCA's Nashville operation and produced hundreds of hits in Studio B. And he was there running the studio when Elvis came for this recording session, during which he ended up cutting almost four dozen songs after a week in the studio.

The prolific output during the fabled 1970 "marathon sessions," which can be heard on *From Elvis in Nashville,* allowed them to bank enough material to last awhile since Elvis's schedule was so full.

RCA's Felton Jarvis produced the sessions and assembled the band that included David Briggs (piano), Norbert Putnam (bass), Jerry Carrigan and Kenneth Buttrey (drums), Chip Young (guitar), Charlie McCoy (multi-instrumentalist) and James Burton (guitar). Al Pachucki served as the engineer.

To put everyone in the Christmas spirit (it was May, after all) and set the mood for a holiday album, Jarvis placed a decorated Christmas tree and fake packages in the studio. Elvis's friend Lamar Fike even showed up one day dressed as Santa Claus.

Despite all the efforts to put Elvis and the studio session players in a holiday mood, cutting a Christmas album was not a priority. Elvis had a hot band and he wanted to jam. But before he could cut loose, he had to oblige the RCA brass and the Colonel. He sang the first two songs—"It Won't Seem Like Christmas" and "If I Get Home On Christmas Day"—with sincerity. But his boredom meter started to peg. He switched genres to Toni Arden's "Padre," an operatic tune he said in a 1958 interview was "his favorite song."

It took him another hour before he could summon the energy to tackle "Holly Leaves and Christmas Trees," a song written by his friend and bodyguard Red West, who was a brilliant writer and actor in his own right.

But it wasn't until the group got to the Charles Brown blues classic, "Merry Christmas Baby," that Elvis demonstrated any real interest during this session. It was the highlight of the evening and, in a way, a letdown because it was the last ounce of gas he had in the tank. When Felton Jarvis asked him for take three of the Christmas classic, "Silver Bells," Elvis shook his head no. He'd had his fill of holiday tunes.

With that, Jarvis called it a night; it was the right call. The session ended around 4:00 A.M. with seven songs in the can. Not a bad night by any stretch of the imagination. They'd resume at 6:00 P.M. the next evening.

The second day in the studio started with a bit of drama. Drummer Jerry Carrigan overslept and failed to show up. He was quickly replaced by Kenny Buttrey, a first-rate Nashville session drummer who worked with Bob Dylan, Neil Young, Simon & Garfunkel, Waylon Jennings, and Jimmy Buffett. Because of that, the session started about ninety minutes late.

"I'll Be Home on Christmas Day," penned by Michael Jarrett, was the evening's first take. Elvis sang it with gusto and some great bluesy phrasing. It was a powerful vocal performance. While preparing for another take, Elvis sang an a cappella version of "The Lord's Prayer," which Jarvis happened to catch on tape. Like all good producers, he instructed his engineer to keep tape always rolling, especially when a great artist like Elvis was in the studio. Elvis nailed two more Christmas tunes before he started showing signs of boredom, and Jarvis felt it was simply best to follow, not lead.

During a break in between mastering "Winter Wonderland" and "O Come, All Ye Faithful," Elvis and the band jammed on "I Got a Woman," "That's All Right," and a blistering eleven-minute version of Bob Dylan's, "Don't Think Twice, It's All Right."

The Colonel didn't hover in the corner of the studio watching everything Elvis did; in fact, even being in the same building while Elvis was recording was a rarity. For the Colonel, it was simply an opportunity to network and to catch up with some old friends. But Chet Atkins was on-site, and the building was wired so that he could listen in on the session wherever he was with the flip of a switch. He heard what was going on and picked up the phone in his office to call the Colonel in another room.

"Your boy is not doing Christmas songs," Atkins plainly informed the Colonel. He nodded to Tom Diskin, which was shorthand that he wanted to see Elvis. Because Tom was so kind and polite, he was the one who always made the approach to Elvis when business had to be discussed. It was his job to walk into the studio and tell Elvis that the Colonel wanted to see him. The two men met in the parking lot to have a heart-to-heart discussion. I looked out the window and saw them leaning on cars, each man speaking his piece. My best guess is that the Colonel told him to cut the Christmas album first and then focus on the other material. Elvis probably told him that, as an artist, he didn't work that way and needed to stay fresh by rewarding himself every now and then with a song he wanted to cut. Their talk lasted about twenty minutes.

Whatever words were exchanged, they ultimately worked it out. It seemed like it was all a game. In the end, both did indeed get their way—the Colonel got his Christmas album and Elvis was able to cut the material that left him artistically satisfied.

Like the pro that he was, Elvis marched back into the studio and finished the remainder of the Christmas tunes, and everyone was relieved. Then he was able to concentrate on his gospel album and the other songs he was itching to do.

Elvis was so loose that during a break he and Red gave a karate demonstration to everyone assembled. Not the wisest thing to do in a studio setting given the expensive gear and equipment in the room. When Elvis disarmed Red, his gun went sailing through the back of Chip Young's handcrafted Conde Hermanos guitar.

Years later, Young said in a 2014 interview that it all started when someone asked Elvis, "If somebody pulled a gun on you, how would you get away from them?" That's all Elvis needed to hear. He loved showing off.

"Ah, that's easy," Elvis replied. "Red, come here, and bring that gun over here."

The rest of the story went like this, according to Chip: "So, Red reaches in his pocket and pulled out a gun. And I said, 'Is that gun loaded?' He said, 'Well I wouldn't carry around an unloaded gun." So I said, 'What about unloading it?' So, he opens it up and bullets fall down on the floor. And I'm thinking, wow! So, he goes over and stands in front of Elvis. And I'm looking at the way that gun is going to go out of Red's hand. We had a bunch of guitars stacked up against a drum booth over there. It was the first night that James Burton had worked with us, and his guitars were there, too. I had my gut-string guitar leaning up, and I said 'Let me move those' and Elvis hit Red's hand, and that gun went flying across the studio—and boom!—right in the back of my guitar. The barrel went inside, and it just stuck. It just hung there."

Young said everyone was laughing like crazy except for him. Elvis told him to go and buy another one and he'd pay for it.

"Later, I gave the guitar to the Country Music Hall of Fame and Museum," Young said. "With that hole in it."

And that is how antiques go from being merely valuable to being priceless. That guitar is probably one of the more valuable instruments in the museum because of that hole, who put it there, and how.

It was the last time Elvis recorded in Nashville, and it was magic. And we heard almost every song on the studio loudspeakers. When the Colonel and I departed for Palm Springs, I knew he was happy. Elvis was carrying the fire again, and everyone could feel it. The King ruled once again. His subjects were happy.

In all, those sessions produced forty-two masters and became the holiday-themed *Elvis Sings the Wonderful World of Christmas*, the Grammy Award–winning gospel album *He Touched Me*, and a batch of hit singles including, "Until It's Time for You to Go," "I'm Leavin'," and "It's Only Love."

As usual, the Colonel's instincts were correct. *Elvis Sings the Wonderful World of Christmas* did phenomenally well. At the time, Christmas albums usually didn't fare well on the *Billboard* charts, but it reached number 3 on the Hot Country album chart and number 1 on the Christmas album chart. It sold three million copies in the US alone and seven million worldwide. Today, any Baby Boomer and Gen Xer will tell you that iconic album cover was in their parents' record collection.

The gospel album that followed—*He Touched Me*—garnered Elvis a Grammy Award and sold a million copies. That was a remarkable feat for the genre. But it paled in comparison to the Christmas album, which several generations have enjoyed throughout the decades.

Over the years, RCA has recycled Elvis's Christmas songs into various packages. *Elvis' Christmas Album* continues to be a perennial bestseller. The RIAA awarded Diamond certification to the Elvis Presley Estate in 2012 for ten million sales of the 1970 version. Since then, the worldwide total is now up to twenty million. *Elvis' Christmas Album* is the best-selling album in the entire Presley catalogue, outpacing classics such as *Elvis Is Back!*, *Blue Hawaii*, *How Great Thou Art*, *From Elvis in Memphis*, and *Aloha from Hawaii via Satellite*.

It's also the best-selling holiday album of all time, beating out distinguished artists such as Nat King Cole, Johnny Mathis, Barbra Streisand, Kenny G, Mariah Carey, and Mannheim Steamroller. That's a 2023 reckoning, by the way. As usual, the Colonel wasn't wrong. His instincts for what the fans wanted almost never strayed.

15

The Colonel's Crew

Colonel Parker managed the most exciting entertainer in the world, yet he wanted his life to be as normal as possible. He was a man of routine, execution, and repetition.

On Monday, January 18, 1971, Colonel took Loanne Miller, Tom Diskin, and George Parkhill to dinner at the Lost Knight restaurant in Las Vegas. It was located inside the Royal Inn on Convention Center Drive. It was a quaint place with good food and within walking distance of the International. After dinner, the Colonel announced he had a surprise. Instead of leaving the building, he walked them to the hotel elevators and punched the button for the top floor. They quickly ascended to the penthouse suite that the Colonel had reserved for the entire engagement. It was a beautiful facility with three bedrooms and a full-service kitchen.

The suite was a refuge from the hectic activities at the International, but it was close enough so the Colonel could be there within minutes if there were any problems. The fans who set up headquarters at the International during an engagement were always waiting to see either Elvis or the Colonel. Both men had extremely high regard for the fans and understood without them they would not be enjoying the fruits of their labor. The Colonel enjoyed engaging with the fans and tried to look out for their best interests by constantly informing them of Elvis's activities and keeping ticket prices as low as possible.

However, because the Colonel and his staff were in Las Vegas for five or six weeks during every engagement, it was important for them to have a place to relax away from the constantly ringing phones in their fourth-floor offices at the International. The Royal Inn proved to be the perfect getaway. On the evenings they used the suite they ordered room service or Loanne cooked dinner. Some nights, George put his culinary skills on display and prepared a gourmet meal for the group.

Every weekend the Colonel returned to Palm Springs to spend time with Marie and monitor her physical condition. While he was on the road, he hired a registered nurse to remain with her in addition to the housekeeper and cook employed on a regular basis. Marie suffered from severe arthritis in her hips. She had undergone hip replacement surgery a few years before, but it did not seem to help. She required a cane when walking, which was becoming more difficult as time went on.

The Colonel loved his Palm Springs home. It was modest as far as the Vista Las Palmas neighborhood went. The interior decoration was all Marie and very feminine. Her collection of cat figurines dominated every nook and cranny. The Colonel collected elephant figurines, which I'm sure reminded him of his days in the carnival.

At the entrance, the first thing visitors saw was a beautiful four-foot-high illuminated photo of Elvis, Priscilla, and Lisa Marie. The backyard, however, was the sun-loving Colonel's domain. The focal point was the barbeque area, which was built entirely of desert rock. It was some fifteen feet wide and stood about five feet tall with built-in ovens, grills, lights, a sink, and related accessories. A large walk-in freezer was built into the back of the house and a pool surrounded by lounge chairs and tables completed the décor. When he was home, Colonel Parker lived in his private, walled-in domain and loved to cook for his staff and friends.

The day before Elvis's opening on January 26, 1971, the Colonel was having fun in the hotel with his "trained bear," which was Grelun Landon from RCA's West Coast office wearing a bear suit. He decided to drop in at the hotel president's office to introduce his new pet.

"Things were not going well in the executive office that day," Loanne Miller recalled. "There were some pretty intense meetings going on with a lot of shouting. Mr. Shoofey was not at his best."

Suddenly the Colonel, with his bear, walked into the outer office where the secretaries sat. He introduced his new pet to Loanne, Marilyn, and Nancy, Shoofey's three secretaries. Colonel Parker then walked into Shoofey's office completely unannounced.

"I held my breath, expecting even more shouting to come out of the office," Loanne said. "No one ever walked into Mr. Shoofey's darkly paneled office without permission. Suddenly the room erupted in laughter, and the Colonel had completely diffused the tension."

When he came out of the office a little later with Shoofey, the three secretaries had cookies ready for the bear. However, the Colonel kept grabbing them from Grelun saying that cookies weren't good for bears, which resulted in more laughter.

The Colonel was also not afraid to wear the bear suit when it came to protecting Elvis.

Shortly after the close of Elvis's 1971 Winter Festival, the Hilton Hotel Corporation took complete ownership of the International and Flamingo hotels. The International was renamed the Las Vegas Hilton and the company logo was added to the Flamingo's well-established name.

When the Colonel negotiated his initial 1969 International contract with Shoofey, one of the clauses called for the entire contract to be renegotiated should Shoofey ever leave the organization. Shortly after the sale to Hilton, Shoofey did leave. The flamboyant Henri Lewin, executive vice president of Hilton's Western Division, was brought in to head the new contract management team. In his first meeting with the Colonel, Lewin insisted that the existing contract was perfectly fine. The Colonel begged to differ. He produced the document and Lewin read it over. Finally, he conceded.

"You're in the driver's seat, Colonel," Lewin said.

"It doesn't mean anything to be in the driver's seat if you don't know how to drive," Colonel Parker replied. Elvis got a nice raise simply because Colonel Parker knew his contracts inside and out, and they were always to the benefit of his client.

As summer approached, Loanne Miller was becoming increasingly unhappy with her job in the International Hotel's executive offices and decided to investigate the real estate field to possibly become an agent or broker. Las Vegas was taking off and both commercial and residential real estate sales were booming. She discussed her plans with the Colonel, who suggested she resign immediately and accompany him and his staff to Lake Tahoe for Elvis's engagement at the Sahara Hotel in July. On June 14, she gave her two weeks notice. Shoofey asked her to stay until a replacement could be found. She finally left the Hilton on July 3, just three days before the Colonel and George were scheduled to fly to northern Nevada and begin preparations.

Compared to the heat of Las Vegas in the summer and its hectic go-go lifestyle, Lake Tahoe was like a breath of fresh air; however, that clean mountain air took some time to get used to thanks to the 6,225-foot elevation. The executive staff at the Sahara Tahoe, under the leadership of Monty Hundley, was top-notch. Not only were they very knowledgeable about their jobs, they had fun at their work. The Colonel and his staff enjoyed working with them too. On Tuesday, July 20, the Colonel directed his decorating crew around the hotel just as they had done at every engagement in Las Vegas. The hotel was transformed into a setting for an Elvis "happening."

The Sahara provided the Colonel with office space in the hotel and a beautiful home nearby, right on the shores of the lake. The hotel was owned by a seagoing ship's officer who had furnished it with many beautiful and unusual items picked up during his travels around the world, especially from the Orient. The Colonel, a former sailor, immediately felt at home. It featured a huge sundeck overlooking the deep, frigid waters of the lake and a large wood-burning stone fireplace in the wood-paneled den. There was even a large bathtub in the master bathroom.

The Colonel fell in love with the house, including its year-round tenant, Fibby, a large, loveable cat who ruled the roost but was gracious enough to allow the Colonel to have his space. Fibby's fur was a blend of various shades of brown, gold, tan, and white, and he loved to be petted. The two of them spent many enjoyable hours sitting on the deck and taking in the magnificent view of the lake and the surrounding mountains.

The Tahoe engagement was another record breaker for Elvis. He set an all-time attendance record for the Sahara, as he had done in Las Vegas. For his two weeks there, he received $300,000. By now Loanne Miller was working full-time in Colonel Parker's office. Her real estate career was put on permanent hold. Show business was fun and exciting, and it was an entirely new world for her to learn. She had a great but demanding tutor. The Colonel was adamant about his daily schedule. No matter what time the staff went to bed, he expected them in the hotel's coffee shop for breakfast at 8:00 A.M. On tour, breakfast was even earlier so they could get an early start to the next city. His orders were followed without question, although many times they didn't make a lot of sense. He often gave orders, and then completely reversed his instructions. It took Loanne many months before she realized that it was not only his intelligence that was behind his decisions but an uncanny intuition. Many times, his staff had trouble following his wishes because they were not logical, and yet somehow, they seemed to work.

Loanne was the first woman to work with the Colonel on a daily, face-to-face basis. For years the Colonel's staff had consisted of men (except for an occasional female secretary for short periods, and they were not privy to the inside operations). With Loanne added to the staff, the situation was different. She eventually became the Colonel's confidante, and his loyal male staff members were not sure she deserved this special privilege. For the first time since any of them had known him, he was taking a close, personal interest in a woman other than his wife. His protective staff undoubtedly feared the worst, that she would take advantage of him. It was only after several years of teaming up with the Colonel that she was able to gain acceptance from the entire staff.

The Colonel was professional and quite formal when it came to conducting business. The language around the all-male staff changed considerably as well. No profanity was permitted in her presence. Only within the confines of his office did the Colonel use the first names of his staff. When he addressed them, it was always, "Mr. Diskin," "Mr. McDonald," "Mr. Parkhill," "Mr. O'Brien," and "Miss Miller," and he expected others to address them that way as well.

In late September 1971, Marie Parker underwent her second hip replacement surgery. While this one was more successful than the first, she continued to complain of pain in her hip. The Colonel realized she could not live alone, although she refused a caregiver. Colonel Parker found himself in the position of asking friends to stay with her in Palm Springs when he was on the road or in Las Vegas or Lake Tahoe. This included Clannie Williams from his Madison, Tennessee, office. She stayed in Palm Springs a few times but eventually told Colonel Parker he'd have to make other plans. Unfortunately, Marie had a sharp tongue and was not the easiest person to get along with. I know this caused the Colonel great consternation because he was loyal to Marie and equally as loyal to Elvis.

The best therapy for Colonel Parker was work. He maintained a strenuous schedule, especially when Elvis was on tour. In every city, he'd meet Elvis's plane when it arrived, and the two would have a briefing, usually on the plane. The hotel and security arrangements would have already been made. On the occasions when there was additional business to be discussed, the Colonel would accompany Elvis to his suite at the hotel where they could continue their talks in private. Even the traveling party had been preregistered at the hotel and received their room keys as soon as they got off the plane. Professional baggage handlers took care of all the luggage and equipment except for Elvis's personal things, which were handled by his staff.

The Colonel arrived early at every venue after having checked it out earlier in the day. When the show began, he'd sit next to the stage, alert to any security issues that might arise. He was ready to protect Elvis with his body if necessary. But Elvis had a well-oiled security team who were top-shelf, even eliciting praise from members of the

Secret Service. There's no doubt in my mind the many hours Colonel spent in front of those blaring loudspeakers accounted for his hearing problems in later years.

As soon as Elvis was safely back in his hotel suite, the Colonel and his staff would depart to the next city. Depending on the distance between concerts, they'd usually arrive in the wee hours of the morning and check into their hotel for a few hours of sleep. Regardless of Elvis's arrival time, the Colonel was usually in the coffee shop no later than 7:00 A.M. After the first few days of a tour, the nights got shorter, and sleep became more precious.

November 17, 1971, would mark Elvis's final public appearance until January 26, 1972, when he returned to Las Vegas. The Colonel and his staff, along with the Management III team, flew to Lake Tahoe to complete the tour settlement reports and rest for a few days.

Gross proceeds from the tour were $1,096,648. After deducting all expenses, the net profit for the tour was $804,000. Of this, Elvis received two-thirds ($536,00) and the Colonel one-third ($268,000). Per their prior contract, souvenir sales were divided fifty-fifty, each receiving $21,250.

At the end of each tour, the Colonel gave out bonuses to everyone for a job well done. All were delighted, except for Vernon Presley, who did not think the additional expenditure was necessary. He expressed his displeasure to his son, who relayed the message to his manager.

"Daddy doesn't think we should be paying out bonuses," Elvis told the Colonel. That situation was rectified by simply putting Vernon's name at the top of the bonus list for $2,500. Vernon suddenly thought the entire bonus plan was a good idea. The Colonel knew exactly how to address every situation with nuance, a touch of psychology, and tons of street smarts.

Loanne Miller became the official RCA Records tours secretary on December 7, 1971, a job she would hold throughout Elvis's touring years. It was tougher than it sounded because she was entering an all-male world. It was like allowing a woman to be admitted to a men's club, and some of these old-school gents were not comfortable with the idea. The Colonel made it clear that she was to be treated with respect. She tried her best to blend into the background as much as possible and didn't expect special treatment from anyone in the organization.

To solidify her position, she began carrying the files and tour information with her on every trip. To save space, she placed all pertinent information in a three-ring binder and carried what they needed in her briefcase. This proved to be extremely efficient because all the information the Colonel needed was available at a moment's notice and was easy to locate.

Loanne learned early on to never carry more luggage on tour than she could handle herself, which meant doing laundry on the road. They were rarely in a town long enough to send out laundry, so she always carried a bottle of liquid soap with her. On one of the tours through the Deep South, the luggage was stored in the nose of the plane, which was not pressurized. When she unpacked the luggage, she found every piece of clothing soaked in liquid soap. The only solution to her predicament was to rinse everything out in the bathtub until the soap was gone. The more she rinsed, the more bubbles filled the tub. After several rinses, everything was soap-free but still wet. When the Colonel came into her room to ask a question and saw her laundry hanging everywhere, he was puzzled.

"What the hell is going on here?" he bellowed. "Why are you doing laundry now?"

Loanne took a deep breath and tried to explain the situation, but to no avail. The Colonel stalked out, muttering to himself, "Women!"

One of Loanne's other duties in every town was to be sure the Colonel had plenty of extra towels and a board under his mattress. She carried his special pillow and his personal clock with her so he could feel more at home in each hotel room. Adjusting to a different bed every night was hard enough but adjusting to a different pillow was next to impossible. She also packed his clothes for every trip and immediately unpacked his luggage when they reached their hotel. Then Loanne would lay out his pajamas and slippers and place his toiletries in the same location in every bathroom. She even carried a special fragrance that she'd use in every hotel room he stayed to give it a homey feeling. Since the Colonel had always traveled with men in the past, he truly appreciated these new luxuries.

During an engagement at Lake Tahoe, a business associate had given the Colonel a special wooden Buddha. Loanne made sure to pack it in his carry-on luggage each time they boarded a tour plane, and then took it out and placed it in front of the Colonel before every take-off and landing. The Colonel would then lean back in his seat, close his eyes, and mumble a chant to himself. He claimed it was something he had learned from Spanish gypsies. On one trip, Jerry Weintraub asked the Colonel what he was doing.

"Jerry, I'm ensuring our safety on this trip," he replied. "The Buddha will now take care of us until we land."

Jerry scoffed. "Colonel, that is foolishness," he said. "The Buddha has nothing to do with our safety."

Soon, the pilot had reached his cruising altitude and the plane was flying smoothly through a clear, blue sky. The Colonel warned Jerry not to laugh at the Buddha because he could be very sorry. Jerry was still smiling and shaking his head when the plane dropped suddenly. Jerry stopped smiling and shouted at the pilot.

"What happened?"

"We don't know, Mr. Weintraub, it must have been an air pocket," came the reply.

"Jerry, I warned you not to laugh at the Buddha," the Colonel reminded him.

"Colonel, the Buddha had nothing to do with what just happened," Jerry replied, and was somewhat short. Just then the plane dropped a second time. This time no one laughed.

"I'm sorry, Buddha, I'm sorry," Jerry repeated several times as the plane continued to bump around. The Colonel picked up the small statue and spoke softly to it.

"He's sorry, Buddha," Colonel said. "He really didn't mean to insult you. He's very sorry about it."

The remainder of the trip went smoothly. From that day on, whenever they boarded a plane and everyone was buckled in for takeoff, Jerry would say, "Colonel, do you have the Buddha?" Then he would look at Loanne and say, "Get the Buddha. Get the Buddha!" Several months later Jerry gave the Colonel a gold ring with a jade Buddha on it.

I don't know what Jerry's religious affiliation was, but I can tell you that Buddha had to be right up there with Jesus and Muhammad.

During the Elvis touring days, Sam Ferguson joined the staff. Like the fictitious Mr. Green who supposedly traveled with Eddy Arnold, the fictional Sam handled all complaints and requests for passes. He was blamed for everything that went wrong. Sam was usually fired and rehired several times on every tour. Unlike Mr. Green, he never got a room. In the last year of his life, the Colonel told Loanne that when Sam realized his traveling days were over, he passed away. It wasn't until later she realized that the Colonel knew his own traveling days were over as well.

On December 15, 1971, the Colonel and George Parkhill flew into Las Vegas to take a truckload of toys to St. Jude's Ranch for Children in nearby Boulder City, Nevada. The Colonel delighted the youngsters by appearing in his Santa suit, just as he had done for the Humane Society in Tampa, Florida, decades before. He had purchased all the toys himself; but, as usual, he insisted there be no publicity regarding the matter. He often played Santa in Palm Springs, charging a hefty fee, which he always gave to local charities. When the Colonel hung up the Santa suit, he passed it on to me. Every year we dropped in at the homes of Frank Sinatra and Liberace with me in the Santa garb, much to the delight of their mothers.

In March 1972, Las Vegas hotels were hit by a citywide strike, which meant this was backed by all the unions. The town went dark. The Las Vegas News Bureau, the publicity branch of the Chamber of Commerce and the top promotional machine for the entire city, called an emergency meeting of all the town's publicity and advertising executives. The main point of business was how they were going to get Las Vegas rolling again after the strike was settled. It was agreed that the best way was to bring in Las Vegas's number one superstar—Elvis Presley—to generate immediate room occupancy and to let the world know that Sin City was back in business. A deal was made with the Colonel, but the strike was suddenly settled before the final arrangements could be made. The hotel continued with *The Wonderful World of Girls*, starring Gene Kelly, which was appearing in the showroom when the strike began.

The Colonel met with Hilton executives on Monday, March 27, to discuss Elvis's personal appearance contract with the hotel. As a result, on April 20 a new contract was signed that would increase Elvis's fee to $130,000 a week, per week, for the next two engagements and $150,000 per week for the three engagements after that. Additionally, the hotel agreed to furnish an advertising budget of $125,000 per engagement.

When the negotiation was settled, the Colonel received a nice letter from Barron Hilton, praising him for his publicity efforts on behalf of Hilton Hotels. It also contained an offer for Colonel Parker to become Hilton's "talent and publicity consultant" for $50,000 a year for a three-year period, ending on December 31, 1974. "We look forward to a long and mutually beneficial association with a truly outstanding individual," Hilton closed.

The Colonel's energy level was amazing. He outworked people half his age even though he was about fifty pounds overweight. This didn't help his back problems. He would never stand when he could sit, but he never stopped going. He was a perfectionist and wouldn't allow himself to become a step slower or miss the slightest detail. Everything had to be in order and double-checked. But he was in good humor most of the time, with a cheerful attitude and the ability to see humor in nearly every situation. If anyone around him was gloomy or a downer, they would be banished from his presence until they returned in a more convivial mood. At an age when most men were planning for retirement, Colonel Parker was revving up.

The Colonel's days were getting longer: he usually worked eighteen hours a day. He didn't need much sleep to exist and was putting the younger crew to shame. He never complained once about the long hours. His business was his life, and he thoroughly enjoyed it. Because he continually underestimated his achievements, he was surprised when they were pointed out to him. He never thought about what he had accomplished. Instead, he was more focused on what he could pull off in the future for his client. And that meant new milestones and records to break.

The spring tour wrapped up at Tingley Coliseum in Albuquerque on April 19. It was the most profitable to date. The tour grossed $1,314,943, which meant, after expenses, Elvis's share of the net was $660,000. The Colonel collected $333,000. They each netted an additional $17,000 from souvenir sales. Of course, there would be additional revenues from the *Elvis on Tour* documentary when it was released in theaters later that year.

Elvis was no slouch in record sales, either, boosted by his new visibility and the public's belief that he was committed again to a recording career. A *Billboard* magazine survey indicated that Mr. Presley was the all-time top recording star from 1955 to 1972 with fifty-five platinum albums (one million or more) and twenty gold albums (sales of 500,000). He topped the Beatles almost two to one.

Shortly after arriving in New York for a four-show stint (June 9–11, 1972) at the legendary Madison Square Garden, which grossed an accumulative $730,000, the Colonel found out through some of his contacts that an experienced bootlegger was planning to tape one of the Garden concerts and have it on the street shortly thereafter. Some of the fans were already looking forward to buying it. The Colonel quickly called his friend Harry Jenkins, who had been a liaison between the Colonel and RCA for many years. He was surprised when told Jenkins had just left the company. The Colonel phoned the people in charge of production and apprised them of the situation.

"We're going to have to record the Garden shows and get an album out as soon as possible," the Colonel explained. "If you don't, your company will be losing a lot of future sales."

The RCA people advised him there was no time to set up complete sound recording equipment to meet the deadline and certainly no way to get an album out as quickly as he wanted. The Colonel persisted, and when he persisted, well, he persisted, if you get the hint. There was no telling this man no when he had his mind made up.

RCA finally gave in, recorded the concert, and made it available in lightning-fast time—it was on sale just a week after the concert. *Elvis: As Recorded at Madison Square Garden* peaked at number 11 on *Billboard*'s Top 200 Album charts and went gold only a month after it was released. Of course, several people wanted to take credit for this undertaking, but make no mistake, that album was totally Tom Parker's brainchild.

The month I obtained my driver's license, Colonel Parker decided he no longer wanted to drive. Almost by default, I became his chauffeur, but I didn't mind. No one wanted to be in a car with the Colonel behind the wheel. He was a terrible driver, because he had to look at you when he spoke rather than keeping his eyes on the road. He was also an aggressive driver.

Driving for Colonel Parker came with great benefits. I met some of the most powerful people in the entertainment business. I got to see him negotiate and network with some of the smartest people in the industry and gained a worldly education in business, law, and psychology that could not be learned in a textbook or taught in a classroom. He was also a great car companion, never short on stories or wisdom to dispense. One of my duties during the "movie years" was to drive Colonel Parker from Palm Springs to Los Angeles, where he lived during the week. On Thursdays I'd fetch him and take him to the Hillcrest Country Club, where he had a standing weekly lunch with Abe Lastfogel, George Burns, Milton Berle, Red Buttons, and Jonathan Winters. I usually sat at the "kiddies' table" with the other men's personal assistants.

After lunch we'd drive back to Palm Springs so he could meet up with Abe at the Spa Hotel the following day. Any Elvis Presley movie business was conducted in the hotel's steam room. Abe and the Colonel could stay in there for a good hour, and they devised an ingenious way to deal with people making pitches to them. Most people can take about ten to fifteen minutes before they must get out, and with Abe and the Colonel smoking cigars in there, many didn't last that long. The ones who really wanted to make a deal found a way to keep breathing and pitching while red-faced, gasping, and dizzy.

One of my other jobs was to locate Marie's cats. They had a bad habit of getting out of the house. One night the Colonel also called the Palm Springs Police Department to aid me in my search. Officer Dick Grob arrived and saw me standing in the street. At first, he approached me with caution, but after I explained I was with Colonel Parker, he eased up. We managed to corral the cats and bring them back to Marie and the Colonel.

Because of how he handled himself, the Colonel remembered Dick and asked for his services again when Elvis and Priscilla were married and spent a few days at the Honeymoon House. Dick sat in a patrol car out front to keep away the paparazzi or anyone else who got any strange notions about invading their privacy.

"I was sitting out in front of the house in a police car that didn't have air conditioning," Grob recalled to the *Las Vegas Sun* in 1997. "This guy walks out of the house with a glass of lemonade, climbs into the car and said, 'Here, it looks like you need this.'"

Presley introduced himself, and the two men spent an hour bantering and listening to the police radio in the patrol car.

"He said, 'Come on in anytime you want more to drink.'"

The pair remained friends, and Grob visited whenever Elvis was in town vacationing.

"Had he not been an entertainer, I think he would have been in some sort of law enforcement," said Dick. "I think he was amazed at the brotherhood that exists among law enforcement people around the world. It transcends races, cultures, everything, much like his music did."

On one occasion there was a car accident at a major Palm Springs intersection near Windy Point. Traffic was at a standstill and Elvis, being the good citizen that he was, got out and started directing traffic. Naturally, his presence created more of a jam.

Elvis gravitated to Dick and wanted to go shooting with him when he was in town. Dick took him to the desert where they practiced, since the station did not have a shooting range. Elvis made a large donation to the department, and they constructed a state-of-the-art (for the time) firing range.

Dick became a trusted friend and associate of Elvis and the Colonel, and ultimately joined Elvis's security team. Later, he became head of security. Dick stayed with Elvis until the end and continued working for Graceland until 1980.

"It was the only job that wasn't a job," Dick said in reflection. "It was an opportunity that a lot of people would have died to have, and I appreciated it."

Elvis loved firearms and acquired an extensive gun collection. He purchased quite a few from a place called Tiny's Gun Shop on Industrial Place in Palm Springs. Tiny, who was actually a very large and jovial man, was introduced to Elvis through Dick.

Tiny would open his shop to Elvis at all hours to accommodate him, and not just to show him guns. The two men genuinely liked each other. On one visit other customers were roaming around the shop, including a young couple Elvis perceived didn't have much money. The young man was showing off a rifle to his girl, peering through the scope with one eye open. Elvis stepped over to them.

"Do you like the rifle?" Elvis asked. A little stunned that Elvis suddenly appeared in front of him, the young man answered, "I love it!" He then showed off the rifle's features to Elvis. When he finished talking, Elvis said, "It's yours."

One night in the early 1970s, Elvis asked me to take him to Germain Bros. Liquor & Food to pick up some soda and a pack of cigarillos. Elvis let me drive his black Stutz, an exquisite and rare automobile. When I pulled up to Germain's, there was one available spot to park, which was right in front. I drove up and slithered into the spot. Elvis was wearing a dark running suit, one of his huge belt buckles, an expensive gold chain draped around his neck, and aviator sunglasses. Elvis thought he was incognito, but that was ridiculous: How could he be?

Our timing was good, as Germain was about to close. Elvis found what he needed, and we stood in line. As we were waiting, I noticed a big lump in Elvis's pants, which slowly made its way from his waist to his ankle. Suddenly it dropped to the floor, making a loud clinking noise. Everybody stopped what they were doing to look at the .357 Magnum on the floor. Then they took two steps back.

The cashier, a young lady, put her hands up as if she were going to be robbed.

"No, no, no," I protested. "This is Elvis and his gun just fell out of his pants."

"Please don't shoot," she begged, putting her hands into the air. She obviously wasn't listening. This didn't go unnoticed by Elvis, who laughed hard.

The cashier wouldn't put her hands down. So, I picked up the gun and placed it on the counter to show her I wasn't going to use it, nor was she being robbed. Just then I noticed another young lady in the back secretly whispering into the receiver of their phone. Elvis was now beside himself.

"Greg, I'm just going to go wait in the car outside," he said, a big smile on his face.

By then I heard sirens in the distance and decided the best course of action was to leave some cash on the counter, take the gun back, and make a beeline toward the front door. When I got to the Stutz, Elvis was holding his sides. He was clearly enjoying this. Luckily, I pulled out of the parking lot and headed back to the Chino Canyon house without any fanfare. Had the Colonel ever found out, I feel certain he would have had me killed.

In my junior year of high school, I began making moves of my own. The first concert I ever promoted was Sonny and Cher in 1966. The occasion was the homecoming dance. I sat on the school's entertainment committee and was charged with booking the evening's entertainment. I had a $750 budget and called the William Morris Agency to see what that could get me. Turns out it was enough to book Sonny and Cher, but just barely. They were a couple of years past their "I Got You Babe" prime, but still a name act. And more important, met our budget.

I had a room reserved for them at the Ramada Inn—a decent enough place—but it wasn't good enough for Sonny. He wanted us to put them up in the Riviera Hotel, certainly the nicest place in Palm Springs at the time, but that just wasn't in our budget. When we finally met, we had a big screaming match. Two decades later, I ran Sonny's mayoral campaign. He had the memory of an elephant and recalled the incident when I brought it up. To Sonny's credit, he and Cher put on a helluva show, even for a high school homecoming.

Sonny and Cher were my entrée into the world of concert promotion, and from there I began booking and promoting shows in Palm Springs and San Bernardino. I booked shows for the Everly Brothers, Fats Domino, the Righteous Brothers, the Lettermen, Emmylou Harris, and Jim Stafford. My go-to place was the Mediterranean Showroom at the Riviera Hotel, which sat approximately six hundred people. The Colonel accompanied me on many of these shows, looking out into the crowd, estimating how many tickets I had sold. And he was usually right. The Colonel loved being around the action even if he wasn't calling the shots. He especially enjoyed watching his protégé in action. He was incredibly proud of me, but he was never short on advice either. ("You're not buying enough ads" or "Don't forget to advertise your oldies acts in the obituaries.")

And Colonel Parker never allowed me to rest on my laurels. He was forever asking, "What are you doing this month? You don't have a show set? Really? There's nothing going on in the Coachella Valley, and you don't have a show?" If the Colonel saw an empty showroom or building, he envisioned a place that could be filled with people. That's just how he operated. The Colonel constantly pushed me to do more, promote bigger shows, and be a mover and shaker.

I began booking so many shows and collecting decent paydays that

I didn't work for the Colonel during Elvis's touring years. He asked me to work for him, but I couldn't take the pay cut. I made much more than the guys on Elvis's payroll booking and promoting my own shows.

The Colonel accepted and respected my decision not to work for him, but I remained in his inner circle for the rest of his life. And that was better than money in the bank.

16

Aloha from Hawaii

In late February 1972, President Richard Nixon made a historic trip to China in an effort to ease long-term tensions and hostilities after years of diplomatic isolation. Not only did this visit strengthen Chinese-American relations, but it also served to encourage progress with the USSR.

I was driving Colonel Parker from Los Angeles to Palm Springs as we listened to a radio broadcast of this event, live via satellite from China. The Colonel's mind went into overdrive as he learned about this new technology, which would allow people to hear and see someone around the world on radio and television. He blurted the first thing that came to his mind.

"What a great way for people everywhere to see and hear Elvis!" he said.

He knew a show by satellite could make entertainment history and Elvis was the perfect worldwide star to pull it off.

But how do you achieve something that has never been done before? I have been around lots of wealthy and influential people. Many of them come up with great ideas such as these, but 99.9 percent of them never get off the drawing board. If they do, there is a team of people doing the nuts and bolts to pull it off. Colonel Parker was a one-man show. He was among that .01 percent who worked tirelessly to realize his vision. This idea, he felt, could be very big . . . but it would need some more thought.

The world was changing, and so was Elvis. Elvis and Priscilla were separated and talk of a divorce was making headlines everywhere. He had been living under the age-old male belief that the husband could play around, but the wife was to stay home and remain faithful and raise their child. Despite Elvis's infidelities, Priscilla had remained faithful for years. She'd finally had enough and told Elvis she was leaving him. He did not take it well, but he was about to meet the wonderful Linda Thompson, who was his main girlfriend for the next four years. Linda and I are friends to this day. Linda's brother, Sam, had worked as a sheriff's deputy before he became Elvis's bodyguard in July 1976. Sam was a trusted friend of Elvis's, and the two men spent hours singing gospel songs together on tour. After Elvis's passing, Sam attended law school and became a very successful lawyer and judge. Later he became a member of the Nevada Transmission Authority and the Public Utilities Commission. Sam was also a warden of a prison for a spell, which is ironic because he's the sweetest guy in the world. He and his wife, Louise, are close friends of mine, and we stay in touch and travel together to Elvis-related events. After his legal career, Sam started a record label with music impresario David Foster, which they later sold to Warner Music. Linda and Sam were two of the few people in Elvis's inner circle who did not do drugs and tried to help Elvis with his addiction. Sam believes, despite all of Elvis's success, deep down he remained humble if not a bit insecure.

"Elvis used to sit up nights and wonder why he had become the King and someone else had not—someone like Jerry Lee. He really did ponder on this issue cosmically: 'Why me?'" Sam said. "He knew he was talented, and he was good looking, and at the right place at the right time. But there were a lot of others out there too. He truly felt humbled by that. He never truly came to grips with it."

The relationship between Colonel Parker and Management III Productions was growing strained. The Colonel was aware that Weintraub was using his power with the Elvis tour to promote his own artist, John

Denver. The Colonel insisted that no other artist ever ride on Elvis's coattails, and Jerry was really pushing the boundaries. The Colonel often spotted Weintraub stepping outside the offices and conducting business that had nothing to do with Elvis. Weintraub also invited other artists he was trying to sign to Elvis's concerts to show off his relationship with the star.

In the world of show business, what Weintraub was doing was an accepted practice, but that did not fly with the Colonel. He was growing more agitated with the situation and Weintraub's swelling ego.

When on tour, Jerry was often on the phone handling his personal affairs and not taking care of business. When their private jet was ready to leave, they'd have to wait while someone ran to get Jerry off the airport phone. The Colonel was also getting reports that Jerry was difficult. The Colonel waited until the tour was over to make his move.

The contract for Elvis's winter tour in November was signed on September 12, listing only three names: Elvis, the Colonel, and RCA Records. Management III Productions was not going to be involved.

With his load lightened, the Colonel was free to think. And he was thinking a lot about turning the satellite idea into reality. He contacted NBC president Tom Sarnoff about selling the show to countries all over the world, and Sarnoff got it done. The eventual tally was thirty-eight countries plus the British protectorate of Hong Kong. The special was not broadcast in Russia, China, Africa, South America, the Middle East, or South Asia.

Parker and Sarnoff set a tentative concert date for November 18 at the end of Presley's winter tour, but it was scrapped at the request of MGM president Jim Aubrey. Wisely, he wanted to avoid the special overlapping with the theatrical release of *Elvis On Tour*, which was scheduled for November 1. He wanted to protect the $1.6 million investment his studio made, which won the award for Best Documentary Film at the 30th Golden Globe Awards the following year. The Colonel agreed to push the special back a few months.

A date was finally set for the satellite show on January 14, 1973; a charity was announced (the Kui Lee Cancer Fund), and a name was given to the special: *Aloha from Hawaii*.

The special also came with a hefty paycheck: Elvis was paid $900,000 (equivalent to $6 million in 2022) from NBC for a one-hour concert.

Before the historic concert was announced in September 1972, at a press conference in Las Vegas, Colonel Parker issued an announcement that outlined several of what he called historic "firsts" for the broadcast:

- This would be the first live concert to be broadcast in its entirety worldwide via satellite.
- This would be the largest audience ever to witness a concert, with expectations "in excess of one billion people."
- This would be the first time in the history of the record industry that an album would be released worldwide simultaneously.

Elvis made an appearance at the press conference with RCA president Rocco Laginestra, who flew in for the event.

"What are we going to say, Colonel?" he asked.

"Rocco, you'll think of something when the time comes," the Colonel replied.

The afternoon conference took place on the Hilton's thirtieth floor inside the Crown Room, which boasted a panoramic view of the entire western Las Vegas valley. The small stage featured a floor-to-ceiling display of fifty of Elvis's Summer Festival straw hats, each with the name of a major foreign country. The media attending the event had no idea what it all meant but would soon find out.

Elvis, sporting a white high-collared suit, aviator sunglasses, and longer-than-usual hair, sat next to Laginestra with the Colonel off to the side. Rocco announced, using RCA's recently unveiled GlobCom satellite and accompanying technology, that Elvis would appear live in Honolulu, Hawaii, and would be seen in virtually every major country in the world either live or on tape delay. Laginestra caused quite a stir when he announced to the attending media this special event would draw more than a billion people from around the planet, instantly making it one of the biggest entertainment events of the twentieth century.

Colonel Parker had scored another first and was giving the world an opportunity to see the world's number one superstar without ever having to leave American soil. Elvis was sweaty and looked distracted.

"How do you pace yourself, so you're up when you need to be up?" a reporter asked.

"I exercise every day, and I vocalize every day," Elvis replied. He may have been slightly exaggerating on that first part. He was tipping the scales at a hefty 195 pounds at that point, which didn't go unnoticed.

NBC named Marty Pasetta as the special's producer-director. He had produced broadcasts of the Oscars, Emmys, and Grammys. He had also helmed *The Smothers Brothers Comedy Hour, The Glen Campbell Goodtime Hour, The Andy Williams Show* and Don Ho's five TV specials, which were highly popular in their day and also filmed on location in Hawaii.

Pasetta did his homework and attended Elvis's Long Beach concert on November 15. He walked away from the show disappointed, feeling Elvis's performance was flat and uninspired.

"He stood there like a lump," Pasetta remembered. "He didn't do anything. I went back to NBC and said, 'Hey, guys, what am I going to do with this guy? How long is the show? Ninety minutes? I can't tap dance that much. It doesn't look like he's going to move.' They said, 'That's your problem.'"

When Pasetta finally met Elvis at Graceland, with his armed bodyguards hovering close by, they spoke for nearly four hours. He spoke about his vision for the show, which included an eighty-foot runway six feet off the ground so Elvis could walk down the center of the audience and have women coo at him. But that presented a problem, not with Elvis, but with the Colonel, Pasetta recalled.

"The Colonel always had the stage ten feet above the floor, and he had guards across the front. He didn't want to have anybody touch his boy," Pasetta said. "When I told this to the Colonel, he had a fit. He said, 'I'm not lowering the stage. I'm going to have my guards there, and he can stand there and sing.' I said, 'That's not going to work on the tube for an hour and a half show.' He said, 'No. I won't do it. You can't do the show.'"

But Pasetta said Presley loved his ideas and, in one of the few instances in his career, he overruled Colonel Parker.

"Elvis said to me, 'The Colonel controls my business. I control my creativity and my music and my show. He has nothing to say about it. That's your rule. You will deal with Joe Esposito,' who was sort of a go-between," Pasetta said. "I talked to Joe, the Colonel . . . everybody. But I tried not to deal too much with the Colonel. I had enough problems getting the show on."

One of the last things Pasetta told Elvis in their marathon meeting was that he needed to drop about twenty pounds. Pasetta said the room went eerily quiet.

"He [Elvis] sat straight, and the guys on either side of him took out their guns and laid them down on the table," said Pasetta. "And if you don't think I was scared, you're crazy."

Pasetta needed Elvis skinny because he was going to film him up close, from his neck to the top of his head. He said he was shooting close because it would capture Elvis's true sex appeal for the camera. All well and good, but he still didn't know how Elvis would react to his bluntness.

"He jumped out his chair. He grabbed me, put his arms around me and said, 'You're the first person who was ever honest to me,'" Pasetta said.

But the goal was easier said than done. A decade earlier—no sweat. But now Elvis was thirty-eight years old, and his metabolism had obviously slowed. But he gave Pasetta his word and Elvis planned to keep it.

Elvis immediately went on a strict diet where he drank lots of protein drinks and boiled minuscule portions of protein and vegetables in hot water. He also went on long daily jogs and extended karate workouts. The diet also included daily injections of protein taken from the urine of a pregnant woman to burn up fat in the system. He wasn't allowed to use anything with fat in it, including lotions, shaving creams, and shampoos.

To Elvis's credit, he stuck with the regimen and lost the weight, about twenty-five pounds in all. He looked great, and he arrived in Hawaii a few days before the concert in fighting shape. All he had to do now was get a tan, not a problem in the Aloha State.

Elvis had a very special relationship with Hawaii and her people, and they responded in kind. When he landed at the airport, he was taken by helicopter to the Hilton Hawaiian Village hotel where hundreds of fans welcomed their hero. Hula dancers swung their hips. Girls in bikinis hugged him, and so many leis were placed around his neck that you could barely see his face. He loved it, of course, but was a little tense. He would be performing live before an estimated billion and a half people around the globe, and he wanted everything to go smoothly.

Things didn't go so smoothly with Loanne who, for some reason, didn't know about the pre-trip to Hawaii. She just landed in Los Angeles, and an agent was waiting for her at the gate. A few minutes later the Colonel approached.

"Hurry," he said, "we don't have much time to catch our flight."

"What flight?" asked a puzzled Loanne.

"The flight to Hawaii," the Colonel said in an exasperated tone.

"But I didn't pack for Hawaii," she wailed.

"Look, if you want to go with us, you had better hurry," the Colonel replied as he turned and walked briskly toward the departure gate. "You can buy what you need when we get there."

Loanne followed along and, upon arrival in Hawaii, had a great time buying muumuus and other island clothes and accessories. It was her first time in Hawaii, and she recalled it as a "very special trip."

Elvis worked hard in rehearsals and had his performance down cold. He had his hair restyled by friend Patti Parry and had designer Bill Belew go to work on a look that would scream, "America!" to the world. Bill—and Gene Doucette, who did the embroidery and design—came up with a white jumpsuit and cape emblazoned with gold studs and approximately 650 red, white, and blue rhinestones on the front and back in the design of an American eagle.

Elvis held a rehearsal show on Friday, January 12, at the Honolulu Convention Center with approximately six thousand people in attendance. Their enthusiasm wasn't blunted by the technical issues experienced by the TV and satellite crew.

"Because it's live, that adds the element of tension," said Phil Arnone, a program director at the time. "Knowing that you only get the one shot, you can't re-tape a number or change anything. You shoot it as it happens. A mistake, a camera shot that is wrong, or a button pushed wrong, or Elvis is flat, you live with all of that because it is a live broadcast. . . . Everyone gets kind of puckered up in that situation."

It got even hairier the next day, which was the day before the show. Someone had cut a few of the power lines going into the venue. Pasetta called his friend Don Ho, who was the most powerful man on the island, and he got the problem fixed within a few hours.

On the day of the show, it was discovered the backstage equipment was creating a humming sound. Pasetta called Ho again who told him to call the navy yard.

"We had a truckload of lead sheets that were brought over two hours before the show, and we lined them up and got our sound back," Pasetta said.

The special, which cost NBC $2.5 million to produce, was filmed on January 14 at 12:30 A.M., to be beamed live to other countries around the world in prime time. (The special wasn't broadcast live in the United States and Canada to avoid a programming conflict with Super Bowl VII. Instead, NBC aired it on April 4, after additional songs and island footage were added to make it a ninety-minute program.)

It was a blockbuster show that proved Elvis Presley was still the King. He came out for an hour and rocked the universe with a powerhouse performance that was beamed out to an estimated 1.5 billion people. He smiled at the audience, locking eyes with them, obviously enjoying himself. He was on fire.

To put it into proper perspective, for a moment in time, a quarter of the world's population stopped what they were doing to watch an Elvis concert. This blew the doors off the Beatles' famous appearance on *The Ed Sullivan Show* in 1964. It was a Herculean achievement that hasn't been duplicated in nearly fifty years.

The special was NBC's highest-rated show of the year and drew rave reviews (*Billboard* wrote that Elvis "dominated the tube with showmanship") across the board. It also raised $75,000 for the Kui Lee Cancer Fund, surpassing its original anticipated amount by $50,000. Elvis led in the giving by paying $1,000 for his ticket.

The soundtrack became Elvis's first number one long player in eight years, topping both the pop and country album charts. RCA employed two record plants full-time to rush-release the quadraphonic album to retail stores three weeks after the concert. It paid off. *Aloha from Hawaii Via Satellite* has sold more than five million copies and is still selling.

The day after the concert, Elvis was supposed to visit the USS *Arizona*—the World War II vessel he refurbished in 1961 with the help of Colonel Parker—with his crew. Sonny, Red West, Marty Lacker, and Joe Esposito went to Elvis's suite at the Hilton Hawaiian Village hotel. The men knocked on the door at the appointed time, getting no response. Finally, Linda Thompson answered the door with a look of dismay on her face.

"He can't go anywhere," she said, shaking her head. One by one, they all went inside, spotting Elvis on the couch, his head lolling back. There was a towel around his neck, and he was sweating profusely. On occasion, they had seen him like this before, specifically in Vegas. When he greeted them, he was slurring his words and could barely keep his eyes open. Their hearts sank. He was seriously messed up.

"Well, I guess we won't be doing anything with him," someone piped up.

"No, it doesn't look like it," said Linda, who looked crestfallen.

The day after one of the greatest performances in entertainment history should have been a moment to savor. Instead, it was marred by an addiction that was just getting revved up.

And Colonel Parker, the man who could move mountains, and often did for his star client, was helpless. Parker could fix anything, but this was something he had no idea how to deal with. He couldn't force Elvis to deal with it. The Colonel has been wrongly accused of enabling Elvis's drug habit. It's utterly ridiculous. Why would he kill a cash cow? And he wasn't cleaning up after him or apologizing for him.

At least not yet.

17

T-R-O-U-B-L-E

Since his live comeback of '69, Elvis Presley had worked almost nonstop; his output of studio work and live performances was unmatched by any other artist of his era. James Brown billed himself as "the hardest working man in show business," but he had nothing on Elvis. Instead of winding down after *Aloha from Hawaii*, Elvis cranked things up a notch in 1973. He performed 168 shows that year—the most of his career. He continued grinding it out because he needed the money, and perhaps he felt obligated to the 112 people he kept on the payroll. Elvis was loyal to everyone in his sphere, which is why they loved him so much. The reality was, he needed to take a nice long break. Not only did he deserve it, but his body must have been begging for the rest.

In late January, Elvis opened his eighth engagement at the Hilton. Even though he still looked trim and fit from his recent weight loss, several critics noted that his energy level was low, and some of his shows lacked zip. His voice was also faltering, and he soon began developing throat problems thanks to the dry Vegas air. He canceled both of his shows on January 31 as well as the late show on February 1. Almost two weeks later, on February 13, history was about to repeat itself. That night Colonel Parker was called into Elvis's dressing room. He told his manager that he couldn't do the show. The Colonel sat down and addressed both Elvis and his father, Vernon Presley, who was on hand.

"The problem is we should have notified the hotel long before now," the Colonel started off. "People are already seated in the showroom and have been served dinner. But, if you can't go on, you can't. Your father will just have to go out and make an announcement."

Vernon paled.

"Son, you can do the show," Vernon said. "I'm not going to go out on that stage and tell people you aren't going to perform. I just can't. Elvis, you must do the show."

He listened to his father. Elvis went out and performed the evening show but canceled the midnight performance. He canceled the second performance on the 14th as well. He started the dinner show on January 15 and performed two songs before he walked off the stage and took the elevator down to his dressing room. The Colonel rushed downstairs and found his star lying on the couch.

"I can't finish the show," Elvis exclaimed. "I just can't."

While the two men talked, the showroom speakers were turned on in the dressing room. They could hear J. D. Sumner and the Stamps and Charlie Hodge performing their comedy routines. Onstage, the rest of the crew didn't know what was going on. They were just trying to keep things going the best they could. After about ten minutes, the Colonel said, "Elvis, just listen to that applause. Your fans love the Stamps' singing. They're all doing a great job." The continued applause got Elvis's juices going. He finally jumped up off the couch.

"I'm feeling a lot better," Elvis declared. "I think I can finish the show."

Elvis ran back onstage and finished what he started. However, he made sure management announced in advance there would be no midnight performance. He completed the engagement as scheduled on Friday, February 23, 1973, but it took almost all his energy to cross the finish line.

Elvis was back at Graceland recuperating when Vernon called the Colonel with a major problem: his son's spending was out of control again and had put a major dent in their bank account. His extravagance was well known. He would lavish gifts on his friends and their wives and give away new cars by the truckload. The same went for furs and expensive jewelry to complete strangers. Graceland itself was a major expense, as were his boys, not to mention Uncle Sam, who was taking a big bite out of his earnings. And with his marriage to Priscilla coming to an end, an expensive divorce settlement was looming ahead.

Priscilla's attorney, Arthur Toll, got her a settlement for an outright cash payment of $725,000 and $4,200 a month in spousal support for a year, plus $6,000 a month for ten years. Priscilla would also receive $4,000 a month in child support and half the price of the sale of their Hillcrest home, as well as 5 percent of Elvis's publishing company. The divorce would cost him about $1.5 million. It was not an unreasonable request given that the two had been together for over a dozen years and had a child together.

Elvis didn't fight the deal because he didn't want any public speculation that he didn't have the money. But the truth of the matter was he really *didn't* have the money then and was forced to make a shortsighted business decision.

For some time, RCA, Elvis's recording label, had been after Colonel Parker to sell all the rights to Elvis's back catalog. His royalties generated around $500,000 annually through repackaging and other artists' covers of his songs. Back then, nobody envisioned CDs, downloads, streaming services, or any technology that supplanted vinyl, but RCA knew how valuable backlists were and offered Elvis $5.4 million for his entire output of recordings.

Vernon had already opened negotiations with RCA to all records Elvis made prior to February 28, 1973. When negotiations hit a snag, he came to the Colonel in Palm Springs to ask him to complete the deal. I was at the house, but not in the same room when this occurred. And the money wasn't just about paying off Priscilla. Elvis revealed he would also lose Graceland.

The Colonel objected on the grounds that the "old catalog"—how Colonel Parker referred to it—was Elvis's annuity and shouldn't be messed with. Besides, he didn't feel RCA was offering enough and that Elvis was practically giving it away. Stars do it all the time now;

Bob Dylan, Bruce Springsteen, Stevie Nicks, and David Bowie (whose estate sold his catalog to Warner Music in 2020) have all sold off their back catalogs, but they did it at the end of their careers. Elvis was not yet forty, and his career was nowhere near over.

Elvis held firm on the matter and wasn't budging.

"Colonel, if you don't do it, I'll just get Ed," Elvis said, referring to his personal attorney, Ed Hookstratten, who represented a who's who of entertainers (Johnny Carson), newscasters (Jessica Savitch) and sports figures (Marcus Allen). I remember sitting with Tom Diskin in another room in Colonel Parker's Palm Springs home, and Tom had his eyes closed and just shook his head. He knew making that deal was extremely shortsighted. It was the only time I ever saw Tom disapprove of something that Elvis did.

The Colonel, at the behest of Elvis, went ahead with the negotiations. He truly felt Elvis's best years were ahead of him, and he would still receive the royalties from those. What no one could foresee was that Elvis would never have another top-selling album or single, and after four years, there would be no more recording, period.

Ultimately, the loser was Lisa Marie (and her heirs), who eventually inherited the estate when she turned twenty-five. Even though Elvis's estate generates millions a year, they own the singer's recordings from only 1973 to 1977. The bulk of his recording material goes right into the pockets of RCA.

On March 1, 1973, there were five separate contracts signed between Elvis Presley and RCA president Rocco Laginesta. The Colonel signed the first four while George Parkhill signed just the third document.

The initial contract stated that for all the master recordings made prior to February 28, 1973, RCA would pay $5 million, one half to Elvis Presley and one half to All Star Shows. In addition, as final settlement of Elvis's record contract of monies held in a guaranteed account on royalties due on sales prior to February 28, RCA would pay $400,000, with $300,000 going to Elvis and $100,000 to All Star Shows.

Contract number two stated that for a period of five years, Colonel Tom Parker would serve as a consultant to RCA Records and assist in the exploration of merchandising rights for an annual payment of $10,000.

The third contract called for the Colonel to (a) assist RCA Records Tours in planning, promotion, and merchandising in connection with the Tour Agreement and (b) assist RCA in planning, promotion, and merchandising in connection with records under the Record Agreement. For these services, the Colonel would receive $75,000 for the first full year and $100,000 for each full year succeeding the first year while the term of the Tour Agreement was in effect. No payments more than $675,000 were to be made. As additional compensation for services furnished, RCA would pay an amount equal to 10 percent of RCA Records Tours net profit.

In the fourth contract, All Star Shows would be paid $50,000 for each such contract year.

Contract number five was an agreement between Elvis and RCA Records for seven years, commencing March 1, 1973. It stated that Elvis would record two albums and four singles per year. For each single, the royalty rate would be fifty cents a copy. For each double album, the royalty rate was one dollar. For any single record sold on their budget label, the rate would be twenty cents, and for any double album sold on the budget label, the rate would be forty cents.

The foreign royalty rates for any single or album sold on the top-price label would be 9 percent of the retail list; on the budget label, the rate doubled to forty cents.

RCA Records also guaranteed Elvis that the royalties accruing each year would not be less than $500,000. All monies were directed by Elvis to be paid 50 percent to Elvis Presley and 50 percent to All Star Shows. The royalty rates paid to Elvis at the time were top dollar. Few people were aware that Elvis's recording costs were *not* deducted from his royalty payments like other major entertainers. This was unheard of in the recording industry at that time and was just another example of the Colonel's astute business negotiations.

When the tour wrapped up in Denver on April 30, 1973, everyone headed to Lake Tahoe for another engagement. It was a time for celebration as George Parkhill had just been appointed vice president of RCA Records Tours.

The seventeen-day Tahoe engagement in May did not go well. The strain from Elvis's separation from Priscilla and the impending divorce was starting to show. Elvis showed up about thirty pounds overweight and was experiencing breathing problems. He had several respiratory treatments and even hired a masseur to pound on his back and break up mucus collecting in his lungs. Many nights he was getting only a few hours' sleep. When he couldn't sleep, he had a doctor come to the hotel and give him a double dose of Valium. (Dr. Nick had a practice in Memphis and couldn't always go on the road with Elvis. Besides, Elvis was a doctor-shopper. If someone couldn't supply him with what he wanted, he simply picked up the phone and called another doctor. At one time he seriously considered buying a pharmacy to keep his supply steady.)

The hotel wasn't faring so well either. The telephone lines were jammed with show reservation requests and the hotel inadvertently overbooked many of the shows. When seventy people with reservations showed up for the early shows, they were turned away and promised seating for the second performance, but didn't get in for that one either. The problem just snowballed.

Elvis had had enough and threw in the towel. He canceled his engagement on May 16 because of illness, five days short of completion. Elvis received his two-third share of the proceeds from the engagement, or $140,000. The Colonel received his one-third share, $70,000. Because Elvis did not complete his scheduled engagement, the Colonel waived the $100,000 promotion fee for All Star Shows. The actual promotion cost was $25,000, which was split between All Star Shows and the Sahara Tahoe. The Colonel never took advantage of situations like this, and always tried his best to see that everyone came out well. He had a strong sense of fairness, which is often overlooked.

On May 19, the Colonel received a letter of thanks from Monty

Hundley, vice president and general manager of the Sahara Tahoe. It praised him as "the most honorable man in show business" for his handling of this prickly situation. Hundley wrote that his association with Colonel Parker "has been one of the highlights of my career in this business."

During the final days of the Tahoe engagement, Elvis and his father learned about the lump sum payment that Priscilla sought as part of her upcoming divorce settlement. Elvis was ranting about how unfair she was being and how she had turned on him. The Colonel calmly told him, "Elvis, just where do you think she had learned these things? There could be only one place. She was a child when she came to live with you, and she learned from watching you and what you did. What you are seeing now is just a reflection of your actions with her."

The comment angered Elvis, and it was the last time they spoke of the divorce settlement.

Elvis was becoming more erratic, and it showed in his performances on the road. One night he'd be fabulous and the next night he would sleepwalk through his set. There was always tension because no one knew what to expect day-to-day.

It was becoming more and more obvious to everyone that Elvis had a serious problem with prescription drugs. For years, the Colonel had refused to believe it. The situation was not unlike a wife who suspects her husband of having an affair. She sees the lipstick on the collar and other signs of infidelity but refuses to believe it. She simply does not want to think about what she would do if her marriage ended, therefore she goes into denial and in her mind the affair doesn't exist. The Colonel was always a very positive person and ready to expect the best to happen while at the same time worrying about what might occur. However, by mid-1973, the Colonel had accepted the fact that there was, indeed, a serious problem, and he didn't know how to deal with it. He knew Elvis well enough to know that he had a strong personality and would not allow anyone to talk to him about it or attempt to tell him what to do. The men who worked with Elvis daily, including his own father, could see the direction he was going but couldn't do a thing about it. The boys, including Red West and Sonny West, were told that if they didn't like the way things were, they could leave.

Through the years following Elvis's death, outsiders have blamed the Colonel, Vernon, and Elvis's entourage for not helping him. The only person who can help someone with a problem like Elvis had is the one with the problem. Without self-motivation, no one can overcome an addiction, no matter what form it might take. Everyone around Elvis tried their best to help him and their incredible loyalty should be applauded instead of criticized. It was something they could not control.

The Colonel was becoming more and more distraught with the situation. Many times, he would come back to the room after trying to talk to Elvis, and tell Loanne, "He is so cunning that he doesn't want me to see him when he is in really bad shape, and when he does see me, he knows that I know. He also realized that I can't do anything without a confrontation and that wouldn't help. It would only make the problem worse."

The Colonel got so frustrated that tears would well up in his eyes. He and Elvis had been through so much and had come such a distance together; he was now unable to help Elvis, try as he may.

The Colonel dictated a letter to Elvis on July 12, 1973, couching in the nicest terms possible, now that the tour was over, he might want to think of some new ideas for his upcoming Las Vegas Hilton engagement. He said that it was perhaps time for a new opening as well as an overhaul of the show. The Colonel was essentially telling Elvis his Vegas show was getting stale and that it wasn't just his opinion, but the opinion of others as well. The Colonel also reminded Elvis that during his last Vegas and Tahoe engagements, five performances were missed and the Hilton went ahead and covered them financially, and he still owed them. Colonel Parker, as always, ended the letter on a positive note but telling Elvis, "Without a doubt you are by far the greatest artist I have ever known and can be even greater if you just believe in yourself half as much as I believe in you."

I'm sure when Elvis read that letter, it stung a little. But it probably paled in comparison to the moment when Elvis climbed the steps of the Los Angeles Superior Courthouse in Santa Monica in October 1973. The occasion was the finalization of his divorce. He hated the idea of ending a marriage, but no longer wanted it hanging over his head.

Twenty minutes later, he and Priscilla came strolling out of the courthouse holding hands and smiled for the waiting press. They hugged and exchanged goodbyes. As she walked away, she turned back to wave. He winked back. They handled this difficulty like true adults.

Elvis was about to embark on a new chapter in his life. I don't want to ruin it for you, but it wasn't going to have a happy ending. The Aloha concert, only ten months before, was to be the zenith of one of the most incredible entertainment careers in American history. If the Colonel had had a crystal ball, he would have urged his boy to retire after that show and exit the stage of public life as gracefully as possible. But ultimately Elvis's story is a tragedy.

18

Prescription for Disaster

After the Tahoe engagement, attorney Ed Hookstratten hired John O'Grady to find out who supplied Elvis with the pills he was taking. O'Grady, a former Los Angeles Police Department narcotics cop turned private detective who did investigations for Hookstratten, reported back to Ed, Vernon, and the Colonel that it was mainly the doctors George Nichopoulos and Elias Ghanem, and the dentist, Max Shapiro.

Between the three of them, Elvis was getting industrial-sized bottles of prescription pills. On one of the labels was a handwritten notation by Dr. Nichopoulos: "to keep sanity."

Many people have pointed to Elvis's divorce from Priscilla as the catalyst for his unraveling, but there was so much more that was going on. No doubt the divorce and the breakup of his family played a role, but so did his declining health, weight gain, and growing lack of interest in his career after peaking on *Elvis: Aloha from Hawaii*. However, the common denominator linking all those things was his escalating abuse of prescription medication.

Bodyguard Sonny West discovered that a prescription in his one-year-old son's name was being filled for Elvis at Schwab's Pharmacy at Sunset Boulevard and Laurel Canyon in Los Angeles. Sonny suspected it was prescribed by Max Shapiro. In Memphis, Elvis's Aunt Delta handed Sonny a package from Elias Ghanem from Las Vegas. He opened the bag and found two plastic bottles with approximately five hundred pain pills in each container. They were still sealed from the manufacturer.

Even with those issues now at the surface, on July 23 Elvis and the Colonel signed a new contract with the Las Vegas Hilton for 1974 and 1975, calling for two fifteen-day engagements a year, each consisting of nineteen performances. Elvis had previously been doing two shows a night for four weeks. The contract called for $150,000 per week with a reduced advertising budget of $75,000 per engagement.

Why in the world would Colonel Parker continue doing business with a man in the throes of an addiction? Remember, these were the days before the Betty Ford Center opened in 1982 and began the long road to destigmatizing addiction. Most of the public, including Colonel Parker, had no clue about how to deal with this pressing issue. I can't speak for the Colonel, but my best guess would be that he figured Elvis was better off working than being back at Graceland spending all day in his bedroom zonked out on pills. If he could work, maybe he would have a moment of clarity and see all the good things in his life and turn it around.

On Monday, July 30, the Colonel and his staff moved into the Las Vegas Hilton to begin preparations for the Summer Festival '73 starting on August 6. The Colonel arranged for the Girls Club of Southern Nevada to run the souvenir booth and receive the proceeds.

The Colonel and his entire staff attended Elvis's opening show to see how he behaved. It wasn't good. For the first few nights he either sleepwalked through his shows or goofed off on stage. At one point he tried to beg off performing, claiming he had the flu. Doctors were not able to confirm this, and he had to agree that he was able to perform. It was becoming more obvious every night that his problem was getting worse. The Colonel and Vernon met to discuss what they could do to help him. "Vernon," the Colonel said, taking a serious tone, "we may have to take him off the road if it gets any worse. Tell him that and maybe that will be incentive enough to get him off this stuff." Several times during the engagement he was on stage for forty-five minutes or less. Many of the fans assumed that Hilton management had told him to shorten his show to get them back into the casino earlier, but this was totally untrue. Wayne Newton, for example, used to appear on stage for two hours or longer with no complaints from management.

During the engagement, Linda Thompson was by Elvis's side and took Lisa Marie to several shows with her. Linda tried to be a positive influence on Elvis, as anyone close to the situation will attest. She did everything she could to make his life better and helped him in every way she could. There was no doubt in anyone's mind that Linda was in love with Elvis and stayed with him until she saw there was nothing more she could do.

The problems concerning his show continued. Fans were getting rowdy, trying to climb onstage many nights. There were also technical issues with his microphones and the sound system, which annoyed Elvis greatly. He did continue to compliment Joe Guercio and his orchestra, however, always recognizing their talent whether in Las Vegas or on the road.

Elvis usually left all his business dealings to either the Colonel or his father. But when he did something on his own, it was usually a doozy. For some reason, he decided to sign the gospel singing group Voice—Donnie Sumner, Sherrill Nielsen, and Tim Baty—to a personal management contract during the Summer Festival in 1973, giving Elvis exclusive rights to the group for recording, rehearsals, arrangements, and writing new material.

The contract stated that all new songs written by the group would be submitted to Elvis Presley Music for publishing and recording. As talented as they were, they had never recorded as a trio and had never written anything of note. They could also book their own personal appearances and concerts, with Elvis receiving no commission, which made no sense. The contract called for them to receive $50,000 a year for two years.

The Colonel took it all in stride and, in fact, had his office type up copies of the agreement that Elvis had written out in long hand. In his letter accompanying the contract, the Colonel did add one final paragraph: "Although I personally would not have made this kind of agreement, I respect your desire to handle this yourself. I am, however, always available to you if you need me for advice."

On Monday, September 3, Elvis agreed to do a special 3:00 A.M. performance to allow other entertainers appearing in Las Vegas to see him. Hilton management gave Elvis an expensive piece of jewelry in appreciation. Just prior to that, an employee named Mario, who worked in the hotel's Italian restaurant, had been terminated. He used to bring food up to Elvis's suite, and they had become friendly. When Elvis found out about Mario being fired, he became very upset. He was venting his wrath before he went on stage for his final performance. The Colonel advised him that whatever the hotel did regarding one of their employees was really none of Elvis's business. Of course, Elvis didn't like hearing that, but it was only common sense not to anger the people signing your paychecks.

The Colonel and his entire staff attended the closing show. From the stage Elvis began to rant about the incident, making derogatory comments about Hilton management, including Barron Hilton himself. Elvis was completely out of line. The Colonel turned to Loanne and said, "I've never been so embarrassed in my life. I want to crawl under the table. I can't believe he just said that. Who does he think he is? How am I ever going to face the Hilton people? He can't get away with this."

The Colonel could be volatile at times and had a hair-trigger temper, especially during the touring years, but that night he was more upset than I had ever seen him before. His entire body was shaking with rage.

"I've had it!" he exclaimed. "I've put up with this nonsense for years, but this is too much. No more. Either he straightens out or we're finished. If he can't stop taking those damn pills, then there is nothing more I can do and I'm getting out. I don't need this crap. I'm quitting."

It was practically World War III that night in the dressing room after the show. The two men raged at each other for what seemed like hours. The Colonel usually gave into Elvis on most matters, but this time he was determined, and didn't feel it was worth the pressure and agony any longer. The Colonel stormed out and returned to the fourth floor.

The next morning, September 4, 1973, he dictated a letter to Loanne for Elvis to read. The Colonel got right to the point by telling Elvis that he had embarrassed Hilton Corporation executives with his little outburst, in front of two thousand people, no less. He told Elvis that he was completely out of line, pointing out that the Hilton had given him major considerations in the past—knocking thousands of dollars off his food, beverage, and suite over the years, and as much as $20,000 on that particular engagement. The Colonel reminded Elvis that they are not judge and jury, but performers and "have a job to do on that stage" without getting involved with hotel employees. Colonel Parker felt that it was unfair of this employee to take his personal problems to him, and that Elvis, in retrospect, would come to understand that he was used in this matter.

Colonel Parker left the letter with Joe Esposito and told him that he wanted to see Elvis when he got up that evening. At midnight he had not heard from him, so the Colonel went to bed. An hour later George Parkhill knocked on his door, saying that he had just received a call from Elvis, announcing that if the Colonel didn't come up to his suite, he was coming down to the Colonel's room. The Colonel quickly dressed and, with George, went up to the thirtieth floor. It was another blowout argument with Elvis threatening to fire the Colonel. An hour later he was back in his room and awakened Loanne.

"Come into the office, please. I have dictation for you," he said.

They worked in the office until 7:30 A.M., when Loanne announced she was going back to bed. She returned to the office three hours later to resume the letter addressed to Vernon Presley. It was alarmingly detached and to the point. The Colonel stated effectively at 1 A.M. on Wednesday, September 5, 1973, he had tendered his resignation with the understanding of a flat settlement on the balance of all contracts in existence. If the settlement was concluded, it would dissolve any and all personal management relationships of any nature for the future,

Prescription for Disaster

and he would make this turnover of Colonel Parker / All Star Shows management as convenient as possible.

Colonel Parker signed the agreement, but it was never returned with Elvis's signature. A cold hard blast of reality blew through the Imperial Suite on the thirtieth floor. The two memos were like incoming nuclear missiles. The boy king had been called on his bluff. Elvis knew the Colonel didn't fool around, but that intensity now had been turned in a direction Elvis never imagined—toward him. The only person in the world who held the line between reality and the bubble he lived in had just burst the bubble.

The same afternoon the Colonel sent another letter to Elvis, asking for him to select one of two settlements he proposed, then sign and date, and their business would be finished. The Colonel was pressing Elvis hard for an answer, ending the letter, "I wish you lots of luck, and I will surely respect the privacy of the confidential nature regarding which of the two settlements is made."

When Colonel Parker didn't hear back from Elvis, he sent him a third letter on September 6. He was clearly pushing for an answer, but all he kept getting were nonresponses. Elvis took the matter up with Vernon, who most likely told him something to the effect of, a) they could not afford paying off the Colonel to the tune of $5 million; b) Elvis had the greatest manager in the world in Colonel Parker; and c) Elvis was being petty and petulant.

I think Elvis also sensed Colonel Parker wasn't bluffing. If he paid him to go away, Colonel Parker was gone. He spent every waking hour of his day thinking of how to promote Elvis Presley to the masses. And if Elvis was going to sabotage himself and the Colonel's efforts, then Parker was going to throw in the towel on their relationship. He didn't need the aggravation at his age. He had his hands full with his wife, Marie, whose condition continued to spiral downward. And, as the Colonel pointed out in his September 6 letter, Elvis was behind delivering on his recording obligations to RCA, the first time this ever happened in their long and fruitful partnership.

When Elvis did finally deliver the album, it wasn't much. *Raised on Rock / For Ol' Times Sake* was a mix of covers and bland originals. But it held a special memory for me.

Elvis cut vocals for a few of the songs at the Chino Canyon house a few months prior and twenty-eight master tracks at Memphis's Stax studios. I guess he wasn't happy with some of the vocals and decided he'd rerecord them in Palm Springs. The Colonel asked me to open the house and help Elvis set up for a recording session, which would be taped by the RCA recording mobile unit parked outside in the carport with engineer Bill Porter camped inside. The first day didn't go so well.

The engineers ran the power from the truck to an A/C cord plugged into the wall, which blew out the panel. Because I had experience working with electricity, I was asked to replace several breakers and rewire the panel to accommodate the new infusion of power. Fortunately, the power blowout occurred during the day while Elvis was sleeping. By the time he woke up around 7:00 P.M., they were ready to roll.

The crew had set up the microphone on the piano where Elvis would do his vocals for "Sweet Angeline" and "Are You Sincere?" I have managed and produced several recording artists, but Elvis was the first I ever saw record a song sitting down. And he sang gospel songs for two hours straight while the guys in the truck got everything ready.

It was the first time I'd ever been able to watch him sing and record.[26] He was truly a natural, but he also worked hard. He spent hours on those sessions making sure to get everything just right. The amazing body of work Elvis left behind speaks for itself.

Sadly, *Raised on Rock / For Ol' Times Sake* performed dismally. It peaked at number 41 on *Billboard*'s Top 200 album chart and failed to chart in the United Kingdom, where his following was even more fervent than the States.

---

26 During the May 1971 Nashville sessions, I didn't actually get to witness Elvis working in the studio. I was only able to listen to those sessions on a speaker in another room.

Prescription for Disaster

The downhill slide had commenced, and it wasn't going to get any better from there on out. Five days after Elvis's divorce was official, he entered Baptist Hospital in Memphis for what Dr. George Nichopoulos called, "a persistent case of recurrent pneumonia." He had been on a charter flight to Memphis and was experiencing difficulty breathing. When he arrived in Memphis, Linda Thompson called Dr. Nick, who checked him into the hospital.

Elvis was bloated, semi-comatose, and in bad shape. A team of doctors worked on him. Initially, they thought he might be suffering from congestive heart failure because of the severe buildup of fluid in his body.

Dr. Nick called Max Shapiro in California and told him Elvis was near death. Shapiro finally told Dr. Nick that he had been giving Elvis daily shots of Demerol. That's when Dr. Nick realized that Elvis had a full-blown addiction.

Elvis was immediately put on phenobarbital and methadone. The latter is commonly used to treat heroin addicts. It relieves cravings and removes withdrawal symptoms. Elvis had never used heroin, but the fact that he was put on methadone meant serious business.

Before he was discharged, doctors David Knott and Robert Fink, both drug addiction specialists, spoke to Elvis privately about the dangers of prescription abuse and recommended he check himself into a hospital. Elvis politely listened but had no intention of entering a place like that, such was his denial.

He remained hospitalized until November 2, 1973. Elvis had put on a considerable amount of weight, presumably because of his use of cortisone, a medication used to fight inflammation.

Colonel Parker heard nothing directly from Elvis through the end of the year. He just kept rolling along, hoping that Elvis would become alert and lose weight. Everyone was glad to see 1973 end and looked forward to a better year in 1974.

The Colonel had heard from various sources that Elvis had sent several of his boys around to investigate finding another manager, including Led Zeppelin's Peter Grant, but not surprisingly, no one wanted to touch Elvis Presley. He was seen as unpredictable and difficult to handle. These gents had dealt with out-of-control rockers all the time, so why take on another?

Not only was Elvis demanding, but he was used to having exclusivity, and the bigger managers wouldn't give up their other clients. The economics simply didn't work for them. It did with the Colonel because he maintained a frugal lifestyle and low overhead that gave him freedom. He loved Elvis like a son and was interested in working with only him.

And speaking of money, Elvis was badly in need of it. There were no tours lined up, which were his best and most consistent source of income. If there were ever any doubts about whether he needed the Colonel, there could be no questions now. Without Colonel Parker, Elvis was just half a partnership, and no one wanted to take a chance with him.

With all the humility and energy he could muster, Elvis finally reached out to the Colonel to inform him he wanted to get back to work as soon as possible. He had momentarily cleaned up his act, and thanks to an introduction by Dr. Nick, had taken up racquetball and resumed his karate workouts to get back in shape.

With those positive steps, Colonel Parker booked a January engagement at the Las Vegas Hilton but cut the workload in half, reducing his usual four-week run to two. It seemed to pay off. Elvis's voice held up as did his health. There were no cancellations this time around. More important, the run was drama-free, and there were no onstage histrionics from Elvis.

This engagement was the first time Elvis and the Colonel had seen each other for quite some time. When they did, it was a classic exchange I witnessed. Colonel Parker, Tom Diskin, my wife, Sherry, and I walked through the kitchen hallway to the backstage of the Hilton showroom to watch Elvis's opening night performance. Sonny West and Charlie Hodge turned the corner and behind them was Elvis. Elvis started walking toward us and locked eyes with the Colonel, smiling widely. Then they began singing in unison "The Hot Dog Vendor's Call":

Prescription for Disaster

A loaf of bread . . . A pound of meat
And all the mustard you can eat
Pickles on the bottom, onions on the top
Put it in your mouth and it goes flippity-flop.

When the two finished singing, they hugged. No apologies were exchanged. Elvis also hugged Sherry and shook Tom Diskin's and my hand. Tom and I walked down the hallway, exchanged a brief glance, and noted that the Colonel didn't say a word about the matter. It's been correctly stated in several Elvis bios that he had a hard time apologizing to people. The same went for the Colonel. They had been together so long there was no need to apologize.

With their relationship back on track, the Colonel took the steps to set up Boxcar Enterprises, which eventually became the sole entity marketing Elvis's commercial rights. Boxcar was co-owned by Elvis and Colonel Parker, plus Tom Diskin, Freddie Bienstock, and George Parkhill, all longtime business associates of Colonel Parker. I was the only paid employee of Boxcar Enterprises, and other than concert promotion, this was my introduction to the record and licensing business. The whole idea behind Boxcar was to provide another income stream for Elvis where he didn't have to do any additional work or performance.

In the beginning, it was a record label with distribution through RCA. It's first release was *Having Fun with Elvis on Stage,* an entire album of Elvis bantering and telling jokes between songs during his concerts from 1969 to 1972. Initially, the hastily released album was sold only at Elvis concerts, but RCA later decided to pick it up, which I'm sure they regretted. Even though it's a collector's item today, *Having Fun with Elvis on Stage* is considered one of the worst albums of all time by fans and critics alike, deeming it hokey and incoherent.

The label even distributed a single titled "Growing Up in a Country Way" by Bodie Mountain Express with Kirk Seeley, who were favorites on the Disneyland and Knott's Berry Farm circuit. The song was written by Chuck Woolery, the famous TV host. Chuck was also the son-in-law of David Nelson (brother of Ricky Nelson) and was at a lot of our functions.

Tom Diskin and I produced and promoted the single. It wasn't very successful, but it garnered them an opening spot on Elvis's concert bill on New Year's Eve in Pontiac, Michigan, which was a big deal.

Boxcar also signed rockabilly singer-songwriter Jody Reynolds from Palm Springs. He had scored a Top 5 hit with "Endless Sleep" in 1958. Whenever Elvis was in Palm Springs, he made it a point to go and see Jody at Howard Manor. Elvis was also there to see Bobby Craig and Ron Coppola, who were in Jody's backing band. Bobby was also a keyboardist for Ricky Nelson and Chuck Berry. They were friends with Elvis and the Colonel and often hung out at the Chino Canyon house. Colonel Parker signed Jody with the intention of funneling songs to Elvis, but Elvis died before recording any of his songs. Reynolds included one he wrote for Elvis, "Yesterday and Today," on an album he released in 1978.

Boxcar truly became profitable only after Elvis's death when his image and likeness became extremely valuable. Luckily for Priscilla and the estate, the Colonel had the foresight to have this set up and was able to utilize it when the time came. Today, Boxcar is an extremely valuable asset to Graceland.

Management III Productions was brought back to book Elvis's next tour, a quick twenty-date jaunt of the South that ran from March 1 to March 20. Almost every show was sold out and the tour grossed $2,310,533.10. After expenses were deducted, Elvis cleared $789,022, while Colonel Parker's take was $394,511. It appeared as if the two men had put their differences aside and returned to the business at hand.

The rest of the year was filled with tours, recording sessions, engagements in Las Vegas and Lake Tahoe, and of course, the requisite spending sprees. Elvis wrote a $50,000 check to George Waite who wanted to produce a new karate documentary called *The New Gladiators*. Elvis wanted to use this documentary to introduce karate to the mainstream like *The Endless Summer* did for surfing and *On Any Sun-*

day did for motorcycle riding. He financed, appeared in, and narrated the documentary, which depicted karate competitors and their training, leading up to tournaments around the world. They filmed roughly thirty-two minutes of film, including a segment of Elvis performing chi exercises on September 16, 1974. A snippet of it was included in the 1981 documentary, *This Is Elvis.*

After he was filmed for *The New Gladiators,* Elvis launched into a ten-day buying spree during which he purchased more than a dozen cars for family, friends, staff, and strangers. He also went big for his cousin, Billy Smith, buying him a 1975 Woodcrest double-wide trailer with three bedrooms so he could live in comfort on the grounds of Graceland. The trailer set Elvis back about $20,000 (equivalent to approximately $157,000 in 2023). Elvis also bought himself a 1973 Stutz Blackhawk, which was his third, dropping a cool $26,500. It had Pontiac's 230-horsepower V-8, a red leather interior, and an 18-karat gold trim package. Elvis was possessive of the car and rarely allowed anyone else behind the wheel. Shortly after midnight on August 16, 1977, he drove it through the gates of Graceland for the last time.

Despite his appetite for spending lots of money, it was a relatively scandal-free period until about August. Elvis's summer stint in Vegas was successful, but as the engagement ended, he was wound up with a lot of aggression. He cussed out a heckler during an August 30 show (dropping an F-bomb on someone who screamed out they hated him), and then, a few days later on September 2, during his final dinner show for the season, he rambled for thirty-eight minutes about his various karate degrees, his divorce from Priscilla ("We just made an agreement to be friends and to be close and to care because we have a daughter to raise"), and a cartoonish liver biopsy. He saved up his most passionate rant for scandalous gossip magazines who surmised he might be "on something," i.e., drugs.

The concert, known by the fans as "Desert Storm," had served as a reminder not to broach the subject with Elvis unless you wanted to be shown the door. But as far as bad shows went, things were about to get a whole lot worse.

On Friday, September 27, 1974, he arrived in College Park, Maryland, disheveled and completely out of it, to start a fifteen-show tour. Sonny West said when he climbed out of the limousine at the hotel, he looked as though he'd been on a huge bender. His hair was a mess, his speech was slurred, and he could barely stand up straight.

Luckily for Sonny, there was a police detail to help with security. Sonny whisked Elvis up to the hotel suite and put him to bed. He then gathered up all the other guys to ask what in the world was going on. Red West said it was a miracle he even got out of bed that morning. And speaking of miracles, Sonny gathered all the security detail together and formed a prayer circle, asking God to help Elvis in these tough times.

After a nap, Elvis headed to the venue. Once there, he dressed in a white peacock jumpsuit, and stepped on the stage.

"I just woke up," he told the crowd of fifteen thousand.

He just about sleepwalked through the performance, hanging onto the microphone for dear life, mumbling unintelligibly, and messing up the lyrics of "Love Me Tender."

The show was cut twenty minutes short. The next night, Elvis was only slightly better.

But it wasn't the quality, or lack thereof, of the show that caught the attention of *The Washington Post* reviewer as much as Elvis's weight gain. In the next day's paper, the reviewer noted Elvis's "paunch," and when Elvis read the piece, he was infuriated. When he took the stage for his second show in College Park, he told the crowd, "Those of you who saw the morning paper, er, the evening paper, whatever it was, they gave . . . they gave me a fantastic write-up. No, they did. Except they said I had a paunch here, and I want to tell you something . . . I got their damn paunch! I wore a bulletproof vest onstage. True. You know in case some fool wants to take a .22 and blow my . . . belly button off."

He also ranted about the tabloids, which had been hinting that Elvis was no longer the boy next door. He told the audience that he was a federal narcotics agent and an eighth degree black belt.

The crowd cheered Elvis on, but school officials made the decision

Prescription for Disaster

that he would never be invited back to the University of Maryland. And they made good on that promise.

Elvis had to push through eleven more dates and an eight-show engagement in Lake Tahoe before he could take a break. And when he did, it was a bizarre choice. In late October, he went to see Dr. Ghanem for help losing weight. Ghanem had added a wing onto his cavernous Las Vegas home for celebrity patients. Once Elvis "checked in," Ghanem put him on a "sleep diet" he concocted, which consisted mostly of liquid nourishment and lots of sedated rest. Elvis stayed with part-time girlfriend Sheila Ryan, a former *Playboy* Playmate.

After two weeks, Elvis walked out ten pounds heavier than he had been when he walked in. In early December, he repeated the exercise with Linda Thompson by his side. The results were pretty much the same: no significant weight loss.

He was in such bad shape that Colonel Parker postponed his annual January engagement at the Las Vegas Hilton to February. On Monday, December 30, 1974, Colonel Parker informed his liaison at the hotel: "I see no way that this artist can be ready to perform at the Hilton January 26, 1975," explaining that it would be, "an inconsiderate solution for us to pursue the possibility and persuade Elvis to perform for this engagement."

Knowing how important it was for Colonel Parker to keep his word, especially to the folks at the Hilton, Elvis knew this postponement was not an easy ask for his manager. But the Colonel bit the bullet and did the right thing. Elvis later thanked him in a telegram for taking care of this piece of business while he was away "recuperating."

Two weeks after his fortieth birthday, Elvis was admitted once more to Baptist Memorial Hospital when he couldn't catch his breath. Dr. Nick told the press that Elvis was having liver problems, but that story was simply for the papers.

While Elvis was in the hospital, Vernon suffered a heart attack at his home on February 5, 1975. He recovered in the room next to Elvis's.

A ray of hope appeared in late March through singer/actress Barbra Streisand and her boyfriend, hairdresser-turned-movie-producer

Jon Peters. They appeared backstage after one of Elvis's midnight shows in Vegas to discuss an idea with him. For three hours they huddled in a room, and after Streisand and Peters left, Elvis came out with a big grin on his face. He was offered the lead role in the remake of *A Star is Born*.

Elvis had always wanted to be taken seriously as an actor, and this was the role that could show everyone he had the chops. It was tailor-made for him, but to take on the part, he'd need to clean up his act and invest his heart and soul in the project. That was exciting to his friends and employees who knew he needed a new creative challenge in his life.

When Elvis said he was going to do the picture, Red West got right in his face and said, "You swear? Shake hands on it!" Elvis shook on it. But a few days later, he sang a different tune.

"You know, Streisand has been known to take control of a picture, and I don't know if I can deal with that," Elvis announced. "And that hairdresser boyfriend of hers might end up directing it, and I might have to slap the shit out of him." But what really bothered Elvis was the prospect of having to lose weight, get in shape, and having the discipline to properly prepare for the role.

Colonel Parker has often been cast as the villain for allegedly demanding too much when contacted about what it would cost for Elvis's services. He said $1 million in salary, $100,000 in expenses, 50 percent of the profits, and a separate deal for soundtrack rights would just about cover it. Then, to kill the deal for good, Parker insisted that Elvis get top billing over Streisand.

Any time Elvis wanted the Colonel to get him out of something, the Colonel did it by making outrageous demands. (This also happened once before in the 1960s when Elvis was approached to make a children's record with Judy Garland. Elvis didn't want any part of it but didn't have the heart to tell Garland no. So, the Colonel put the price into the stratosphere and got him out of the deal.)

Elvis hitting the age of forty wasn't a milestone that he embraced. The *National Enquirer* had published a nasty story headlined: "Elvis at 40—Paunchy, Depressed and Living in Fear." It wasn't far from the truth.

Sex symbols have a harder time getting older and often fight it with all their might. Often, that means turning to plastic surgery to turn back the hands of time. In Elvis's case, he had excised some fatty tissue underneath his eyes and had his double chin tightened. This might have made him feel better about himself, but his behavior was getting more bizarre all the time.

In an Asheville, North Carolina, hotel room after a show, Dr. Nick said he was going to cut off Elvis's supply of medication. Elvis showed his displeasure by pulling out a Beretta pistol and waving it around. The gun accidentally went off, and the bullet ricocheted off the television and a chair and was spent by the time it thumped Dr. Nick's chest.

"Son, good God almighty!" Vernon exclaimed. "What in the world made you do a thing like that?"

"Aw, hell, Daddy, so I shot the doc," Elvis said blithely. "No big deal. He's not dead." Elvis was a very caring person and took a liking to everyone in his sphere. But that statement underscores how his personality was undergoing a sea change.

At the second show in Asheville, Elvis was unhappy with the tepid response from the audience. He even passed around a request box hoping to whip up some interest and enthusiasm, though that didn't fly. But what he did next almost triggered a riot.

During a break in between songs, Elvis twisted off a ring, bent down, and handed it to a man in the front row. A woman rushed the stage, and Elvis gave her a ring. Then he tossed one out into the crowd and started handing jewelry to members of the band. The crowd went bananas, and so did Vernon, who was watching the show from the wings with his hands on the sides of his head. Elvis got his roar of approval, but it cost him thousands of dollars in jewelry.

One night in the dining room of the Imperial Suite in Las Vegas, Elvis took out a gun, put his feet up on the dining room table, and shot out the ornate chandelier. At Graceland, he blasted a black commode to pieces because he decided he no longer liked the color.

He also spent $140,000 on fourteen Cadillacs and gave them away. One went to a complete stranger, who just happened to be in the showroom at the time. She was checking out a very expensive model when Elvis sidled up to her and asked, "Do you like it?" She did, and next thing she knew, Elvis bought it for her.

When cars weren't enough, Elvis started buying planes. He bought himself a Jet Commander, which is a small corporate jet, and a G1 prop plane for Colonel Parker, who politely declined the gift because it would cost so much to maintain the aircraft. One of Colonel Parker's favorite sayings was, "How much does it cost if it's free?" In this case, it would have been a lot. He decided it would be much easier and cheaper to charter a plane than own one.

Then Elvis decided to upgrade to a Convair 880, a four-engine jet previously owned by Delta Airlines with a hundred-passenger capacity. That set him back about $250,000, and he spent another $800,000 having it customized by an outfit in Dallas.

The 129-foot plane he called the *Lisa Marie* had a bedroom (with a seat belt over the queen-sized bed), three closed-circuit TVs, a six-seat conference room, a lounge area with gold-plated seat belt buckles, a fake fireplace, two half baths outfitted with gold wash basins with flecks of twenty-four-karat gold and brass fixtures imported from Spain. To give it his personal touch, he had the "TCB" logo painted on the tail. It was about $400,000 a year in operation costs.

While the *Lisa Marie* was getting its makeover, Elvis shelled out close to $900,000 for a Lockheed business jet called the JetStar[27] to use in the meantime.

Elvis gave Dr. Nick a $200,000 interest-free loan to build a home out of redwood. The staff payroll alone was about $100,000 a month, and Graceland's monthly upkeep came to around $40,000.

Why do I keep bringing up Elvis's finances? I guess to show that he toured constantly to chase a checkbook and that almost all his de-

---

27 Elvis's ten-seat JetStar was originally owned by *Hustler* publisher Larry Flynt. Today it's known as *Hound Dog II* and is currently on display at Graceland.

Prescription for Disaster

cisions were not based on art, but on commerce. Elvis carried over a hundred people on his touring payroll, and as a road manager, concert promoter, and music veteran, I can tell you that is very excessive, especially back in the 1970s. Elvis was making close to $2 million a year at this time, but his expenses and spending habits were always above what he made.

Colonel Parker has always been criticized for not steering Elvis in another direction, but the truth of the matter is that Elvis Presley was steering the ship, and his usual port of call was the bank. The Colonel didn't tell him how to spend his money. He told him how to make it. Tours were fast and easy cash grabs, but after Elvis met his payroll, paid Uncle Sam, and then indulged himself, the money did not last. This was not a sustainable model by any means, but the bottom line was that Elvis did not respect money. It had been a very long time since he'd driven a truck, operated a drill press, stared down not making rent, or had only a baked potato for dinner. The Colonel's memories of riding the rails hungry and owning one pair of pants were still fresh.

Yes, tours were a fast way to grab cash, but between the onstage rants, the rambling, and being banned from a campus, the tabloids—never a stupid bunch to begin with—were beginning to draw lines between the dots. Elvis could hole up in Graceland all he wanted. They could see through the walls.

The storm clouds were gathering, and the sky was growing black. The svelte heartbreaker with the golden voice, country charm, and star presence was now gone. In his place, something slipped and slithered in the dark, something that did not want to be seen.

19

Auld Lang Syne

Elvis Presley started America's Bicentennial off on a high note. He performed a New Year's Eve concert on the last day of 1975 in Pontiac, Michigan. Approximately 62,500 people showed up at the Silverdome to hear the legend sing, cheer him on, and get a glimpse of the King of Rock 'n' Roll.

It was a historic show in many ways. It was the first time Elvis performed on New Year's Eve since 1955 and was one of the first musical artists to perform at the venue. The show also had the highest attendance of any Elvis concert.

The concert was not without its faults. Elvis had received a death threat a few days before the show. Police disclosed to Sonny West on his advance trip to set up security that a mentally challenged male threatened to kill Elvis. However, the guy threatened every celebrity who visited the area, so the cops didn't feel it was a serious problem. As a precautionary measure, they did place the person in custody before Elvis arrived and released him after he left town.

Because the stage was so massive—it was twenty-five feet high and placed in the middle of the stadium—a special tunnel had to be constructed for Elvis to get from the dressing room to the stage. The entire field had to be covered in plywood, but the construction crew had to wait until the end of the football season to get started. It was a good thing the Lions didn't make the playoffs that year!

During the show, Elvis felt vulnerable. He performed at the fifty-yard line on a ten-foot riser surrounded by speakers. The elevation of the stage made him feel especially at risk but was necessary to ensure that all sixty thousand fans would have a good view of him and his stage show because there were no jumbo screens as there are at today's concerts. Adding to Elvis's discomfort was the fact that the TCB Band and the orchestra were set up on a different level of the riser and the separation caused issues with the sound.[28]

The evening kicked off with the Bodie Mountain Express as the opening act. I'm sure these hardened Detroit fans didn't expect to see a bluegrass band sporting diapers and playing their hearts out when it was near freezing outside, but they got an A for effort and chutzpah. No doubt this was a prank by Colonel Parker, who loved putting people on.

Pat Upton, a singer I managed at the time, was the evening's middle act. Pat was going to be on Boxcar Records after his lead vocal on the hit "More Today Than Yesterday" by Spiral Starecase. Pat also worked for years with Ricky Nelson but quit just before the awful plane crash that took Ricky's life in 1985. All this is to say that Elvis and Colonel Parker were helping me out by including Pat on the bill. Elvis reminded me later it was indeed a favor, but in a good-natured way.

As the Elvis portion of the concert got underway, Al Dvorin mentioned to Colonel Parker that Elvis's souvenir scarves were not selling so well. The Colonel thought for a moment and then told Al to go up on stage and announce to the fans to act quickly and buy a souvenir scarf so Elvis could spot them in the crowd. Sure enough, there were no scarves to be found at the merchandise booths by the end of the show.

There was also an unfortunate incident while performing "Polk Salad Annie" when Elvis ripped the seat of pants and had to leave the stage to change his jumpsuit. When he finally got back to the stage, he promptly ripped a second pair of pants.

---

28 The most noticeable moment was when Elvis performed "My Way." He had to stop halfway through the song to hear what the TCB Band was playing. He lost his timing for a while.

At midnight Elvis led a ten-second countdown and watched balloons drop from the ceiling. He fumbled through "Auld Lang Syne" because he didn't know the words, but the audience appreciated his effort, and everyone went home happy. People who were there still say it was the greatest show they'd ever seen.

The Colonel and his staff didn't get back to their hotel rooms until 5:00 A.M., giving them less than three hours of sleep before they hopped on a plane back to Las Vegas. They finished the show reports that afternoon with the production reviewed by the Colonel's team.

The report was astounding: the Pontiac date grossed $800,000 and would go down as Elvis's most profitable concert ever, and that helped him to recoup some of the fortune he had squandered the year before on planes, cars, and gifts to his friends. As a result of its success, plans were immediately put in place for another New Year's show in 1976.

It was obvious that touring was by far the best way to supplement the badly depleted Presley bank account. Elvis informed the Colonel he wanted to go back on the road as soon as possible. No tour arrangements had been made since he was hospitalized in August, and it would take time to get everything in order. Plus, there was the matter of the canceled recording sessions that were owed RCA Records, per their contract, a real thorn in the Colonel's side. On January 7, 1976, the Colonel addressed the matter to Elvis in a letter. He had to remind Elvis that they had had to postpone recording four times in the past three months due to illness. However, they still owed RCA two albums and four singles for their 1975 contract. The Colonel stated they could not bill them for their 1976 contract until that obligation was fulfilled. He said he was making arrangements for Felton Jarvis to record him the first week in February at Graceland with a mobile recording unit. He signed off, "Again, Happy Birthday, Happy New Year, and keep playing the organ."

To give context to the last line of the letter, the Colonel had gifted Elvis a beautiful $5,000 Lowrey organ, which Sherry and I delivered to the Las Vegas Hilton as a Christmas present a month earlier. Knowing

I owned a music store in Palm Springs for several years, Elvis asked, "Did the Colonel pay full retail?" hinting that he wanted me to get my full profit on the sale.

"He sure did." I smiled.

It seemed like the two men were on much better footing than the previous year.

Vernon Presley, now back in action after his heart attack and a brief stay in the hospital, wrote a letter to the Colonel on January 16, 1976. He mentioned that Elvis had heard some upsetting things through some of his "guys" (i.e., Lamar Fike and Joe Esposito) about his financial situation. Vernon had asked Colonel Parker not to mention Elvis's finances in the future.

The Colonel dictated a letter to Loanne that same day in response to Vernon's concern. It was classic Colonel Parker. He not only issued a denial but said he dealt with it by speaking to Elvis directly. The Colonel asked him to put whomever accused him of leaking financial information to him on the line. When Elvis did not give the phone over to anyone, the Colonel nipped it in the bud quickly. He concluded, "If I had to contact you or Elvis when I heard a rumor, I would be on the phone every day."

That letter ended that conversation rather quickly.

In the latter part of January 1976, Elvis flew to Las Vegas, although he was not scheduled to appear there until the end of the year. He and Colonel Parker had agreed on a new contract that resulted from the return of the airplane Elvis had given him for his birthday the previous summer. At that time, the Colonel said he would prefer a larger share of the profits, which he would work to create, and Elvis agreed.

The January 22 contract indicated that the Colonel had given a lot of thought to the fact that he was often working eighteen-hour days. Elvis did not require a high-priced public relations firm because the Colonel single-handedly did that job, which saved Elvis several thousand dollars a month. The Colonel advertised, publicized, and always promoted in a first-class manner to ensure the maximum attendance at all of Elvis's appearances. In fact, the two men had an agreement. If you ever attended an Elvis concert, you might remember there was a segment in the show where the houselights went up and Elvis surveyed the room. He told the audience he wanted to see what they looked like. That much was true. But the real reason was that the Colonel made a promise to Elvis that every ticket in every venue would be sold out, and if Elvis saw an empty seat anywhere, he could walk offstage with the Colonel's blessing. But that never happened because the Colonel was diligent in selling out every show.

Also under the Colonel's direction, Elvis was protected from the media, which was what Elvis wanted. The Colonel did all the wheeling and dealing and took the heat for any problems. Elvis handled only the entertainment portion of the agreement. And the contract more than reflected that.

Fans and critics alike have criticized the Colonel for "taking 50 percent," but that doesn't tell the whole story regarding this particular contract, which was actually a joint venture agreement that turned out to be a very bad deal for the Colonel. The language specifically spelled out their independent obligations to the partnership and was based on the net proceeds as opposed to the gross number, which is normally used in management agreements (15–25 percent is standard). The Colonel's contract was unique because of his exclusivity to Elvis Presley.

The 1976 contract that Colonel Parker and Elvis Presley operated under is commonplace today and conducted under a limited liability company where the artist provides his/her entertainment skills and services, and the manager acts as a member-manager of the LLC. They both have an equal say. That's exactly what the 1976 agreement was. For example, manager Irving Azoff and the Eagles are partners in their venture. So are many other big acts and managers. But in the case of the last agreement with Elvis, all the costs came off the top in this agreement, but it was geared toward the artist. Years later, Jerry Weintraub and I were asked to do a summation of the deal for Lisa Marie's court-appointed guardian, Blanchard Tual. After a detailed look at this contract, both Jerry and I agreed we would not have accepted that deal because it was not very profitable for Colonel Parker being based on what was left over after Elvis's touring expenses, and sometimes there was nothing left. The venture paid all touring expenses, including the four planes, a hundred-plus people on the payroll, hotel, food, ground transportation, and per diems, before the Colonel saw any profit. The truth is, Colonel Parker took on more risk than Elvis and got very little in return.

Their relationship did not yield fruit in other ways. The Colonel rarely, if ever, took a vacation because he simply didn't know how. Someone once asked him when he was going to take a vacation.

"What would I do on a vacation?" he asked. "The thing I enjoy most is my work."

But Elvis was starting to take the fun out of that. It got harder and harder to coax Elvis to live up to his obligations, most especially where it concerned his recording contract for RCA. He was so passionless about making music that he didn't even want to leave Graceland to record *From Elvis Presley Boulevard, Memphis, Tennessee,* so RCA brought the recording studio to him. They parked a mobile unit outside Graceland; it contained a control room to mix the sound. To improve the acoustics, the technicians placed expensive equipment in the den, such as baffles and partitions to separate Elvis and the musicians, just as they would be in the studio.

Producer Felton Jarvis assembled several members of Elvis's road band and a few Los Angeles and Nashville session musicians to play on the tracks. J. D. Sumner and the Stamps were there, as was soprano Kathy Westmoreland.

Elvis showed up for the first session wearing a police uniform—something he obtained while on a recent trip to Denver, Colorado, where he knew and befriended members of the department. Elvis liked and respected law enforcement, collected police badges and guns, and enjoyed hard-boiled cop movies like *Bullitt, Dirty Harry, The French Connection,* and *Across 110th Street.* I think deep down he fancied himself as a kick-ass crusader who worked quietly with law enforcement to rid society of the vermin who didn't play by the rules. How else can one account for his behavior during those sessions?

According to his bodyguards Red and Sonny, Elvis would record in the den then slip into his bedroom, ranting and raving about wiping out Memphis drug dealers whom he blamed for getting his stepbrother, Ricky Stanley, hooked on heroin. Elvis bailed him out and pulled some strings to get the charges dropped.

Sonny and Red were summoned to Elvis's room during a break from the recording. They saw his weapons strewn about the floor—pistols, automatic weapons, rifles, and even rocket launchers. This was overkill, even by Elvis's standards. Hell, anyone's standards. The police don't use rocket launchers. At least not in America.

Elvis then handed them a list of names and police-profile pictures, preparing Red and Sonny as if they were at a mission debriefing. The biggest threat they had ever faced were overzealous teenage girls, jealous boyfriends, and a few drunks who jumped on stage courtesy of some liquid courage.

"These sons of bitches need to be wiped out," Elvis declared.

His plan was quite simple: slip out the back of Graceland, knock off these drug pushers, and then come back and record some hits. It would be just like in his movies such as *Speedway* or *Blue Hawaii*. One good sock at a bad guy, and then belt out "Rock-A-Hula Baby." Well, at least he was thinking somewhat about his career.

"You're getting into something very heavy here, Elvis," Sonny warned. Elvis waved him off.

"Hell, the police want them," he countered. But the one Elvis himself especially wanted was a local hood who ran a pool hall. According to Elvis, this thug knocked Ricky down with a pool cue, and now Elvis was going to take him out himself.

The Wests manage to cool Elvis down and convince him to put off the mission for a while, thinking perhaps it was just a phase.

Elvis's recording sessions were flat and uninspired. He simply wasn't interested. Felton Jarvis had hoped to get at least twenty tracks out of the session, but Elvis called it quits after a dozen.

Before this time, Elvis would mostly take pills between engagements, but now he was doing it all the time, and it showed in his performances. He slurred his words, forgot lyrics, and occasionally had to resort to cue cards to get through songs, when and if he felt like completing them.

When Elvis returned from the road, his usual pattern was to head into his room for a few days of rest and recuperation. Those R & R sessions began getting longer and longer, and sometimes they'd lapse into weeks before he had to be dragged out of his room to go on tour again.

But that was not where he wanted to go. There were no drugs out there. He fell into every predictable pattern addicts have: reject any suggestions at detox, at all costs. If you must kick, scream, cry, explode, threaten, do it. Have a problem, like running out of breath between songs or gaining weight? Find a fix. Have an oxygen tank backstage to take hits from between numbers and wear loose clothes. Your people cut off your dealers? Fire them. You still need people? Hire new ones who are too intimidated to do anything about it, no matter what they see. You want to go work for the other King? Go ahead. There is no other King.

They were all helpless. The King was mad. And in the words of a real mad king, George III, "Everyone who does not agree with me is a traitor and a scoundrel."

20

Way Down

There are very few unknown stories in the Elvis World. Everything has pretty much been told, dissected, regurgitated, and rewritten. There are not one, but two websites offering a daily fact about Elvis ("Give us this day our daily Elvis . . ."). And then there's social media. Pages about Elvis on Facebook are countless, as are the ones on Google. Elvis fans are unmatched even by *Star Trek* fans. There is no detail undeserving of their attention. Untold Elvis stories, recordings, gossip, or trivia are *gold* in their realm.

I have one and it involves Elvis and Ronald Reagan. Well, sort of.

The first of nine tours in 1976 was scheduled for March 17–22, opening in Johnson City, Tennessee, and closing in St. Louis, Missouri. As usual, the advance crew arrived at the first venue two days early and set up headquarters at the local Holiday Inn. On opening day, the Colonel got up at 3:30 A.M. and went to the airport to meet Elvis, who was arriving in the *Lisa Marie*.

Two days later, when the Colonel and his people landed in Charlotte, North Carolina, on the 19th, and checked in at the Downtowner Motor Inn, they were surprised to see Secret Service agents on their floor. The Colonel had just entered his room when agents knocked on his door, asking for a few minutes of his time. Sonny West headed up the advance crew and had grown a full beard. He was always an imposing figure, but with a beard he really stood out. The Colonel initially thought the Secret Service was a little nervous about Sonny's personal appearance and set their sights on him. A short time later, the Colonel found out that California governor Ronald Reagan was staying on the same floor, which accounted for the presence of so many federal agents. When they discovered the Colonel was in charge, they all relaxed. He had been completely checked out years ago as a trusted friend of Lyndon B. Johnson. The Colonel had also met Reagan on many occasions.

A short time later, Reagan's people approached the Colonel and confided they were having trouble transporting the governor to his next location, where he was scheduled to speak. The Colonel said he would be happy to lend a charter plane to Reagan (he always had a backup just in case) but had to make arrangements with chief pilot Jim Walker. Little did the Colonel know he was doing a big favor to a future president of the United States.

The first tour of the year lasted a week and covered only four cities, as Elvis used Johnson City as his home base. The short tour netted Elvis $350,000. The Colonel's take was $175,000.

Although the contract signed two months earlier called for all net profits to be divided 50/50 between Elvis and the Colonel, Vernon had asked the Colonel to continue receiving 33.3 percent until Elvis could get his finances straightened out. The Colonel agreed to this, and the January 22 contract never actually went into effect. When Elvis died, the Colonel was owed a large sum of money by Elvis, for which he could have gone to court, but decided not to pursue it.

"How could I possibly take money from Lisa Marie?" he asked when the subject came up later. He never did receive the monies due to him from the revised contract.

When the tour ended in St. Louis on March 22, the Colonel and his staff had already headed for Lake Tahoe, where they would spend three days at the Sahara, completing reports and relaxing before heading off to their respective homes.

By April 5 they were all gathered back in Las Vegas, working on the next three tours. The Colonel was putting together shorter tours to make sure Elvis was able to complete them. He also began planning for Elvis's next appearance at the Las Vegas Hilton in December.

It was during this period that Barbara Walters, now making a well-publicized $1 million a year under contract with ABC, called Colonel Parker. She wanted to interview Elvis for one of her specials.

"Certainly, Miss Walters, we'd be happy to oblige," the Colonel said. "The fee is $50,000." That was his standard answer to such requests. Walters balked.

"Colonel Parker, we do not pay for interviews," Walters said.

"Miss Walters, you are making $1 million a year for what you do, and it is well-deserved. Looking at it from that perspective, don't you think Elvis is worth his $50,000 fee?"

Put like that, it made sense to Walters, who said she'd give the matter some thought. The Colonel then added a little zinger.

"By the way, Miss Walters," he said, "if I had been negotiating your new ABC contract, I would have said you were worth $2 million!"

The interview never took place.

The Colonel and his crew continued to put in long hours at the Hilton office, working on the next three tours and a ten-day residency in Lake Tahoe. The Colonel would spend a full day in the office and pass his evenings in the casino. While I'm mentioning Colonel Parker's gambling, it's been said he racked up so much debt that he kept signing contracts with the Hilton that practically made Elvis an indentured slave. Again, pure nonsense.

Loanne Miller and I had a nice lunch with Barron Hilton after Colonel Parker passed in 1997. We talked a lot about the Colonel, including his supposed gambling debts. Hilton dismissed those rumors with the wave of a hand.

"There are gamblers who will stop when they lose a car or home, but the Colonel was not like that," Hilton said. "The Colonel stopped playing when he should have. Elvis *never* did a show to service the Colonel's gambling debt."

Hilton, in fact, laughed hard at the recollection because before Elvis stepped foot in Las Vegas, he had to be paid in advance. Vernon Presley saw to that.

"Besides, the Colonel was a big attraction when he was on the floor," Hilton said. "He was good for business."

Loanne also confirmed this assertion was outrageous. "Did he have debts? No, he paid as he went," Loanne said. "I can verify that because I was the person who quite often paid the gambling debt; he sent me down to clear it. I would take care of that. He never gambled something he didn't have, and he was always very careful to make sure there was enough money to take care of Marie if she lived to be a hundred and fifty."

The second tour of the year was another short jaunt with eight shows in six cities, starting in Kansas City and ending in Spokane, Washington. Elvis's share was $380,000 and the Colonel received $190,000.

While appearing in Denver on April 23, Elvis went on another automobile shopping spree. He bought four Lincoln Continentals for his cop buddies in Denver and bought Judy West, Sonny's wife, a white Cadillac Seville. Pat West, Red's wife, got a new Eldorado, and Elvis's girlfriend, Linda Thompson, also got a Seville.

He also purchased a light blue Cadillac Seville for the Colonel. But there was one catch: the Colonel wanted me to go to Colorado to fetch it for him. I had just gotten home from being on the road with Ricky Nelson and was pooped. I did not want to go to Denver, but it was the Colonel. It was hard to say no to him because I knew he needed my help. I flew to Denver the next day and drove it back in a two-day stretch. When the car arrived in Palm Springs, it sat in the carport most of the time. By then, the Colonel had basically stopped driving.

Later, the Caddy was part of the memorabilia that the Colonel gave to Elvis Presley Enterprises, and it's now on display at Graceland. All told that Cadillac shopping spree cost Elvis about $70,000.

Denver television reporter Don Kinney heard about the spree and broke the story on the local news. He ended his news report with a joking aside, "By the way, Elvis, if you're listening out there and you've got an extra one of those Cadillacs, I sure could use one." The next day, a brand-new Cadillac Seville was delivered to Kinney's station. Elvis did it just to blow the guy's mind.

Of course, there was a price to be paid for that largesse. Elvis had to continue funding that lifestyle, and he did so by constantly being on the road. After discussions with both Elvis and his father, the Colonel was assured Elvis wanted to continue touring. He said he wanted to perform in front of his fans and do little else. When he was at home at Graceland, he spent most of his time upstairs in his darkened bedroom. At least when he was touring, he had to get up and get dressed. He had a purpose. The Colonel and Vernon were extremely worried about Elvis's purpose in life and felt that touring helped him live a somewhat normal (for him) life. Sure, it was a Band-Aid, but it was the only good option available to them.

On Wednesday, May 26, the Colonel met with Tom Hulett to discuss their apprehensions about Elvis's condition. However, in keeping with Elvis's request to continue touring, the Colonel booked the third tour of 1976 to begin May 27, opening in Bloomington, Indiana, and wrapping up at the Omni in Atlanta on June 6. Tour Three consisted of twelve shows in eleven days with Elvis earning $553,501 and the Colonel receiving $276,750.

At the Civic Center in El Paso, Texas, on June 2, Elvis again caused problems for the security people by passing out scarves and urging fans to rush down to the ringside area to receive one. This was a difficult problem for the Colonel to handle since Elvis seemed determined to overlook the fact that security costs were going to escalate, and there was a possibility that security personnel would even refuse to work his shows. There was also the threat of lawsuits from injured fans. Everyone was relieved when the tour ended without further incident. But there always seemed to be trouble lurking around the corner.

Earlier in the year Dr. Nichopoulos and Joe Esposito brought a promotional idea to Elvis regarding opening a string of racquetball courts around the country under his name. Near the end of his life, racquetball was Elvis's only form of exercise. Joe Esposito and Dr. Nick thought it would be a great investment for them, but wanted Elvis to put up the money. The first of fifty franchised Elvis Presley Center Courts would be built in Memphis. Elvis signed the contract without consulting the Colonel and never read the fine print. He naively thought he was just lending his name to the venture. It was not until the promoters asked for an $80,000 advance on the $1.3 million he had agreed to underwrite that Elvis asked the Colonel for help.

The Colonel was irate, which is when he worked his best. He notified T. Michael McMahon, vice president of the proposed racquetball project, that he and Elvis had a long-standing contractual agreement that prohibited Elvis from lending his name and support to any venture without their mutual approval. The deal was quickly nullified.

Communicating with Elvis was becoming extremely difficult. The Colonel would call and leave messages, but the calls were never returned. On June 15, Colonel Parker wrote a letter to Elvis. In it he explained that he was busily coordinating the next two tours, focusing on advertising, hotels, airports, ticket sales, etc. When Joe Esposito went on vacation for a week, no one on Elvis's staff had been in contact with him. Since the Colonel never took a vacation himself, this seemed inexcusable that no one was getting back to him with any details as the tours were nearing the eleventh hour.

This letter underscores how little Elvis and the Colonel interacted during this period given that the Colonel was Elvis's sole rainmaker. Elvis wasn't mad at the Colonel. He truly respected him and was simply avoiding him because he knew the Colonel would hear in his voice if he was slurring or didn't have his head on straight. The relationship changed over the years, but the respect was always there.

Colonel Parker celebrated his sixty-seventh birthday in Landover, Maryland, where Yanique Diskin, Tom's wife, furnished the cake. This was part of Tour Four, which started on June 25 at Buffalo's Memorial Auditorium and ended July 5 at Memphis's Mid-South Coliseum. Elvis performed thirteen shows in eleven days; for that, he received $749,000 while the Colonel took in $374,500. They also each received a $32,000 check for concession sales.

The following week, Vernon Presley, with Elvis's consent, gave termination notices to Red West and Sonny West as well as bodyguard Dave Hebler. Vernon told them that they were making a few changes and scaling back on expenses. They were all shell-shocked, especially Red and Sonny, who were like brothers to Elvis. They each received one week's severance pay.

The common denominator among these three men was that they did not look the other way when Elvis's problem spiraled out of control. In fact, they got in his face several times about it, and it finally cost them their jobs. By cutting them loose, Elvis was cutting the last ties to his sobriety. It's another hallmark of an addict: get rid of the people hassling you, if possible. For Elvis, that wasn't a problem.

Elvis normally did a masterful job of hiding his habit from Colonel Parker, but when he went back on the road for the fifth tour of that year, the cat was out of the bag.

On Saturday, July 31, Elvis had a two-day stay in Hampton Roads, Virginia. The Colonel was at the airport to meet Elvis's plane when it arrived from Hartford, Connecticut. He didn't return to the hotel until 3:30 A.M. and was extremely upset. He had tried to talk to Elvis about the scarf issue and the fan security, but Elvis was so out of it that it was no use.

"What can I do?" the Colonel wondered aloud to Loanne. "The real Elvis is sharp and clever and would understand. But the person I saw tonight didn't even recognize me! He is too out of it to respond. He is like another person. No one knows how much I miss the real Elvis. If only I knew how to bring him back."

Everyone else on the tour was also concerned about Elvis's condition but were helpless to do anything about it.

"I had never seen Colonel Parker so discouraged and so disheartened," Loanne recalled to me.

That morning he dictated a letter to Elvis, conveying the issue with the scarves once more. He said that in addition to a frantic surge to the front of the stage this created, small children and adults were getting shoved around. Security personnel were also worried about possible riots starting by those who didn't get a scarf. This scenario could possibly result in several lawsuits, not to mention insurance rates increasing for the venues hosting Elvis concerts.

It was obvious the Colonel was trying a very tactful and psychological approach. Elvis had previously been told many times about these problems but continued to ignore the situation.

Tour Five did not sell out in advance, as evidenced by the advertising costs. An ordinary tour would require an advertising budget ranging from $10,000 to $40,000 to ensure filled houses at every venue. Advertising costs for the latest tour ran a record high $213,739. Elvis did make $550,000 and the Colonel $275,000 despite the additional promotional costs.

As Elvis returned to Memphis to relax for three weeks, the Colonel and staff returned to Las Vegas to wrap up plans for Tour Six and to lay the groundwork for three additional tours to complete the busiest concert year in Elvis's entire career.

Artie Newman, a veteran assistant casino manager at the Hilton and friend of the Colonel's, had pleaded with him for months to talk with a prominent Japanese businessman who was also a valued casino customer of the hotel. He had a business proposition to discuss with the Colonel and was using Artie as an intermediary. The Colonel finally gave in to his friend and let Artie set up a meeting.

The businessman and an associate walked into the Colonel's office in the MGM Studio in Culver City with an interpreter. After introductions were made by the interpreter, they all sat at a conference table. The man who wanted to bring Elvis to Japan handed over a cashier's check for $1 million. The Colonel placed his hat over the check, pulled it toward him, then peeked underneath.

"Well, that's fine for me," said the Colonel. "But what about Elvis?"

Tour producer Charlie Stone, who was present at that meeting, recalled what happened next.

"There was so much talking back and forth between these men in

Japanese, but nothing was translated back." Stone laughed retelling this to me in 2023. "They didn't know how to deal with that situation."

The Japanese promoter did not want to meet the Colonel's price, and the conversation soon ended. Elvis never did appear in Japan or Europe or tour outside of America save for a brief engagement in Canada. But he was making plans to go overseas. I have in my possession a certificate of insurance Elvis Presley took out on himself and the *Lisa Marie* to fly to England, Germany, and Japan, where he was planning a tour in 1977. Charlie Stone had flight tickets in his briefcase and was headed to London to book the 12,500-seat Wembley Arena for an entire week (it was the first time they had seven days available), but then Elvis died. Elvis was looking forward to playing in these three countries where he had a fervent and loyal following.

The millions of overseas fans who make up a large part of the fan base that has kept Elvis's memory alive for the past four and a half decades unfortunately never got to see him perform in person. Many critics and pop culture historians have blamed this on Colonel Parker and say that because he was a Dutch citizen and didn't hold a passport, he held Elvis back. Once again, another falsehood. Given Colonel Parker's connection to many people who held power—Lyndon Johnson, Jimmy Carter, and Ronald Reagan—getting a passport issued would not have been a problem. I'd seen the Colonel call a few presidents and they'd pick up the phone on the first or second ring. Besides, the Colonel didn't need to fly to a foreign country to oversee Elvis in concert. He could have sent an advance team and a road manager to handle the operations overseas.

But there were other considerations for why Elvis didn't tour overseas at that time: Elvis's traveling medicine cabinet and his fascination with guns. They traveled wherever he did. He didn't just carry a piece; he had several sidearms on his person almost all the time. At Sonny West's wedding, a few years before, he had two pearl-handled pistols tucked inside his waistband and a derringer stashed in his boot. Mountain men didn't walk around that heavily armed. Between the guns and the drugs, Elvis broke laws in practically every state he visited. Go to a strict country like Japan or Saudi Arabia locked and loaded like that or with a stash of drugs? Forget about it.

Paul McCartney found that out the hard way a few years later, in January 1980, when he brought a large quantity of marijuana into Japan. Not only did it make international headlines and embarrass the ex-Beatle, but he had to spend nine days in jail, refund millions in ticket sales, and offer up several mea culpas once he got out of the pokey. That easily could have been Elvis.

Whatever problems Elvis may have had, in the States he was still the King. As a wise Elizabethan poet once wrote, "the greatest slave in a country is generally the king of it." More and more, his kingdom was his dark bedroom in Graceland.

And if he didn't change his life, that room would become a sepulcher.

21

Baseball, American Pie, and Chevrolet

No matter how down Elvis Presley got in his personal life, professionally he remained very much in demand. His concerts still sold out. His record sales, though not the chart-toppers of yesteryear, still generated enough profit to make RCA Records executives happy. His songs still played on the radio as did his movies on syndicated television. And there was always someone knocking on the Colonel's door to approach him with a big idea.

In August 1976, the Colonel received a letter from Tom Sarnoff, an executive vice president at NBC, regarding the network's plans for a fiftieth anniversary show. The network went on the air on November 15, 1926, with a gala four-hour radio program originating from the ballroom of the Waldorf-Astoria Hotel in New York City. Of course, television didn't come into play until a dozen years later, with NBC's broadcast of the opening ceremonies of the New York World's Fair on April 30, 1939. With that, NBC began a regular television service, and by 1951 had established a coast-to-coast television network. Five years later, the world got a glimpse of its first rock 'n' roll star thanks to the medium.

The Colonel had already turned down Sarnoff's requests to use clips of Elvis's early television performances on the network, but Sarnoff persisted and asked him to reconsider given their shared history.

The Colonel replied in his inimitable style in a letter to Sarnoff. He pointed out that showing a clip of Elvis without compensation was unfair to his client. However, he would consider an arrangement of six one-minute or thirty-second commercials for one of Elvis's concerts or hotel engagements. The Colonel said he would try his best to work with him, which was not only fair but reasonable. And it was, but Sarnoff did not see it that way.

Sarnoff's reply was short and to the point, stating that it was not possible to offer up commercials in exchange for the clip. "I guess we'll have to resign ourselves to the fact that Elvis will not be on [NBC's anniversary show]," he ended the letter.

On August 18, the Colonel decided to take his communication problem with Elvis to Vernon in the form of a letter. It stated that he had pinned down two of Elvis's employees, asking if Elvis had received his messages. They indicated yes but that Elvis did not want to see or speak to the Colonel. He was baffled and said the last time he had seen Elvis was in Fayetteville, North Carolina, and was very thankful for the advice he had given him regarding a sticky situation involving a possible lawsuit. He stated that he would not arrange for the next tour unless they cleared up the matter like "grown-up, intelligent people."

The Colonel's frustration with the entire situation continued, and on August 20, just a week before Tour Six was scheduled to begin in San Antonio, he dictated a series of letters.

The first was to Elvis since he still wouldn't communicate by telephone. He reiterated to Elvis that since he wanted to do more concerts each month (because he needed the money), the Colonel still wanted his guidance and input on his touring and recording schedule. He also reminded Elvis that they owed RCA six singles and three albums to complete the 1976 contract. The Colonel said it had been ten days since they had last spoken and that he had left many messages for him. He said that he could only do so much for Elvis given their lack of communication.

The same day he sent a letter to Tom Hulett. It was the first time the Colonel had put in writing to Management III Productions his doubts about the future of the tour business because of the "uncertain availability of Elvis." He also stated that unless Elvis adhered to the proper medication and treatment, he would not sign off on any long tours. The Colonel said they could no longer take the responsibility of signing contracts and building commitments, except for one tour at a time. "We had some close calls on the last tour, and we cannot take those chances again. I will go over this with you in person next week," Colonel Parker wrote.

Finally, he penned a short note to Tom Diskin, sharing his dismay about Elvis and the state of their relationship. The Colonel sounded almost desperate, telling Diskin it would be a miracle if they would complete or even start the tour given their current circumstances. And if they canceled, Elvis would put the blame on them and not take responsibility for his actions. He stated that Elvis had not contacted him in ten days and he had no idea of Elvis's condition.

Colonel Parker thought very carefully before writing these letters. Life wasn't much fun anymore worrying about Elvis and watching Marie's health deteriorate before his very eyes. Elvis was also nearly impossible to reach, which perplexed the Colonel and discouraged him from making any plans. His new demeanor was entirely opposite from his basic nature.

Tour Six opened on August 27 in San Antonio, Texas, with the Colonel arriving two days early and staying at the Palacio del Rio. The tour consisted of sixteen performances in thirteen days.

Elvis's concerts were becoming more and more lethargic. He was extremely overweight, slurring his words and forgetting lyrics. The press was becoming brutal in its reviews. On August 28, an afternoon concert in Houston was especially disastrous, and critics from both the *Chronicle* and *Post*, longtime Elvis advocates, tore him apart after four thousand fans walked out of the show.

"Elvis Presley has been breaking hearts for more than twenty years now and Saturday afternoon at the Summit—in a completely new and unexpected way—he broke mine," wrote the *Post*'s Bob Claypool. "In short, the concert was awful—a depressingly incoherent, amateurish mess served up by a bloated, stumbling and mumbling figure who didn't act like 'The King' of anything, least of all rock 'n' roll. It made for a sad, pitiful afternoon."

While many hard-core fans maintained that the show was "great," many more demanded their money back.

The Colonel and staff arrived in Mobile, Alabama, in a pouring rain. To add to their problems, they discovered ants in their beds. In Macon, Georgia, there were roaches in their room. The bug spray got liberal use on that tour.

It was in Macon where they received word that Red West, Sonny West, and Dave Hebler were going to write a "tell-all" book about Elvis. No one wanted to believe it. Everyone on the tour was stunned even though Elvis (through his father Vernon) had unceremoniously sacked them. Years later, Sonny West said that he and the others were cut loose with very little pay and limited prospects and needed the money.

In some of the smaller towns where Elvis played, Colonel Parker had to rely on local funeral homes to supply the limousines. They always hoped they wouldn't be needed for other reasons, and there were few scheduling problems. However, in one small town, the Colonel was advised that a widow had scheduled her husband's funeral at the same time as the show. She thought about it and decided her late husband would have wanted her to represent both at the concert since they were such avid Elvis fans and had already purchased their tickets. She asked the funeral home to postpone the services until after the show had left town. Not only did she attend the concert, but she also brought along a photo of her husband and placed it on the seat next to her.

"It's the least I could do for him," she said.

Despite the poor performances on that tour, financially it did well. Elvis earned $600,000 while Colonel Parker took home half that amount. Souvenir sales were down, earning each of them only $12,360. This was possibly caused by disgruntled fans not wanting any merchandise after a poor performance.

If there were any doubts about this, critical reviews kept pouring in, and on September 14, 1976, the Colonel sent a stack of them to Vernon Presley with an enclosed letter. Colonel Parker explained that word was spreading fast about Elvis's bad performances as well as rumors about his drug and sleeping-pill habits. He said the letter was actually meant for Elvis to read and he was hoping that Vernon would show it to him to snap him out of his reverie. He said their problems were starting to snowball and that they were having a "great deal of trouble booking buildings due to the press reports being released from some disastrous concerts and the many complaints." He wrote that more than four thousand people walked out of his Houston concert and that he could no longer cover up for Elvis. He said that Elvis was now being watched closely by the media and that if Elvis wanted, he could dispel all the rumors by improving his health and performances.

As if he didn't have enough to worry about, the Colonel continued to worry about Marie as well as Elvis. On September 20, he flew with her to Florida in a private plane so she could see her son, Bobby. He hoped that seeing Bobby would improve her condition. Unfortunately, she did not recognize him. It was the Colonel's last hope, and the lack of favorable results frustrated him. He felt that all he could do from that point on was to see that she received the best around-the-clock care possible. He had already lost his wife to illness, although her body would continue to survive for another decade.

Marie hung in there, but many around Elvis did not. That November, Linda Thompson decided that she could no longer stick around and watch Elvis self-destruct. Linda also suspected—rightly so—that Elvis was courting other women. But it was the drug habit that was the real rub. She once said that she could keep Elvis alive for another five years or she could wake up one morning and find him dead. When you know someone who is heavily using hard drugs, that's a common thought; that one day you're going to walk in and find them dead. Both options were beginning to wear her out and age her internally. The sad part was, Linda never stopped loving Elvis. She was and is a very special lady. She went on to have a very successful songwriting and acting career.

A few weeks after Linda left, George Klein introduced Elvis to nineteen-year-old Ginger Alden.

Elvis played his last Sin City engagement in December 1976. From all reports, his performances had become weak and bizarre. He read lyrics right off the sheet and was likely to declare, "I hate Las Vegas!" His career careened from legitimate superstardom to ludicrous, and Elvis had become a caricature of himself.

Bill Burk of the *Memphis Press-Scimitar* had known Elvis since the 1950s and was there for his closing night. He filed a story that shook up everyone back in Tennessee and that turned out to be most prescient. After sitting through Elvis's closing night performance at the Hilton, Burke wondered in print if this might be Elvis's last Vegas engagement based on "groupies who openly expressed concern for him [Presley]." He didn't come out and say Elvis had a drug issue, but one could surmise that based on his column.

Years later, Burk confirmed to my coauthor Marshall Terrill that when he wrote that piece, he had been aware of Elvis's problem from insiders since 1973, but was kept under strict orders from his boss to keep his lip buttoned.

"The people think of Elvis as baseball, hot dogs, apple pie, and Chevrolet," Burk was told by his editor. "And we will never *ruin* that image."

Elvis wasn't a star. He was an icon. It would be like finding out that George Washington lied about something, or that Franklin Roosevelt knew ahead of time the Japanese were going to attack Pearl Harbor. That's why the fans kept coming back despite the lousy reviews. Those writers couldn't be right. They made a mistake. It had to be. The boy had just had a bad night—that's all. He would be fine tonight. The people were in as much denial as Elvis was.

All of it would be over in less than a year.

22

Under New Management

Elvis Presley spent his last birthday on Earth at his home in Palm Springs, enjoying time with his new girlfriend, Ginger Alden, and her sister Rosemary. I usually saw Elvis when he came to town because I either picked him up at the airport or had to unlock his Chino Canyon Drive home, turn on the lights or get the air-conditioning unit going.

I remember the Colonel and I were called to duty when Elvis took a break in between touring, and he decided to make a stop in Palm Springs. The municipal airport was a tiny white building at the time, which could barely handle the *Lisa Marie*, a very large plane. But it was either that or fly into the Ontario Airport, which was about seventy-five miles west of Palm Springs.

We had organized a few rental cars for Elvis and some members of his entourage. The cars were driven by Woody Logan and his son Ricky. The two were landscapers for Elvis and the Colonel. They parked the cars on the tarmac near the Combs Gates Aviation hangar.

Delta was the major airline at the airport, and they were not willing to lend their air stairs to anyone, including Elvis . . . so we had to improvise. The Colonel and I were in my red pickup truck, thinking that we'd drive it under the door of the plane and Elvis could step right into the bed of my pickup truck. But the placement of the main cabin door was a good ten feet from the ground and there was no way we were going to ask Elvis to jump. We had to do some fast thinking.

I looked around and spotted a truck with a ladder welded to the bed parked outside the Combs hangar. I walked to the truck, looked inside, and lo and behold, the keys were in the ignition. I couldn't find anyone to ask about borrowing it, and I knew it was tantamount to stealing, so I hesitated. That's when the Colonel screamed at me.

"Damnit, Greg!" he yelled. "What's the holdup?"

"No holdup at all, Colonel," I said, jumping into the truck. I drove it over to the *Lisa Marie* and backed it up to the plane. The stairs abutted the door perfectly, but it wasn't exactly sturdy. In fact, they were rickety.

Elvis was a good sport about the whole thing and stepped off the plane onto the ladder and into the bed of the truck. Everyone who was there had a good laugh. An interesting side note: Elvis ended up spending $700,000 to install stairs on the *Lisa Marie*, which was almost three times the cost of the actual plane!

The day after they arrived, Elvis called his dentist, Max Shapiro, in Los Angeles because he wanted his teeth checked. Elvis encouraged him to make a house call in the desert and offered to pay for his airfare and provide overnight accommodations. Max brought his eighteen-year-old fiancée, Suzanne, with him. Max was in his sixties and not a good-looking man.

After Max examined Elvis's teeth, Ginger took a seat in a chair in the master bedroom. Max offered to file her lower teeth to even them out. While he was working on her teeth, he casually mentioned to Elvis that he was contemplating marriage but couldn't decide where they'd hold their nuptials.

Elvis asked them if they had a marriage certificate. Max said they always carried it on them.

"Why don't you get married here?" Elvis asked. Max was caught off guard and stopped working on Ginger's teeth. Elvis said he would supply the venue, the jeweler, and someone who could marry them: Elvis's friend Larry Geller, who could legally perform marriages. How could he say no to that offer?

Elvis sent an emissary to the jeweler's store on Palm Canyon Drive.

He was asked to bring an array of rings to the listed address for a secret ceremony, and he refused. Elvis then dispatched Dick Grob to the merchant's place of business, as Grob knew the owner. When Dick arrived, he spoke freely to the man.

"You know this is for Elvis Presley, right?" was all Dick had to say. The jeweler assembled a nice collection for the wedding and was glad he did. Elvis bought a large quantity of rings that day and didn't even bother to look at the price tags.

Meanwhile, when Max saw my wife Sherry's teeth and braces, he asked her how long the braces had been on, and his reaction to her response was, "That's ridiculous! Greg, go get your needle-nose pliers." I did as he said, and when I came back, Sherry was sitting in a chair with Max looking into her mouth. When I handed him the pliers, he took off the braces immediately and threw them away, saving us a trip and a large bill from the dentist.

Colonel Parker didn't think the story was so funny when he heard about it. He did not like Max Shapiro and thought of Sherry as a daughter. Sherry cooked a lot of meals for the Parkers and constantly looked after Marie when the Colonel was on the road. She held a special place in the Colonel's heart.

"Why in the world would you let that man take off Sherry's braces without anesthesia?" the Colonel asked in an angry tone, one of the few times he was disappointed in me. "Do not allow him around your wife ever again."

After Shapiro and Suzanne[29] exchanged their vows and left the house, Elvis asked Larry and Rosemary to come into the room. One of his favorite books was *The Prophet,* and he began to read from its passages on marriage.

---

29 Suzanne Shapiro experienced a short and difficult life. According to court documents, she was given to a religious cult as a child and most likely married Shapiro because she had nowhere else to go or was escaping the cult. At age thirty-four, she was brutally beaten, raped, and shot execution-style by two brothers in Los Angeles. They were sentenced to life in prison without the possibility of parole.

"Ginger, I haven't asked you before, but I would like us to get married, and I want Larry to do it the same way he married Dr. Max and Suzanne, so what do you think? Do you want to?"

Ginger was stunned and momentarily at a loss for words. Finally, she spoke, but not much.

"Sure," she said excitedly.

Elvis presented Ginger with an engagement ring a few weeks later on January 26, 1977. It was made from a diamond taken from one of his rings made by jeweler Lowell Hays. After Lisa Marie went to bed, Elvis took her into the dressing room in his bathroom at Graceland, got down on his knees, and presented her with a small green velvet box. Inside was a magnificent ring with a large diamond in the center surrounded by six smaller stones.

"Will you marry me?" he asked. She nodded her head, then said yes.

There was hope that Elvis would finally get his act together. Here was the proverbial love of a good woman, carrying with her the promise of a new start. But it didn't take long for Elvis to fall back into his bad habits. He abandoned a recording session set up in Nashville by Felton Jarvis, keeping a group of musicians waiting around for days, claiming that he had a sore throat. In desperation, RCA technicians brought their equipment to Graceland and waited three days, but again, Elvis never recorded. He requested that they make backing tracks, and he would lay the voice in later. RCA bent over backward for Elvis even though he wasn't bending much for them.

He did, however, go on a ten-city tour of the South from February 12th to the 21st. He insisted that Ginger accompany him. She was a good motivating factor for Elvis, as he did his best to impress her, providing a new spark to his concerts.

Beyond the tour, Elvis went out of his way to woo Ginger. Often, that meant busting open the wallet and showering her with gifts. He bought her a Cadillac, expensive jewelry (including a sparkling TLC diamond necklace), and clothes, in addition to flying her entire family to Las Vegas. He also spent close to $100,000 taking a group of thirty people, including Ginger and her sisters, on an extravagant trip to Hawaii. Whenever Elvis did something, no expense was spared.

"What profiteth it to gain the world if you couldn't share your good fortune with your friends?" Elvis said to hairstylist and friend Larry Geller.

After several failed attempts by Felton Jarvis to get Elvis to record new material, he rented an eight-track machine to record Elvis on the road. But Elvis was often tired and stumbled through the songs. RCA decided to release *Welcome to My World*, a compilation of previously released country material and a pair of live tracks to satisfy the fan base. The art-be-damned effort received a tepid response, charting at number 44 on *Billboard*. (It later went platinum after Elvis's death.)

Tour Two should have been easy with only eight performances, including two in Norman, Oklahoma, and two in Alexandria, Louisiana. On March 26, Joe Esposito asked to meet with the Colonel. Elvis, he reported, had "chipped a tooth" before the show, and to those on the inside, this was a sign there were going to be problems relative to the medication he was taking. In other words, he was slipping into that gray world where no one could reach him. There were more "tooth troubles" on the 28th. The tour seemed grim, and Elvis's boys were doing everything in their power to keep him from going into that state, but he was clever when it came to circumventing their actions.

They also saw more concern in the Colonel's demeanor than they had previously observed. On March 29, they flew into Baton Rouge, Louisiana, to make sure the hotel accommodations were ready for Elvis, who would arrive after the show that night. The next two shows were in Alexandria, but Elvis stayed in Baton Rouge and flew back after both performances. The Colonel went to the airport that night to see Elvis and check things out for himself. He returned to the hotel miserable over what he saw.

It was pouring rain in Mobile when the advance crew arrived, which didn't help the emotional atmosphere. The Colonel and Tom Hulett were debating whether they should even attempt a show that night in Baton Rouge but decided to give it a shot. The Colonel desperately hoped that knowing he had a concert to do, Elvis would pull himself together and keep going. Without the concerts to prepare for, no one knew what would happen to Elvis. The only thing that seemed to hold his attention was performing for his fans. He could be in a stupor before going onstage, but once there, some inner reserve would take over and he was able to perform.

The show began in the Louisiana State University Assembly Center, but at intermission an announcement was made that Elvis was unable to perform because of illness. The communiqué brought howls of protest from a crowd estimated at more than thirteen thousand people.

Dr. Hypolite T. Landry, a Baton Rouge physician, issued the following statement: "My examination of Mr. Presley reveals that he has an acute case of gastroenteritis and fatigue. It is my recommendation that he cancel his performance tonight and the remainder of his tour and be hospitalized for treatment and rest."

Dr. Nick accompanied Elvis back to Memphis on the *Lisa Marie*, where he was hospitalized at Memphis Baptist. Back in Mobile, Alabama, Tom Hulett was on the verge of a nervous breakdown. Elvis's behavior and canceled shows were causing him nightmares. The Colonel announced that the rest of the tour was canceled. He was on the phone constantly for the next several days, working on "postponement dates" for Mobile, Macon, and Jacksonville. He had also placed ads in the newspapers in the three cities with the announcement that the canceled shows would be rescheduled. This prevented the problem of refunding all the money for the canceled shows. Those who wanted a refund received it, but almost everyone kept their tickets to use on the rescheduled dates.

They all returned to Las Vegas to finish the tour reports and complete arrangements for the next three tours. Fortunately, the Colonel's old friend, Eddy Arnold, was in town and dropped by to visit, which brightened the day. The Colonel took his staff to see Eddy's show at the Sahara Hotel.

On April 12, the Colonel called Elvis to advise him about a CBS-TV special that would be filmed on Tour Five. He hoped this would be the impetus needed to get Elvis back on track. He remembered that *Elvis: Aloha from Hawaii* four years before had motivated him to get in shape and thought the new TV special would have the same effect.

During this difficult period, the Colonel and Vernon often talked about the elephant in the room. Both men were upset and frustrated about the best way to help Elvis, or if they could help Elvis at all.

Elvis's exploits were becoming regular fodder for the tabloid media. The *National Enquirer* ran a cover story on Elvis with an unflattering picture and the sensational headline: "Elvis's Bizarre Behavior and Secret Face Lift," which was a regurgitation of a *Star* story that ran a few weeks before. That headline blared: "Elvis, 42, Fears He's Losing His Sex Appeal."

In late April, a story ran in the *Nashville Banner* that Colonel Parker was selling Elvis's management contract to a group of West Coast businessmen. The newspaper cited several "authoritative sources" in the music industry for the piece, and stated the reason was the Colonel's gambling habit and the fact that the two men had not spoken in almost two years. They even quoted Parker, who denied the allegations.

"The whole story is a fabrication by somebody," he said while prepping a show in St. Paul, Minnesota. "I'm here, I'm working with Elvis, I'm in good health, and I don't have any debts—at least none that I can't pay.

"I have no idea how this story got started. It just sounds like one of those phony deals, and I don't know why newspapers pick up on this stuff. I've been working with Elvis all along, and I intend to keep right on working with him."

He was being creative with the truth. The Colonel was working for Elvis. Elvis wasn't working with anyone except his "doctors."

About a year before the *Nashville Banner* story broke, Colonel Parker and I attended a Billy Graham Crusade at the San Diego Stadium on March 31, 1976. We were there to visit the manager of the facility, who was a friend of the Colonel's. In fact, Colonel Parker was on a first-name basis with every building manager of every venue in the country.

This was simply a social visit to see an old friend and become more familiar with a fairly new venue, possibly one where Elvis might play someday. Elvis usually performed at the San Diego Sports Arena, an indoor arena built in 1966, which sat about twelve thousand people. The stadium was massive and had the capacity for seventy thousand seats, and Billy Graham packed the place.

As we were talking in this gentleman's office located behind the box-office area, we couldn't help noticing the large laundry baskets filled with money, most likely from food and beverage concessions and merchandise. Anytime Colonel Parker saw that amount of cash, he got inspired. I could practically hear his brain percolating.

As we were driving back to Escondido to visit Lawrence Welk at the Welkome Inn, the Colonel was smoking a cigar and looking out the window.

"You know, I think Elvis would love to sing gospel music to a large audience," he said. "He could draw huge crowds like the one we just saw and perhaps get inspired again. Perhaps it might get him out of his funk and save Elvis."

Whenever Elvis played his piano and sang at home, it was always gospel songs. Whenever he sang in between takes at the recording studio, it was gospel. Same with soundchecks. He grew up on gospel, loved singing it, loved hearing it, loved to hear others play it. It was his passion music.

This was the first time in a while that I had seen Colonel Parker excited. He had been down on Elvis for the past year, and their level of communication was at an all-time low. The next day the Colonel called Elvis in Memphis and while I couldn't hear what Elvis said on the other end of the line, I was in the Colonel's Palm Springs office and could tell he was very receptive to the idea. He seemed to have Elvis's undivided attention because they talked on the phone for a long time, and this was a period when Elvis wasn't taking his calls.

The idea would be to take Elvis off the road for a while and let him regain his health. When he felt better, he would record a gospel album and take it out on the road and play in large stadiums. One of the details I picked up on was that Elvis really liked the idea of having a hundred-person choir backing him in every city that would volunteer their time just as they did for a Billy Graham Crusade. A director would rehearse them a day before the show and get them ready for Elvis.

To do all of this, they'd need a large infusion of cash. The money would cover Elvis's overhead to keep him off the road, for the gospel album (distributed on the Colonel's and Elvis's new label, Boxcar Records), and to build a whole new road show. The Colonel felt the only way to pull this off would be to take on a new financial partner. And if they were to do this, it had to be done discreetly. But where to find someone like that?

My bookkeeper, Bob Stewart, had as clients Rudolph "Rudy" Weyerhaeuser Driscoll, Sr. and his wife, Margot. They were multimillionaires and philanthropists tied to the billion-dollar Weyerhaeuser fortune; the American timberland company has produced a variety of products such as lumber, paper, and fodder for livestock since the 1800s.

Rudy thought the idea of owning a piece of Elvis Presley sounded intriguing. Margot was a former ballet dancer who was a big Ricky Nelson fan. And I just so happened to manage him.

These refined folks, who sat on boards, supported the arts, bestowed endowments on research universities, and ran their own foundation were perhaps looking for a little excitement and a foot in the door of the entertainment industry. I really didn't know their motivation, but they were very nice and classy people. They wanted to meet Colonel Parker right away.

I called him at his house and explained who I was with and what they were interested in doing. He told me to bring the Driscolls to his house. They met, hit it off, and spoke for several hours.

The Colonel got down to brass tacks: he wanted $10 million, which he and Elvis would split right down the middle. In addition, Rudy would put up the money for some additional projects, which he was happy to do. He'd also keep the Colonel on as Elvis's manager. For that, Rudy would get 25 percent of all future earnings. The Colonel would give up 25 percent of his back end while Elvis still retained his 50 percent share.

To compensate me for setting up the meeting, Rudy asked me what I wanted. I knew Ricky Nelson needed some national exposure to help him make a big comeback, so they agreed to bankroll a television special to the tune of $200,000. That ended up being *It's All Right Now*, which was directed by Taylor Hackford and aired in syndication in 1978. The Driscolls were listed as the executive producers. And if that wasn't enough, they leased out an entire floor in a high-rise building at 6430 Sunset Boulevard (today it is known as the CNN Building) in the heart of Hollywood and gave me a spectacular office filled with high-end furniture, posters, gold records, and filing cabinets filled with Elvis stuff. The office, which had a sign on the door that read MARGO ENTERPRISES INC. was a virtual shrine to the King. The Colonel had a tiny office at the RCA Building across the street, and it was nowhere near as nice as mine. We both got a kick out it, and he enjoyed ribbing me about my luxurious accommodations and how he was going to be parking himself in my office to conduct business. In fact, he once tossed me out of my office to hold a meeting with Abe Lastfogel. I laughed, then went downstairs to the Jolly Roger, a restaurant on the bottom floor, to grab a bite to eat. I took no offense. It was a pleasure that I could do something nice for Colonel Parker.

The Driscolls were not only extraordinarily kind but serious ballers! When they placed a $10 million check in Colonel Parker's hands, he knew these folks were the real deal. It was probably the largest amount of money he ever held in his hands, but when it came down to it, the Colonel couldn't cash the check. He didn't give me a reason why he never went through with it, but he couldn't bring himself to go to the bank and deposit it. If I were to guess, there was probably some concern that Elvis couldn't hold it together and the Colonel might be on the hook for that seven-figure check. The Colonel had a hard enough time making people whole while on tour, and this was exponentially more.

The Driscolls understood and were nothing but gracious about the Colonel's change of heart. With Elvis becoming unreliable while simultaneously hemorrhaging cash on Cadillacs, expensive jewelry, and Hawaiian vacations, holding on to that check may have been the Colonel's insurance policy for both of them.

23

Always Elvis

On April 12, 1977, Colonel Parker called Elvis Presley to advise him about the CBS-TV special that would be filmed later that year. Better yet was the paycheck: $750,000. The fee was split between Elvis and the Colonel under their last agreement, which was struck on January 22, 1976.

Loanne was present when the Colonel received a phone call from a CBS vice president introducing himself. During the conversation, she overheard the Colonel say, "Don't worry about me. As long as I get what I want, you'll have no problems with me." That statement summarized the Colonel very well.

During this difficult period, the Colonel and Vernon talked often about how to get Elvis out of his funk. Both men were frustrated and at a loss about the best way to help Elvis.

Tour Three of 1977 was scheduled to begin in Greensboro, North Carolina, on April 21. The advance staff arrived two days early to begin final preparations for the twelve-city, thirteen-day tour. On April 20, the Colonel received one phone call after another from Memphis. The news wasn't good.

They didn't know if Elvis would be able to start the tour the next day. The Colonel was on the phone and pacing the floor most of the night. The next morning the Colonel, who was having breakfast at the Hilton, was interrupted with another phone call. It was Dr. Nick.

He said he would have Elvis on the plane in time for the next concert. You can bet the Colonel breathed a sigh of relief.

For almost five decades, Colonel Parker has received endless grief for pushing Elvis to go out on the road when he wasn't his best. That's an easy thing to say, but when an artist asks you to plan a tour and you've locked in a date, booked the venue, paid for advertisements, and actively promoted the show, and fans have spent their hard-earned money to see Elvis, it isn't so easy to pull the plug. Then there's the liability that most people aren't aware of when it comes to a canceled show. The advertising dollars spent to promote the show, which run into the tens of thousands, are gone. In Elvis's case, RCA Records Tours guaranteed him $50,000 a show plus percentages. The venue has potential revenue from concessions, which includes food, alcohol, and merchandise on the line. All these separate entities are significantly impacted by the cancellation of a show.

And, in addition to the venues, the hotels, airlines, caterers, off-duty cops, disc jockeys, program directors, radio shows, and everyone associated with the concert have their bottom line affected. It's hard to call those people the next time you need attention for your artist to get them to make the investment. Then there're the fans who are irate and want their money back. Cancellations, plain and simple, aren't good for the concert business.

The Colonel also knew that if more concert dates were canceled, they would have a rough time booking future shows. This tour was crucial, as the venue people were watching to see if Elvis was able to live up to his commitments.

One of the few bright spots at this time, the *Moody Blue* album, was recorded by RCA at several of the stops on this tour. It was his twenty-fourth and final "studio" album, though it was a hodgepodge of live and studio work with a half-dozen tracks recorded at Graceland over a two-year period. It was released in July 1977, and eventually went double platinum.

The stress was beginning to show on the Colonel. When he returned to the hotel in Green Bay, Wisconsin, he began shouting at Loanne over a minor matter.

"Why are you acting like this?" she asked him. "Why do you get upset with me, but you forgive others for their errors, even when they really goof?" The Colonel gave her a hard look before he spoke.

"Look, I put up with crap all day, and for the sake of the show I have to keep my mouth shut. But there are times when I must blow off steam, or I'll explode. Who can I shout at except you?" he explained. "You're supposed to understand, not get mad. So, help me when I need to shout, or else I'll just blow up and there will be no more Colonel." From that day on, Loanne not only accepted his shouting directed at her, but she also provoked him when she could see he was under great stress. He always felt better after his volcano exploded in her direction.

Elvis opened Tour Four in Knoxville at the University of Tennessee Stokely Athletic Center on May 20. Elvis left Memphis for the 387-mile flight to Knoxville and barely made it in time for the concert. He sang twenty-two songs, including a medley of his early hits. Afterward, a doctor saw Elvis backstage and noted that he was pale, swollen, and lacked stamina.

The Colonel was very upset when he returned to the Executive Inn that night and had another restless night. The press reviews were mixed on this two-week tour, some complimentary and others not.

His show in Philadelphia on May 28 didn't go over so well, with reporter Matt Damsker, writing a review in *The Evening Bulletin*: "Elvis '77 is paunchy, puffy, lumbering, frequently off-key, apparently under-rehearsed (he had to read the first verse of 'My Way' from a page of sheet music) and, for all that, the most outrageously condescending showman I have ever seen." Damsker added that Elvis appeared as if he had just roused from a drunken slumber and that his speech was slurred. "There are dolphins who perform more affectingly," Damsker stated.

In Jacksonville on the 30th, Elvis left the stage for about thirty minutes in the middle of the show. However, when he did return, he performed well. At 3:45 the next morning, the Colonel went to Elvis's room for a meeting. He was frustrated and needed Elvis's assurance that he would be able to finish the tour. A repeat cancellation of a show after the audience had been seated would have dire consequences, and the Colonel needed to be prepared if Elvis had any doubts about his ability to go on.

During the closing days of the tour, the Colonel was becoming more and more upset. Another "cockroach" hotel in Macon didn't help his disposition. The Colonel needed to be in control, and there was no way he could sway what was happening at this point. His uneasiness gave way to nightmares. He could see years and years of frustration ahead of him and no way to prevent it. He never imagined that Elvis wouldn't be around, but the Colonel just didn't know what condition he would be in.

Despite the earlier canceled shows, no one thought that the next tour would be the last. In the minds of everyone involved, Elvis, like Muhammad Ali, could get back to fighting form if he really wanted to do so. In retrospect, it seems strange that everyone felt Elvis could change.

It began all over again on June 15 when they flew into Springfield, Missouri, to set up Elvis's first appearance on Tour Five two days later. Elvis didn't even walk onto the stage until 10:30 that evening. On the 19th, CBS-TV began filming in Omaha for the next special.[30] The Colonel celebrated his sixty-eighth birthday in Indianapolis on Sunday, June 26, and Elvis gave one of his finest performances in months. About eighteen thousand attended the Market Square Arena show, unaware that it would be his last.

Upon his arrival in Indianapolis, RCA presented Elvis with a plaque commemorating the pressing of the two billionth record at their Indianapolis pressing plant. The presentation and the concert

---

30 The CBS special was culled from footage in both Omaha, Nebraska (June 19), and Rapid City, Iowa, (June 21). Much of the footage from Omaha was deemed unusable because of sound and performance issues.

were cause for celebration. After the show, Elvis and Ginger attended a party with friends and family, who all returned to Memphis together.

Colonel Parker left for Las Vegas right after Elvis's plane had landed for what would be his final concert ever. The tour settlements were completed in Las Vegas and work began on Tour Six, which would commence in Portland, Maine, on August 17, 1977.

Shortly before the start of Tour Six,[31] *Elvis: What Happened?* the salacious book by Red West, Sonny West, and Dave Hebler was published by Ballantine Books. It had an initial print run of 400,000 copies, which were shipped to bookstores nationwide on August 1. Rupert Murdoch coughed up $125,000 for the rights, which would later be excerpted in the *Star*, a tabloid that was a rival publication of the *National Enquirer*.

It was an unabashed and messy tell-all that revealed many of Elvis's issues, among them his affection for guns and his abuse of prescription drugs, and included some sordid episodes that the three men had divulged to Australian writer Steve Dunleavy, giving the book a tabloid bent.

The controversial book was serialized in England and Australia a few months prior, causing quite a stir among foreign fans and press, before it was released in the United States. Through his contacts (a fan in the publishing industry), Elvis had the opportunity to read an advance copy. The material alternately embarrassed, enraged, and frightened him. Naturally, he felt betrayed by the three men.

"Man, I loved those guys," Elvis would say to anyone within earshot. "Why would they do this to me?"

The Colonel also felt betrayed. He was genuinely shocked that they could have been so disloyal to Elvis after all the years they had been in Elvis's employ. He especially took a shining to Sonny West, whom

---

31 Tour Six cities included Portland, Maine (August 17–18); Utica, New York (August 19); Syracuse, New York (August 20); Hartford, Connecticut (August 21); Uniondale, New York (August 22); Lexington, Kentucky (August 23); Roanoke, Virginia (August 24); Fayetteville, North Carolina (August 25); Asheville, North Carolina (August 26); and Memphis, Tennessee (August 27–28).

he had personally taken under his wing and trained to be to one of the top security chiefs in the business. Elvis confided to the Colonel that he was reluctant to face his fans on the tour, as well as his nine-year-old daughter, Lisa Marie.

"How can I ever face my little girl?" he agonized out loud.

The Colonel had protected Elvis for years in every possible way, and with the publication of this paperback book, his work had been ruined. The Colonel gave his star the best common-sense advice he could summon at the time.

"Elvis, the best way to handle this book thing is to do such good shows that no one believes that trash could possibly be true," the Colonel said. "Be positive and concentrate on proving the book wrong by getting yourself in the best possible shape." The Colonel was nervous about the tour, but he knew it was important that Elvis not be aware of his uneasiness.

After the CBS crew began filming the TV special, they interviewed Vernon Presley in his office at Graceland. He gave major kudos to Colonel Parker.

"Colonel Parker is an honest man, and I think that's where the big organization and big togetherness comes, you know," he said. "Once you find out you don't have to worry about a guy being your manager, what he will do for you, how he handles it—you do the show, and everything works out right."

In hindsight, I'm not so sure *Elvis in Concert* was such a good idea. It showed Elvis grossly overweight and far from his peak. Some parts were disturbing, showing him sweating profusely and struggling with tone and breath control.

I know Elvis was happy with the easy money grab, but when it was aired a few months after his death, family, friends, and fans alike were horrified by what they saw. *Elvis in Concert* was never released on videocassette or DVD, and the estate has no plans to ever release the special. According to them, Elvis was visibly "far from his best in the way he looked and the way he performed." I completely agree.

RCA Records released a soundtrack album in conjunction with the broadcast of the television special. The double album augmented the televised performances with a second album of additional recordings made during the Omaha and Rapid City concerts. The concert soundtrack album was released in October, 1977, and reached number 5 on the *Billboard* album charts. It eventually reached triple platinum status.

The advance crew for the sixth tour of the year gathered at the Sheraton Inn on Maine Mall Road in Portland, Maine, on August 15, 1977. They were warmly greeted by General Manager Banns Eckert. The Colonel's entire staff of George Parkhill, Pat Kelleher, Tom Hulett, Charlie Stone, Al Dvorin, and Loanne had dinner together that night with Marty Moore of Concerts West. They discussed plans for the August 17–18 concerts at the Cumberland County Civic Center, and each person confirmed that their duties were covered. Many fans waited for days in line to see the two scheduled Portland concerts, a place where Elvis had never performed before.

After dinner, the Colonel puffed on his always-present Cuban cigar and entertained the group with stories and jokes. It was a pleasant dinner, and everyone was prepared for the tour.

At 8:00 A.M. on August 16, 1977, they all met for breakfast at the inn to review their duties for the day. They had lunch at the hotel as well, not knowing the world as they knew it would soon be turned upside down.

Shortly after 4:00 P.M., the Colonel received a call from Joe Esposito in Memphis, informing him that Elvis had been taken to Baptist Memorial Hospital. The Colonel was dubious. He chose to believe that Elvis, whatever was ailing him, would rebound and make a full recovery. However, he was solemn when he came into the room where Loanne was working. A few minutes later the phone rang. It was Vernon.

"Colonel, my son is gone," he wept. "What will I do?"

Sometime in the afternoon of Tuesday, August 16, 1977, Colonel Parker called me in Los Angeles. I was at entertainer Ricky Nelson's house in Laurel Canyon. He had successfully shed his teen idol image and was enjoying his newfound reputation as one of the pioneers of the country-rock that Jackson Browne, Linda Ronstadt, and the Eagles were making popular. (Randy Meisner, a future Eagle, played in Nelson's Stone Canyon Band before making the leap to the Eagles in 1972.) I had been Ricky's manager for a few years and his booker for many years before that. We were close and spent a lot of time together strategizing his career and, other times, just shooting the breeze.

A few minutes before Colonel Parker's call, Ricky's maid came downstairs to his music room and told us about a disturbing news report announcing that Elvis Presley was dead.

We were both in shock. Even though Elvis's behavior and habits were known to those who were close to him, including Ricky, it took us by surprise. He was a vital force, and we all thought somehow he'd miraculously bounce back and return to his former glory. Now he was in Glory.

Initial reports had listed cardiac arrhythmia or heart failure as the official cause of Elvis's death. But that really didn't matter at that moment. All that mattered was that the world lost the greatest musical entertainer of all time, and everyone associated with Elvis lost a friend.

He was forty-two.

When the phone rang, I sensed it was Colonel Parker.

"Greg, would you mind going to Palm Springs?" he asked. "I'd like for you to check in on Marie and look in on Elvis's house. I have a few things to take care of here, and then I have to fly to Memphis." Of course, I would, I replied. Nothing more was said. I understood what was going on and wanted to help in any way I could.

Colonel Parker and his crew remained at the Sheraton in Portland, Maine, to take care of business. Loanne Miller said the Colonel gathered the troops and delivered an inspiring message.

"The Colonel gave us a little talk 'cause we were all just torn up," Loanne told Joanna Johnson in 2004. "He said, 'I'm sorry, this is hard. Just because he's gone, we're still working for him, it will always be Elvis and the Colonel till the day I die. He will always be there for me. Make him proud of us.'"

The Colonel knew there'd be a big run on Elvis records and merchandise, and so he placed a few key calls and made deals to ensure that all contracts were legitimate, supply chains were in place, and that the demand was met. He also had to call all the promoters to cancel the next leg of the tour and offer refunds[32] to ticket holders. It's exactly what Elvis would have expected of him.

He implored RCA Records to press as many Elvis records as possible, even getting them to reactivate a pressing plant in England slated for closure, keeping it open for a few more months. They pressed millions of records, and much of his back catalog went gold or platinum. Anything attached to Elvis literally flew off the shelves.

He worked with Factors Etc. Inc. owner Harry "The Bear" Geissler to create a line of merchandise to stop bootleggers from manufacturing or commercially exploiting Elvis's image and likeness. Geissler specialized in the T-shirt heat transfer business and made a mint on images of Farrah Fawcett-Majors of *Charlie's Angels* fame, which enabled him to purchase licenses for *Rocky, Star Wars,* and *Superman*. He paid a tidy sum for an exclusive merchandising deal with Boxcar Enterprises and received a percentage of all sales.

Colonel Parker knew there was work to be done but has been heavily criticized for not breaking down or showing some sort of emotion in the immediate aftermath of Elvis's death. I look at it differently. He knew there was going to be an onslaught of demand for records, memorabilia, and anything fans could get their hands on. He was looking out for the Presley family and Elvis's legacy, just as he always did.

Ricky Nelson accompanied me on the two-hour drive to Palm Springs. When we arrived at Elvis's Chino Canyon home, we could not believe our eyes.

It was a zoo.

More than a hundred and fifty people had gathered in front of the home and were spilling out onto the street. Then to my horror, I

---

32 As it turned out, only 60–65 percent of Elvis fans wanted refunds for Tour Six, knowing the tickets would be future collector's items.

discovered the front iron gate, which posted a NO TRESPASSING sign, had been breached.

Inside there were about three dozen fans, acting like complete savages, taking whatever mementos they could get their hands on—anything that wasn't nailed down. A few of them were also tearing up the red-and-black carpet in the living room, which baffled me at the time. A few weeks later, one-inch portions were being sold in the classified section of *Rolling Stone* magazine. It was such an invasion of Elvis's privacy. The only other time I've heard of such ghoulish behavior was when Depression-era outlaw John Dillinger was shot by the FBI in Chicago in 1934. Crowds gathered around the spot where he was killed and dipped their handkerchiefs in his blood.

I immediately called the Palm Springs Police Department, and then ran everyone out of the house. Ricky held the front iron gate open to ensure they left, but once the realization hit them that another musical idol was in their midst, they had the temerity to hit him up for an autograph on the way out of the house they had just robbed! Ricky was flummoxed.

"I feel very weird about signing autographs right now," Ricky said, who normally would have obliged under almost any circumstance. "Elvis just died . . ." Ricky loved Elvis and was angered by the request. He did not sign one autograph that day.

Finally, a few squad cars arrived and restored the peace. They assigned a detail to the house until the fans left, which wasn't until a week later.

Once Elvis's house was secured,[33] Ricky and I headed to Colonel Parker's home, about eight blocks away. When we arrived, a scene of another kind was unfolding. The street was lined with press trucks and media, all looking to get a statement from the Colonel. That wasn't

---

33 After Elvis's death, Vernon Presley hired me to handle the sale of the Chino Canyon home, arrange for some vehicles to be transported to Memphis, and finish some construction odds and ends on the house. He also gave me all of the storage boxes and other Elvis stuff that had been left in the back of the garage.

going to happen. He was too busy looking after Elvis's estate and finalizing the details for his funeral. He just didn't have the time or emotional energy to expend on dealing with the press.

I can tell you this: the Colonel was a wreck. Somehow, he was still able to keep it together. And he was being unfairly judged for that. I'm referring specifically to the fact that many have judged him for showing up to Elvis's funeral in a Hawaiian shirt and baseball cap. I must kindly remind them that once Colonel Parker discovered the news that Elvis was dead, he flew from Portland, Maine, to Memphis the following day. The only clothes he had were on his back or in his lightly packed suitcase. As long as I knew Colonel Parker, he did not own a suit. Elvis's service took place two days after he passed and there simply wasn't time for him to go shopping for a suit. And, honestly, Elvis would've gotten a kick out of the Colonel showing up for his funeral in a Hawaiian shirt and baseball cap. I know he would have smirked and said, "Well, that's the Colonel."

After I checked in on Marie, I stepped into the Colonel's office, where the phone was ringing off the hook. He asked me to personally field his calls, which were overwhelmingly from the press and a few friends looking to offer their condolences. When the media called the house, I politely told them that the Colonel was not going to be making a statement now or anytime soon regarding his feelings about Elvis.

Vernon Presley, who was also an emotional wreck, asked J. D. Sumner to plan and carry out his son's private funeral services. The first took place in the music room at Graceland on Thursday afternoon where Elvis was lying in state in a nine-hundred-pound seamless copper casket. At 1:00 A.M. Wednesday, Vernon had called C. W. Bradley, a minister at the Wooddale Church of Christ, who had been a friend of the Presley family for about a decade. He immediately agreed to do the service and was assisted by the Reverend Rex Humbard of Akron, Ohio, who also had a special relationship with Elvis and had visited him backstage at the Las Vegas Hilton the year before. Most of the music was performed by the Stamps Quartet, who sang, "How Great Thou Art" and ended the service with "Sweet, Sweet Spirit."

The service at the Forest Hill Cemetery mausoleum was attended by about a hundred and fifty mourners, including Sammy Davis Jr., Ann-Margret and her husband Roger Smith, guitarist Chet Atkins, actor George Hamilton, Priscilla and Lisa Marie Presley, and Colonel Parker.

The night before, James Brown and Caroline Kennedy paid their respects, but they did not stay for the services. As it turned out, Kennedy was not there to pay her respects but to get a scoop. When she missed a deadline for the New York *Daily News* (where Kennedy interned while in college), she later sold her story to *Rolling Stone*. Many in Elvis's inner circle lost respect for her when it ran. Vernon, who especially felt burned, so aptly put it, "She not only insulted the memory of Elvis, she insulted her own family name."

Although the entire cemetery had been closed to the public for the burial services, approximately a hundred thousand people stood on the street outside as the forty-nine-car procession (including sixteen white limousines) pulled through the gates where Elvis would be interred in a crypt a few hundred yards from his mother's grave.[34] Once the funeral procession moved inside the cemetery, several bystanders in the street tried to break through police barricades.

The funeral ended up costing just under $50,000—a grand send-off for the King—but an expense the estate could hardly afford. Elvis had about a million dollars in a checking account and virtually nothing in savings.

Colonel Parker had been enlisted by Vernon to continue running things for the estate, which he did. And thank goodness. The estate's worth was estimated at $4.9 million at the time of Elvis's death, but that figure was deceptive. The cash-poor estate had mounting bills, and keeping Graceland functional and operational was expensive. The Colonel was needed more than ever. He not only saved the estate but helped make it what it is today.

---

[34] A few months later, the remains of Elvis and Gladys Presley were moved to the Meditation Garden at Graceland.

Always Elvis

After the funeral, the Colonel headed to Tampa, Florida, where he stayed with Clyde Rinaldi's family, whom he had known and done business with since the 1940s. The Rinaldis provided a haven where the Colonel could grieve privately. And trust me, that man grieved for Elvis. He was truly devastated. A big part of his life was over. The Colonel loved entertainment, and he was a tiger. He spent hours plotting, planning, scheduling, negotiating, and making deals. He was born to be Elvis Presley's manager, and his life changed in the snap of a finger. For twenty-two years, from the moment he woke up in the morning, each day of his life revolved around Elvis. What did he have to look forward to if Elvis wasn't around to create opportunities for him? Most of all, the two were friends. They traveled together, lived near each other, grilled steaks and watched TV, laughed and joked around, and most of all, they triumphed together. Elvis's meteoric rise to become the top entertainer in the world simply would not have been possible without the Colonel's foresight, guidance, and connections.

When Colonel Parker finally got back to Palm Springs about a week later, we sat out in his backyard under shade, and the two of us cried like a pair of little boys. Of course, he never showed that side of himself to the public. And he wouldn't. That just wasn't his way.

Sadly, Colonel Parker was never the same man after Elvis Presley died. He was a man of indefatigable energy and capability, but the spark was gone. Elvis was his North Star, the light he traveled by. When Elvis died, so did a piece of Colonel Parker, and that's the God's honest truth.

Was the Colonel disappointed in Elvis? Yes, sure he was. To the Colonel, it was all so avoidable. He expected Elvis to have some fun—he was the King, after all—but this thing with the prescription drugs was a mystery to him. Why would anyone do that when they had what Elvis had? Mostly, he was upset that all the great work they had done together had been destroyed. This magical thing they had created and put together was now overshadowed by scandal.

About a year later, some of the spark returned. That's when Colonel Parker staged a ten-day fan festival called *Always Elvis*. The gathering took place at the Las Vegas Hilton where Elvis reigned supreme during twice-annual concert runs from 1969 to 1976. In conjunction with the festival, the Colonel, Vernon, and Priscilla dedicated a life-size bronze statue of Elvis in the hotel lobby.

For a fifteen dollar admission fee, fans were treated to a five-screen, thirty-two-projector multimedia documentary featuring Elvis's home movies, movie clips, film outtakes, and early concert footage in the hotel's new two-thousand-seat showroom. The ninety-minute documentary, *Always Elvis*, later toured the country.[35]

The site also included displays of costumes Elvis wore in the movies and in concert, guitars and personal items, as well as vendor and exhibitor booths selling all types of Elvis memorabilia and merchandise. These included concert photos, dinner plates, wastebaskets, music boxes, and bumper stickers ("Elvis Didn't Die—He Moved to a Better Town" was a big hit). Fans could also meet Charlie Hodge, who had a booth where he could meet fans. He gladly signed autographs (for a $5 fee), posed for pictures, and told lots of Elvis stories, as did Canadian-born comedian Jackie Kahane, who toured with Elvis from 1972 to 1977. He had been hand-selected by the Colonel, who heard him open for Wayne Newton one night in Las Vegas.

"In all the time I was with him, I never had a cross word with Elvis. I did have one confrontation with Colonel," Kahane said in 2000, a year before he died. "He hated to have his picture taken. I had gotten a new camera and was taking a picture of the plane, the *Lisa Marie*, and I didn't see Colonel sitting on the stairs of the plane. He called me over to him and in very vulgar terms told me off. I stood my ground, yelled right back at him, and finally said, 'Remember I can get another

---

35 *Always Elvis* was an attempt to replicate the success of *The Beatles: Away With Words*, a traveling multimedia show that toured the United States in the early to mid-seventies. For a time, it satiated the appetites of hardcore Beatles fans who were still reeling from their breakup.

job, you can't.' With that we both broke into laughter, shook hands, and never had a bad word after that."

But by far the biggest celebrity in the crowd that day was Colonel Parker.

I was sitting with him in his booth, which was surrounded by gold record awards received by the Presley estate since Elvis's death. I witnessed people lining up twenty-deep to meet the Colonel, just to shake his hand, get a picture taken with him, and thank him for bringing Elvis to the masses. One young man in his mid-twenties came up to the booth and delivered a special message that especially touched Colonel Parker.

"I just want to thank you for the way you handled Elvis's career," he said.

"You hear that?" the Colonel smiled at *Los Angeles Times* reporter Robert Hilburn, who was covering the event. "That's worth all the criticism."

In the days following Elvis's death, Colonel Parker wrote a special poem about Elvis, and he offered it to fans at the convention for $1, the proceeds going to charity. I think the last four lines speak volumes on how he felt about Elvis:

The boy became a man and he carried on,
To make us happy with his songs.
We will play your songs from day to day,
For you never really went away.
The Colonel

And if there is any doubt how the Colonel felt about Elvis, I'll defer to an August 15, 1989, article written by *Chicago Tribune* columnist Bob Greene. After spending a week in Elvis's suite at the Las Vegas Hilton—sleeping in the King's bedroom, brushing his teeth in his bathroom, and eating room service in his dining room—Greene was tipped off that Colonel Parker was in the hotel's coffee shop. Being the good scribe that he was, Greene sought out the famed manager. The columnist was under the impression, like many were, that Colonel Parker got 50 percent of whatever Elvis took in and that he "kept him on the road, displaying him like a circus animal in small cities."

Greene spotted Colonel Parker almost immediately. He was sitting at a table sporting a white yachting cap, his cane sitting on the next chair.

When Greene introduced himself to the Colonel, who was now eighty years old, he was "no longer the fearsome-looking former carny," but a man who offered undiluted conversation.

They talked for a good while, and near the end of the interview, Greene wanted to know if he could ask his subject a stupid question.

"If it's stupid, don't embarrass yourself," the Colonel said. "Don't ask it."

"Do you miss him?" Greene asked.

The Colonel didn't hesitate to answer.

"Every day," he said. "There's not a day I don't think about him. A lot of days I cry."

24

Colonel Parker Reconsidered

The public narrative began to dramatically shift on Colonel Parker at the start of the 1980s.

What set the ball in motion was the death of Vernon Presley on June 26, 1979, at sixty-three years old from cardiac arrest. He had been ill with heart ailments for some time. When Elvis died, Vernon was named executor and trustee of the estate and received a salary of $72,500 a year for fulfilling those duties. In addition to Vernon, Elvis's beneficiaries were his grandmother, Minnie Mae Presley, and his only child, Lisa Marie Presley.

Elvis's will stated Vernon could, at his discretion, provide funds to other family members as needed. But after his 1979 death and Minnie Mae's passing in 1980, that left Lisa Marie as the sole heir to his estate. However, his will stipulated that her inheritance was to be held in trust until Lisa Marie's twenty-fifth birthday on February 1, 1993.

At the time of Vernon's death, the estate had generated $4.9 million according to probate court documents. That was mostly the Colonel's doing. The estate went from being in the red to going into the black in a little more than a year after Elvis's death thanks to the 160 licensing contracts the Colonel negotiated on behalf of the estate. Shortly before his death, Vernon named Priscilla as the estate's executor. Vernon's death triggered a court appearance because a new executor had been named.

Priscilla showed up for the first hearing with Joe Hanks—Elvis's former accountant—and representatives of Memphis's National Bank of Commerce, later named "successor co-executors." This was a more complex setup where it concerned the Colonel, who had an exclusive deal with Vernon after Elvis's death.

The new executors weren't looking to change things or rock the boat. In fact, they wrote the Colonel a warmhearted letter, essentially telling him it would still be business as usual. The co-executors went to Memphis probate court for approval of the compensation agreement with Colonel Parker. It was merely a formality, and the executors had planned on continuing using the Colonel's services and guidance. However, Probate Judge Joseph Evans, for whatever reason, felt this arrangement needed a closer examination, and appointed Blanchard E. Tual, a thirty-eight-year-old Memphis attorney who was seven years out of law school, to do a deep dive into Colonel Parker's agreements with the estate to "represent and defend the interests of Lisa Marie." Based on Tual's findings, Evans would render a final decision.

Tual spent several months combing through all the agreements between Colonel Parker and the Elvis Presley Estate. The Colonel complied with every request, making available all of his records to the court. Tual presented in September 1980 his research and analysis in a blistering three-hundred-page document now known as the Original Report.

Essentially, Tual charged that Colonel Parker's salary—half of all income Elvis or his estate received—was excessive. He also claimed that the Colonel and RCA Records had conspired to steal millions from the estate, and the Colonel took a kickback from the label. Tual said the deals Parker made for Elvis, particularly those made from 1970 to 1977, cost his client millions in potential earnings and denied his estate substantial income.

The report was especially critical of the 1973 deal in which RCA Records paid $5.4 million for Elvis's master recordings—a deal the Colonel tried to talk Elvis out of making. But Tual lay the sole blame at the Colonel's feet, which was uninformed, unfair, and hard to take back.

The report also implied that Colonel Parker was so deep into the hole in terms of gambling debts owed to the Las Vegas Hilton that he was no longer serving Elvis at all, and in fact was working *against* Elvis's best interests. But where he got this information is suspect because certainly not one of Colonel's business associates at the Hilton would ever tell him that, which leads me to believe his sources either weren't in the know or had an axe to grind.

Tual concluded at the time: "Elvis was shy and unassertive. Parker was aggressive, shrewd, and tough. His strong personality dominated Elvis, his father, and all others in Elvis's entourage."

Elvis Presley shy and unassertive? I don't think he could ever be accused of those two personality traits.

Another Tual statement: "The Colonel was a very strong-willed, domineering person who I think had total control over Elvis. I think Elvis was . . . intimidated by him."

These comments are not only laughable but demonstrate to me that all his hours of research did not give Tual the slightest understanding of their relationship. Elvis was not naïve, shy, or unassertive as Tual declared. Elvis was not intimidated by anyone and certainly not the Colonel. He was very strong-willed and set the financial tone with Colonel Parker early on, according to Joseph Hanks, who served as Elvis's accountant from 1969–1977.

"Colonel Parker told me in the early going when they got started that he tried to advise Elvis about things like that [tax shelters and investments], and Elvis told him, 'You take care of the money coming in, and me and my daddy will take care of it going out,'" Hanks told Stephen G. Tompkins, a reporter for the Scripps-Howard News Service. The Colonel adhered to Elvis's wishes and followed that mandate their entire working relationship.

The Colonel brought great opportunities to Elvis and made him an estimated $100 million over their twenty-two-year relationship. But according to Tual, he cheated Elvis out of millions. That was rich, because Tual's guardianship certainly didn't come cheap. He presented Judge Evans, who appointed him to investigate the Presley-Parker relationship, a bill for $155,000 in October 1981.[36] He claimed that he worked between 1,500 and 1,600 hours on behalf of Lisa Marie Presley, getting close to $100 an hour—an amount that was top dollar for an attorney in the South. Even Judge Evans thought that amount was an overreach and decided to give him $15,000 less than he requested.

"I thought $155,000 was a little high," Evans said in the article. "He is still serving and will be entitled to another fee later. I thought he was well compensated." Tual remained mum on the subject when a UPI reporter asked him for comment.

Regardless, Tual's interpretation of their business relationship tainted the public image of the Colonel—he was vilified in the media and by Elvis fans, many of whom quickly turned on him. These allegations also strained his relationship with the Presley Estate, but that was tainted by the probate court. Based on the report, Judge Evans brought down the hammer on Colonel Parker and ordered the co-executors for the Presley Estate to file suit against him and RCA Records for "fraudulent business practices." The estate complied, but, I believe, were reluctant to sue. They knew the Colonel's heart and how he felt about Elvis. He was family to them.

"The estate was forced by the state of Tennessee to proceed," Loanne Miller said in 2004. "In fact, the estate refused to make charges against the Colonel, and that's in the court record. The judge [Evans] ordered them to proceed, or they would be replaced. So, there was never the problem between the estate and the Colonel, that's another one of those stories."

The Presley Estate was truly between a rock and a hard place. They were forced to bring a suit that sought to sever Parker's existing relationship with the estate. Colonel Parker replied with a countersuit in Nevada, and RCA also filed suit against the estate in federal court in Nashville. A settlement was finally reached, with the estate essentially buying the Colonel out for $2 million for his "right, title and interest in

---

36 In 2023 dollars, $155,000 would be worth approximately $500,000.

all Presley related contracts." He received regular payments from the estate until 1987 as well as $225,000 for the Colonel's shares in Boxcar Enterprises.

In turn, RCA agreed to pay the Presley estate $1.1 million to settle all disputes.

As they were signing the final settlement papers, Priscilla smiled at Colonel Parker and said, "I wish you were my manager." To this very day she remains a staunch supporter of the Colonel and constantly defends him in the press. She even defended him to actor Tom Hanks, who portrayed Colonel Parker in the 2022 Baz Luhrmann film *Elvis*, when he and his wife, Rita Wilson, took Priscilla to dinner. Hanks already had his mind made up about Parker before he even stepped foot in front of the camera, calling him a "scoundrel." Then he got the other side of the story from Priscilla.

"I was expecting to hear stories about the distrust she had for Colonel Tom Parker over these many years," Hanks told a reporter for *Variety*. "And she said, 'No. He was a wonderful man, and I wish he was alive today. He took really great care of us.'"

He sure did. But that's not the narrative the public is willing to believe after all these years despite Priscilla's protestations.

With all the legal hurdles cleared between the Presley Estate and Colonel Parker, Elvis's life, career, and legacy could now be fully explored. That was set in motion when Priscilla Presley enlisted Jack Soden, then a thirty-five-year-old stockbroker from Kansas City, to become executive director of the Graceland division of Elvis Presley Enterprises, Inc. Together the two prepared Graceland for a public opening on June 7, 1982. Prior to Graceland's opening, Memphis tourism was in the doldrums. Graceland quickly became the cornerstone of the tourist industry for the city and the region.

Graceland has hosted more than twenty million visitors, and is second-most-visited homes. (The others are the White House; the Biltmore Estate in Asheville, North Carolina; 1892 Bishop's Palace in Galveston, Texas; and Hearst Castle in San Simeon, California.) In 1991,

Graceland was placed on the National Register of Historic Places. In 2006, it was designated a National Historic Landmark.

Today Graceland hires up to 450 employees a year, both full- and part-time, and has an estimated $150 million economic impact on the city of Memphis. In 2019, the estate earned approximately $39 million. Some years, the estate earns even more. According to a 2020 *Forbes* magazine article, the estate is worth somewhere between $400 to $600 million.

Colonel Parker would be proud of how Priscilla Presley, Lisa Marie Presley, and Jack Soden have sought out an amazing team of partners in Joel Weinshanker and the Authentic Brands Group (Jamie and Corey Salter) to keep Elvis Presley not only fresh and relevant in the twenty-first century, but to retain his status as the biggest entertainer in history as well.

Even before the 1983 lawsuit with the Presley Estate was settled, Colonel Parker picked up the phone and called Jack Soden shortly after the opening of Graceland and made a peace offering. He told Soden that despite his lawsuit with the Presley Estate, he was willing to help him in any future endeavors involving Elvis and Graceland. At this point, everyone associated with the estate was a bean counter or lawyer, and they didn't know the music business or how to run a museum attraction featuring an artist of Elvis's stature. The Colonel didn't want to see Elvis's legacy disappear or Graceland to fall into someone else's hands.

Soden took Colonel Parker at face value, and they developed a nice friendship over the years. Their relationship continued to bear fruit for Elvis Presley Enterprises, who invited Colonel Parker to work on special projects for them in the coming years. The biggest harvest came in 1990 when Colonel Parker unloaded the large collection of Elvis items he had packed away in four buildings outside of Nashville. It contained scrapbooks of news clippings, magazine articles and ads, original contracts for movies and television appearances, letters, telegrams, invoices, and even fan mail going back to

1955. The collection also included multiple samples of original souvenir and promotional memorabilia through the years, including the original pressing plates and artwork from which they were made. And he had numerous newsreels and interview audiotapes, acetate recordings, original copies of every record Elvis ever released, and thousands of original photographs and negatives spanning Elvis's entire career.

Colonel sold the items, which filled seven semitrailer trucks and weighed an estimated thirty-five tons, for a bargain basement price of $2 million. The collection, which even included Elvis's 1957 gold lamé suit, considered one of the most iconic rock outfits in history, was a wise investment for the estate as the collection is probably worth a hundred times the original asking price more than three decades after the sale. It's also a safe bet the collection spawned several projects for Elvis Presley Enterprises, including new and exciting displays at Graceland to keep the faithful coming year after year.

My relationship with Colonel Parker did not end after Elvis's death. In fact, we drew closer to each other. My family and I spent numerous weekends with the Colonel and almost every holiday with him and Marie, even though she couldn't speak at this point. My children knew them as "Aunt Marie" and "Colonel." He, in fact, named my twins Suzanne Marie and Thomas Andrew when he came to the hospital to visit Sherry with a roomful of Elvis Presley hound dogs and teddy bears for Sherry and the kids. While I was scurrying back from Los Angeles, he posed as her husband and filled out the birth certificate paperwork, naming the two the children after he and Marie. It was a gag, but Sherry and I decided to keep the names.

He doted on our children, played games with them, and taught them funny little songs and poems, including "The Hot Dog Vendor's Call" from his carny days. On birthdays, he'd call them on the phone and play them "Happy Birthday" on his harmonica. He also did that for me and my wife, Sherry, and his gardener, Woody Logan. In fact, if you did not get a phone call from Colonel Parker on your birthday, it meant you were in trouble.[37]

The Colonel loved Sunday brunch, and we usually dined at the Ingleside Inn, Lord Fletcher's, and Howard Manor in Palm Springs, and a family restaurant called Hayden's in nearby Desert Hot Springs. I also accompanied the Colonel on a lot of his visits to the grocery store, where he loaded up on meats and all sorts of specialties. He talked a lot about his Dutch past as we strolled down the aisles and admired the variety of goods available to shoppers.

"I would dream to have this kind of selection and bring this kind of food home to my family," he once said. "We couldn't have dreamed this!"

The Colonel never forgot to count his blessings, and perhaps he regarded it as one when Marie Parker finally—and mercifully—passed away on November 25, 1986, of chronic brain syndrome. She was seventy-eight. Marie's quality of life had declined steadily over a decade, but the Colonel provided around-the-clock love, protection, and care with a staff that included wonderful caregivers. They include Teresa Davis, Mary Estler, Nina Garcia, and Polly Valdivia. Nacho Garcia took care of the grounds and watched over the ladies. Every one of them loved Marie and played board games with her for hours.

After her death, the Colonel moved to Las Vegas, where he had two things going for him: a familiar home and someone who deeply cared for him.

Barron Hilton's friendship with Colonel Parker extended well beyond Elvis's passing, and the two not only remained friends, but the Colonel was still on an annual retainer for entertainment advice. People might say that Hilton was being overly kind, but he probably knew

---

[37] I was present when Colonel Parker called Lyndon B. Johnson at the White House to wish him happy birthday. He called the switchboard operator, told her who he was, and a few minutes later the president called him back at his Palm Springs office. The Colonel pulled out his harmonica and started playing "Happy Birthday." Johnson got a big kick out of the kind gesture.

what most others didn't understand: The Colonel and Elvis were brand ambassadors for the Hilton since 1969. Not only did they bring the Hilton name great recognition during Elvis's twice-annual residency in Sin City, but while on tour, they also made a point of staying at a Hilton Hotel whenever they could.

Loanne Miller, who had worked with Colonel Parker since 1970, married him on October 19, 1990, a few years after Marie's passing. She was twenty-five years younger than Colonel Parker, and she not only understood him, but went to great lengths to take care of him. She kept him in good humor and health, making sure he took his medications and shuttling him to doctor's appointments. He would not have lived as long as he did without Loanne, and for that, she earned our love and respect. Besides, she was just a great lady and a real joy to be around. She was very special.

Despite his new address, I still saw Colonel Parker about once a month. Ricky Nelson often played Las Vegas, which gave me an opportunity to visit with the Colonel and Loanne. They lived in a high-rise apartment on a golf course behind the Hilton, and later moved into a nice townhome. He liked the slot machines, roulette wheel, and craps table, jokingly saying that gambling was his form of exercise.

The Colonel loved Las Vegas and being around the action. He lived and breathed show business and, in addition to Barron Hilton and Alex Shoofey, he was very friendly with Milton Prell of the Sahara and casino mogul Steve Wynn of Wynn Resorts. Many of his friends, including Eddy Arnold, Jerry Lee Lewis, Roy Orbison, Rick Nelson, Frank Sinatra, and George Strait[38] performed there, and Colonel Parker and Loanne could usually be found in the audience on their opening

---

38 Colonel Parker advised George Strait to stretch his artistic legs and act in a movie. He took the Colonel's advice and accepted the starring role in *Pure Country*. The 1992 film performed decently at the box office, but really cleaned up in video sales and rentals. The soundtrack became the best-selling album of Strait's career to date. Around the same time, he also advised Las Vegas hotel mogul Steve Wynn to sign an exclusive deal with a talented performer from Canada. Her name was Celine Dion.

nights. Everything was comped: from backstage passes, the ticket to the show, a nice dinner, and everything else the Colonel could extract from these artists. He was still a carny at heart.

The Colonel lent his name to charitable causes, and he not only cut these nonprofits a check but also showed up in person for fundraising activities and dinners, especially where it concerned the Las Vegas SUN Summer Camp Fund. He helped them raise thousands of dollars each year to provide less fortunate children a summer camp experience away from the stifling heat of Southern Nevada. He honestly believed that America was the greatest country in the world and was grateful that it gave him the ability to earn a nice living and enjoy a nice life.

The Colonel was also a soft touch when it came to former members of the Memphis Mafia. He might have been sentimental, though he didn't show it. I know for a fact he lent a few of them money when they were down-and-out or going through a rough patch, and I have the canceled checks to prove it. He also wrote many letters of endorsements to prospective employers so these individuals could be hired. Even though they worked for Elvis Presley, which carried a lot of weight in those days, many of them found the transition to "civilian" life tricky and hard. A letter of commendation from Colonel Parker often meant working or collecting an unemployment check.

He also forgave some of the men. I know that Sonny West made amends with the Colonel for his participation in *Elvis: What Happened?* when he visited him in Las Vegas. I doubt if the book was actually brought up in conversation, but the two men had one major thing in common: they loved Elvis Presley, and that was enough. Time and wisdom seemed to heal those old wounds. Besides, these two had spent many years and experienced something very special together. They knew it was better to bury the hatchet than let any bad feelings linger. Now, I'm not saying this was the case with all the Memphis Mafia, and I doubt this bothered the Colonel in any way. However, he was more than willing to see anyone who wished to see him. Many of them did and found their visits fun and exciting.

Even though Colonel Parker was in his twilight years (he was now in his eighties), there was still no shortage of entertainers clamoring for his services. The Colonel would wish them success and offer all the free advice they'd ever need, but it was always a hard no. He didn't need the money or the aggravation. And besides, Elvis was a hard act to follow.

"I've had the greatest," he'd say. "Anything else would be a step down."

He did make an exception of sorts by advising Ricky Nelson's sons Matthew and Gunnar about a year after their father's death.

Gunnar Nelson explains: "Greg McDonald brought us down to the Colonel's house in Palm Springs. We were still nursing our wounds and hanging out aimlessly, spending money we didn't have, impressing people that didn't matter. Greg heard it in our voice when we called him in Palm Springs and figured we needed a father figure. He picked us up in Los Angeles and took us to the Colonel's house. The funny thing was, everything in that house was blue—and I mean everything!

"He asked us to tell our story, and we told him that we were the only unsigned band in history to be the musical guests on *Saturday Night Live*, but we'd broken up immediately after the performance. I was playing the drums at the time and wanted to come up front and sing alongside my brother Matthew. We told him we were very frustrated because we couldn't seem to get the right guys for our new band. Without missing a beat, the Colonel looked up and said, 'You boys don't need a band. Ever. Just you two and two acoustic guitars. That's it.'

"I was a headstrong kid, still in my late teens, who'd always played in rock bands on the LA club circuit, looking at this old guy and thinking, *Yeah, his time has passed. What the heck does he know?* The irony, looking back, is that every huge break in mine and Matthew's career—from getting signed to Geffen Records to playing in front of 66,000 people in Erie, Pennsylvania—was that our success was due to *no band, two brothers with two acoustic guitars*. That old man was a genius!

"As Nelson, we have sold ten million albums, scored a number one hit '(Can't Live Without Your) Love and Affection,' had a bunch of Top Ten singles, and have sustained a career for more than three decades. But if we'd only listened to his advice from the beginning, we would have ten-folded our career in a fifth of the time. What did the Colonel know? Are you kidding me?! I'm such a schmuck not listening to him from the very beginning.

"But we're listening to his advice *now* . . . that's for sure!"

The Colonel admitted that over the years he had an opportunity to cash in on a book he was writing with Loanne called *How Much Does It Cost if It's Free?* However, he spurned numerous offers—many in the seven-figure range—because he felt publishers didn't want to hear the truth about their relationship and only wanted the dirt on Elvis.

"I'd tell them I'm not a dirt farmer," he quipped.

Colonel Parker made fewer and fewer public appearances as time went on. He tipped the scales at three hundred pounds, walked with a cane, and still smoked his beloved cigars. He did, however, manage to keep his mind sharp and alert. He woke most mornings around 5:00 A.M., called old friends and associates, dictated letters to Loanne, and concocted promotions that didn't go anywhere. But he never tired of the action, and it never left his blood.

I brought Colonel Parker back to Palm Springs in 1994 so he could receive a star on the Palm Springs Walk of Stars. The Walk of Stars was established in 1992 to honor and recognize celebrities, politicians, authors, playwrights, screenwriters, and pioneers who have lived at one time or another in the desert village. It was very helpful for Palm Springs downtown redevelopment, which was just starting to pull through a long recession dating back to the late 1980s.

I bought stars for Elvis, Ricky Nelson, and Colonel Parker, all in front of the Welwood Murray Library. It was at the intersection of Tahquitz Canyon and Palm Canyon Drive smack dab in the center of Palm Springs. It's where the heaviest pedestrian traffic flowed, and the place where I felt they would get the most eyeballs. But the library wasn't happy with my purchase. In fact, they were furious with me because they felt their benefactor should have had his star located on the same exact spot. However, they didn't have the foresight or the gumption to shell out the money. They sent me a nasty gram stating they were going to "turn the matter over to their attorney" and discuss this with city hall.

And they did. The city manager, Norm King, called me, and we laughed about it.

"When people come to Palm Springs, they're going to want to have their picture taken with Elvis, Ricky, and the Colonel . . . and probably not Welwood Murray," I said. He agreed and assured me the city would not pursue the matter. However, the story made the front page of the Palm Springs *Desert Sun* and the Riverside *Press-Enterprise*, which only drew more people to the event. More than a thousand people showed up for the dedication, including twenty Elvis tribute artists. Colonel Parker was ecstatic that so many people showed up to pay their respects.

Barron Hilton jetted in Colonel Parker and Loanne from Las Vegas, and Elvis Presley Enterprises sent Jerry Schilling as their representative, and I picked them all up at the airport. After a meal, we headed over to the ceremony. When the Colonel stepped out of the car, the crowd greeted him with thunderous applause and cheers. Mayor Lloyd Maryanov[39] officiated the event and unveiled the three stars.

I would say it was one of Colonel Parker's happiest days in his later years. It was a big day for the Colonel and one of the happiest days I'd ever spent with him. We even shared a running joke that I paid $7,500 apiece for the stars and didn't get a discount.

---

39 Maryanov was not a big fan of mine. I was Sonny Bono's campaign manager the year Maryanov ran against him for mayor. He got his butt handed to him in the race, and he knew I was the strategist that served up his weaknesses to the public. We put our differences aside that day and shook hands. Colonel Parker also was a helpful strategist in the race, even coming up with the slogan, "It's Time for a Change."

"Back in the day, I would have charged $25,000 to put Elvis's name on the sidewalk," he chuckled.

The Colonel rarely left his apartment in his ninth decade but mustered the strength to attend an eighty-fifth birthday bash thrown by Barron Hilton in June. Both Priscilla Presley and Jack Soden were in attendance, as were many of the Colonel's friends and associates from the past. Barron Hilton even had classy five-and-a-half-by-nine-inch programs printed for the affair, which was held at the Hilton Center. On the cover, it featured a side profile of a smiling Colonel Parker sporting a ten-gallon cowboy hat. The masthead of the program read: "Our Colonel."

Perhaps the best surprise of all—Governor Bob Miller declared June 25, 1994, as Colonel Tom Parker Day in Nevada. That was a day before the Colonel's birthday . . . but it was the thought that counted.

The last few years of Colonel Parker's life were not kind. Father Time was catching up to him, and he suffered from diabetes, arthritis, gout, and other health issues. He was essentially housebound near the end. That finally came on Tuesday, January 21, 1997, when he died of complications from a stroke. He was eighty-seven.

I was in the south of France on vacation with my family when I received word of Colonel Parker's passing. Loanne called me in the middle of the night to let me know that he died quickly. She said I was the first call. The Colonel would have wanted it that way, she said.

Of course, I knew the end was near, and I shed more than a few tears that evening. He was a father figure and nothing but kind to me. I had known him since I was a kid, and he was a large part of my life. I owed my entire career to this man. He took me in because he saw a child much like the child he had been in his youth. I needed stability, an education, and a nudge or two in the right direction. I lived with him and Marie, left for school each day from their home, and came home to sit by the Colonel while he cooked on the grill, rolled a cigar in his mouth, and told me stories about his days traveling the world and living the carny life. I asked a million questions of him, and he answered each one thoughtfully and with patience. He taught me his trade and craft and introduced me to the life I live now. I would not have what I have now or be the person I am now without him. He smiled every time I walked into the room. How can you ever possibly repay someone who was everything to you?

His funeral was held at the Hilton Hotel four days after his passing. It was attended by a gathering of people from his past and present: Eddy Arnold, Sam Phillips, Jerry Weintraub, Phyllis McGuire, Steve Wynn, Jack Soden, and Priscilla Presley, who gave a touching and funny eulogy.

"Elvis and the Colonel made history together, and the world is richer, better, and far more interesting because of their collaboration," she said. "And now I need to locate my wallet because I noticed there was no ticket booth on the way in here, but I'm sure that the Colonel must have arranged for some toll on the way out."

Even Colonel Parker would have laughed heartily at the gentle but funny barb and tipped his hat to the beautiful lady who had a special place in his heart.

Over the years, Colonel Parker's reputation remains tainted, especially with new offerings such as Luhrmann's 2022 film *Elvis*, the musical-drama which paints Elvis as a caged bird and the Colonel as a greedy opportunist constantly lurking in the shadows. The funny thing about Colonel Parker is that he was like a human peacock. He enjoyed being recognized and commanded attention and respect. The shadows are the last place you'd find him. In this new retelling, Elvis was a "showman" and the Colonel was a "snowman" who routinely victimized and undermined his client throughout their two-decade partnership. The movie did not highlight many of the Colonel's great accomplishments, which were innovative and now part of the fabric of the entertainment industry. I could write an entire book on all the things the movie got wrong, but I don't want to waste that much ink on the film.

Sadly, for younger Elvis fans who have no other point of reference, this 159-minute biopic will likely be the last word for them. But those who knew and loved Colonel Parker, including Priscilla Presley,[40] will always defend him. And so will I . . . to my death.

Elvis Presley Enterprises forgave the Colonel for errors he might have had in judgment—few, if any—a long time ago, but most Elvis fans still haven't been able to do the same. That's sad. If they had been in a dressing room or backstage with the two of them during those epic years, they would know the truth in a second. The Colonel would no more have duped Elvis than he would have kicked a puppy. But every epic needs a villain as well as a hero. That person cannot be one and the same. The myth demands someone else be blamed for all of Elvis's missteps and mistakes. The fingers pointed at the Colonel after Elvis's death have never unflexed. It's not fair. He loved the fans as much as they loved his boy. Perhaps future generations will read this book and have a kinder view of Colonel Tom Parker.

After all, he's the man who brought them Elvis Presley, the greatest show on earth.

---

40 Even though *Elvis* was given the thumbs-up by Elvis Presley Enterprises, Priscilla Presley has been adamant in recent interviews that Colonel Parker was not a heavy or a villain, and that her former husband was fortunate to have him as a manager.

Greg, Sherry, and the Colonel. Courtesy of Greg Marshall

ACKNOWLEDGMENTS

An adult's life is widely informed by what happens to him in his formative years. The memories of childhood may be distorted in the mind by time and experience; nevertheless, the formation is based on the adult's memories of what happened. When the French writer Marcel Proust bit into a madeleine, it triggered a series of memories that led him to recall his entire early life in the seven-volume novel *In Search of Lost Time*.

In Tom Parker's case, it wouldn't be a small sponge cake that brought him back to childhood. What is written here about Parker's early years and professional career Colonel Parker related directly to me, which gives you, the reader, an exclusive insight into his life. This is important because the story is straight from the horse's mouth, not from an outsider or third party. And much of what you've read—about his poverty-stricken childhood on a Dutch farm, his peripatetic early life bumming across America, voyaging around the globe in the merchant marine, and learning his trade as a traveling carny—has never been told before. Those experiences shaped his life and led him to his life of fame.

I am literally the last man standing who can tell his story.

He never cared to tell his story and neither did his other employees—Tom Diskin, George Parkhill, Jim O'Brien, or Loanne Miller, who became his second wife, and later, widow. Jerry Weintraub, a close associate of Colonel Parker's, did write a chapter about his dealings with the legendary manager in his 2010 memoir, *When I Stop Talking, You'll Know I'm Dead*. Take note: Weintraub didn't have one bad thing to say about the man. And never once did he suggest that the Colonel cheated his primary client, nor anyone else for that matter.

"People later said the Colonel stole from Elvis, took too much, or did not treat him right. He was vilified. But as far as I'm concerned, none of that's true," Weintraub wrote. "The Colonel never stole anything from Elvis. If he had, I would have known it. I was there."

And as I've said before, so was I.

This literary endeavor was not a solo effort; it took an entire team to help me tell this story. The authors would like to thank the following people in alphabetical order for their contributions to this book: DJ Argo, Bruce Banke, Scott Bennett, Tim Brinkman, Art Browning, Jim Browning, Wren Budden, James Burton, Louise Burton, Alan Bush, Stephen Chambers, Chris Christian, Bobby Craig, Gina Craig, Mike Curb, Alicia Dean, Doug Galloway, Nacho Garcia, Jim Gissy, Paul Gongaware, Dick Grob, Melissa Grob, Harley Hatcher, Dick Heckmann, Cara Highsmith, Richard Jans, Michael Johnson, Patrick Lacy, Angie McCartney, Ruth McCartney, Jack Magids, John Meglen, Gunnar Nelson, Matthew Nelson, Ricky Nelson, Willy Nelson, Martin Nethercutt, Loanne Parker, Peter Pawling, Barbra Reinecke, Judy Reynolds, Chad Schlosser, Scott Seckel, Tony Seidl, Jimmie Snow, Jack Soden, Charlie Stone, Linda Stone, Jim Sykes, Linda Thompson, Louise Thompson, Sam Thompson, Jimmy Velvet, Ray Walker, and Tina M. Walls.

My wish in this literary endeavor is for others to experience and get to know Tom Parker as I experienced him—as a real human being. My hope is that everyone has read this with an open mind and, hopefully, an open heart.

SELECTED BIBLIOGRAPHY

Guralnick, Peter, and Ernst Jorgensen. *Elvis Day By Day*. New York: Ballantine Books, 1999.

Leigh, Barbara, with Marshall Terrill. *The King, McQueen and the Love Machine*. Xlibris Corporation, 2002.

Mansfield, Rex and Elisabeth, with Marshall and Zoe Terrill. *Sergeant Presley: Our Untold Story of Elvis' Missing Years*. Toronto, Ontario: ECW Press, 2002.

Presley, Priscilla Beaulieu, with Sandra Harmon. *Elvis and Me*. New York: G. P. Putnam's Sons, 1985.

Stone, Charles. *My Years with Elvis and the Colonel*. Erwitte, Germany: Praytome Publishing, 2009.

West, Sonny, and Marshall Terrill. *Elvis: Still Taking Care of Business*. Chicago: Triumph Books, 2007.

INDEX

Abbott, Jerry 11
ABC Studios 11
Aberbach, Jean 9
Aberbach, Julian 9
Across 110th Street (film) 289
Acuff, Roy 66, 78, 79
Adams, Nick 114
Adele 213
Adler, Renata 193
Adventures of Ozzie & Harriet, The (sitcom) 114
Alan Ladd Hardware 206
Alden, Ginger 307, 308, 309, 311–312, 323
Alden, Rosemary 308, 310
Allen, Marcus 260
Allen, Steve 12, 13, 124
"All Shook Up" (song) 125, 143
All Star Shows, contract for 260–261
Aloha from Hawaii 250, 266, 314
Aloha from Hawaii via Satellite (album) 228, 255
Always Elvis (documentary) 332

Always Elvis (festival) 331–332
American Sound Studio 197
Andy Williams Show, The (TV show) 251
Anka, Paul 214
Annenberg, Walter 162
Ann-Margret 3, 166–167, 330
"Anytime" (song) 71
Arden, Toni 224
"Are You Lonesome Tonight?" (song) 130, 134, 135, 223
"Are You Sincere?" (song) 272
Arnold, Eddy 65, 68–77, 83, 91, 101, 107, 128, 218, 223, 238, 313, 343, 349
Arnone, Phil 254
Aspinall, Neil 175
Association of Country Entertainers 79
Atkins, Chet 223–224, 225, 330
Aubrey, Jim 249
"Auld Lang Syne" (song) 286
Austin, Gene 55–59, 65
Authentic Brands Group 340

Autry, Gene 52
Avalon, Frankie 181
Axton, Mae 99
Azoff, Irving 288

Baby, the Rain Must Fall (film) 161
Bachwick, Bill 206
Back in the Saddle Again (Autry) 52
Baker, Conway 44
Baker, Herbert 111
Banke, Bruce 48, 201–202, 204
Barnum, P. T. 4, 51
Barrow, Tony 175
Bashful Brother Oswald 78
Bassett, Terry 215
Baty, Tim 268
Beatles, The 2, 171–180, 255, 332n34
Beatles and Me on Tour, The (Davis) 175
Beatty, Warren 139
Beaulieu, Captain 187, 188
Beaulieu, Priscilla *see* Presley, Priscilla
Belew, Bill 254
Berle, Milton 9, 11, 12, 124, 241
Berman, Shelley 214
Berry, Chuck 161, 178, 181, 276
Bicknell, Alf 175
Bienstock, Freddy 183, 203, 275
"Big Hunk o' Love, A" (song) 126
Billboard magazine 240
Bishop, Joey 137, 214
Black, Bill 87
Black, Cilla 178

Blackman, Joan 154
Blue Hawaii (album) 228
Blue Hawaii (film) 141–142, 154, 161, 290
"Blue Suede Shoes" (song) 103, 176
Blythe III, William Jefferson 70n4
Bodie Mountain Express 275, 285
Bogart, Humphrey 102
Bonja, Ed 162
Bonnie and Clyde (film) 194
Bono, Sonny 347n38
Boone, Pat 162–164, 214
Bowie, David 260
Boxcar Enterprises 275, 276, 327, 339
Bradley, C. W. 329
Bray, Buddy 218
Breda city 16–17, 33, 42
Briggs, David 224
Brooks, Garth 79
Brossette, Stan 158–160, 191–192
Brown, James 257, 330
Browne, Jackson 326
Buffalo (United States) 297
Buffalo Springfield 181
Buffett, Jimmy 225
Bullitt (film) 289
Bullock, W. W. 92–93
Burk, Bill 307
Burns, George 102, 241
Burton, James 205–206, 224, 227
Buttons, Red 74, 241
Buttram, Pat 52
Buttrey, Kenneth 224, 225

Index

Bye Birdie (film) 166
Byrds, The 181

Cagney, James 102
Camp Shows 102
"Can't Live Without Your Love and Affection" (song) 346
Capitol Records 174
Capote, Truman 170
Carey, Mariah 228
carnival tours 46–52, 55–57
Carrigan, Jerry 224, 225
Carson, Johnny 260
Carter, Jimmy 300
Cash, Johnny 91, 223
Cash, June Carter 223
Catholic Weekly, The (newspaper) 12
Cat on a Hot Tin Roof (film) 161
"Cattle Call" (song) 72
CBS-TV 319, 322
Change of Habit (film) 197
Channing, Carol 114
Chaplin, George 142
Charro! (film) 196, 197
Checkerboard Jamboree (WMAK radio) 72
Chin, Tom 56–57
Christian, Chris 162
Chronicle (newspaper) 304
Civilian Conservation Corps (CCC) 38–39
Clambake (film) 181, 185
Clark, Dick 129
Clark, Petula 197
Claypool, Bob 304–305
Clift, Montgomery 161

Clinton, Bill 70n4
Coco, Imogene 13
Cole, Nat King 228
Comic Sammy Shore 207
Concerts West 215–216
Cool Hand Luke (film) 194
Coppola, Ron 276
Corey, Wendell 110
Cortes, Louise 43
Cortes, Sonny 43
Country Music Hall of Fame and Museum 227
Cowboy Copas 78
Craig, Bobby 115, 276
Cramer, Floyd 141, 223n24
Crowther, Bosley 140
Cummings, Jack 166–167
Curtiz, Michael 119

Daily Express (newspaper) 175
Daily News (newspaper) 12
Damsker, Matt 320–321
Davis, Ivor 175–177
Davis, Jimmie 60
Davis, Oscar 83, 84
Davis, Richard 175
Davis, Teresa 342
Davis Jr., Sammy 114, 137, 208, 330
Dean, James 103, 161
Defiant Ones, The (film) 161
Delaney, Joe 87
DeMille, Cecil B. 112
Denver, John 214, 222, 248–249
Desert Sun (newspaper) 347
Diamond, Neil 197
Dillinger, John 328

Dion, Celine 213, 343n37
Dirty Harry (film) 289
Disc Jockey Convention (Miami, Florida) 130
Diskin, Tom 10, 70–71, 84, 88, 103, 112–113, 159–160, 219, 221, 225, 229, 260, 274, 275, 276, 304
Diskin, Yanique 297
Diskin Sisters, The 70
"Don't Be Cruel" (song) 125, 143
"Don't Ever Take the Ribbons from Your Hair" (song) 71
"Don't Think Twice, It's All Right" (song) 225
Doors, The 181
Dot Records 163
Double Trouble (film) 181
Doucette, Gene 254
Dowell, Buford 148
Drifting Cowboys 78
"Drinkin' Hadacol" (song) 78
Driscoll Sr., Margot 316–318
Driscoll Sr., Rudolph "Rudy Weyehaeuser" 316–318
Duke 52
Dunleavy, Steve 323
Durante, Jimmy 102
Dvorin, Al 10–11, 70, 71, 115, 129, 285, 325
Dylan, Bob 180, 225, 259–260

Eagles 288, 326
Easy Come, Easy Go (film) 183, 194
Eckert, Banns 325
Eddy Arnold (Streissguth) 76
Eddy Arnold Show (radio show) 72

Ed Sullivan Show (TV show) 107–108, 171, 172, 255
Edwards, Vince 139
Egan, Richard 104, 105
Eisenhower, Dwight D. 116, 141
Ellington, Buford 141
Ellis, V. H. 98
El Rancho Hotel 73
Elvis (album soundtrack) 196
Elvis (film) 339, 349
Elvis (Goldman) 30, 142n14
Elvis: As Recorded at Madison Square Garden (album) 241
Elvis: That's the Way It Is (documentary) 219
Elvis: What Happened? (West, West, and Hebler) 323, 344
Elvis' Christmas Album 222, 228
Elvis Is Back! (album) 228
Elvis on Tour (documentary) 240, 249
Elvis Presley Center Courts 297
Elvis Presley Enterprises 108, 295, 339, 340, 341, 347, 350
Elvis Presley Music 8, 268
Elvis Sails 125
Elvis Sings the Wonderful World of Christmas (album) 227
"Endless Sleep" (song) 276
Endless Summer, The (documentary) 276
Epstein, Brian 3, 173–176, 178
Erickson, Leif 168
Esposito, Joan 190, 219–220

Esposito, Joe 135, 155, 160, 175, 178, 185, 190, 201, 220, 252, 255, 270, 287, 296, 297, 312, 325
Estler, Mary 342
Eugene, Clarence *see* Snow, Hank
Evans, Joseph 336, 337–338
Evans, Mal 175
Evening Bulletin (newspaper) 320
Everly Brothers 181
"Everybody Loves That Hadacol" (song) 78

Fabian 181
"Fame and Fortune" (song) 136
Fargo, William G. 4
Fawcett-Majors, Farrah 327
Federal Deposit Insurance Corporation (FDIC) 46
Feudin' Rhythm (film) 73
Fike, Lamar 30, 224, 287
Fink, Robert 273
Flaming Star (film) 140
Flynt, Larry 282n26
Follow That Dream (film) 157
Fontana, D. J. 141
"Fool Such as I, A" (song) 126
Forbes (magazine) 340
Fortas, Alan 175
Fortas, Jo 175
Fort Barrancas (Pensacola, Florida) 43–44
Foster, David 248
Four Seasons, The 214
Foxx, Red 212
Franklin, Aretha 197

Frank Sinatra's Welcome Home Party for Elvis Presley (TV show) 135–136
Freeman, Joan 168
Freeman, Y. Frank 119
French Connection (film) 289
From Elvis in Memphis (studio album) 197, 228
From Elvis in Nashville 224
From Elvis Presley Boulevard, Memphis, Tennessee (album) 289
From Memphis to Vegas/From Vegas to Memphis (album) 209
Fun in Acapulco (film) 139, 164–165
Funny Girl (film) 201

Gable, Clark 117–118
Gaedel, Eddie 129
Galfund, Allan W. 125–126
Gamble, James 4
Garbo, Greta 158
Garcia, Nacho 342
Garcia, Nina 342
Gardner, Dave 141
Geffen Records 345
Geissler, Harry "The Bear" 327
Geller, Larry 175, 309, 310, 312
Germany 35–36
"Get Back" (song) 173
Ghanem, Elias 266, 279
G.I. Blues (film) 137–138, 140
Girl Happy (film) 169
"Girl of My Dreams" (song) 56
Girls! Girls! Girls! (film) 158
Gissy, Jim 47n3

Gleason, Jackie 8, 9, 136
Glen Campbell Goodtime Hour, The (TV show) 251
Gold, Wally 134
Goldberg, Lou 183
Goldman, Albert 30, 142n14
"Good Luck Charm" (song) 171, 223
"Good Rockin' Tonight" (song) 82
Graceland estate 113, 115–116, 184, 289, 339–340
Graduate, The (film) 194
Graham, Billy 315
Grand Ole Opry 67, 68, 72, 142
Grant, Cary 205
Grant, Peter 273
Great Depression 25, 38–39, 44, 45, 47, 49
Greene, Bob 333–334
Greene, Shecky 10, 201
Griffith, Andy 13
Grob, Dick 242–243, 310
Gross, Ben 12
"Growing Up in a Country Way" (song) 275
Guercio, Joe 205n20, 268
Gunfight at the O.K. Corral (film) 105

Hackford, Taylor 317
Hadacol Tour 78–79
Hair 212
Haley, Bill 161, 181
Hamilton, George 2–3, 330
Hanks, Joe 336, 337
Hanks, Tom 39
Hard Day's Night, A (album) 174

"Hard Headed Woman" (song) 119, 126
Hardin, Glen D. 205
Harlow, Jean 158
Harrison, George 173, 179
Harum Scarum (film) 169–170
Having Fun with Elvis on Stage (album) 275
Hawaii 39–40
Hays, Lowell 311
Hayworth, Rita 102
Hazen, Joe 181–182
"Heartbreak Hotel" (song) 7, 113, 143, 176, 193, 223
Hebler, Dave 305, 313
Help! (album) 174
Hendrix, Jimi 215
Hepburn, Katharine 102, 158
He Touched Me (album) 227–228
Hewlett, Bill 4
"Hey Jude" (song) 173
Hilburn, Robert 333
Hill and Range publishing company 8, 203
Hillsborough County Humane Society 60–63
Hilton, Barron 162, 239, 269, 294, 342, 343, 347, 348
Hilton Hawaiian Village 253, 255
Hilton Hotel Corporation 47, 48–49, 75, 167, 206, 221, 231, 232, 239, 250, 257, 264, 267–270, 274, 279, 286, 294, 299, 307, 319, 329, 332, 333, 337, 343, 349
Hirshan, Leonard 103
Ho, Don 251, 254

Hodge, Charlie 155, 185, 258, 274, 332
Hoedown (film) 73
Holiness movement 145
"Holly Leaves and Christmas Trees" (song) 224
Honolulu Advertiser (newspaper) 142
Hookstratten, Ed 184, 260, 266
Hoover, Herbert 45
"Hot Dog Vendor's Call" (song) 274–275
"Hound Dog" (song) 12, 13, 125
Houston Livestock Show 218
How Great Thou Art (album) 228
"How Great Thou Art" (song) 329
How Much Does It Cost if It's Free? (Parker and Parker) 346
Hoxie Bros. Circus 47
Hughes, Howard 146n15
Hulett, Tom 215–216, 296, 303, 312, 313, 325
Humbard, Rex 329
Hundley, Monty 232, 262–263
Hutchins, Chris 175

"I Don't Hurt Anymore" (song) 81
"I Feel Fine" (song) 178
"If I Get Home On Christmas Day" (song) 224
"I Got a Woman" (song) 225
Ike 212
"I'll Be Home on Christmas Day" (song) 225
"I'm Leavin'" (song) 227
In Cold Blood (Capote) 170
"Indescribably Blue" (song) 193–194
International *see* Hilton Hotel Corporation
"In The Ghetto" (song) 198
In the Heat of the Night (film) 194
It Happened at the World's Fair (film) 158
It's All Right Now (TV show) 317
"It's Now or Never" (song) 134, 223
"It's Only Love" (song) 227
"It Won't Seem Like Christmas" (song) 224

Jacobson, Max 186
Jagger, Dean 119
Jailhouse Rock (film) 112
Jamboree Attractions 81, 85, 87, 88
James, Harry 9
James, Mark 198
Japan 39
Jarrett, Michael 225
Jarvis, Felton 224–225, 286, 289, 290, 311, 312
Jefferson Airplane 180, 181
Jenkins, Harry 183, 203, 214, 240
Jennings, Waylon 223n24, 225
Jessel, George 141
Joey Bishop Show, The (TV show) 13
John, Elton 213
"Johnny B. Goode" (song) 178
Johnny J. Jones Exposition 47
Johnson, Joanna 326
Johnson, Lyndon B. 128, 292, 300, 342

Jolson, Al 102
Jones, Carolyn 119
Jordanaires, The 12
"Just a Little Lovin'" (song) 72

Kahane, Jackie 332
Kanter, Hal 111
Kaye, Danny 215
Kaye-Smith Enterprises 215–216
Kelleher, Pat 325
Kelly, Gene 112, 239
Kennedy, Caroline 330
Kennedy, John F. 165
Kenny G 228
"Kentucky Rain" (song) 198
Kerkorian, Kirk 162, 198–201, 205
Kid Galahad (film) 119, 158, 165
King, Norm 347
King, Pee Wee 65, 70
King Creole (film) 119, 121, 124
King Jr., Martin Luther 180
Kinney, Don 295–296
Kissin' Cousins (film) 167
Klein, George 186, 190, 307
Kleiner, Dick 192
Knott, David 273, 275
Kufferath, Arnold 43
Kui Lee Cancer Fund 255

Lacker, Marty 175, 255
Lacker, Patsy 175
"Lady Madonna" (song) 173
Laginestra, Rocco 250–251, 260
Lake Tahoe 232, 235, 237, 262, 293, 294
Landon, Grelun 230, 231

Landry, Hypolite T. 313
Lange, Hope 140
Lansbury, Angela 154
Lastfogel, Abe 101–102, 103–104, 169, 241, 242, 317
Las Vegas 27, 73–74, 199–213
Las Vegas Hilton *see* Hilton Hotel Corporation
Las Vegas News Bureau 238–239
Las Vegas Review-Journal (newspaper) 212
Las Vegas Sun (newspaper) 212, 242
Laughton, Charles 107–108
Lawford, Peter 137
LeBlanc, Dudley J. 78, 79
Lee, Jerry 248
Lee, Peggy 205
Leiber and Stoller 9
Lemmon, Jack 102, 170
Lennon, John 89, 173, 176–179
Lewin, Henri 231
Lewis, Jerry 102, 139
Lewis, Jerry Lee 161, 181, 343
Liberace 11, 201, 238
Lisa Marie plane 282, 292, 300, 308, 309, 313, 332
Little, Barbara 186
Littlefield, "Little Willie" 78
"Little Less Conversation, A" (song) 196–197
Live a Little, Love a Little (film) 195
Livingston, Alan 174
Logan, Ricky 308
Logan, Woody 308, 341
Long, Earl 78
"Lord's Prayer, The" (song) 225

Index

Los Angeles 27–28
Los Angeles Herald Examiner (newspaper) 141
Los Angeles Times (newspaper) 193
Louisiana Hayride (TV show) 10, 111
Louisville & Nashville Railroad Company 137
Love Me Tender (film) 12, 104, 105, 108, 110, 278
Love Me Tender (song) 136, 208
Loving You (film) 110–111
Luhrmann, Baz 339, 349

MacArthur, Douglas 39
Madison Square Garden 240–241
"Make the World Go Away" (song) 72
Management III Productions 215, 216, 248, 249, 276, 303–304
Manilow, Barry 213
Mansfield, Rex 131
Martin, Dean 102, 139, 205
Martin, Freddie 10
Maryanov, Lloyd 347
Mathis, Johnny 228
Matthau, Walter 102
Mayer, Louis B. 167
McCalla, Irish 12
McCartney, Paul 173, 177, 178, 301
McCoy, Charlie 224
McDonald, Sherry 153, 274, 275, 286, 310, 341
McDonald, Thomas 144–146
McDonald, Zella 144
McGraw, Tim 80
McGuire, Phyllis 349
McKenzie, Bill 215
McMahon, T. Michael 297
McPherson, Aimee Semple 27–28
McQueen, Steve 139, 161
mechanical royalties 222n23
"Meeting Tonight" (song) 148
Meisner, Randy 326
Memorial Auditorium (Buffalo) 297
Memphis 297
Memphis Boys, The 197
Memphis Mafia 30, 113, 136, 175, 183, 185, 191, 344
Memphis Press-Scimitar 307
"Merry Christmas Baby" (song) 224
Metro-Goldwyn-Mayer (MGM) 158, 166, 169, 181, 194, 195, 219
"Milkcow Blues Boogie" (song) 82
Miller, Bill 200–201
Miller, Bob 348
Miller, Loanne *see* Parker, Loanne
Models and Melodies 56
"Mohair Sam" (song) 178
Moman, Chips 197, 198
Monroe, Marilyn 156
Moody Blue (album) 320
Moore, Mary Tyler 197, 325
Moore, Ruth Brown 113
Moore, Scotty 87, 141
"More Today Than Yesterday" (song) 285
Morgan, Jane 214
Morris, Phyllis 211
Morrison, Norman 180
Mossman, Sterling 142

Mother Maybelle and the Carter Sisters 78
Muhoberac, Larry 205
Murdoch, Rupert 323
Music Operators of America 129
"My Blue Heaven" (song) 56
"My Way" (song) 285n27

Nadel, Arthur 185
Naff, Nick 202–203
Nashville Banner (newspaper) 314
Nashville Sound 223
National Broadcasting Corporation (NBC) 196–197, 250, 251, 254, 302
National Enquirer (newspaper) 314
National General Pictures 197
Neal, Bob 83–84, 85, 86–88, 92, 96–99
Nelson, David 276
Nelson, Gunnar 345
Nelson, Matthew 345
Nelson, Ricky 114–115, 124, 139, 181, 205–206, 276, 285, 295, 316, 317, 325–328, 343
Nelson, Willie 223n24
Neutrality Act (1939) 58
New Gladiators, The (documentary) 276–277
Newman, Artie 299
Newman, Jimmy 199, 200
Newman, Paul 112, 161, 173
Newton, Wayne 268, 332
Newton-John, Olivia 79
New York Times, The (newspaper) 140, 193
Nichopoulos, George 186, 266, 273, 296
Nick (doctor) 262, 273, 274, 279, 281, 297, 313, 319–320
Nicks, Stevie 260
Nielsen, Sherrill 268
Niven, David 102
Nixon, Richard 247

O'Brien, Jim 219
"O Come, All Ye Faithful" (song) 225
O'Day, Pat 215
Official Snowmen's League of America, Ltd. 162–164
O'Grady, John 266
On Any Sunday (documentary) 276–277
O'Neal, Patrick 202
"One Night" (song) 126
On Stage (album) 219
Orbison, Roy 343
Original Report 336–338
Orlando, Tony 3

Pachucki, Al 224
Packard, Dave 4
"Padre" (song) 224
Paget, Debra 12, 104
Palm Springs 3, 4, 11, 21, 29, 84, 115, 144, 146, 152, 165, 170, 173, 189, 190, 192, 205, 206, 227, 259, 260, 272, 276, 287, 295, 308, 315, 327, 328, 331, 342, 345, 346, 347
  Colonel's crew and 230, 234, 238, 241–243, 245, 246

Index

Palm Springs Walk of Stars 346
Pap and His Jug Band 78
Paradise, Hawaiian Style (film) 174, 194
Paramount Pictures 119
Paramount Studios 103, 104n8, 110, 111, 130, 138, 154, 158, 164, 168, 173–174, 183, 194
Paramount Theater 104–105
Parker, Colonel Tom 1
  in American military service 38–44
  back in Holland 32–33
  charitable causes and 344
  childhood and youth of 15–23
  city life for 23–24
  death of 348
  early years at America for 25–29
  efficacy of 2
  gambling and 294–295
  in handling business dealings 4
  humor sense of 130–131, 160
  immigration to United States 36–38
  legal adoption of 31–32
  loyalty of 3
  marriage to Loanne Miller 343
  as mega-manager 2
  Original Report on 336–338
  on religion 22
  rumours about 30–31
  at Sells-Floto Circus 53–54
  ship job for 33–35
  ship travel to America 24–25
  split with Arnold 76–77
  temper tantrums of 157
  trip to Germany 35–36
  trip to Spain 35
  as veterinarian 60–63
  see also individual entries
Parker, Loanne 44, 202, 203–204, 210, 219, 229–238, 253, 264, 269, 270, 287, 294, 295, 298, 319, 321, 325, 326, 338, 343, 347, 348
Parker, Marie 54, 55, 69, 73, 100, 106–107, 152, 190, 230, 234, 242, 271, 295, 304, 306, 310, 326, 341, 342, 348
Parkhill, George 203, 229, 232, 238, 260, 262, 270, 275, 325
Parry, Patti 175, 254
Parton, Dolly 223n24
Pasetta, Marty 251–252, 254
Pat Boone Sings Guess Who? (album) 163
Pearl, Minnie 142–143, 223
Pensacola (Florida) 43–44
Perkins, Carl 161
Peters, Jon 280
Phillips, Dewey 82
Phillips, Sam 84–85, 90–94, 349
Pierce, Webb 78, 86
"Polk Salad Annie" (song) 285
Pomus, Doc 9
Pontiac (Michigan) 284–286
Porter, Bill 272
Post (newspaper) 304
Prell, Milton 190, 343
Presley, Elvis Aaron 1, 82
  animosity towards 105–107
  cancellation of shows and recordings of 257–258, 286, 313, 320, 321, 327

Presley, Elvis Aaron (*continued*)
  charitable aspects of 2
  Christmas albums and 222–228
  Comeback Special of 195, 197, 201, 214, 222
  concert for *Arizona* Memorial fund 141–143
  contracts and business dealings of 8–10, 12–13, 260–261
  death, and aftermath 326–329
  divorce with Priscilla 265
  film career of 104–105, 110–111, 113, 119, 121
  funeral services of 329–330
  Graceland estate and 113, 115–116, 184, 289
  importance of 89–90
  Lennon on 89
  marriage with Priscilla 189–192
  military service of 117–132
  promotion of 108–109
  RCA Victor and 96–98
  relationship with Priscilla 131–132
  Tahoe engagement and 257–265
  see also individual entries
Presley, Gladys 86, 87, 88, 106, 109, 110–113, 121, 330n33
Presley, Lisa Marie 193, 210, 230, 260, 268, 288, 311, 324, 330, 335
Presley, Minnie Mae 109, 335
Presley Pattern 111
Presley, Priscilla 90, 131–132, 175, 184, 186, 187–192, 210, 230, 242, 248, 259, 263, 276, 330, 332, 336, 339, 348, 349, 350
Presley, Vernon 86, 87–88, 96, 106, 110, 112, 113, 121, 165–166, 184, 235, 257, 258, 267, 270, 271, 279, 281, 287, 293, 295, 296, 298, 303, 306, 314, 319, 324, 325, 328n32, 329, 330, 332, 335
Press-Enterprise (newspaper) 347
Procter, William 4
Prophet, The (Gibran) 310
Prowse. Juliet 138
Public Works Administration (PWA) 46
Pure Country (film) 343n37
Putnam, Norbert 224

Radio Luxembourg 176
Rainmaker, The (film) 103
Raised on Rock/For Ol' Times Sake (album) 272
Ralston Purina feed company 69–70, 72
"Ramona" (song) 56
Randolph, Boots 141
RCA Records 139, 141, 210, 228, 235, 241, 249, 255, 259, 260–261, 275, 286, 302, 312, 324, 327, 336, 338, 339
RCA Record Tours 320
RCA Studio B 223, 224
RCA Victor 71, 76, 81, 87, 91, 92, 93, 125, 134, 183
Reagan, Ronald 292–293, 300
Recording Industry Association of America (RIAA) 111, 228
Red, Hot & Blue (WHBQ radio) 82
Reeves, Jim 223n24
Refried Elvis (Zolov) 138
Revolver (album) 173
Reynolds, Jody 115, 276

Index

Rich, Charlie 178
Richard, Little 181
Rinaldi, Clyde 331
Ringo 177–178
Rio Bravo (film) 161
Roberts, Oral 145, 148
Robinson, Edward G. 102
Rocky (film) 327
Rogers, Will 102
Rogers & Cowan 139–140
Rolling Stones, The 181
Romero, Alex 112
Ronstadt, Linda 326
Roosevelt, Franklin Delano 46, 58
Ross, Diana 213
Rotterdam 23–24, 35
Roustabout (film) 168
Rubber Soul (album) 173
Ryan, Sheila 279

Sacks, Manie 87
Sahara Tahoe 232, 263
Sanders, Denis 219
Sanders, Harland 60
Sands, Tommy 114, 193
Saperstein, Hank 108
Sarnoff, Tom 195, 249, 302–303
Saturday Night Live 345
Savitch, Jessica 260
Schechter, Irv 160, 181–182
Scheff, Jerry 205
Schilling, Jerry 155, 175, 347
Schroeder, Aaron 134
Schulten, Marjorie 122, 123
Scott, Lizabeth 110
Seeley, Kirk 275
Seller, Peter 177
Sells-Floto Circus 53–54

Shapiro, Max 266, 273, 309–310
Shapiro, Suzanne 310
Sheena, Queen of the Jungle 12
Sholes, Steve 7, 95, 97
Shoofey, Alex 199–201, 203, 204, 209, 210, 220, 231, 232, 343
Shoofey, Teri Lynn 203
Shuman, Mort 9
Sidney, George 166–167
Siegel, David 47n3
"Silver Bells" (song) 224
Simmons, Jean 112
Simon & Garfunkel 181, 225
Sinatra, Frank 2, 87, 136, 137, 190, 192, 205, 238, 343
Sinatra, Nancy 131, 137, 192–193
Smith, Billy 175, 277
Smith, Carl 78
Smith, Jo 175
Smith, Roger 330
Smothers Brothers Comedy Hour, The (TV show) 251
Snow, Hank 76, 78, 79–81, 85–89, 91, 98–99, 107
Social Security Administration 46
Soden, Jack 339, 340, 348, 349
"Something" (song) 173
Spain 35
Speaks, Leonard 44
Spector, Phil 9
Speedway (film) 192, 290
Spinout (film) 181, 194
Spiral Starecase 285
Springfield, Dusty 197
Springsteen, Bruce 260
Stage Show (CBS-TV) 8, 9, 103
Stamps 258, 289
Stamps Quartet, The 329

Stang, Arnold 9, 124
Stanley, Ricky 290
Stanwyck, Barbara 168
Star Wars (film) 327
Stay Away, Joe (film) 194–195
Steamroller, Mannheim 228
Steiger, Rod 161
Steve Allen Show (TV show) 107
Stewart, Bob 316
Stewart, Jimmy 117
Stewart, Rod 213
Stone, Charlie 216–217, 299–300, 325
Strait, George 343
Streisand, Barbara 201, 205, 228, 279
Streissguth, Michael 76
Strickling, Howard 158, 159
"Stuck on You" (song) 134, 136, 223
Sullivan, Ed 12, 107–108, 124, 136
Sumner, Donnie 268
Sumner, J. D. 258, 289, 329
Sun Records 85, 90
Sun Studios 85
Superman (film) 327
"Surrender" (song) 134
"Suspicious Minds" (song) 198
"Sweet, Sweet Spirit" (song) 329
"Sweet Angeline" (song) 272

Tamblyn, Russ 112
Taurog, Norman 154, 195
Taylor, Elizabeth 158
TCB Band 205, 285
"Teddy Bear" (song) 111
TelePrompTer Corporation 119
"Tennessee Stud" (song) 72
Texaco Star Theater 9
"That's All Right" (song) 82, 225
"There's Been a Change in Me" (song) 71
"These Boots Are Made For Walkin'" (song) 192
This is Elvis (documentary) 277
Thomas, B. J. 197
Thomas, Danny 102, 168
Thomas, Kevin 193, 194
Thompson, Linda 248, 255–256, 268, 273, 279, 295, 306
Thompson, Sam 248
Thunder Road (film) 161
Tickle Me (film) 169
Tily III, H. Coleman 94, 96
Timex 135
Tingley Coliseum tour 240
Tiny ill and His Orchestra 78
Toll, Arthur 259
Tompkins, Stephen G. 337
Tracy, Spencer 102, 158
Trouble with Girls, The (film) 196
Tual, Blanchard E. 288, 336, 337–338
Tubb, Ernest 65, 223
Tucker, Hoxie 46–47
Tucker, Sophie 124
Tucker, Tanya 3
Turner, Lana 102
Turner, Tina 212
Tutt, Ronnie 205

Index

TV Guide 196
Tyler, Judy 112

United Artists 186
"Until It's Time for You to Go" (song) 227
Upson, Dean 68
Upton, Pat 285

Valdivia, Polly 342
Vallee, Rudy 195
Van Ander, Roscoe 44
van Kuijk, Adam 15, 19, 23
van Kuijk, Andreas Cornelius *see* Parker, Colonel Tom
van Kuijk, Maria 15, 42
Variety (magazine) 194
Veeck, Bill 129
Viva Las Vegas (film) 166, 169
Voice group 268

Waite, George 276
Wald, Jerry 161–162
Walker, Jim 293
Wallis, Hal 102–103, 104, 105, 110, 119, 130–131, 154–155, 181–182, 183, 194
Wall Street Journal, The 110
Walters, Barbara 294
Warner, Jack L. 146, 147
Washington Post, The (newspaper) 278
Wayne, John 139
"Wear My Ring Around Your Neck" (song) 126
Webb, Del 199, 202
Weinshanker, Joel 340

Weintraub, Jerry 214–216, 220, 222, 237–238, 248–249, 288, 349
Weiss, Steven H. 215
Welcome to My World (album) 312
Wells, Henry 4
Welwood Murray Library 346–347
West, Judy 295
West, Mae 102
West, Pat 191, 295
West, Red 155, 175, 191, 220, 224, 226–227, 255, 264, 278, 290, 298, 305, 323
West, Sonny 155, 173, 175, 220, 255, 264, 266, 274, 278, 284, 290, 292–293, 298, 300, 305, 323–324, 344
Westmoreland, Kathy 289
"What a Fool I Was" (song) 71
"What Put the Pep in Grandma" (song) 78
Wild in the Country (film) 140, 161, 194
William Morris Agency 73, 101, 150, 160, 181, 183, 184
Williams, Audrey 78
Williams, Clannie 234
Williams, Esther 9
Wilson, Rita 339
Winters, Jonathan 241
"Winter Wonderland" (song) 225
"Witchcraft" (song) 136
Wonderful World of Girls, The (TV show) 239
Wood, Natalie 188
Wood, Randy 163
Woolery, Chuck 275–276

Works Progress Administration (WPA) 46
Wynn, Steve 343, 349

"Yesterday" (song) 173
"Yesterday and Today" (song) 276

"You're My World" (song) 178
Young, Chip 224, 226, 227
Young, Neil 225

Zenoff, David 190
Zeppelin, Led 215, 273
Zolov, Eric 138

ABOUT THE AUTHORS

Tom McDonald

Greg McDonald is an entertainment producer who got his start in show business with Colonel Tom Parker, who knew him when he was a teenager. He managed Ricky Nelson for seventeen years, ran Sonny Bono's mayoral and congressional campaigns, and was president of Trans Continental Records (Backstreet Boys, NSYNC, and O-Town). He's also produced several feature films, television series (*Making the Band*), and large-scale concerts. McDonald manages Colonel Tom Parker's show business assets, including his name, likeness, and image. He resides in the Palm Springs area with his wife, Sherry.

Marshall Terrill is a veteran film, sports, and music writer and the author of more than thirty books. They include bestselling biographies of Steve McQueen, Elvis Presley, Johnny Cash, Billy Graham, and Pete Maravich. His book *Steve McQueen: The Life and Legend of a Hollywood Icon* is in development to be made into a feature film. He also executive produced the 2017 feature film documentary *Steve McQueen: American Icon* and the 2022 documentary *Johnny Cash: The Redemption of an American Icon*. He resides in Tempe, Arizona, with his wife, Zoe.